Globalisation and Jurisdiction

Globalisation and Jurisdiction

Edited by Piet Jan Slot and Mielle Bulterman
Europa Instituut, Leiden University

Final editing TGV, Leiden
Lay-out   AlphaZet prepress, Waddinxveen

ISBN 90 4112 307 5

Printed in the Netherlands

Contents

Foreword

The theme Globalisation and Jurisdiction has been a topic of special interest ever since I was involved in the US Grand Jury investigation of the European shipowners' cartel in the mid seventies. After some initial publications,[1] I was finally able to develop this subject further during my sabbatical at Stanford Law School during the academic year 2000-2001. My interest was stimulated by many memorable presentations of colleagues and distinguished visitors. Several important topics of this theme were subsequently discussed during a workshop in June 2001 that I was able to organise under the auspices of the European Forum of the Stanford University. The basic idea was to study the way in which the law has responded to the strongly increasing globalisation. During the Stanford Seminar we looked at different sectors and phenomena: the banking sector, antitrust, transport law, international taxation, conflict of law rules as well as international private law, and intellectual property rights. The workshop generated a wealth of material for thought and study. Thus the occasion of the 40th anniversary of the Europa Institute of the Leiden University provided an excellent opportunity to continue the search into this fascinating topic. It is an area on which a lot has been written[2] but at the same time there is not a lot of research that looks at the overall aspects of the regulation of global international trade. These subjects were presented during the Leiden seminar and followed by an extensive discussion.

These presentations are presented here in a more formal and extensive format. Some additional topics have been included to provide an even more extensive treatment of the topic.

Piet Jan Slot

---

1   P.J. Slot, 'National Regulation of Maritime Transport and International Public Law', *Netherlands International Law Review,* Vol XXVI (1979), p.329-346 and P.J. Slot & E.Grabant, 'Extraterritoriality and jurisdiction', 23 CMLRev. (1986), p. 545-567.
2   Vide the enormous amount of literature on the topic of extraterritoriality.

Introduction

Piet Jan Slot and Mielle Bulterman

Ever since international economic relations were established law has been developed to shape them in a satisfactory manner. Conversely, changes in the law have sometimes preceded, and thus fostered, international economic intercourse. The spectacular growth of the international economy over the past decades has called for a more intensive role for the law and probably also for a different kind of law. This has led to a panoply of new legal instruments and procedures as well as a resuscitation of the traditional and established forms. At the same time there is constant need to reflect on the appropriate level of jurisdiction for prescribing as well as enforcing such rules. Although there is a substantial amount of legal writings documenting and commenting upon the legal instruments created in different sectors of the economy and commenting on the jurisdictional issues involved, efforts to systematise such instruments seem to be largely absent. In this context the question arises whether the traditional concepts of public and private law jurisdiction and the principles underpinning them are still adequate to deal with international commerce and movement of persons and companies.

The theme 'globalisation and jurisdiction' was chosen with the purpose of finding answers to this question. To achieve this aim, the theme was reflected upon both by scholars and practitioners. The involvement of practitioners in the discussion made it possible to achieve an overview of the legal developments in some selected sectors which display particularly interesting features: international securities and banking, internet, tax and antitrust. For every sector the question can be asked: what are the challenges posed by globalization and how has the law been reacting to them? An overview of these developments provides valuable input for the second purpose of the discussion, the academic debate on jurisdiction and globalisation. Which problems are encountered? To what extent have traditional concepts of jurisdiction accommodated the requirements of a global economy? To what extent have these traditional concepts been adapted and new ones developed to solve these problems?

The first contribution of Johnston and Powles provides a rich general overview of the themes and problems related to political and economic globalisation. Their exploration of the phenomenon of globalisation and the responses to globalisation in some specific fields makes it clear that the problems encountered in a globalising world are not new. Nevertheless, these problems occur both more frequently and in a new context, making their solution necessarily more complex. They demonstrate that globalisation can no longer be analysed as the inevitable product of the natural economic order. Nowadays there is a lot more to it. In particular the political element plays a much stronger role in the process. Consumerism and environmentalism organised on a worldwide scale have given this process an unprecedented impetus. Witness for example the actions in Seattle on the occasion of the meeting of the WTO or the pan-European action against the dumping of the Brent Spar into the North Sea. To this has to be added the ever-increasing power of multinationals. All this leaves a complex picture of globalisation providing no immediate clues for allocating jurisdiction.

Subsequently, they proceed with a brief summary of the traditional approaches to jurisdiction both in international public and private law. In this context they point to the greater acceptance of the role of international dispute settlement bodies.

On the basis of an analysis of the responses to globalisation in different fields, they demonstrate that different approaches are applied in the various fields affected by globalisation. They point out that the nature of the transactions and the conduct to be addressed necessarily has an impact on the approach taken to jurisdiction. Furthermore, such efforts should respect the rule of law; if not, jurisdictional competition will be short-lived as foreign judgments may not be accepted in other jurisdictions.

It appears from their brief survey that some sectors such as international transport have found satisfactory ways of dealing with concurrent jurisdiction issues. Others, such as taxation and securities, are struggling with competing interests. A sectoral approach does not necessarily preclude the development of a unified theory of jurisdiction. Such a theory requires the flexible reinterpretation of otherwise relatively unchallenged axioms. This finding is, by and large, confirmed by the subsequent contributions that focus on specific areas of law affected by globalisation.

Wautelet examines the contribution international private law can make to solve the problems related to globalisation. He commences his article with F.A. Mann's classic article on the subject. In it Mann proposed the now generally accepted distinction of the different types of jurisdiction:

* jurisdiction to *prescribe* (i.e. to make its law applicable to activities and relations, whether by legislation, regulation or determination of a court)
* jurisdiction to *adjudicate* (i.e. to subject persons or things to process of courts)
* jurisdiction to *enforce* (i.e. to induce or compel compliance, through courts or by use of executive, administrative, etc.).

Wautelet notes that conflict-of-law rules of international private law do not necessarily have an impact on the jurisdiction of States. Conflict-of-law rules in the strict sense serve *private* interests: they determine which law is applicable to a given relationship and do not necessarily impact on the sovereignty of the (foreign) State whose law is declared applicable. However, international-

ly mandatory rules or *règles d'application immediate* do impinge on the jurisdiction of the State applying its rules to a case before their courts.

On the other hand general international public law does not impose limits on the jurisdiction of municipal courts. In the absence of a general, well-defined international framework for jurisdictional claims uniform rules on jurisdiction have to be established by agreement between States. Such agreement has been achieved within the European Union, but is still lacking at a
global level. Private international jurisdiction is defined as adjudicative jurisdiction in what are essentially private matters. Wautelet goes on to three general principles which are accepted by most jurisdictions:

- Territorialism is not the sole justification/limitation of jurisdiction
- Consent constitutes a satisfactory base for jurisdiction
- Prohibition of 'exorbitant' or 'improper' fora (genuine link)

The theoretical questions raised by first point – the demise of territorialism as
the basis for jurisdiction – are further explored in the contribution of Michaels.
It is obvious that as long as the State is territorial, State jurisdiction must be territorial. It is also clear that globalisation has an impact on territoriality.

Wautelet notes that consent has gradually won acceptance as a satisfactory basis for jurisdiction. This has also led to acceptance of other forms of dispute settlement and in particular arbitration. Such acceptance has taken time.
Nowadays arbitration is also accepted even if the controversy involves special
policy considerations. This development in turn has given rise to enforcement
issues.

The third principle that can be discerned is that of a minimum connection,
sometimes also referred to as the genuine link. In the end this principle boils
down to a simple prohibition of discrimination against foreigners.

Wautelet identifies two main problems that stand in the way of a general
agreement on jurisdiction. The first is an issue of legal technique: should such
an agreement identify rules for granting general or specific jurisdiction? The
second is a question of principles. Which principles should be guiding the delimitation jurisdiction? Even more important is the question of what weight or
priority should be given to these principles.

Meeusen's contribution complements Wautelet's article very well because it
demonstrates that international private law rules may well be designed to
serve public-law purposes. This is clearly demonstrated by the rules of the EU
discussed by him. The EU rules on private international law such as the Brussels I convention, and more recently regulation 44/2001, have been characterised by the ECJ as an attempt to facilitate the achievement of the common
market. This phenomenon is greatly expanded with the provisions of article
65 EC providing a clear competence for the Community to enact rules in the
field of judicial cooperation in civil matters. Meeusen's contribution demonstrates that substantive harmonisation of international private-law rules can
proceed when the participating countries share common goals and values.

The goals are enumerated in article 61 EC and the values in article 6 EU as well as in the case law of the ECJ on general principles of community law.

Rogerson addresses the English courts' approach to jurisdiction over foreign activities of multinationals. In her view the English courts' approach may constitute a useful antidote to the possibility of powerful multinationals to structure their operations in such a way as to escape liability in jurisdictions where their subsidiaries do business. Nevertheless, she characterizes the approach of English courts to jurisdiction over foreign activities of multinationals as un-principled and finds their reasoning flawed. If the 'natural forum' is abroad English proceedings in general will be stayed. However, in practice, proceedings may continue if the claimant would otherwise be deprived of a 'legitimate advantage' available in the English court. Such an advantage for a claimant may be both procedural and substantive. An obvious procedural advantage – over proceedings in civilian jurisdictions – is the party-driven rules of discovery of evidence. A substantive advantage is the possibility to hold one tortfeasor among many wholly liable. Rogerson points out that the substance of the claim may still depend on the application of English law. Unfortunately, the two key cases discussed by her have left this issue unanswered.

She suggests that the incorporation of the defendant multinational company in England, the location of its head office there and the fact that they control the activities of their subsidiaries from England would constitute a better and more equitable basis for jurisdiction than the application of the principle of 'legitimate advantage.' But the fact is that it is very easy for a multinational company to structure its business so as to ensure that the subsidiary is doing its own business and not that of the company.[1] Against this background, Rogerson concludes that the English courts' approach has redressed the balance somewhat, even if its reasoning is flawed. It is interesting to compare the practical approach of English courts to the position under the US Alien Tort Statute cases dealt with in the contribution by Bekker. Even though at first sight the US statute involves only cases where the claim is based on an infringement of public international law it may, of course, yield results similar to those of the approach followed by the English courts.

Michaels takes the challenges to both the legitimacy and the intelligibility of the traditional concepts as a result of globalisation as the guiding argument for his article. After discussing the erosion of the traditional concept of territoriality, his claim is that it no longer gives an adequate picture of the world and consequently can no longer serve as a fundament for a law of jurisdiction. He

---

1   A notorious example of such a practice, not mentioned by Rogerson, is the practice of setting up 'single ship companies' in the maritime sector. Such legal constructs allow shipowners to avoid liability and the enforcement of claims against them by way of arresting vessels. Thus, to give an example, claims for damage caused by pollution by one vessel of the 'parent' company can be circumvented because other ships cannot be arrested as they belong to legally different entities.

illustrates his points by discussing several decisions that have been the talk of the town among lawyers recently: the *Yahoo!* decision, the problems with e-commerce and antitrust suits involving claimants outside the US.

To overcome these problems, territoriality has not been abolished as a basis of jurisdiction but made more flexible by means of the adoption of the effects doctrine. In a globalised world, however, the application of this doctrine does not always produce a satisfactory outcome. Firstly, due to the fact that economic markets are no longer local, any localization appears arbitrary. Secondly, in a globalized world economy, everything has an effect on everything. In this context, Michaels in his article suggests six possible solutions. These are respectively: anarchy, universalisation, collaboration, re-territorialisation, re-conceptualizing territory, and finally, doing away with territory.

Universalisation offers a solution in some exceptional circumstances as exemplified by the International Criminal Court. Re-territorialisation is feasible in some ways, but the question is more whether it is desirable. Re-conceptualising territory might be a solution for areas like the *Yahoo!* case and e-commerce. Such jurisdiction would not have to be State jurisdiction but may be exercised within specific business communities. All in all, his article challenges us to continue the search for a more appropriate foundation for jurisdiction, which is what this publication attempts to do.

The demise of territorialism as the basis for jurisdiction noted by Wautelet is also apparent in the contribution by Miller and Baker. They discuss the enforcement of the US antitrust law through private-law suits based on competitive injury to themselves. They discuss the jurisdiction to apply US antitrust law to trans-border situations. Miller and Baker focus primarily on the application of the effects doctrine in 'non-import' cases. They point out that nowadays the question is not so much whether the US can exercise jurisdiction but much more 'where should jurisdiction be exercised given the increased exercise of jurisdiction by other nations.'?

In 1982 the Foreign Trade Antitrust Improvements Act (FTAIA) was adopted in order to reduce the risks to US enterprises of being charged with antitrust violations where it was clear that the alleged restraint was not directed and did not affect the US market. It provides that the Sherman Act shall not apply to conduct involving trade or commerce (other than import trade or import commerce) with foreign nations unless it has a direct, substantial and reasonable effect on commerce within the United States or on a domestic firm competing for foreign trade. The act left open serious questions in situations where the facts were mixed in the sense that there is at least some activity and general effect in the USA.

The lower courts of the US are having a difficult time to apply the FTAIA in a consistent manner: conflicts between courts are clear and growing. This is illustrated by cases such as *Kruman* v. *Christie's International plc.* in which a class action was brought by foreign purchasers and sellers of art outside the USA. The district court rejected the claim since the plaintiffs could not prove that *their injury* was a result of the effect on US commerce. This judgment was reversed by the Court of Appeals for the second circuit, which held that if there was a conspiracy that injured both US and foreign purchasers, then the foreign purchasers could sue in the US courts even if they themselves lacked injury in the US. Miller and Baker conclude that confusing rules and different approaches are applied to what are in the end similar cases in terms of key elements. There seems to be consensus, however, on the following points: (1) the FTAIA has set forth the sensible basic rule that there is no role for US courts where there is no effect in the US; (2) the (potential) effect in the US must be substantial, i.e. not *de minimis*; (3) there is nothing inherently wrong with giving exporters a cause of action when they have been excluded from a market, particularly where they may have a difficult time litigating abroad. They also observe that government enforcement agencies have every incentive to cooperate with each other and to defer to each other when jurisdictional issues are difficult.

Becker provides an interesting overview of the recent resuscitation of the 190 years old 'Alien Torts Claims Act.' This Act vests US federal district courts with jurisdiction of any civil action by an alien for a tort committed in violation of the law of nations. Recently, there have been a host of claims brought before US courts seeking relief for such violations.

Unfortunately, the current state of US law is such that it is unsettled whether the Act confers a claim or private right of action. There are conflicting judgments from the second and ninth circuit Courts of Appeal. Becker argues that there are good grounds for questioning the existence of such a right. If, however, the Act does create such a right the next question is what the evidentiary are for proving violations of international law. Such violations can only be based on treaties or universally accepted and clearly-articulated and discernable rules of customary international law.

Wouters, De Smet and Ryngaert provide further examples of claims brought under the Alien Torts Claims Act. They also provide a brief comparison with the Belgian 'Genocide Act.' They note that the Alien Torts Claims Act does not, unlike the Belgian Act, grant absolute universal jurisdiction. Furthermore, the Foreign Sovereignty Act and the Act of State Doctrine preclude claims against foreign States. Moreover, jurisdiction under the Act is of a civil nature, not criminal. They express doubts whether a universal torts jurisdiction, as provided for by the Alien Torts Claims Act, is the most suitable instrument to deal with gross violations of human rights and norms of international law. In their opinion, multilateral mechanisms would be a better option provided, of course, that such mechanisms are supported by powerful states.

It is interesting to contrast the demise of territorialism as the basis for claiming jurisdiction by national courts with the approach of the European Court of Human Rights (ECrtHR) on the question of State liability for acts taking place or having effect outside its borders. This issue is addressed in the contribution of Lawson. Article 1 of the European Convention on Human Rights (ECHR) provides that the Contracting Parties shall secure to everyone 'within their jurisdiction' the rights and freedoms set out in the Convention. In some cases, the ECrtHR has held that States can be held responsible under the ECHR for action which took place outside their borders. Noteworthy examples are the cases brought against Turkey by individuals complaining about the infringement of their rights in northern Cyprus. However, the Court has also made it clear that it is not prepared to assume jurisdiction over all extraterritorial actions of the contracting parties. In *Bankovic* the ECrtHR observed: 'Article 1 must be considered to reflect this ordinary and essentially territorial notion of jurisdiction, other bases of jurisdiction being exceptional and requiring special justification in the particular circumstances of each case'. It continues: 'The Convention was not designed to be applied throughout the world, even in respect of the conduct of the Contracting States. Accordingly, the desirability of avoiding a gap or vacuum in human rights' protection has so far been relied on by the Court in favour of establishing jurisdiction only when the territory in question was one that, but for the specific circumstances, would normally be covered by the Convention'.

Thus it is clear from the case law of the ECrtHR that there are to be limits in its jurisdiction. Somewhat unhappy with this limitation, Lawson argues that such limits should not apply when there is a direct and immediate link between the extraterritorial conduct of a State and the alleged violation of an individual's right.

The second point of agreement mentioned by Wautelet, i.e. that consent constitutes a satisfactory base for jurisdiction, is followed up by Brenninkmeijer and Shelkoplyas in their contribution on the relevance of Alternative Dispute Resolution (ADR) in a globalising world. ADR is an attractive method to solve conflicts between parties, who are operating in multiple jurisdictions. One of the reasons to have recourse to ADR, instead of to a national court, is that the latter has to apply legal rules of national law which might be ill-suited to govern complex international transactions. While acknowledging that ADR may play a role in the resolution of international disputes, Brenninkmeijer and Shelkoplyas stress that ADR cannot truly compete with existing means of litigation and arbitration. Most importantly, in the absence of a universal system of recognition and enforcement, ADR can only be successful when the parties are prepared to comply with any agreement reached. If not, recourse to traditional means, such as arbitration or a national court, is still necessary to solve the dispute. The authors observe that while ADR originally was perceived as a market-driven phenomenon, it is increasingly getting governmental attention. Within the European Union, for example, the European Commission has published a green paper on alternative dispute resolution in civil and commercial law. This development must be applauded since the European Union and States can contribute to creating an environment favourable for further evolution of ADR. At the same time there is cause for caution: the Community legislator must be careful not to restrain its development and evolution by putting in place a rigid regulatory framework. It is observed that the courts of the EU have also employed ADR techniques. The authors note that this may raise delicate issues when important legal principles are at stake. Such principles can better observe the conventional dispute resolution systems.

The process of globalisation does not only give rise to questions concerning the jurisdiction of (inter)national courts over extra-territorial or cross-border situations, it also gives rise to important questions concerning the jurisdiction (to *prescribe*) of the national legislator. Rebane and Marx focuse on the application to foreign companies of the US corporate governance standards as laid down in the Sarbanes-Oxley Act. The enactment of the Sarbanes-Oxley Act is a logical response to the corporate scandals involving multinational corporations. This is also demonstrated by the fact that the US has not been the only State to adopt corporate governance rules: within the European Union corporate governance reform has been evolving for the past several years. Rebane and Marx conclude that the Sarbanes-Oxley Act should not be viewed simply as an overreaction by the US government to US corporate scandals, but rather, as a constructive basis for improving corporate governance standards worldwide.

As a global organisation, the UN obviously can make an important contribution to the establishment of worldwide standards. Bulterman describes some of the jurisdictional problems that may be encountered when the UN is acting as a world legislator. She focuses on the implementation of the UN financial sanction regime enacted following September 11, 2001. These sanctions are decided upon by the UN Security Council and implemented by the UN Member States. The current practice of the UN financial sanction regimes makes it clear that genuine global jurisdiction, namely the imposition of sanctions on specific persons and entities by the UN Security Council, gives rise to fundamental questions from a legal protection perspective. At a UN level there is no court available where individuals affected by the UN sanction regime can challenge decisions affecting them. At the national level, as well as the regional level, the EU courts are available but they are only competent to rule on national or regional rules implementing the UN regime. Such courts do not have jurisdiction to rule on the lawfulness of the UN sanction regime. The UN financial sanction regime demonstrates clearly that respective roles of the different levels of jurisdiction and their interaction need further clarification.

Another sector affected by the process of globalisation is labour law. Heerma van Voss signals two developments in labour law: the internationalisation and constitutionalisation of labour law. He argues that both trends fail to meet the challenges of globalisation. Subsequently he provides a brief overview of some of the main elements of the EU policy on labour law. In his view the EU efforts will not be sufficient to meet the challenges of globalisation. Closer cooperation between industrialized countries will be required; furthermore new policy instruments with an emphasis on coordination and evaluation of best practices may be needed.

Fox's contribution constructs an economic-efficiency-based theory of optimal areas for securities disclosure. It addresses two questions: what level of government should be the one regulating disclosure? And second, which one or ones should regulate any given issuer? The starting point of his study is an analysis of issuer disclosure in general. He observes that issuers will not disclose at their optimal levels if we rely on market forces alone. As often with regulatory issues, market failure constitutes the key rationale for regulating issuer disclosure. His study centres around two key interrelated assumptions. The first is the level of trans-border trade. The second is the extent to which a particular government is responsive to the needs of its residents. His approach of optimal regulatory areas establishes a framework for analysing the debates in Canada, the USA and the EU about the appropriate level of legislation. Fox concludes that for Canada and the USA a single regulatory area is the optimum, while for the EU it is a close call whether it is the EU or the individual Member States.

SOME CONCLUDING OBSERVATIONS

The process of globalisation has not (yet) altered the fact that the nation-state still forms the basis for the exercise of jurisdictional powers. Thus the question how the law has responded to the challenges posed by globalisation is essentially still a question of the impact of globalisation on State jurisdiction. However, there are signs that the traditional role of the nation-state may be eroding because jurisdiction is no longer exclusively exercised on a territorial basis.

Wautelet's and Rogerson's contributions show that international private law is still largely characterised by a national approach. At the same time there are important trends in the direction of an international approach. This is on the one hand exemplified by several sectoral agreements i.e. in the field of air and maritime transport, and on the other hand by efforts, in particular by the EU, to approach international private rules as a tool for facilitating the achievement of the internal market. The latter is clearly borne out in Meeusen's contribution. There is now an impressive body of Community law addressing international private-law and tailoring it to the needs of the internal market.[2] A related trend is the enactment of public-law rules setting aside private law rules for achieving objectives of the Community such as the protection of the consumer, the environment[3] and the national labour markets.[4] Such a development is less likely at an international level because it requires a consensus on the substantive rules involved. Such a consensus may only occur at a sectoral level as noted above. The example of the European Union also shows

---

2   This started with the so-called 'Paris Memorandum', an administrative agreement between maritime authorities of several Western European countries and gradually led to an EC directive on this subject as well as several regional agreements sponsored by IMO.
3   See the examples given by Johnston and Powles at p. 7, 8 and Meeusen in paragraph 18.
4   A clear example of the latter is directive 96/71 concerning the posting of workers in the framework of the provision of services, [1997] OJ, L 18/1-6. The preamble of this directive provides an extensive statement on the rules on contractual obligations as laid down in the Rome Convention of 19 June 1980 and the reason for setting these aside with the purpose of affording protection to local labour.

that the distinction between public-and private-law jurisdiction becomes more and more arbitrary.

It is a traditional method of the law that in the absence of a consensus on substantive rules procedural rules are established. Once such rules are put into practice this may lead to the gradual development of substantive rules. The exchange of information enables parties to evaluate each other's approach and methods; this in turn may increase the willingness to discuss the cases on the merits. Examples of this method can be seen in international antitrust cooperation, referred to below, and the gradual emergence of rules on Port State Control in the maritime transport sector. There is also an increasing acceptance by the traditional jurisdictions that parties may choose freely which court will hear their dispute, as well as the freedom to opt for arbitration or some other form of dispute settlement procedure such as ADR. A similar development may be observed in the public-law sphere, e.g. the WTO dispute settlement system.

In the area of public law there is the constantly recurring issue of unilateral exercise of jurisdiction as exemplified, inter alia, by the earlier US antitrust policy towards foreign conduct, the US antifraud regulation and the Sarbanes-Oxley act. As the developments in the area of antitrust law show the possibility of cooperation as opposed to unilateralism only occurs once there is a substantial alignment of interests and a concomitant harmonisation of policies. This has happened over the decade between the USA and the EC through the conclusion of two cooperation agreements, the first one in 1991 and the second one in 1998. In 2002 a joint working group published 'Best practices on cooperation in merger investigations.' Earlier the agencies had agreed on Administrative Arrangements on Attendance, allowing officials of the three agencies to be present at hearings of the other agencies. Both the EC Commission, the DOJ and the FTC publish annual reports on the cooperation.

Fox's contribution raises the important question whether or not similar efficiency-based analyses of optimal regulatory areas in other sectors in the global economy lead to similar answers. This question can only be answered by looking at such studies. Economic theory has amply discussed the issue of optimal currency areas. It would seem that Fox's basic assumptions about the level of trans-border transactions and the responsiveness of the government to the needs of its residents will also be relevant for other sectors of the economy. Of course, the exact impact of these assumptions will differ per sector. Some sectors are highly globalized while others are still very local. Similarly, the level of governmental responsiveness will differ from sector to sector. A systematic analysis of these elements across the different sectors of the economy may be highly instructive for the study of the proper allocation of jurisdiction in a globalizing world economy. These elements also provide an indication why sectors such as the maritime and air transport sector have long been viewed as requiring worldwide regulation.

It is interesting to compare the possibilities for private parties to bring claims against other private parties based on Common Law rules of jurisdiction in the UK as described by Rogerson with the claims brought in the USA under the Alien Torts Act. The latter type of claim is primarily addressed towards breaches of public international law. This includes claims against companies as well as governments. These are claims for egregious breaches of international public law. In the case of the UK, courts may assume jurisdiction when claimants would be deprived of substantial justice by being forced to litigate abroad.

The broad jurisdiction of some national courts over extra-territorial conflicts may be contrasted with the reluctance of the European Court of Human Rights in its landmark decision on *Bankovic* to rule on the extra-territorial activities of the States subjected to its supervisory powers. It would be a paradox – to say the least – if States could be held responsible before foreign national courts, but would escape jurisdiction of international courts.

As this study shows globalisation creates an interactive process whereby governmental initiatives enable the private parties to try new actions; conversely, private action may solicit governmental and judicial responses.

The kings of the world and their dukes' dilemma: Globalisation, jurisdiction and the Rule of Law[*]

Angus Johnston and Edward Powles

1 INTRODUCTION

Ever since international economic relations have been established, law has been developed to shape and facilitate them in a satisfactory manner. Conversely, changes in the law have sometimes preceded, and thus fostered, international economic intercourse. The spectacular growth of the international economy over the past decades has called for a more intensive role for the law. This has led to a panoply of new legal instruments and procedures as well as a resuscitation of the traditional and established forms. Although there is a substantial amount of legal writing documenting and commenting upon the legal instruments created in different sectors of the economy, efforts to systematize such instruments seem to be largely absent. At the same time, the question arises whether the traditional concepts of public and private law jurisdiction and the principles underpinning them are still adequate to deal with international commerce and the movement of persons and companies.

In this paper we seek to examine how the process of political and economic globalisation constantly influences the development of jurisdictional rules and vice-versa. In particular, we intend to analyse these developments by reference to the rule of law, not least in order to show that the apparently arid and technical legal rules and doctrines in fact conceal a deep and rich substratum of complex social and political conundra. Thus, we begin in section 2 with an overview of the phenomena associated with ever-increasing political and economic globalisation. Section 3 follows with a brief review of the traditional approaches to jurisdiction and the mounting difficulties which may be seen through the cracks therein.

In section 4, we turn to consider the rule of law (in the context of privatisation of governance) and the rule of laws (in the sense of apportionment of global jurisdiction) and discuss the practical difficulties experienced in vari-

[*] This paper is an expansion and restructuring of a report on a seminar on 'Globalisation and Jurisdiction' held at Stanford University, Palo Alto (California) on 22 June 2001, which has been developed by further presentations by Angus Johnston at California Western School of Law, San Diego (California) on the 'The Rule of Law: Creating an Effective Legal Environment for the Global Economy' (14, 15 and 16 November 2002) and the Leiden Europa Instituut 50th Anniversary Lustrum Seminar on 'Globalisation and Jurisdiction' (5 and 6 December 2002). The authors would like to thank Andrew Lang, Morten Broberg and the various participants at the Stanford, San Diego and Leiden seminars for their helpful suggestions and criticisms. Any errors or inaccuracies which remain are entirely our own work and responsibility.

ous parts of the international economy. We consider methods of addressing such difficulties by reference to specific economic sectors: the use of bilateral treaties in the context of revenue law; the phenomenon of multilateral harmonisation in the context of international air and maritime transport; and the acceptance of substantive diversity in the context of securities regulation. We also consider the impact of procedures and politics with particular reference to United States and E.C. competition law. *En route*, we hope to highlight certain recurrent themes. We will note the interrelationship between jurisdictional rules and substantive law; the conflicting trends towards unified jurisdictional theory on the one hand and fragmentation and sectoralisation of jurisdictional rules on the other; and, in particular, the competing pulls of public and private arenas and which is in the driving seat in these different sectors – who are the 'Kings' and who are their 'Dukes' in the modern arena?

2   GLOBALISATION

To move to a more general and theoretical level, these political, economic and legal developments need to be placed within the broader context of increasing discussion of the phenomenon of 'globalisation'.[1] It is uncontroversial that the jurisdictional and regulatory issues referred to above arise with more frequency (and often potency) as a result of a number of 'globalising' trends. However, isolating the precise meaning of the term 'globalisation' in any given context can be fraught with difficulty. For our primary purposes here, the key notion is clearly one based upon economics, trade and finance: the increase in the speed and quantity of 'flows'[2] between states (or regions) of investment, people and information. These increased flows can create new areas or spaces, which are no longer tied to nation states alone. Ideas of globalisation and universalisation in this sense concern matters such as international financial products (such as Eurobonds[3] and currency swap agreements) and homogenizing developments in certain industries (such as Microsoft's Windows operating system), to name but a few random examples.

   These phenomena often force a move *beyond* the nation state, in a number of different directions. The move could be 'up', in the sense of shifting powers and responsibilities to international organisations of varying depth, intensity and resources. It is sometimes forgotten that these forces may also contribute to shifts downward, in terms of the devolution of power to local or regional levels: this can be seen in the dynamics of long-established relations within

---

1   We are indebted to conversations with Andrew Lang for this (admittedly very brief) coverage of the globalisation issue and acknowledge that any attempt to conceptualise globalisation is likely to be inherently contestable.

2   To use the conception of globalisation developed in Held & McGrew, Goldblatt & Perraton, *Global Transformations* (Polity, Cambridge, 1999), see pp. 14 -16 for an outline.

3   Bonds (debt instruments) which are issued in a non-domestic currency (an example being a yen-denominated issue in London).

Federal states, between the Federal and 'state' level, but more recent examples include classically unitary states such as the United Kingdom (albeit not without certain teething troubles). Finally, and extremely importantly, these globalising tendencies can suggest a trend towards 'contracting out' of nation state-based regulation and enforcement: good examples are provided by S.W.I.F.T.'s rule book on inter-bank transfers, the handling of most disputes concerning documentary credits by the I.C.C.'s Banking Division.[4] Another development in the field of private initiatives moving ahead of public regulation is the increasing introduction of (often publicised) internal corporate policies and practices: these include such matters as codes of practice (covering behaviour towards employees and even competitors) and systems of emissions trading internal to certain corporate groups.

Nevertheless, these forces cannot be separated from their surrounding social and political context. Indeed, the thesis that 'globalisation' is somehow an inevitable product of the natural economic order of our modern world seems ever less sustainable. Granted, revolutions in technology and the acceptance of the general capitalist economic model do play an important role in driving much of the process adverted to in the previous paragraph. In many areas, these dynamics lead to attempts by certain sectors to set up satisfactory systems of self-regulation and dispute settlement (such as S.W.I.F.T. and the I.C.C. on documentary credits, mentioned above, and the creation of I.S.D.A.[5] to provide framework agreements to cover negotiated swaps and derivatives).[6] However, this process is by no means divorced from politics. In fact, serious national and bloc interests are often at stake and states do not hesitate to rely upon these to play their part in shaping that same process: the development of régimes to promote and regulate electronic commerce[7] illustrates the perception of national governments of the importance of the issue and the de-

---

4   We are indebted to Boris Kozolchyk's presentation ('International Contracts') at the Stanford Seminar, 22 June 2001 for this example.

5   The International Swaps and Derivatives Association. We are indebted to colleagues for this intriguing example.

6   Even here, to assert the absence of any political dimension would be to present an incomplete picture. For some, the rise of such 'user-driven' methods of co-ordination amounts to a paradigmatic illustration of the so-called 'privatisation of governance'. Indeed, parallels could be drawn with the role of the World Bank and the IMF in their introduction of structural adjustment conditions as part of loans to struggling economies, or with the role played by some Non-Governmental Organisations (NGOs) in the implementation of national or international development aid programmes. To borrow an argument from English administrative law in deciding on the 'public' nature of a particular body: in the absence of such initiatives it is likely that some form of more 'traditional' government institution would need to step in to fill the gap (see, e.g., *R* v. *Panel on Takeovers and Mergers* ex parte *Datafin plc* (1987) Q.B. 815 – discussed most recently and helpfully by Bamforth in (1993) *Public Law* 239).

7   See the often controversial Digital Millennium Copyright Act 1998 in the U.S.A. and the European Community's new Directive on certain legal aspects of information society services, in particular electronic commerce, in the internal market – Directive 2000/31/EC [2000] OJ L178/1.

sire to (be seen to) promote its position or to control its effects.[8] The politics of
the system are often exposed in cases concerning competition law rules and
their extraterritorial application and enforcement, where sharply differing national philosophies (as well as inconsistencies internal to one country's approach)[9/10] are sometimes made explicit. Equally, these disagreements in competition law cases also act as a strong incentive to develop co-operation between national competition authorities, to attempt to alleviate the practical
problems that such overlaps and differences can create.[11]

   This undoubtedly political element also makes clear the link to issues of
public perception and popular involvement in (and protest against) the various processes involved. The paradox of the increased flows referred to above
is that one might expect people to be brought closer, both to each other and to
their governments. Yet the moves 'up'[12] and 'out' are often seen as 'stretching'

---

8   E.g., by injecting notions of consumer protection into the jurisdictional régime to be ap-
    plied: see the EC's Distance Selling Directive (Directive 97/7/EC [1997] OJ L144/19), es-
    pecially Article 12 thereof which prevents consumers from waiving their rights by means
    of an explicit choice of law clause in the contract. See also the combined effect of Articles
    15(1)(c) and 16(1) of the 'Brussels I Regulation' (Regulation 44/2001/EC [2001] OJ L12/1),
    whereby a 'consumer may bring proceedings ... in the courts for the place where the con-
    sumer is domiciled' against a business which directs its business activities into the con-
    sumer's country (which could clearly cover instances of e-commerce).
9   See Rosenthal and Knighton's discussion of the American approach to the uranium sup-
    ply situation after World War II: first, encouraging increased production in other coun-
    tries; then, passing an embargo on imports of uranium in response to American uranium
    producers' complaints about depressed prices due to overcapacity and, finally, refusing to
    intervene in a private suit brought by Westinghouse against the cartel adopted by foreign
    producers in response to the American embargo (Rosenthal & Knighton, *National Laws
    and International Commerce – The Problem of Extraterritoriality* (RIIA, London, 1982 –
    Chatham House Paper No. 17, pp. 20-21.) More generally (pp. 32-35), they also draw at-
    tention to the dispersed nature of power in the Federal executive in the U.S.A. due to the
    existence of a number of 'semi-independent' regulatory and prosecution agencies, which
    causes difficulties for the State Department in formulating any coherent overall strategy
    with respect to questions of extraterritorial jurisdiction. It also has implications for en-
    forcement within the U.S.A. – see the recent Microsoft trial, settlement and reactions by
    certain states to the outcome.
10 The further complication in the American situation is the role played by the individual
    states and their claims to enforce rules within their jurisdiction: see Griffen, 'Reactions to
    U.S. Assertions of Extraterritorial Jurisdiction' (1998) ECLR 64, p. 70, who notes that the
    U.S. 'Antitrust Enforcement Guidelines for International Operations' (1995), published by
    the Department of Justice and the Federal Trade Commission, 'do not purport to represent
    the views of state attorneys general – nineteen of whom initiated the *Hartford Fire* case'
    (drawn from Baker *FTC Watch* No. 421 at 4 (Oct. 24, 1994)).
11 See the various bilateral agreements in the competition field: e.g. the U.S.A. has agree-
    ments with Germany, Canada and (two with) the European Community. Furthermore,
    October 2001 saw the launch of an interesting analogue to the private, commercial co-op-
    erative ventures discussed in the foregoing text, with the establishment of the Internation-
    al Competition Network. This is a means to allow frequent contacts, projects and ex-
    changes of ideas between competition *authorities*: see the following internet address for
    more details: <http://www.internationalcompetitionnetwork.org>.
12 See the notion of national 'voice' developed by Weiler in the context of the history of the
    European Union, in 'The Transformation of Europe' (1991) 100 Yale L.J. 2403; reproduced
    (with a new afterword) as Ch. 2 in his *The Constitution of Europe* (C.U.P., Cambridge, 1999).

the links of legitimacy and accountability between the governors and the governed. The current E.U. Convention on the Future of Europe, under the presidency of Valéry Giscard d'Estaing, is one of the most visible manifestations of the appreciation of these difficulties by those who hold public power, as well as (ostensibly?) an attempt to address the problems thus raised.

When one adds a consideration of the role of private commerce, the picture becomes even more complex. For some, the increasing power of the multinational corporation[13] can allow it both to influence national (and international) public policy-making[14] and to require traditional sources of public power to rely upon the corporation's capacity (and willingness) to self-regulate.[15] This level of influence is then argued to alienate individuals still further from those who govern them, because the democratic ties act as little more than window-dressing: a means of providing formal legitimacy for institutions which in fact pay little heed to the real 'will of the people'. When these allegations are added to the oft-cited feeling of alienation on the part of 'civil society'[16] from general involvement in the important aspects of (even the national) political process, the pressures which lead to popular protest on certain issues become clearer. Very often, the gripe is not only a divorce from the actual involvement, but also a feeling of disassociation from the results which are achieved: this can undermine the legitimacy of the *output* of that process, which can lead to calls for greater *input* into the process, in the hope of seeing a greater proportion of (politically) acceptable[17] results. Thus, civil society is said to be excluded by such effectively 'secret' decision-making, whether this be at national or supranational political levels, or in the realm of important and influential decisions taken by private and politically unaccountable actors such as corporations. These complaints have often been made within the con-

---

13   See, for background, Navaretti, Haaland & Venables (CEPR), 'Multinational Corporations and Global Production Networks: the Implications for Trade Policy' (Report for the European Commission, 2002).

14   See, e.g., Sell, *Private Power, Public law – The Globalization of Intellectual Property Rights* (C.U.P., Cambridge, 2003).

15   This is a point of particular interest and importance when applied to the media industry. The large media groups have a huge influence on the content of and the approach to the political agenda, even to the point of being decisive factors in securing electoral success for a particular campaign. This can be true of global, regional, national and sometimes even local issues. As far as self-regulation is concerned, in the U.K., in the absence of any developed law protecting privacy, many people who suddenly find themselves and their lives 'newsworthy' must rely upon the self-restraint of the media to regulate its intrusions into their lives, rather than any legal protection. For some, this is a reflection of the importance which British society attaches to freedom of expression and the vital role of the press (or, alternatively, a recognition that those who court celebrity must face the consequences of the notoriety which has brought them success, fame and fortune). For others, this is a result of the political 'masters' being beholden to the press for their power and its maintenance – who would dare to introduce measures to curb the freedom of the press, when it has the ability to destroy a political career or even party?

16   For a recent and interesting enquiry into the nature and existence of this phenomenon on a global scale, see Keane, *Global Civil Society?* (C.U.P., Cambridge, 2003), especially p. 40 et seq.

17   At least, to the aggrieved elements of civil society.

text of the European Union, being seen as a democratic and/or legitimacy deficit of the EU, its institutions and law-making procedures. It is thus easy to see that such difficulties are highly likely to be exacerbated in the much looser, less integrated international system.

On the other hand, it should be noted that this alienation and discontent is by no means a universal phenomenon: for example, in many large, international infrastructure projects, private initiatives are very careful to involve non-governmental organisations ('NGOs') and local civil society in the processes of planning and execution.[18] In such cases, it may often be the case that the local population and the NGOs have greater confidence and trust in these private bodies than they hold in their own national governments, especially if there is a long and clear history of corruption and inefficiency on the part of such governments.[19] This may be said to tie in well with the increasing scepticism with which national electorates are said to view national politics.

---

18   We are grateful to Tom Heller for raising this point at the Lustrum Seminar in Leiden, 5 and 6 December 2002. *Quaere* whether this is sometimes occasioned by a condition of, for example, World Bank support for such projects. This would be an interesting example of a partial shift 'up' from, combined with a form of 'contracting out' of, the nation state paradigm achieving an increased level of connection with the local population, which might otherwise have been significantly alienated by such a project going on in its 'back yard'. (Equally, it should be noted that this by-passing of domestic institutions is by no means a universally welcome phenomenon: see Weiss (ed.), *State in the Global Economy – Bringing Domestic Institutions Back In* (C.U.P., Cambridge, 2003).) Three further comments are, perhaps, appropriate here: first, one significant pressure for such initiatives on the part of corporate investors may well be the need to maintain a corporate image and reputation to satisfy investors and shareholders, suggesting that there are cases where the private interest and an increased participatory element can co-exist and may even mutually reinforce each other; second, the frequency and depth of the involvement of local civil society and NGOs in such projects is undoubtedly very variable. Finally, such investment and infrastructure projects are only one (albeit an important) part of the phenomenon of increasing private party involvement in quasi-governmental roles. To extrapolate too far from these admittedly extremely interesting (and often rather encouraging) examples may be a dangerous exercise.

19   In the environmental field, however, the recent history of the Western world suggests that much of society places greater faith in a transparent planning process which is independent from government and promoters and which guarantees a measure of involvement for any interested private citizen. Furthermore, recent UK government reform proposals (see the Green Paper, subsequent policy statements and the Planning and Compulsory Purchase Bill available at the following internet address:
     <http://www.planning.odpm.gov.uk/consult/greenpap/greenind.htm>) suggest an increasing impatience with the lengthy delays which are caused by such a system of impact assessment and consultation, especially when coupled with the rather strong procedural rights stemming from European Community Law in this field – see Directive 85/337/EC [1985] OJ L175/40 (as amended by Directive 97/11/EC [1997] OJ L73/5). These delays can be a major factor in discouraging altogether investment in vital areas, such as the construction of renewable power generation facilities: this point was stressed throughout the U.K. Cabinet Office Performance and Innovation Unit's publication, *The Energy Review* (February 2002) (see <http://www.cabinet-office.gov.uk/innovation/2002/energy/report/TheEnergyReview.PDF>).

So, these arguments about private commerce and civil society clearly do not all run in one direction.

Another angle on the role of commerce is that it itself feels alienated (or at least poorly served) by the national process of government, due to a perception that attempts to participate at the national level are often ineffective. This can occur, either because there are significant differences between the current national government's policy priorities and those held to be vital by the corporation, or because there is a perception on the part of corporations of the need for a genuine international reaction to a particular phenomenon, which will not be achieved by means of the national political process. Market forces may often demand a more rapid and 'internationalised' solution than any individual state will be able to provide.

However, outside the area of direct market participants, this aspect of alienation has sometimes erupted into popular protest; furthermore, this protest has become increasingly co-ordinated across national boundaries, taking advantage of the very technology and communications revolution which some would present as the apotheosis of globalisation.[20] In this way, protests against the World Trade Organisation, the G8 meeting in Genoa and the E.U.'s Gothenburg European Council have all acquired great publicity in the last few months and years, albeit in a manner which has focused more on particular institutions or groups than particular issues. For example, great public pressure from environmental movements has led to increasingly strict rules on liability for maritime pollution,[21] after wide publicity for previous environmental disasters and their impact (such as the *Exxon Valdez*; more recent examples include the sinking of the *Erika* off Brittany in 1999 and that of the *Prestige* off the Spanish coast in November 2002). Yet when environmental concerns bite closer to home, such as during the rise in taxes on petrol in the United Kingdom for ostensibly environmental reasons, popular protest decried the high prices and demanded reductions, without any significant reference (by anyone, including government or environmental groups) to the underlying environmental dangers.[22] While the motivations behind the petrol protests did not

---

20   See Hall & Biersteker (eds.), *The Emergence of Private Authority in Global Governance* (C.U.P., Cambridge, 2002), especially Ch. 5 (Sassan) – she focuses on the *use* of these new tools of information technology, arguing that an understanding how these tools are employed by private actors in organising and managing global markets is just as (if not more) important than investigating the development and proliferation of the tools themselves.

21   See the International Convention on Civil Liability for Oil Pollution Damage 1992 (obliging ship owners to take out compulsory insurance and setting up a system of strict liability for oil pollution damage) and the International Convention on the Establishment of an International Fund for Compensation for Oil Pollution Damage 1992 (to cover victims whose losses are not adequately compensated under insurance value arising under the Civil Liability Convention). See Forbes (2003) *New Law Journal* 10 (10 January 2003) for a brief discussion concerning the recent *Prestige* disaster.

22   Perhaps because there is no (convincing) evidence that the extra revenue has actually been used to attempt to deal with the environmental problems raised by extensive car usage? Or because there is no evidence that the increase in taxes has had any deterrent effect, in encouraging drivers to use less environmentally damaging modes of transport?

even seem to be uniform across the different countries,[23] there was nevertheless evidence of genuine international links: reports suggested that protest
leaders in France, Belgium, Germany and the UK were in contact via mobile
telephones. Finally, the Warsaw Convention on civil liability in air transport
potentially affects *everybody* who flies, without any say for them whatsoever
in the process of its formation, application and amendment.[24]

This all tends to suggest that the coalitions of interest which lead to large-
scale public protest are of a shifting nature, often containing elements whose
goals are as mutually inconsistent as those against which each element is
protesting. Given the huge variety of issues at stake and the differences in particular national situations and sensitivities (e.g. UK animal welfarism),[25] these
differing intensities are perhaps unsurprising, but they also make any general explanation of such trends and articulation or responses an extremely difficult task. That said, this variety also underlines inescapably the highly political nature of any development and operation of a system of legal rules dealing
with matters of jurisdiction and conflict of laws.

3   THE BASIC FRAMEWORK: TRADITIONAL APPROACHES TO JURISDICTION

The basic presumption is that globalisation, in the widest possible sense, may
call for a new understanding and application of the traditional concepts of ju-

---

23   E.g., in the United Kingdom, it seems that some were tired of the fact that direct French ac-
      tion always seemed to get results in France, while more conciliatory tones in the UK
      seemed to be easily ignored by policy-makers.
24   On which, see section 4.2.2.2, below. A recent and highly contentious illustration is pro-
      vided by the class actions in the U.K. and Australia against airlines, claiming compensa-
      tion for injuries and even deaths caused by Deep Vein Thrombosis. The key preliminary
      issue is whether or not the Warsaw Convention's term 'accident' is capable of including
      the development of blood clots caused inside the body by the conditions on long-haul
      flights. To date, the High Court in London has ruled that such injuries are not 'accidents'
      within the Convention ([2003] 1 All E.R. 935, although Nelson J. did grant the claimants
      permission to appeal), while an Australian court (the Supreme Court of Victoria in *Povey*
      v. *Civil Aviation Safety Authority* [2002] VSC 580) has taken the opposite view (see *The
      Times*, 21 December 2002, p. 4). The consequences of the outcome of these cases for inter-
      national (and mass) tort litigation will be extremely interesting.
25   Vividly expressed in the protests over live animal exports, which often led to blockages or
      restrictions on trade. This brought in elements of EC law, as traders argued that failure by
      the police to secure passage for their lawfully traded goods amounted to a measure hav-
      ing equivalent effect to a quantitative restriction under Article 29 EC: see *R* v. *Chief Consta-
      ble of Sussex* ex parte *International Traders Ferry* (1998) 3 WLR. 1260 (as well as similar cases
      such as *R.* v. *Coventry C.C.* ex parte *Phoenix Aviation* (1995) 3 All ER 37). Of course, this rais-
      es complex issues concerning attempts by one EC Member State to pursue its own domes-
      tic goals in a particular area, even where that pursuit on its own territory also claims an
      ability to influence events in other countries, by, for example, preventing exports because
      the rules in the importing state fail to live up to certain standards (see further Case C-5/94
      R v. *Ministry for Agriculture, Fisheries and Food* ex parte *Hedley Lomas Ltd.* [1996] ECR. I-
      2553 and Case C-1/96 *R* v. *Ministry for Agriculture, Fisheries and Food* ex parte *Compassion
      in World Farming* [1998] ECR I-1251).

risdiction as well as for the formulation of new principles on which those concepts are based. If it was ever possible to allocate jurisdiction on the basis of the ordering concept of national sovereignty alone, the globalisation of the national economies and developments such as the internet have led to a situation where this is no longer possible.

We must make a brief review of the traditional doctrines and processes used to allocate jurisdiction. The orthodox conceptual distinction is usually made between public and private international law, broadly reflecting the division between public and private laws.[26]

3.1   The approach in public international law

The bases which are supported by state practice for the assertion of legislative and judicial jurisdiction have been expressed in terms of five principles: territoriality, nationality, the protective principle, passive personality, and universality.[27] It would seem that one or more of these principles should be present for a state to have jurisdiction, despite the view of the PCIJ in the *Lotus* case[28] that jurisdiction may be assumed in the absence of contrary prohibitive rules. The 1935 Harvard research on jurisdiction was directed at jurisdiction over crime, but much of the debate relating to public international law extraterritorial jurisdiction has gravitated around quasi-criminal matters, most notably US antitrust law. Actions based on such matters, although typically civil in form, can be viewed as the exercise by a state of its public powers.[29]

It may be seen that these principles – which are not all accepted by every state – attempt to provide a link between the persons or act involved and the

---

26   See Lowe (1984) 33 ICLQ 515, at pp. 519-525 (discussing submission clauses in the context of US measures relating to the Trans-Siberian gas pipeline).

27   Harvard Research, Draft Convention on Jurisdiction with respect to Crime (1935); Introductory Comment, 29 A.J.I.L., Supp. 435 at p. 439. Passive personality jurisdiction – based on the nationality of a person injured by an offence – was not endorsed by the researchers (see pp. 578-9). It has found some support in state practice – e.g., *United States* v. *Yunis* (1988) 681 F Supp. 896 in the context of aircraft hijacking, where universal jurisdiction was also invoked. See, further, Neale and Stephens, International Business and National Jurisdiction (Clarendon Press, Oxford, 1988), Ch. 2. An alternative approach is provided by Podgor, 'Extraterritorial Criminal Jurisdiction: Replacing 'Objective Territoriality' with 'Defensive Territoriality'' (2003) 25 Studies in Law, Politics and Society 117.

28   *The Lotus Case (France* v. *Turkey)* (1927) PCIJ Ser. A. No. 10. The robustly positivist paradigm of statehood espoused by the Permanent Court has not escaped criticism – see, e.g., Brierly (1928) 44 LQR 144.

29   It is arguable (see, section 3.4) below that the chasm between public and private international law is neither as deep nor as unbridgeable as the traditional approach may imply. The analysis of antitrust cases in terms of public international law, with the invocation of the doctrine of effects, serves to amplify the competing public interests at play.

state which asserts jurisdiction.[30] The territorial principle is the clearest – a state clearly has competence with regard to its own territory.[31] The possibility of concurrent jurisdiction is implicit in the Harvard analysis – it is evidently possible for the interests of multiple states to be engaged by a single transaction or criminal offence.

Global developments have gradually and inexorably led to a change in the scope of the orthodox principles. Examples abound. The interpretation by a majority of the House of Lords in the *Pinochet* case[32] of the Torture Convention[33] and associated UK legislation shows an unprecedented reliance on international law.[34] The resulting restriction of sovereign immunity, and the corresponding effective widening of the sphere of operation of universal jurisdiction, can on one view be seen to reflect shifting values in a changing world order.[35] In the commercial sphere, the *Lotus* formulation of objective territorial jurisdiction has, notoriously, been treated by some states as covering the economic effects experienced in one country precipitated by acts committed in another.[36] Initial antipathy[37] towards such a fluid and controversial application of territorial jurisdiction has in many cases been supplanted by the development of concepts of comity and reciprocity, which have pervaded a number of fields.[38] On the other hand, the use of extraterritorial jurisdic-

---

30   Such a 'linking point' was discussed by the District Court of Jerusalem in *Attorney-General of the Government of Israel* v. *Eichmann* (1961) 36 ILR 5 at paras. 31-35, citing Dahm's *Anknüpfungspunkt* ('link') in his *Zur Problematik des Völkerstrafrechts* (1956). It is further reflected in the U.S. courts' approach to assessment of jurisdiction by reference to the due process clause of the Fourteenth Amendment to the U.S. Constitution. See *International Shoe Co.* v. *Washington*, 326 U.S. 310 (1945), where the test is developed as one of the 'minimum contact' necessary to satisfy due process.

31   *Island of Palmas Case* 2 U.N. Rep 829 (1928), at pp. 838-9.

32   *R.* v. *Bow Street Magistrates* ex parte *Pinochet Ugarte (No. 3)* (1999) 2 WLR 827.

33   Convention against Torture and Certain Other Cruel, Inhuman or Degrading Treatment or Punishment (1984).

34   See Hopkins [1999] CLJ 461. The speech of Lord Millett is particularly radical; 'Customary international law is part of the common law' (*R.* v. *Bow Street Magistrates* ex parte *Pinochet Ugarte (No. 3)* (1999) 2 WLR 827, at p. 912), on which see Collier (1989) 38 ICLQ 924.

35   On which, generally, see Robertson, *Crimes Against Humanity* (Penguin Books, London, 2000), in particular pp. 368-400.

36   Notably, of course, in the U.S. antitrust cases, beginning with *United States* v. *Aluminum Co. of America* 148 F. 2d 416 (1945).

37   In the form of diplomatic communications and, more seriously, blocking legislation: see, e.g., the Protection of Trading Interests Act (1980) and generally Lowe, *Extraterritorial Jurisdiction* (C.U.P., Cambridge, 1983), pp. xvii-xx.

38   Examples include positive and negative comity agreements between the US and the EC on the enforcement of competition policy; bilateral tax treaties; securities agreements; and reciprocity clauses in EC legislation. A useful illustration of reciprocity is found in the 2nd Banking and Public Procurement Directives: see Eeckhout, *The European Internal Market and International Trade: A Legal Analysis* (Clarendon Press, Oxford, 1994), Ch. 2, p. 307 et seq. and Ch. 9.

tion to implement foreign policy has – unsurprisingly – given rise to serious objections.[39]

3.2   *Approaches in systems of private international law*

In an increasingly global economy, national courts must be prepared to deal with cases determining civil rights and liabilities where international elements are present.[40] It is harder to make generalisations about private international law, given the diverse ways in which different legal systems approach it. It might be observed that it is often the case that the great masses of unilateral curial determinations of competence to hear individual cases are suggestive of an approach pregnant with unruly casuistry. Nonetheless, certain trends can be detected. A number of theories have been advanced. It is often argued, for example, that the realisation of reasonable and legitimate expectations of the parties is fundamental to the conflict of laws.[41] Intriguingly, customary international law does not appear frequently to be invoked as the basis for the resolution of conflicts,[42] but there have been important developments in conventional law.[43] Notably, the EC has recently enacted a Regulation on jurisdiction and the recognition and enforcement of foreign judgments[44] which has superseded the 1968 Brussels Convention,[45] streamlining certain of its provisions. Equally important is the increasing preparedness of US courts to hear claims brought by foreigners.[46]

The EC has given further impetus to the unification of private internation-

---

39   Particularly forceful objections were made by a number of states and the EU in relation to the US D'Amato and Helms-Burton Acts (concerning sanctions against Libya and Iran in the former, and against Cuba in the latter). This legislation contains particularly draconian penalties against those not adhering to the U.S. régime. See Regulation 2271/96 [1996] OJ L309/39 and Lowe [1997] CLJ 248 and (1997) 46 ICLQ 378.

40   The problem is not as new as might be imagined. See section 5 for Shakespeare's summary of some the intermeshing interests which drive international litigation.

41   See, e.g., (from the English conflicts jurisprudence), Dicey & Morris, *The Conflict of Laws* (Sweet & Maxwell, London, 13th ed. 2000), section 1-006; Cheshire and North's *Private International Law* (Butterworths, London, 13th ed. 1999), p. 32.

42   See Kahn-Freund, *General Problems of Private International Law* (Sijthoff & Noordhoff, Leiden, 1980), p. 41: 'Customary international law is an arid source of rules for the conflict of laws'. A useful analysis of the relationship and distinction between public and private international law is given by Collier, *The Conflict of Laws* (Cambridge University Press, London, 3rd ed. 2001), Ch. 23.

43   Which approach Kahn-Freund welcomes: *General Problems of Private International Law* (Sijthoff & Noordhoff, Leiden, 1980), p. 43.

44   Council Reg. No. 44/2001/EC, [2001] OJ L 12/1, which entered into force on 1st March 2002: see footnote [8] above.

45   Convention on Jurisdiction and the Enforcement of Judgments in Civil and Commercial Matters 1968. A number of bilateral conventions are also superseded by the Regulation (see Article 69 of the new Regulation).

46   See the recent 'rediscovery' and use of the Alien Tort Claims Act in the U.S.A.

al law within the Community through a Convention on choice of law in contract.[47] Progress continues to be made with respect to the unification of internal laws – notable past examples include the Warsaw Convention[48] and the
1980 U.N. Convention on Contracts for the International Sale of Goods.[49] Bodies such as UNCITRAL and UNIDROIT are dedicated to the further harmonisation of domestic laws, to avoid conflicts *ab initio*, insofar as this may be possible. Regional conventions to the same end have also been concluded.[50]

3.3   *The role of international dispute settlement bodies*

Although our primary focus is necessarily on the jurisdiction of states' courts, a
cognate issue is the ability – of states and of individuals – effectively to contract out
of the municipal judicial apparatus. A proliferation of international dispute settlement machinery is apparent; with this proliferation has come a corresponding
and healthy widening of the material competence with which states are prepared
to endow certain of the specialist fora. This trend, which may be observed across
a range of fields, is indicative of a desire and need to replace the lottery inherent in
the traditional jurisdictional rules with a more certain, structured approach.

The phenomenon exists at all levels – inter-state, private and mixed. Disputes can be extracted, wholly or in part, from the national arena and settled
in accordance with predetermined standards. A certain structural elegance
emerges. The creation of dispute settlement bodies by state consent involves
the explicit consideration of matters of jurisdiction. Potential conflicts can be
identified and negotiated at the outset (including *political* conflicts of interest, which are arguably much better dealt with by politicians than by judicial
bodies under the mantra of 'comity'). The result is substantially increased
ante hoc certainty. Although firmly rooted in classical international law, these
developments lend new colour to transnational litigation. This is particularly the case with mixed arbitration, where an ever decreasing need to resort
to traditional techniques of diplomatic protection can be observed.[51] A clear
example is the International Centre for the Settlement of Investment Disputes ('ICSID'):[52] a reasonably clear-cut jurisdictional structure and a good
track-record for the satisfactory resolution of disputes provide a stable climate in which inward investment can operate and be encouraged. A coherent substratum of jurisdiction leads to greater substantive efficiency.

---

47   E.E.C. Convention on the Law Applicable to Contractual Obligations 1980 (the Rome
      Convention) [1980] OJ L266.
48   Warsaw Convention 1929, amended at The Hague in 1955, providing uniform rules for
      the carriage of persons or goods by aircraft for reward. See section 4.2.2.2 below.
49   Prepared by the United Nations Committee on International Trade Law (UNCITRAL).
50   See in particular David, 2 *International Encyclopedia of Comparative Law*, pp. 181-188.
51   Discussed generally in Collier and Lowe, *The Settlement of Disputes in International Law*
      (O.U.P., Oxford, 1999).
52   Ibidem, pp. 59-73.

The progress towards greater acceptance of dispute settlement procedures, with varying degrees of delocalisation, is manifest. The trend may be observed over diverse fields ranging from criminal tribunals[53] to the widespread recognition and enforcement of foreign arbitral awards.[54] This presents a profound challenge to the traditional autarchic paradigm.

3.4   *Fresh approaches to jurisdiction? Paths towards (some) effective international co-operation*[55]

We are thus presented with a mass of loosely interrelated principles. Alongside this is a coherent body of evidence – in the form of the proliferation of international agreements – that states are unwilling, at least in certain fields, to leave critical matters of jurisdiction to an uncertain and shifting body of jurisprudence. The diffuse classical concepts used to distribute jurisdictional competence contribute little to legal certainty. It must be questioned whether the colossal discretion left to states in delimiting their own jurisdiction[56] is conducive to a satisfactory climate for contemporary international relations.

For our purposes, the public and private international law dichotomy is possibly overstated and conceals important conceptual and theoretical overlaps. Both branches of law represent emanations of states' ability to exercise their legislative and judicial (and indeed executive) powers.[57] The public interests of a state pervade private international law through mechanisms which exclude foreign law[58] and the ability to refuse recognition and enforcement of a foreign judgment; this reflects the fact that even the sphere of civil law does

---

53   Notably those established by Security Council Resolutions 827 and 955, dealing with atrocities perpetrated in the Former Yugoslavia and Rwanda respectively; and the International Criminal Court (established by the 1998 Rome Statute, subject to ratification). The jurisdiction of the U.N. Tribunals is markedly different from that of the I.C.C., which does not generally enjoy primacy over local courts (Rome Statute, Article 17).

54   Exemplified by the 1958 New York Convention on the Recognition and Enforcement of Foreign Arbitral Awards 330 UNTS 38.

55   For an overview of some important and interesting fields in which international co-operation has effectively developed see McClean, *International Co-Operation in Civil and Criminal Matters* (OUP, Oxford, 2002).

56   Emphasised with particular clarity in the *Barcelona Traction, Light and Power Co. Case* (1970) ICJ Reports 3.

57   Mann, *Further Studies in International Law* (Clarendon Press, Oxford, 1990), Ch. 1. Brownlie, in *Principles of Public International Law*, (Clarendon Press, Oxford, 5th ed. 1998), p. 302, notes that civil liability is ultimately subject to enforcement through procedures which include criminal sanctions. See also Akehurst (1972-1973) 46 BYIL 145, at 187.

58   For the operation of this in England, see Cheshire and North, op. cit., Chapter 8. An obvious example of such an exclusionary mechanism is the use of mandatory rules. As to whether the converse ever holds, and parties are *obliged* to plead and prove a foreign law rather than rely on English substantive law, see Fentiman, *Foreign Law in English Courts* (Clarendon Press, Oxford, 1998), esp. pp. 66-77.

not represent a field in which individuals enjoy unqualified autonomy.[59] The overlap between public and private law is exposed by those very areas in which controversy over extraterritorial jurisdiction has arisen: notably, this has occurred in the fields of antitrust and securities regulation.[60] Characterisation in terms of 'public' or 'private' is not necessarily analytically helpful. Instead, precise countervailing interests and problems must directly be identified.

The primitive reality of national sovereignty remains the ordering concept in both public[61] and private[62] international law. This, unadulterated, is unlikely to fulfil modern requirements of transactional efficiency and the needs of globalisation.[63] Indeed, external sovereignty can now only be understood in the light of ever-increasing interdependence; it is vital that the conceptual framework provided by jurisdictional rules reflects this. The principles which underlie such rules are inevitably transient, not immutable *sub specie æternitatis*. It is essential that regard be had, in particular, to the nature of the transactions and to the conduct regulated, which nature will necessarily impact upon the ap-

---

59   On which generally, e.g., Zimmermann, *The Law of Obligations*, p. 713 et seq. The coincidence between doctrines which effectively circumscribe transactional freedom in a system of domestic law on the one hand, and in its private international law on the other, is not always exact. Such inexactitude may be symptomatic of chauvinism, if not plain atrophy, in that system of private international law.

60   See sections 4.2.2.3 and 4.4 below.

61   Exemplified, for example, in Articles 2(1) and 2(7) of the Charter of the United Nations, and U.N. General Assembly Resolution 2131 on Non-Intervention.

62   Despite Kahn-Freund's rejection of customary international law as a source for the resolution of conflicts (see his *General Problems of Private International Law* (Sijthoff & Noordhoff, Leiden,1980), at p. 39), the starting point for private international law is that it is predicated on raw territoriality. See, e.g., *The Siskina* [1979] A.C. 210, 254 'the general rule that the jurisdiction of the English court over persons is territorial' (*per* Lord Diplock). This general rule is eroded by the use of exorbitant jurisdiction; and, significantly, by the recent approach taken to multinational corporations – see *Lubbe* v. *Cape plc (No. 2)* [2000] 1 WLR 1545 (HL) – discussed by Muchlinski [2001] 50 ICLQ 1 and Sinclair [2001] LMCLQ 197.

63   See Guzman, 'Choice of Law: New Foundations' (2002) 90 *Georgetown Law Journal* 971 (see also <http://papers.ssrn.com/sol3/delivery.cfm/000731650.pdf?abstractid=237802>), who uses public choice theory and economic principles to approach questions of choice of law, arguing that the purely selfish behaviour of nations inhibits global efficiency. This raises a key issue: if the basic approaches to jurisdiction discussed in the text thus far do not produce efficient or effective results, then who will have the power and (crucially) the *incentive* to take into account a welfare circle beyond that of just the nation state? Within the systems in the U.S.A. and (increasingly) the E.U., this sort of welfare calculus does already take place, including as it does tricky questions of winners and losers at the sub-Federal level in making any broader accommodation across the whole geographical area. A good example of this latter point is provided by the recent increases in steel tariffs on imports into the U.S.A.: while it might be said to serve the interests of the domestic American steel producers, it also creates significant economic costs for domestic American consumers of such steel (such as car manufacturers), due to increased steel prices and weaker competition from imports. And this is all *before* any *global* economic welfare assessment is made of the economic impact of such tariffs (including effects felt by steel exporters in Europe and Asia, for example).

proach taken to jurisdiction. So, while the proposition that in the case of real estate, the courts of the *situs* have jurisdiction and apply their domestic law in respect of it seems elementary,[64] a very different analytical approach will obviously be required for jurisdiction over, for example, the internet.[65/66]

In a world where the very nature of international transactions can give rise to interest in a plethora of states, and a corresponding multiple concurrence of jurisdiction, critical questions emerge. The international system is saturated with challenges to the traditional approaches to jurisdiction and cases illustrating current difficulties; obvious recent examples include the French *Yahoo!* Decision,[67] the United States' Digital Millennium Copyright Act 1998[68]

---

64 A manifestation of the linking point doctrine: closeness of connection is used to justify jurisdiction. Use of the *lex loci delicti* in respect of torts (the place where the tort occurred) is also 'intuitive' (although there may be room for debate as to where the *locus* is in the case of a trans-border tort).

65 The *Yahoo!* decision (*UEJF et Licra c/ Yahoo! Inc. et Yahoo France*, 22 May 2000, *Tribunal de Grande Instance de Paris*) exposes the difficulties inherent in allocating jurisdiction over cyberspace. The internet provides almost virtually unlimited opportunities for the commission of transnational crimes and torts: one is potentially subject to the laws, and prescriptive jurisdiction, of all states. Clear concern exists relating to, say, the possibility of a statement, lawful in the state of its maker, being defamatory according to the law of another state – concern which contributed to impediments in negotiations on a draft Convention on Private International Law at the Hague.

66 It should be noted here that such expansive conclusions as to jurisdiction have by no means been confined to Europe. The attitude of Minnesota state law towards the internet has been made clear in ringing tones: '[o]nce the defendant places an advertisement on the Internet, that advertisement is available 24 hours a day, 7 days a week, 365 days a year to any Internet User until the defendant takes it off the Internet' (*Minnesota* v. *Granite Gate Resort, Inc.*, No. C6-95-7227, 1996 WL 767431 (Minn. Dist. Ct. Dec. 11 1996, Minn. Ct. App. 1997). Thus, any argument that the defendant had never mailed to, advertised in or delivered to Minnesota was easily rejected: accessibility was the key, was simple to prove in the internet context and clearly could apply both to other U.S. states and to web sites based in foreign countries. However, other cases in the U.S.A. take a more restrictive approach: see, e.g., *CompuServe Inc.* v. *Patterson* 89 F. 3d 1257 (6th Cir. 1996), discussed by Mitrani (2001) 7 Int. Tr. L. 50.

67 Above, n. 65. Yahoo! auctioned Nazi memorabilia on its US site; sales of such memorabilia are legal in the United States, but not in France. The action against Yahoo! was successful on the basis that the site could be accessed by French citizens and there was no effective way to avoid this. The jurisdictional complexities are evaded by means of a somewhat anodyne recital: 'Attendu que ... les éventuelles difficultés d'exécution de notre décision sur le territoire des Etats-Unis, invoquées par Yahoo Inc., ne sauraient fonder à elles seules une exception d'incompétence'. Perhaps unsurprisingly, the American courts have held that they have personal jurisdiction over LICRA (*Yahoo! Inc.* v. *LICRA* 145 F.Supp. 2d. 1168 (2001)) and have granted a summary judgment declaring that the First Amendment of the U.S. Constitution precludes the enforcement within the United States of the order made by the Paris court (*Yahoo! Inc.* v. *LICRA* case C-00-21275 JF, judgment of 11 November 2001 (U.S. District Court of Northern California, Judge Fogel)).

68 Which criminalises the development of technological tools which can violate copyright. The first case under its provisions failed (*Financial Times*, 18 December 2002) and the DMCA has attracted much criticism on both technological and constitutional grounds (see, e.g., Dixon, 'Breaking into Locked Rooms to Access a Computer Source Code: Does the DMCA Violate a Constitutional Mandate When Technological Barriers of Access Are Applied to Software?' (2003) 8 Va. J.L. & Tech. 2).

and the *G.E./Honeywell* merger saga.[69] The increase in the use of international tribunals and the expansion of the subject-matter which is deemed arbitrable (including disputes involving mandatory rules such as antitrust and securities regulations)[70] are further indications of a changing approach. One must question whether a proliferation of fora is sensible or practical: jurisdictional competition is not without its benefits, but unfettered and cynical forum shopping can be both undesirable and unpredictable in terms of attaining any meaningful system of global regulation.

It must therefore be asked whether developments in various sectors of the economy indicate a progression to a new and possibly more efficient approach to the apportionment of international jurisdiction. Linked to this is a compelling question: is such sectoralisation inevitable; or does it disclose the germ of a nascent, uniform approach to the theory which underpins jurisdiction?

4   GENERAL THEMES AND PROBLEMS: THE LENS OF THE RULE OF LAW

One way of approaching these issues is to examine different sectors of the economy and the types of structures, rules and practices that have developed to shape and organise that economic activity. The use of the Rule of Law in this context might seem slightly problematic, given that concept's strong ties with state-based, national legal systems. As will become evident, its role in our discussion is something of a semantic one. We use the concept of the Rule of Law to help to organise questions of which *actors* are involved in making and developing transnational régimes, which set(s) of rules apply to any given situation and how these rules are formulated, developed and inter-related on private or public, national, bilateral or multilateral levels. Nevertheless, this semantic device should not obscure the point that economic activity beyond the national boundaries of a traditional *Rechtsstaat* still requires an effective 'state of law' to provide a structure of sufficient predictability and reliability within which to operate. These characteristics are well known to any theory of the

---

69   Case No. COMP/M.2220 General Electric/Honeywell (Commission Decision of 3 July 2001), available at <http://www.europa.eu.int/comm/competition/mergers/cases/decisions/m2220_en.pdf>; the Commission declared the proposed merger incompatible with the common market and with the EEA Agreement and thus prohibited its completion, after the American authorities had much earlier given the deal the green light.

70   Arbitrators are generally obliged to apply certain mandatory rules to disputes before them (for an example in the context of competition law, see case C-126/97 *Eco-Swiss China Time* v. *Benetton* [1999] ECR I-3055). See, generally, M. Blessing, 'Mandatory rules of law versus party autonomy in international arbitration' (1997) 14/4 *Journal of International Arbitration* 24. An interesting future development may be the question of whether or not, within the EC, any of the principles of the E.C.H.R. (or any future legally binding EC human rights instrument) should be treated as mandatory rules for these arbitration purposes.

Rule of Law,[71] but, in a complex and multi-faceted international system, their fulfilment is often more difficult, both to formulate, develop and enforce. Different sectors have different requirements, tendencies and actors and, as a result, display the basic attributes of the Rule of Law to greatly varying degrees and achieve these results in many different ways.[72] In what follows, we seek to show many of these different methods and illustrate their operation in a number of sectors of economic activity. Drawing together this variety of areas and comparing their common and distinct characteristics may help to suggest future strategies for addressing the problems and opportunities presented by questions of jurisdiction in an economically globalising world.

4.1   Rule of 'law' – the 'privatisation of governance'

As suggested above,[73] one common general phenomenon that has been identified by globalisation theorists is the idea that once traditional governmental functions are increasingly being performed by private entities, especially multinational corporations. Interesting examples are provided by various forms of self-regulation adopted in particular sectors: these are usually organised by a voluntary 'buy-in' to the system, which then adopts a code of rules and agreed dispute resolution bodies and mechanisms.

At the same time, it has been noted that this shift to the 'private' sphere has not always been to the detriment of public confidence and (the perception of) accountability. Furthermore, in certain sectors the move has not been towards a privatisation of governance at all, but rather towards increased activity on the part of governmental actors in securing an international regulatory framework for such activities. In this vein, the example of some of the jurisdictional rules on transport is discussed below, in the context of multilateral harmonisation;[74] recent moves by national governments concerning the internet (including E-commerce rules[75] and attempts to gain the technology to monitor internet usage and communications) may be seen in a similar light, although

---

71   See, e.g., from the vast literature, Raz, 'The Rule of Law and its Virtue' (1977) 93 *Law Quarterly Review* 195 (also in his *The Authority of Law* (1983), Ch. 11) and Summers, 'The Principles of the Rule of Law' (1999) 74 Notre Dame L.R. 1691 for discussion and development of the content of the Rule of Law; Fallon, 'The Rule of Law as a Concept in Constitutional Discourse' (1997) 97 Columbia L.R. 1 for a discussion of the ideas underlying the various contested concepts of the Rule of Law; and the recent article by Tamanaha, 'The Rule of Law for Everyone?' (2002) 55 *Current Legal Problems* (forthcoming), which discusses different versions of the Rule of Law and how these may affect the application and implementation of the Rule of Law in many different circumstances.

72   Many different means are available: reliance on national law and national systems, privately developed régimes, international co-ordination (via treaties both bilateral and multilateral and in supranationally empowered International Organisations such as the E.U.), etc.

73   See, above, section 2, 'Globalisation'.

74   See, below, section 4.2.2.2.

75   In the EC, see Directive 2000/31/EC [2000] OJ L178/1.

here the move is not 'up' to international harmonisation, but is commonly a reassertion of the traditional territorial paradigm of jurisdiction.[76]

4.2   Rule of 'laws' (or the Rule of whose law and whose courts)?

4.2.1   Problems

A number of common problems will emerge from our examination of various sectors of the global economy. In particular, serious systemic difficulties are endemic. Questions of procedure may be arid but, if chaos is to be avoided, they must be addressed in an area of law where procedure can often drive substance.

Multiple interests over common situations and transactions inevitably have clearly led to a multiplication and concurrence of jurisdiction. Some scholars have argued that such concurrent jurisdiction is undesirable and should be abandoned where possible in favour of exclusive jurisdictional régimes.[77] If this were possible, it would provide a rigid superstructure of jurisdiction which would certainly be conducive to legal clarity. Certainly, where feasible, this is welcome.[78] It leads to self-sufficiency both at the jurisdictional and, as a result, at the substantive level.

Concurrent jurisdiction need not, however, be viewed as an evil. It is true that tactical litigation is a consequence through the process of 'forum shopping': but – despite the pejorative tone often associated with the expression – this is not necessarily to be deprecated. Jurisdictional competition is potentially beneficial.[79] At any rate, it is inevitable where harmonisation of substantive law, or of jurisdiction, cannot be negotiated.

A rather more immediate problem is how the many international and domestic judicial bodies determine their own competence in the light of this pullulating international jurisdiction.[80] What machinery exists to enable such

---

76   See, e.g., cases such as *Yahoo!* (n. 65 above) and *Minnesota v. Granite Gate Resort, Inc.* (n. 66 above).

77   See Mann, n. 57 above.

78   Obvious examples include the WTO and ICSID régimes.

79   As some economic analyses of securities regulation suggest – see section 4.2.2.3 below. An enthusiastic, cheerful and oft-quoted endorsement of the merits of a relatively unbridled, *laissez-faire* consumer approach to forum shopping (or at least, the ability freely to litigate in England) may be found in the judgment of Lord Denning, M.R. in *The Atlantic Star* (1973) QB 364, 382: 'No-one who comes to these courts asking for justice should come in vain ... . The right to come here is not confined to Englishmen. It extends to any friendly foreigner. He can seek the aid of our courts if he chooses to do so. You may call this 'forum shopping' if you please, but if the forum is England, it is a good place to shop in, both for the quality of the goods and the speed of service'.

80   The ability of a court or tribunal to determine its own jurisdiction (often referred to as 'la compétence de la compétence', or 'Kompetenz-Kompetenz') is a common feature of many conventional bodies. Of related interest is the lively and ongoing debate about the position of EC law and the ECJ *vis-à-vis* national law, national constitutions and national courts: see especially *Brunner v. Treaty on European Union* [1994] 1 CMLR 57 and the comments of Herdegen (1994) 31 CML Rev 235.

unilateral determinations of competence to be made in a meaningful way?

Some traditional tools are available. A degree of legal certainty and fairness is achieved, for example, by means of the doctrine of *lis alibi pendens*[81] and various forms of jurisdiction agreement. Although, in the broader scheme of things, this could be criticised as being unacceptably ad hoc and devoid of conceptual nicety, it is useful in a system where the reality of increasing multilateral jurisdiction still falls to be analysed through the crude orthodoxy of unilateral jurisdiction. Yet it is important to grapple directly with the awkward systemic questions which arise where jurisdictional régimes overlap. Such overlaps can occur between different layers of *international*-level rules, as well as in the more frequently discussed realm of concurrent claims to jurisdiction by multiple *national* regimes.

A slightly shocking and highly apt illustration of the serious problems which may arise is given by the award of the arbitral tribunal convened under Annex VII of the United Nations Convention on the Law of the Sea (the 'UNCLOS') in the *Southern Bluefin Tuna* case.[82] The dispute concerned allegations by Australia and New Zealand that Japan was in breach of certain provisions of the UNCLOS. The central jurisdictional problem was that Japan's alleged over-fishing of southern bluefin tuna gave rise to questions of substantive obligations arising under both the UNCLOS and a trilateral Convention for the Conservation of Southern Bluefin Tuna (the 'CCSBT') which the parties had concluded in 1993. The arbitral tribunal, while accepting that issues were raised under both treaties, decided that there was only a single dispute; it further found that this dispute 'centred' around the CCSBT and so declined jurisdiction.

This is concerning. There was a single *factual* dispute, it is true; but this gave rise to two distinct *legal* disputes. The failure to recognise this fundamental distinction has serious consequences.[83] Questions of law under the UNCLOS arose, were live and fell to be decided by the tribunal; avoidance of these by means of a dubious process of characterisation is scarcely acceptable. It is certainly relevant to consider whether a doctrine of pre-emption existed

---

81 Where a tribunal declines or stays jurisdiction if the same matter is being litigated elsewhere. This is a common tool in many systems of private international law and can also be found in instruments which establish international tribunals.

82 *Australia and New Zealand v. Japan*. The award of 4th August 2000 on admissibility and jurisdiction in this case may be found on the ICSID website at the following internet address: <www.worldbank.org/icsid/bluefintuna/main.htm>. See Bialek's summary of the primary issues ([2000] Melbourne JIL 153) and Boyle (2001) 50 ICLQ 447, who glumly concludes '*caveat piscator*'.

83 Not least the environmental consequences. The UNCLOS is a constitution for the oceans, broadly aimed at balancing conservation and exploitation: this must be solved in an *ad hoc* way, not by evading the issue by the ruthless denial of jurisdiction. One of the few good things that can be said about the case is that it highlights the need for careful and considered choice of an appropriate forum. It is arguable that a tribunal convened under, for example, Annex VIII of the UNCLOS, in which the matter would be analysed scientifically rather than legally, by a panel of experts, would have been more appropriate for a complex environmental dispute of this nature.

which might replace the *lex generalis* with a *lex specialis*. In the absence of the specific identification of this,[84] we are left with serious problems. In the first place, it is hard to ignore the bizarre precedent which the case appears to set – namely, that states can avoid obligations under a multilateral treaty by concluding a local treaty, so long as it contains some form of dispute resolution mechanism.[85] Besides this, there are wider issues. As we have seen, it is inevitable that a single event may trigger multiple jurisdictional interests. In particular, it will often be the case that inter-relationships between various multilateral treaties are complex. Thus, incidental questions of law will fall to be decided. It is essential that tribunals and courts recognise this and act appropriately of their own motion. There is an obvious, dangerous risk of fragmentation if this is not done.

Broadly speaking, therefore, there is no reason why concurrence of jurisdiction should not be handled satisfactorily at the local level; but it is critical that judicial bodies are aware of the broader jurisdictional picture. Aside from the question of prescriptive jurisdiction, the related matter of enforcement jurisdiction is naturally also of particular relevance here; indeed, it deserves an equal analytical weight.[86] The functional importance of choice of law must also be borne in mind, including at the legislative level.[87] If individual tribunals are successfully to resolve conflicts from a global, rather than a local, perspective, then it is of course critical that the conflicts process be viewed in the round.

Aside from difficulties arising from *concurrent* jurisdiction as viewed unilaterally through the eyes of individual tribunals, it is also important to consider problems associated with the need for co-ordination where jurisdiction is *divided* between various authorities. This can prove elusive. Competition law provides us with a wealth of examples, of which the *GE/Honeywell* saga is

---

84   In this context it is worth noting that Article 64 UNCLOS clearly envisages the possibility
      of regional machinery to serve the broader aspirations of the treaty.

85   Typically, one would expect bilateral treaties to be subservient to multilateral treaties, in
      that they are often concluded to provide mechanisms to implement a multilateral goal.
      This is particularly so in the case of the *Southern Bluefin Tuna* dispute – the CCBFT was
      meant to be parasitic on the UNCLOS. Analogies with the Antarctic Treaty, which were
      drawn by the majority of the arbitrators, are concerning since this agreement is exceptional in that it is predicated on carefully defined *dis*agreement.

86   It is arguable that prescriptive (or 'legislative') jurisdiction, on the one hand, and enforcement jurisdiction, on the other, are in reality two sides of the same coin. To consider them
      separately is to give a misleading picture of the true ambit of any jurisdiction asserted. It
      is, however, appropriate to make the distinction, given the continuing and unfortunate
      tendency of various judicial bodies to regard questions of enforcement as procedural
      pedantry, rather than an integral part of the overall question of jurisdiction. Classic examples are provided by the attitude of the French court in the *Yahoo!* case (n. 65, above) and
      the U.S. Supreme Court in *Hartford Fire Insurance* 509 U.S. 764; 113 Sup. Ct. 2891 (1993).
      See, also, Slot (2001) 38 CML Rev. 1573, p. 1579 et seq.

87   See, e.g., Guzman 'Choice of Law – New Foundations' (2002) 90 *Georgetown Law Journal* 971
      (see <http://papers.ssrn.com/sol3/delivery.cfm/000731650.pdf?abstractid=237802>):
      e.g. at pp. 4, 15-16 and 31 (transcript).

(no doubt) only the latest instalment.[88] The results in that case vividly illustrate the need for effective and pro-active co-operation.

We will now examine some more sector-specific examples of possible ways of dealing with these difficulties of jurisdictional overlap. A recurring theme throughout is the clear political dimension with such problems and the means for their solution: important foreign policy aims are often secured via claims to hold jurisdiction over certain entities and activities.[89]

4.2.2   Mechanisms for dealing with such problems[90]

4.2.2.1   Bilateral Treaties
When relations between two states disclose difficulties due to possible overlaps in claims to jurisdiction, a natural reaction is to try to agree on how to deal with the problems which such overlaps can create. Bilateral treaties are thus a common means for achieving a greater degree of certainty in these relationships, to the benefit both of the authorities and of those subject to these two national regimes. One well known example is the development of agreements between the E.C. and the U.S.A. regarding co-operation in competition law matters and we will return briefly to this issue in section 4.4 below; however, we will discuss here the basic position under the law of taxation.

The ambit of states' claims to jurisdiction to levy taxes is an area of particular interest and importance.[91] To the extent that extraterritorial jurisdiction is in issue, the interests of only a limited number of states fall to be considered.[92] There is therefore scope carefully to consider the nature and scope of any competing interests. This is not a merely academic matter, for this is an area in which particular care must be taken to deal with overlapping jurisdiction. It is clearly in states' interests to avoid situations in which some form of economic activity gives rise to a liability to tax under the revenue law of more than one

---

88   See above, note 69.

89   See, in particular, the references in what follows to securities regulation and antitrust law and their claims to exercise extraterritorial jurisdiction. This will be highlighted in section 4.4 below.

90   Both in the context of bilateral and multilateral accommodations between states, the creation of independent dispute settlement bodies is often a favoured solution: see section 3.3 above. In the private sphere the massive growth in the use of arbitration is a reflection of a similar tendency, whether using ad hoc tribunals convened under contract or taking advantage of so-called 'privatised' arbitration régimes or dispute resolution bodies (such as the I.C.C.'s Banking Division and its regulation of documentary credits). In this private sphere, the interesting (and, as ever, highly political) question is raised of the inter-relationship between these régimes and important national and regional priorities: see n. 70 above.

91   The brief analysis here is based on the presentation by van Raad at the Stanford Seminar, '*Jurisdiction to Tax – An Overview*'. For further detail see Martha, *The Jurisdiction to Tax in International Law – Theory and Practice of Legislative Fiscal Jurisdiction* (Kluwer, Den Haag, 1989). In addition, interesting broad systemic points are made by Mann, n. 57 above, pp. 13-15, 19-22 and 28-30.

92   Typically two: for example, one might consider the position of German investors realising a capital gain on the London Stock Exchange; or, a U.S. citizen earning income in France.

jurisdiction. Such double taxation[93] is a powerful disincentive to continue the economic activity in question – *ceteris paribus*, the pattern of the activity will be skewed.[94] There is thus a clear need for international co-operation at the highest level.

Two broad bases exist to support a state's jurisdiction to tax.[95] Most importantly, it may be based on the location of the source of the income[96] which is to be taxed – 'source jurisdiction'. Alternatively, it may be based on the personal status of the person who is to be taxed. This has been described as 'domiciliary jurisdiction'.[97] For convenience, we will adopt this term. It should be noted that it is a little misleading, for (as discussed below) it is not exclusively based on domicile, which is a somewhat technical and limited construct. Both tests have been said to reflect the overarching principle of 'economic allegiance'.[98] They must be examined in outline.

(I) Source jurisdiction
First we should consider source jurisdiction. This is generally accepted as the primary basis for the assertion of jurisdiction. This should come as no surprise. Taxes are a raw exposition of the exercise of sovereign authority, as traditionally understood; it follows from this (on just about any model of statehood) that they are primarily territorial in application.

In the 1923 Report on Double Taxation[99] various categories of sources of income were analysed. A number of these were considered to have a stronger economic allegiance with source (or 'origin') than domicile: land and houses; business enterprises of an immovable character; movables with a fixed location dependent on the land[100] and movables ordinarily not capable of a fixed location. In short, the Report recommended that 'corporeal wealth' – income derived from immovables and tangible movables – be subject to the tax jurisdiction of the source state.

As far as business income is concerned, Article 5 of the 1927 Draft Conven-

---

93   An even higher multiple of tax burden is of course theoretically possible. Happily, it would appear to be rare.

94   As it will be – albeit in a different manner – if *no* state asserts jurisdiction. In this situation, the point is not that no tax could be claimed, but rather that no state attempts to enforce its admitted claim to tax.

95   Considered by the authors of the 'Report on Double Taxation' submitted to the Financial Committee of the League of Nations (Geneva April 5th 1923, published by the Economic and Financial Commission of the League (doc. E.F.S.73.F.19)). Various bases were considered, including political allegiance, location of wealth, residence, etc.

96   Or, indeed, capital. The position is discussed above in relation to taxes on income. The principles underlying taxes on capital are not materially different; indeed, the theoretical jurisdiction for *source* jurisdiction is stronger in the case of charges to capital taxes.

97   A phrase coined in the 1987 ALI study *Federal Income Tax Project – International Aspects of United States Income Taxation* (General Reporter: David R. Tillinghast), 6.

98   A concept split up into four elements: origin, situs, domicile and enforceability or legal status.

99   See n. 95, above.

100 Such as equipment and cattle.

tion for the Prevention of Double Taxation[101] provided that taxation should be levied in the countries in which the entrepreneur possesses a 'permanent establishment'.[102] Where there is more than one such country, the tax should be apportioned between the countries in accordance with the proportion of the income generated in each. The 1927 Draft Convention also made provision for interest income and dividends to be assigned to the source country of the income.[103]

(II) Domicile jurisdiction

The second basis of jurisdiction focuses on the person receiving the income. It has various manifestations. In the case of individuals, the main possible tests are citizenship,[104] residence[105] and domicile.[106] The implementation and application of these varies considerably between states.

As far as companies are concerned, there are two principal ways in which a body will be regarded as having separate corporate personality in a state: namely, either by incorporation under that state's company law, or by having its administrative seat in that state (*siège réel*). Often, countries apply the test which determines corporate personality in their domestic law to the question of exposure to worldwide tax liability.[107] Another concept which is frequently to be found is that of 'effective management', or some variation thereon.[108] As ever, different states require differing levels of management to satisfy this criterion.

The 1923 Report on Double Taxation recommended that certain types of income ('intangible wealth') had a closer economic allegiance to domicile rather than source: movables dependent on an individual (such as money), securities and loans and professional income.

(III) Practical implementation of international revenue jurisdiction

It is hard to escape the conclusion that much of this is rather vague. One might wonder how states could ever co-ordinate revenue activities given a rather

---

101   Prepared by the League of Nations Committee of Technical Experts in conjunction with their report, *Double Taxation and Tax Evasion* (Doc. C.216.M.1927.II).

102   A vague threshold term, the definition of which varies among the domestic law of states and various treaties.

103   Articles 3 and 4. The tax treatment of royalties was not considered; various subsequent models take varying views on this.

104   This is rare; it is most notoriously used by the United States.

105   A concept which is inherently vague, and varies considerably between states. The U.K., for example, uses two separate residence tests: residence (where an individual mainly lives in a tax year) and ordinary residence (where an individual usually lives).

106   Very crudely speaking, a domicile of choice is where an individual is, and intends to stay indefinitely. The law of domicile is (necessarily) artificial and complex: for its operation in English law, see Collier, op. cit., Ch. 5.

107   By contrast, many countries which use the *siège réel* doctrine to determine corporate personality use incorporation as a test (whether exclusive or not) for worldwide tax liability.

108   Such as 'place of management and control'; 'central management and control'; 'real management and control'.

broad set of possible jurisdictional bases which are often rather esoterically worded, and are implemented in so many different ways. On top of this, domestic difficulties in enforcing foreign revenue laws only serve to add to the problem.[109]

States typically seek to avoid such ambiguities by concluding bilateral tax treaties.[110] The majority of the trading nations – even within the EC – enter into such agreements in order to create a stable tax environment; specific interests which states have can be negotiated at the outset. To this end, information exchange agreements between tax authorities exist,[111] exemplifying positive comity in much the same way as EC-US agreements on competition law co-operation.[112]

On a procedural note, most domiciliary states recognise the precedence of source jurisdiction, and accordingly will offer relief for any double taxation which arises. As ever, this is not as efficient as *ex ante* apportionment of jurisdiction, but it at least represents an appreciation of the need for co-ordination.

Although practical co-operation is the immediate goal, and very welcome in all its forms, the theoretical underpinnings must still be considered carefully. The distinctions drawn between various streams of income in the 1923 Report may have to be reconsidered in the light of modern patterns of trade and commerce. It is true that the notion of 'economic allegiance' remains a rational and useful foundation for exclusive fiscal jurisdiction. Identification of where such economic allegiance lies today in relation to particular streams of income may however give rise to difficulties.

A live example of this is the impact of modern technological advances. For example, does an internet server situated in a country constitute a 'permanent establishment', which might give rise to a tax liability in that country?[113] Or, how can the traditional domiciliary jurisdiction doctrine of 'effective management' operate where directors of a company run it from different countries via

---

109 An example of this is the principle that English courts will not enforce a claim based on foreign revenue laws (see, e.g., *Municipal Council of Sydney* v. *Bull* [1909] 1 K.B. 7; the principle was reaffirmed by the House of Lords in *Government of India v. Taylor* [1955] A.C. 491. The logic of this is dubious. There is no magic in the ritualistic incantation of the supposed rule which lacks any shred of theoretical or practical justification – see Collier, op. cit., pp. 368-9).

110 See Vogel, *Double Taxation Conventions* (Kluwer Law International, Den Haag, 1997).

111 A good example is Council Directive 77/799/EEC of 19 December 1977 [1977] OJ L 336, p.15) providing for mutual assistance by authorities in Member States regarding direct taxation. A recent illustration of the wide operation of this is Case C-420/98 *W.N. v. Staatssecretaris van Financiën* [2000] ECR I-2847. The effective exchange of information is the focus of proposals in respect of a review of withholding taxes under EC law.

112 See the comments below on competition law.

113 A subsidiary question is how much of the overall income generated can be attributed to the server for the purposes of apportioning any tax.

semi-permanent communication?[114] The OECD's Committee of Fiscal Affairs is currently discussing how such developments should impact on the conduct of international commercial activities; reappraisal of source and domiciliary jurisdiction would seem to be essential.

Thus, while the doctrinal framework in this area is at base sound, its application must be reassessed with care. It is not only theoretical consistency which is essential: it must be accompanied by moves towards simplifying and co-ordinating enforcement régimes.[115] Indeed, such simplification is essential before more complex models of international taxation can properly be considered: for example, the substitution of more sophisticated apportionment doctrines in place of the somewhat simplistic weight-based tests to reflect economic reality.

4.2.2.2   Multilateral harmonisation

Analytically, it is not a large jump from the ideas of bilateral organisation of international jurisdictional issues and consequences to dealing with such questions on a broader, multilateral basis. Indeed, such an approach can arrange the prior allocation of jurisdiction over certain issues with sufficient certainty to dispose of most conflicts, while arranging for mechanisms to deal with those cases where disputes over the interpretation of those rules of allocation arise. The conclusion within the E.C. of the Brussels Convention on Jurisdiction, Recognition and Enforcement of Judgments[116] provides a clear example of this approach, while the more recent moves to include such elements in Directives on particular issues such as consumer protection and E-commerce reflect a similar approach.[117] However, it should be recognised that these initiatives occurred in the context of a far-reaching international organisation which bears many federal characteristics.

Yet there are examples of certain sectors where a similar trend can be observed, even between states outside the framework of such integrating international organisations: the transport sector will be used here to illustrate this

---

114   Similar issues arise in the context of the *siège réel* and the freedom to establish companies within the EC: see, most recently, Case C-212/97 *Centros Ltd.* v. *Erhvervs- og Selskabsstyrelsen* [1999] ECR I-1459 and Case C-208/00 *Überseering BV* v. *Nordic Construction Company Baumanagement GmbH* (European Court of Justice, not yet reported (5 November 2002) and the discussion in Wymeersch, 'The Transfer of the Company's Seat in European Company Law' (*ECGI Law Working Paper* No. 08/2003) (also available on the internet at: <http://ssrn.com/abstract=384802>).

115   An example of this is the difficulty in applying for relief under the UK Double Taxation Treaty, which involves undergoing a somewhat irksome two-stage process. Provisional Treaty Relief has recently been introduced in an attempt to improve the position of the taxpayer.

116   Recently adopted as an EC Regulation – see section 3.2 above.

117   See, e.g., Directive 2000/31/EC [2000] OJ L178/1 (on e-commerce) and the Distance Selling Directive (Directive 97/7/EC [1997] OJ L144/19), especially Article 12 thereof which prevents consumers from waiving their rights by means of an explicit choice of law clause in the contract.

point.[118] This facet of the global economy is of interest for us for rather different reasons than the other sectors under consideration. It is useful to consider it precisely because, so far as jurisdiction is concerned, it is an unusually *uncontroversial* area. It has given rise to few serious conflicts along the lines that have been encountered elsewhere. Our focus will, therefore, be to highlight, in outline, some of the approaches which have been taken to deal with (or pre-empt) jurisdictional problems[119] and then to consider just why appreciable controversy seems to be so much less prevalent.

The interest of two jurisdictions, as a minimum, is implicit and obvious in a journey between states. Various mechanisms have been implemented dealing with both substantive and jurisdictional matters in the public and private fields. A number of examples can be used to illustrate these.

The Chicago Convention[120] reflects the important customary international law rule to the effect that each state has 'complete and exclusive sovereignty over the air space above its territory'.[121] It details conditions under which bilateral air transport services may take place; other treaties regulate safety. It has led to approximately 1000 bilateral treaties.[122] The Chicago International Air Services Transit Agreement[123] grants contracting states the privilege to fly across the territory of other contracting states without landing, and the privilege to land for non-traffic purposes.[124]

There are also rules which inhibit participation in the market for provision of air transport services. An interesting example is the E.C. Council Regulation 2407/92 which prevents Member States of the Community granting licences to air transport undertakings unless, *inter alia*, they are controlled by E.C. nationals.[125]

So far as international maritime law is concerned, examples of regulation

---

118   Interesting examples of this phenomenon in other sectors may be found in McClean, *International Co-Operation in Civil and Criminal Matters* (OUP, Oxford, 2002). See, in particular, Chapters 7-10 which discuss drug trafficking (which, the author notes, was one of the first fields in which states moved to a substantial level of international co-operation), money laundering, terrorism and the proceeds of crime.

119   The presentation by Slot at the Stanford Seminar is the basis for the substantive law considered here.

120   Chicago Convention on International Civil Aviation 1944 15 U.N.T.S. 295; U.K.T.S. 8 (1953), Cmnd. 8742. The Convention has been superseded for EC Member States by the third liberalisation package of 1992. Scheduled flights are excluded from the Convention, and are dealt with by sets of bilateral and multilateral agreements.

121   Ibidem, Article 1. See also *Nicaragua Case (Merits)*, I.C.J. Rep. 1986, p. 14 at p. 111. The rule is unsurprising, and reminiscent of the doctrine of *cuius est solum eius est usque ad coelum et ad inferos* - 'to whomsoever the soil belongs, he owns also to the sky and to the depths'.

122   The award in the *Air Services Agreement Case (France v. United States (1978)* 18 R.I.A.A 416) provides a notorious example how such agreements can be enforced by self-help.

123   171 U.N.T.S. 387; U.K.T.S. 8 (1953) Cmnd. 8742. It is known as the 'Two Freedoms' Agreement. A separate agreement, known as the 'Five Freedoms' Agreement (also concluded at Chicago in 1944) is more extensive, but has been ratified by few states.

124   Ibidem, Article 1.

125   The Regulation is a stark exception to the fundamental principles enshrined in the EC Treaty of freedom of establishment (Article 43 EC) and freedom of individuals from third countries to establish themselves in the Community in order to slide down the razor blade of the internal market (Article 48 EC).

may be found in the U.N. Code of Conduct for Liner Conferences[126] and a mass of important I.M.O. and I.L.O. treaties, which deal with such matters as safety, pollution control and manning conditions.[127]

Further certainty (and harmonisation) comes in the form of the principle of port state control.[128] In the E.C., for example, this has been expressly adopted as the principle underlying the enforcement of international standards for ship safety, pollution prevention and shipboard living and working conditions.[129]

A few aspects of jurisdiction in the private law sphere should also be considered. As far as maritime law is concerned, the traditional position (in what might be described as the *laissez-faire* era) was that there was a great deal of private, and very little public, regulation. An obvious example is the limitation of carriers' liability for individual shipments.[130] Private international law generally was widely used on top of this type of regulation.

As far as air transport is concerned, there is less of a history of private law regulation and international unification has been limited. The obvious example of such unification is the Warsaw Convention,[131] which provides uniform rules for the carriage of persons or goods by aircraft for reward (including the limitation of carriers' liability).[132]

What can we draw from these (admittedly disparate) examples? A theme which is recurrent in this sector is that of public law superseding private law.[133] In the contexts in which this trend has taken place, it has been in the form of harmonisation – both of jurisdictional rules and of substantive law. Thus, an intriguing progression may be observed: namely, the migration of regulation from the *private* to the *public* arena. This migration is not particularly profound in the sense that such a private to public shift is arguably more of metaphorical than of actual content,[134] but the usual *purpose* of the change – to effect harmonisation of some sort – is significant. It is a trite but true generalisation that juris-

---

126 Convention on a Code of Conduct for Liner Conferences 1974. The Code regulates certain liner trades. It is implemented by internal régime in the EC, embodying for example the principle of freedom to provide services, and cabotage.

127 As is the case with the Code, the key principles and standards in these treaties have been implemented in the EC.

128 A useful overview can be found in Hare, *Flag, Coastal and Port State Control: Closing the Net on Unseaworthy Ships and their Unscrupulous Owners* (Sea Changes, Vol.16 1994, p. 57).

129 Directive 2001/106/EC of the European Parliament and of the Council of 19 December 2001 amending Council Directive 95/21/EC [2002] OJ L19/17.

130 The Hague Rules (subsequently the Hague-Visby Rules, and recently the Hamburg Rules).

131 Warsaw Convention 1929, amended at The Hague in 1955. See Diederiks-Verschoor, *An Introduction to Air Law* (Kluwer Law International, The Hague, 7th revised ed., 2001).

132 Ibidem, articles 17-30 deal generally with the details and extent of carriers' liability.

133 A nice example is the Convention on Civil Liability for Oil Pollution in 1969, which severely eroded a well-established private limitation of liability régime.

134 But see section 3.4 above, where we seek to challenge the extent of the perceived dichotomy between public and private law jurisdiction.

dictional problems may be solved (or at least, evaded) by harmonisation of domestic laws. In the field of transport, such harmonisation is rife.

What is it that makes harmonisation so appropriate in this field? Why is
extraterritorial prescriptive jurisdiction simply not usually in issue? How is it
that relatively clean apportionment of jurisdiction between the interested
states is possible? It is probable that the answers to the questions lie mainly in
the fact that states' interests are likely to coincide in matters of the substantive
law which is used to regulate transport. There is a great deal of consensus as
to the appropriate international standards in this area; as a result, states are
happy to harmonise both substance and jurisdiction to a significant degree.

In the absence of such consensus, however, the desirability of relying
upon multilateral harmonisation to resolve jurisdictional (and substantive) issues is, perhaps, more questionable.[135] In the field of competition law, attempts have been made under the auspices of the O.E.C.D. to develop statements of principle on 'effective action against hard-core cartels' (1998) and 'co-
operation concerning anticompetitive practices affecting international trade'
(1995).[136] Attempts by the E.C. to encourage the development of binding rules
of international competition law, however, have met significant resistance
from the U.S.A. in particular: there are reservations about embarking upon
such a process.[137] The suggested alternative to the development of a body of
international rules in this field is to test more fully the limits of co-operation
between the various enforcement authorities: a development of particular interest along these lines is the establishment of the International Competition
Network.[138] The difficulties of the negotiation and conclusion of such international agreements have been all too clear in recent years: the conclusion of the
Kyoto Protocol and its subsequent history are potentially worrying examples
of possible future trends. Thus, ideas of multilateral harmonisation as the logical final destination are much more sector and policy-specific than might appear at first blush. So, in many sectors of the economy, there may be more
mileage in a further possible approach, to which we now turn.

---

135   See, e.g., the comments made (section 4.2.2.3, below) concerning securities regulation.

136   See, for a brief summary of their earlier development, Ham 'International Cooperation in
      the Antitrust Field and in particular the Agreement between the United States of America
      and the Commission of the European Communities' (1993) 30 CML Rev. 571, 573-576.

137   For earlier examples, see: Klein, 'A Note of Caution with respect to a WTO Agenda on
      Competition Policy' (Speech to the RIIA, London; 18 November 1996) (available on the in-
      ternet at the following address:
      <http://www.usdoj.gov/atr/public/speeches/jikspch.htm>) (*viz*: hard to reach agree-
      ment, danger of a 'lowest common denominator' approach, going beyond core WTO con-
      cerns, dangers of dispute settlement procedures encroaching on national sovereignty);
      Varney, 'The Federal Trade Commission and International Antitrust' (Speech to the Ford-
      ham Corporate Law Institute 23rd Annual Conference on International Antitrust Law &
      Policy, New York; October 17, 1996) (available on the internet at the following address:
      <http://www.ftc.gov/speeches/varney/fcli_96.htm>) *viz*: yet to test the limits of co-op-
      eration between enforcement authorities: need to push this further, both bilaterally and in
      the OECD.

138   To which we will return in section 4.4, below.

4.2.2.3 Embracing diversity? Régime competition and the example of securities regulation

As mentioned above, the regulation of securities markets gives rise to serious jurisdictional problems.[139] In particular, the extraterritorial application of states' regulatory régimes is potentially problematic and may give rise to undesirable conflicts of interest and distortion of transactional efficiency. There is a clear need to address such problems, given the increased mobility of capital in markets which are rapidly becoming internationalised. Investors and issuers alike are prepared to engage in transactions on a global scale; it is necessary for the international legal order, and individual legal systems, to respond to their needs.

The aggressive use of extraterritorial jurisdiction presents the usual, unacceptable problems. A classic example is U.S. antifraud securities regulation, which combines the doctrines of conduct and effects; the latter frequently leads to odd results and the quality of justice seeming somewhat strained. Thus, in *Schoenbaum v. Firstbrook*,[140] a transaction involving shares in a Canadian corporation was held to be subject to U.S. antifraud rules. This was so notwithstanding the fact that the transaction occurred entirely in Canada. It was the effect of the transaction on the U.S. capital markets, rather than the nature of the conduct, which gave rise to jurisdiction.[141]

There is a deep-seated reluctance to adopt more flexible jurisdictional rules. Instead, states' regulatory régimes are applied extraterritorially and *en bloc*. Thus, various reasons are put forward for the wide jurisdictional ambit of U.S. securities law.[142] These include, for example, the protection of domestic investors, the wider protection of domestic capital markets and protecting the international

---

139 See also Fox: 'Mandatory Disclosure in a Federal System: The EC Example', presentation at the Leiden Europa Instituut 50th Anniversary Lustrum Seminar on 'Globalisation and Jurisdiction' (5th and 6th December 2002).

140 405 F. 2d 200 (2d Cir. 1968), cert. denied 395 U.S. 906 (1969). The disconcertingly broad reach of U.S. securities law is analysed in detail in Choi and Guzman, 'The Dangerous Extraterritoriality of American Securities Law' (1996) 17 Nw. J. Int'l L. & Bus. 207 (hereafter, 'Dangerous Extraterritoriality').

141 It is true that in this case, the stocks were listed on a U.S. exchange, thus providing an arguably adequate jurisdictional link. This notwithstanding, it has been used to justify an unqualified application of the doctrine of effects – see, e.g., *Des Brisay* v. *The Goldfield Corporation* 549 F. 2d 133. See also section 4.4 below for a discussion of the doctrine of effects in US anti-trust law.

142 Considered, and largely dismissed, in 'Dangerous Extraterritoriality', pp. 219-228. The article focuses on issue of securities and the reach of the antifraud rules. It should be emphasized that some safe harbour provisions do exist in the U.S. securities legislation to allow offers of securities to certain categories of American investors (notably SEC Rule 144A established in April 1990 which allows issuers in private placements to avoid the rigorous disclosure required for public offerings). Furthermore, even when a jurisdictional rule is rather expansive, once it is clearly established it then sets a parameter around which legal advisers must operate. Often, in practice this certainty is as useful as more nuanced jurisdictional rules; however, if a better incentive can be given to such advisers and companies without the sacrifice of certainty then progress may be made. How this is to be done is one of the difficult problems with which Choi and Guzman seek to grapple.

reputation of domestic companies. None of these is particularly compelling.[143]

Quite on the contrary, it may well be in states' interests to adopt a more flexible approach to regulation. The blunt application of extraterritorial laws has a number of undesirable side effects. Very considerable risks are inherent in such an approach. At a crude level, (safe harbour provisions aside), it acts as a serious *prima facie* disincentive for issuers to make offerings to U.S. investors. This is highly likely to skew investment and trade patterns. Thus, a greedy scramble for jurisdiction perversely leads to a serious risk of restricting liquidity in the international capital markets. Individual investors will be unable to enjoy as diverse a portfolio of investments as might be desirable. At any rate, it has the potential to increase the cost of overseas securities transactions, thereby inhibiting capital mobility.

There are very serious criticisms of, in particular, the U.S. securities régime.[144] Attempts to regulate foreign activities which have a perceived impact on the U.S. securities markets are arguably dangerously flawed. Difficulties with service and enforcement aside (weighty though these are), the classic indicia of heavy-handed extraterritoriality are manifest. Notably, interference with the securities régimes of other countries is inevitable, and the range of transactions to which the laws can apply is virtually without limit.

Broader political concerns also exist. For example, early in 2001 the U.S. Securities and Exchange Commission (SEC) promulgated rules requiring foreign firms to disclose their corporate activity in states subject to U.S. government sanctions such as Iraq and Libya.[145] This has ominous overtones of past instances in which executive foreign policy has indirectly been implemented through the use of extraterritorial jurisdiction.[146]

In the light of all this, it is clear that some more principled approach must be sought. Three broad jurisdictional structures are possible.

First, we might expect an approach to the global regulation of securities to be founded exclusively in the reassuring and comfortable cement of territoriality. There are viable theoretical arguments in favour of this. By way of illustration, we will use the example of straight equity securities: shares.[147] Shares, not to mention companies themselves, are patent – although admittedly po-

---

143   A more detailed analysis of the various arguments may be found in 'Dangerous Extraterritoriality', pp. 219-228.

144   See 'Dangerous Extraterritoriality'; also, Choi & Guzman, 'Portable Reciprocity: Rethinking the International Reach of Securities Regulation' (1998) 71 Southern California L. Rev. 903, pp. 908-914 (hereafter, 'Portable Reciprocity').

145   See *The Economist*, 19 May 2001, p. 77.

146   Notable examples being the Helms-Burton and D'Amato Acts: see n. 39, above.

147   The same arguments apply equally to debt and hybrid securities, with the caveat that in respect of more exotic forms of security (and in particular certain complex derivative products), states' regulatory regimes tend to differ more markedly. There is not space here to discuss associated private international law problems of characterisation and choice of law relating to intangible movables, which are as serious as they are currently unresolved. In fact, there are embarrassing and gaping difficulties in the English conflict of laws relating to the simple assignment of a debt: see Collier, op. cit., p. 256; Cheshire and North, op. cit., Ch.13; Moshinsky, 'The assignment of debts in the conflict of laws' (1992) 108 LQR 591.

tent – legal fictions. They are creations of the legal system which they inhabit. Their existence is artificial and abstract and derives from a (domestic) legal suspension of disbelief. This is of course not to deny their manifest utility – shares may at root be lies, but if so, they are benign, elegant and virtually indispensable lies. And yet, given that shares exist only by virtue of recognition by the legal system which defines the corporate form to which they attach, it seems reasonable to expect that their nature, rights attaching to them, and their regulation all be subject to definition by that self-same legal system. Thus, as a company may be incorporated in England and Wales under the companies' legislation of that legal system, it seems wholly rational for the regulation of shares in such companies to be regulated by that same legal system. Thus, on a relatively orthodox analysis, a global securities market which is compartmentalized along national boundaries seems a rational solution.

This analysis is perhaps not consistent with the realities of modern commerce. Shares may indeed be a fiction, but no more so than is any other legal concept. At any rate, it seems a little futile to become engaged in the metaphysical debate. The stark fact of worldwide trade in shares is evidence enough of their perceived, practically tangible, existence. Very different legal systems the world over agree on the essential qualities of shares. The second option would therefore be to attempt to establish international co-operation directed specifically at international securities regulation. This is theoretically highly attractive, although it has received a certain amount of criticism.[148] It is admittedly a radical solution; not so much a case of re-inventing the wheel, as standardising it globally. The feasibility of this depends largely on the ability of states to agree on jurisdictional homogeneity, which is likely to induce – at least to a degree – a certain amount of substantive homogeneity.

It could be argued against this that the marked diversity which can be found in various régimes should be welcomed. Approaches to fundamental issues aimed at equalising the position of investors and issuers – such as disclosure requirements, the avoidance of fraud and market manipulation, *inter* very many *alia* – vary widely across different jurisdictions.

The third approach therefore, a refinement of sorts on the first, would be to accept this diverse range of global régimes and to encourage competition amongst them.[149] Such competition should deflect the benefits of regulation firmly towards investors by dissuading regulators from acting selfishly. The process is ultimately aimed firmly at investor protection.[150] Some unease has been expressed at this approach; commentators have argued that there is, for

---

148   Choi and Guzman in 'Portable Reciprocity', pp. 915-916, while acknowledging the theoretical validity of such an approach, are sceptical about the possibility of its implementation in practice. In particular, they draw attention to the difficulties of negotiating such an agreement, and its eventual enforcement.

149   Markham, 'Super Regulator: A Comparative Analysis of Securities and Derivatives Regulation in the United States, Great Britain and Japan' (*Brooklyn Law Review*, forthcoming) for an analysis of regulatory competition in selected domestic spheres.

150   Choi, 'Channeling Competition in the Global Securities Market' (2003), *UC Berkeley School of Law Public Law and Legal Theory Research Paper* No. 111.

example, a risk that allowing choice of régimes will lead to a 'race-to-the-bottom': a lowest common denominator of regulation.[151] This is indeed a possibility, but it is only *one*, fairly marginal, possibility. It is indeed likely that a competitive régime market and the resulting opportunities for regulatory arbitrage will lead to a greater or lesser degree of change in the substantive law of certain of the participating régimes. But there is no particular reason why this should result in a 'race-to-the-bottom' or, for that matter, a 'race-to-the-top'. These are merely extreme points on a wide scale, in which much more subtle modifications to domestic law may take place. This can in fact be desirable and is indeed a manifestation of a wider and important phenomenon: the potential for good jurisdiction to make good law. It is likely that substantive law will be shaped and refined in the light of a suitable nexus of jurisdiction.

One particular version of the above approach deserves particular consideration. Choi and Guzman advocate the implementation of 'portable reciprocity'.[152] This goes beyond standard reciprocity agreements, which are already used on a limited scale.[153] In essence, the individual issuer of securities would be given the choice of régime with which to comply. Transactions may then take place anywhere; the régime travels with the securities. Niche markets would almost certainly arise: the choice of régime would then become part of the investment risk, which would fall explicitly to be considered by investors. This form of delocalisation would carry with it the usual technical problems: its introduction would be fraught with difficulties both of negotiation and enforcement and a whole lot else besides. Indeed, the co-ordination required to allow the operation of such a system of 'issuer choice' may well prove as difficult as the negotiation of any 'traditional' multilateral agreement. The proposal remains an interesting one, however: and indeed a reminder of the true nature of delocalisation, rooted as it is in traditional geographic boundaries. The very difficulties encountered above highlight this metaphorical aspect of jurisdiction, for it is in fact inevitable that delocalised régimes are implemented at a local level. Orthodox international law analysis precludes any form of truly floating, abstract jurisdiction. Local difficulties remain to be addressed and, in the case of a portable reciprocity régime, these are considerable.

Subtle arguments (mainly economic rather than legal) will dictate the optimal jurisdictional structure to encourage efficient trade in securities. Whatever the precise model, whatever degree of interdependence be considered attainable and desirable, it is absolutely clear that the myopic (if not entirely blind) and chauvinistic assertion of extraterritorial jurisdiction is a considerable hindrance. Some form of radical rethinking of the system at the global level is essential.

---

151   See, e.g., Fox, 'Securities Disclosure in a Globalizing Market: Who Should Regulate Whom?' (1997) 95 Michigan L. Rev. 2498. Detailed consideration is given to the possible outcomes of this strategy in Choi & Guzman, 'National Laws, International Money: Regulation in a Global Capital Market' (1997) 65 Fordham L. Rev. 1855.

152   'Portable Reciprocity', pp. 914 et seq.

153   Such agreements typically allow countries inter se to apply a predetermined and mutually acceptable régime to transactions involving each other's securities within their jurisdictions.

4.3   Rule of Law or Politics?

As adverted to above, the resolution of jurisdictional difficulties by means of multilateral negotiations on the international plane can be extremely awkward in practice: even within permanent supranational institutional structures with considerable powers and scope, such as the E.U., history suggests that reaching agreement on sensitive matters can often prove virtually impossible (tax harmonisation, worker participation in corporate governance to name but two contentious examples), although the pressures of outside forces may often force even the most reluctant of hands (e.g. growing calls for a harmonised, E.C.-wide approach to the problems of asylum-seekers and immigration in Europe). The complexities of competing national and/or regional politics and policies can often bar the way to progress.

The political influence also extends to the application of certain developed legal tests, often placing the courts which must apply these tests in extremely uncomfortable positions. One interesting example of such difficulties is provided by U.S. Antitrust law.

Traditionally, national competition rules have sought to protect and promote the process of competition within one country, for the benefit of the consumers within that country. There may well be occasions where the economic standing of that country would be better served by tolerating certain practices directed at foreign markets, which would be condemned if carried out internally to that state. The tolerance (and even encouragement) of export cartels provides a well-known and apposite example,[154] which shows that the welfare of *foreign* consumers is not a matter traditionally accorded much weight in the enforcement of national competition law. This territorial focus, however, was soon found to be too limited to address many of the practices which might affect *national* consumers. After all, in the absence of complete national self-sufficiency, exposure to often significant quantities of imports brought with it the ability for the conduct of foreign firms (or at least the 'foreign conduct' of firms, outside the national territory) to affect conditions on the national market.[155] The rapid growth of international trade has served only to underline and extend this influence which can be brought to bear by actors and actions outside the national territory. This was undoubtedly a major pressure behind the extension of national jurisdiction in the competition law field to extraterritorial matters. The massive growth in the volume of international trade, combined with the trend towards mergers involving already huge corporations and the conclusion of strategic alliances between firms has led to a world in which there are ever more truly global firms, whose economic conduct can never see its effects isolated within the territory of a single state.[156] The basic positions taken by the courts and executive

---

154   See, e.g., the U.S. Webb-Pomerene Act 1918.
155   See *United States* v. *Aluminum Co. of America (Alcoa)*, 148 F.2d 416 (1945) and the *Uranium Cartel Litigation* (e.g. *In Re Westinghouse Uranium Contracts Litigation*, 563 F.2d 992 (1977)).
156   See Van Miert, Foreword to the *European Commission's XXVIIIth Report on Competition Policy* (1998), pp. 3-4.

agencies in the USA and the EC reflect this increasing focus upon the international nature of today's potentially anti-competitive conduct.

In the USA, the blunt statement in the famous *Alcoa* case – that 'it is settled law ... that any state may impose liabilities ... for conduct outside its borders that has consequences within its borders which the state reprehends' – has been modified by subsequent judgments. Today, it seems tolerably clear that the courts will ask whether or not the conduct in question had a direct, substantial and foreseeable effect on American commerce.[157] More controversial is the extent to which this potentially wide-ranging formulation can be limited.

One clear example of such a limit is the defence of 'foreign sovereign compulsion', where the defendant company pleads that being compelled to respect the requirements of U.S. law would necessarily place it in breach of the criminal law of another country.[158] This defence would seem to require a good faith attempt by the defendant to secure a waiver from the 'foreign sovereign' of the application of its criminal law: only if this cannot be secured will the U.S. courts allow the defence[159] and even then it seems that it could still be open to the U.S. court to impose sanctions upon the defendant,[160] although where the foreign sovereign order concerns substantive (as opposed to procedural or evidential) matters U.S. courts do seem to show significant deference to foreign law.[161] Furthermore, this defence will only be available where the foreign sovereign's involvement *requires* the very conduct which U.S. law seeks to override: where there is mere approval by the foreign state without compulsion, the U.S. courts will not take the view that such conduct by the defendant is therefore sufficiently 'required' or 'mandated' to fall within the defence.[162]

---

157 See the Foreign Trade Antitrust Improvements Act 1982, concerning foreign commerce other than import commerce, and cases such as *Timberlane Lumber Co.* v. *Bank of America*, 549 F.2d 597 (1976), at p. 613 (*per* Judge Choy): the 'effect' can be actual or intended; some cases suggest that 'substantial' means no more than 'not de minimis' (see *Dominicus Americana Bohio* v. *Gulf & Western*, 473 F. Supp. 680 (1979), at p. 687 (*per* District Judge Robert L. Carter)) and the 'foreseeability' of such effects is tested objectively (see *United States* v. *General Electric Co.*, 82 F. Supp. 157 (1949). Overall, there is a fairly clear test for legislative jurisdiction here, subject to the point in the Restatement para. 415(3) which requires that the 'exercise of jurisdiction is not unreasonable'.

158 *Société Internationale* v. *Rogers*, 357 U.S. 197 (1958), concerning the order to disclose banking records held by a Swiss bank, where such disclosure would have been a criminal offence under Swiss law.

159 *United Nuclear Corp.* v. *General Atomic Co.*, 451 U.S. 901 (1981).

160 See *In Re Westinghouse Uranium Contracts Litigation*, 563 F.2d 992 (1977).

161 *Interamerican Refining Corp.* v. *Texaco Maracaibo*, 307 F. Supp. 1291 (1970).

162 See *United States* v. *The Watchmakers of Switzerland Information Center Inc.* 1963 Trade Cases ¶70,600 (S.D.N.Y. 1962), *order modified*, 1965 Trade Cases ¶70,352 (S.D.N.Y. 1965) (cited in the *Timberlane* case (above, n. 157, at p. 606): 'the defendants' activities were not required by the laws of Switzerland. They were agreements formulated privately without compulsion on the part of the Swiss Government. It is clear that these private agreements were then recognized as facts of economic and industrial life by that nation's government. Nonetheless, the fact that the Swiss Government may, as a practical matter, approve of the effects of this private activity cannot convert what is essentially a vulnerable private conspiracy into an unassailable system resulting from foreign governmental mandate'.

The real centre of debate, however, has concerned the idea of a restriction of the American courts' jurisdiction on general grounds of comity with other nations.[163] This notion can be conceived of, either as a matter to be taken into account before the court concludes that it possesses jurisdiction in the first place,[164] or as a question subsequent to the establishment of jurisdiction, where the court asks whether that jurisdiction ought to be *exercised* in the instant case.[165] Both conceptions have found support among American judges, but it seems that the weight of authority favours the latter approach, confining the comity question to an examination of the propriety of exercising a jurisdiction which has already been found to exist. The general comity doctrine was developed in the *Timberlane* case,[166] where Judge Choy held that, given admitted jurisdiction, 'there is the additional question, unique to the international setting, of whether the interests of and links to the United States – including the magnitude of the effect on American commerce – are sufficiently strong, *vis-à-vis* those of other nations, to justify an assertion of extra-territorial authority'. This mandated a balancing approach, to be conducted by the consideration of the weight of a number of factors.[167]

---

163 Acknowledging, of course, that the 'foreign sovereign compulsion' idea is one expression of such ideas of comity.

164 See the forceful dissent of Justice Scalia in *Hartford Fire Insurance Co.* v. *California*, 509 U.S. 764; 113 Sup. Ct. 2891 (1993), at p. 2920 – *viz*: 'The 'comity' they refer to is not the comity of courts, whereby judges decline to exercise jurisdiction over matters more appropriately adjudged elsewhere, but rather what might be termed 'prescriptive comity': the respect sovereign nations afford each other by limiting the reach of their laws'; see further the minority opinion of Judge Adams in the *Mannington Mills Inc.* v. *Congoleum Corp.*, case (595 F.2d. 1287 (1979), at pp. 1299 and 1301 (esp. at p. 1301, n. 8)). If this were the approach adopted, then it would overcome the objection of F.A. Mann that, if a court has jurisdiction, it must exercise it (see 'The Doctrine of International Jurisdiction Revisited After Twenty Years' (1984) 186 R.d.C. 9, reprinted as Ch. 1 in his *Further Studies in International Law* (Clarendon Press, Oxford, 1990)).

165 See the views of the majorities in the cases of *Timberlane* (above, n. 157) and *Mannington Mills* (above, n. 164): e.g. '[h]aving concluded ... that there is subject matter jurisdiction, the question remains whether jurisdiction should be exercised' (*Mannington Mills*, at 1294).

166 *Timberlane Lumber Co.* v. *Bank of America*, 549 F.2d 597 (1976), at p. 613.

167 The full list (as augmented by the *Mannington Mills* judgment (see n. 164, above) is: 'the degree of conflict with foreign law or policy, the nationality or allegiance of the parties and the locations or principal places of business of corporations, the extent to which enforcement by either state can be expected to achieve compliance, the relative significance of effects on the United States as compared with those elsewhere, the extent to which there is explicit purpose to harm or affect American commerce, the foreseeability of such effect, the relative importance to the violations charged of conduct within the United States as compared with conduct abroad' (all from *Timberlane*, n. 157, above, at 614), the 'possible effect on foreign relations if the court exercises jurisdiction', 'if relief is granted, whether a party will be placed in the position of being forced to perform an act illegal in either country or be under conflicting requirements by both countries', 'whether an order for relief would be acceptable' in the U.S.A. 'if made by the foreign nation under similar circumstances' and 'whether a treaty with the affected nations has addressed the issue' (all from *Mannington Mills*, pp. 1297-1298).

The large number of factors and their inherent complexity, allied to the quasi-constitutional status often accorded to the Sherman Act as a statement of the American economic philosophy of free competition, have led to scepticism on the part of foreign companies and governments as to the extent of protection offered by this comity test. This was exemplified by the *Uranium Antitrust Litigation*, both in terms of the actions of the U.S. Government in its investigation of the foreign cartels (which had been set up in response to the closure of the U.S. market to foreign uranium producers) and in the reaction of the U.S. courts to attempts by foreign governments to explain why jurisdiction should not be exercised by the U.S. in these cases. As the U.S. Court of Appeals (Seventh Circuit) exclaimed, 'shockingly to us, the governments of the defaulters have subserviently presented for them their case against the exercise of jurisdiction';[168] by all accounts, this caused significant embarrassment to the U.S. Government in its foreign relations, especially since the Department of State had encouraged the submission of such *amicus* briefs.[169] On the other hand, it should be noted that there is some evidence of the success of such contributions by foreign governments in the conduct of other international antitrust cases.[170]

The *Hartford Fire Insurance* case, however, suggests a more limited reading of the comity doctrine, where Justice Souter seemed to equate it with the more specific defence of foreign sovereign compulsion. Since the United Kingdom only *allowed*, but did not *compel*, the conduct complained of (a London re-insurer's decision to boycott certain types of insurers, thus removing certain types of insurance cover from the U.S. market), there was no reason to decline jurisdiction. Justice Scalia's powerful dissent, however, provided clear support for the retention of the more accommodating balancing approach laid down in *Timberlane* and recorded in the Restatement (Third) of Foreign Relations Law of the United States (see §403(1) and (2) thereof).[171] In spite of this dissent, the First Circuit Court of Appeals in the *Nippon Paper* case[172] held that such extraterritoriality allowed the bringing of a *criminal* prosecution against a Japanese company which had participated in a cartel to fix the price of fax paper to be sold in the U.S.A. The main judgment here, while commenting

---

168   *In re Uranium Antitrust Litigation* 617 F.2d. 1248 (7th Cir. 1980), at p. 1256.
169   See (1979) 73 A.J.I.L. 122, p. 125 for a partial reprint of the letter sent by the Solicitor General on 2 May 1978.
170   Griffin, 'Foreign Governmental Reactions to US Assertions of Extraterritorial Jurisdiction' (1998) ECLR 64, at 72, n. 66) cites such cases as *Conservation Council of Western Australia* v. *Aluminum Co. Of America* 518 F.Supp. 270 (W.D. Pa. 1981) (where the claim was dismissed due to lack of jurisdiction) and *Natural Resources Defense Council* v. *Nuclear Regulatory Commission* 647 F.2d. 1345 (D.C. Cir. 1981) (where an *amicus* brief from the Philippines Government seemed to contribute materially to the court's narrow reading of the extraterritorial scope of environmental and other regulatory statutes).
171   Indeed, Lowenfeld, who drafted the sections of the Restatement in question, has gone on record to register his disagreement with the interpretation given by the *Hartford Fire Insurance* majority of the Restatement's provisions: see (1995) 89 AJIL 42, esp. at p. 51.
172   *United States* v. *Nippon Paper Industries Co.* 109 F.3d. 1 (1st Cir. 1997).

that the *Hartford Fire Insurance* decision had 'stunted' the comity concept in antitrust cases, simply applied the *Hartford Fire Insurance* majority's reasoning that even wholly foreign conduct was caught by the Sherman Act. Any examination of the concept of 'reasonableness' was cursory and treated as covered by the authority of *Hartford Fire Insurance*,[173] although it should be noted that such conduct was also illegal in Japan (so no issue of conflict between the mandatory rules in Japanese law and U.S. law was raised here).

The history of the general comity concept in U.S. antitrust law has thus been a rather chequered one. It should be remembered that in cases of enforcement by an executive agency, the U.S. 'Antitrust Enforcement Guidelines for International Operations' (1995)[174] provide that comity *will* be taken into account in any decision on whether to bring an action or to seek specific remedies: here, 'comity' is defined using factors similar to those in *Timberlane*. However, these guidelines also emphasise that, once a decision is made, this amounts to a 'determination by the Executive Branch that the importance of antitrust enforcement outweighs any relevant foreign policy concerns'. It is also stressed that the courts should not try to substitute their view on the 'proper role' of this comity issue where such a determination has already been made. Indeed, in its *amicus* brief in *Hartford Fire Insurance* itself, the Department of Justice argued that no comity analysis by the court was necessary where the executive had already decided that action should be taken against the foreign company.[175] Of course, the flaw in this apparent safeguard lies in the multiple parties which can seek to enforce U.S. antitrust law: private actions may also be brought against foreign companies, where the authorities will have little influence over a plaintiff's decision to sue or the decision of the court in the case at bar.[176]

So, the U.S. courts developed comity principles but then recoiled from the consequences of applying the reasoning on such politically sensitive issues with a huge impact on international relations, hence the step back in *Hartford Fire Insurance*. Clearly, comity is now largely dead as a balancing concept applied by the *courts* in U.S. antitrust law. However, given the point in the previous paragraph about the multiple potential 'enforcers' of U.S. antitrust law, a

---

173   Interestingly, in his concurring opinion, Judge Lynch *did* examine the balancing test for comity laid down in the Restatement and *Timberlane* and yet *still* found that the balance in the *Nippon Paper* case lay in favour of U.S. jurisdiction. In his analysis, only the North American markets were targeted and the effects on the American market were foreseeable and direct. 'The only factor counseling against finding that the United States' antitrust laws apply to this conduct is the fact that the *situs* of the conduct was Japan and that the principals were Japanese corporations. This consideration is inherent in the nature of jurisdiction based on effects of conduct, where the *situs* of the conduct is, by definition, always a foreign country. This alone does not tip the balance against jurisdiction' (ibidem).

174   Antitrust and Trade Reg. Rep. (BNA), Special Supplement (6 April 1995), available on the Justice Department's Web site: <http://www.usdoj.gov>.

175   See 'Brief of the United States as *Amicus Curiae* Supporting Respondents', in *Merrett Underwriting Agency Management Ltd.* v. *California*, 509 U.S. 764 (1993) (No. 91-1128) at p. 27.

176   See, e.g., Jones and Sufrin, *EC Competition Law – Text, Cases, and Materials* (O.U.P., Oxford, 2001), p. 1045.

decision to return to 'foreign sovereign compulsion' as the only possible defence on such matters has a similarly significant impact upon international relations – it will not always be possible for the Federal enforcement agencies to act as a filter in such cases. In such scenarios, as well as in cases of great political importance for the Federal enforcement agencies, the 'rule of politics' may still cause serious difficulties for companies and regulators alike.

4.4   Rule of Procedures

Issues of overlapping jurisdiction can raise difficult questions of co-ordination, which can be especially tricky in the face of marked differences in the substantive rules which have a claim to cover a particular situation. On a case-by-case basis, the rules of private international law seek to provide a system allowing courts to resolve some such questions. Equally, the roles of various investigative and enforcement agencies increasingly involve the need for co-operation with their counterparts in other states or organisations. The arrangements for bilateral co-operation and information exchange between tax authorities (discussed above in section 4.2.2.1) are a good example of this development, while the increasing frequency and density of interactions between competition authorities provides another important illustration.[177]

In section 4.3, we covered the difficulties faced by the U.S. courts in dealing with the acknowledged impact of national antitrust rules upon situations and companies located outside U.S. territory. Just because the courts have recently withdrawn from the application of comity principles in individual cases, however, does not imply that the issues potentially covered by comity have disappeared. While the courts no longer feel themselves able to conduct such (political) balancing exercises, the enforcement authorities have developed a range of approaches designed to address many of these matters pre-emptively.[178] The E.C. has entered into agreements on such co-operation with the U.S.A.[179] and Canada;[180] despite some high profile cases which have

---

177   Due to constraints of space, coverage here is necessarily brief. For further details on these issues, see Zanettin, *Co-operation between Antitrust Authorities at the International Level* (Hart Publishing, Oxford, 2002).

178   E.g., the OECD's principles on 'co-operation re anticompetitive practices affecting international trade' (1995) (available at: <http://www.europa.eu.int/comm/competition/international/3a04en.html>).

179   Agreement between the European Communities and the Government of the United States of America regarding the application of their competition laws (Decision 95/145/EC, ECSC [1995] OJ L95/45; Agreement between the European Communities and the Government of the United States of America on the application of positive comity principles in the enforcement of their competition laws [1998] OJ L173/26.

180   Agreement between the European Communities and the Government of Canada regarding the application of their competition laws [1999] OJ L175/50 (see also the following internet address: <http://www.europa.eu.int/comm/competition/international/bilateral.htm>).

caused genuine controversy,[181] the evidence concerning day-to-day contacts suggest that much good and smooth co-operation does occur.[182] The most important methods used include exchange of (non-confidential) information and close co-operation in the conduct of investigations where information and/or companies are located in the other authority's territory. Given the fact that differences between the E.C. and the U.S.A. still exist as regards the substantive rules which apply to any given case,[183] this dialogue can serve more than just the practical purpose of case management and information acquisition. Such contacts can foster greater mutual understanding of approaches and the ability to foresee (and, where possible, avoid) difficulties more easily.

The problems which remain are often brought into sharpest relief due to disparities in the *procedural* constraints which apply in the systems which claim jurisdiction over a particular competition law situation. The *GE/Honeywell* merger and its treatment on both sides of the Atlantic provided a vivid illustration of the consequences of adherence to the time limits under which investigations must be conducted. As a result, not only did the final substantive results of the U.S. and E.C. investigations differ, but the former delivered a decision long before the latter, resulting in severe commercial uncertainty for those involved in the deal.[184] While various efforts to remove such problems via the international harmonisation on the W.T.O. level of *substantive* rules have met with some resistance,[185] attempts to deepen dialogue between competition authorities have met with more success. The E.C.-U.S. and E.C.-Canada agreements were adverted to above; within the E.C., the U.K., French and German authorities have recently adopted a common notification form for merger clearance, in response to an increasing need to co-operate on mergers which have elements in more than one E.C. Member State.[186] On an international level, various competition authorities have joined together to form the International Competition Network (I.C.N.).[187] In September 2002, after signif-

---

181 See, in particular, *Boeing/McDonnell Douglas* (Decision 97/816/EC [1997] OJ L336/16 (especially paras. 11 and 12 of the decision) and *GE/Honeywell* (Case No. COMP/M.2220, Commission Decision of 3 July 2001; see: <http://www.europa.eu.int/comm/competition/mergers/cases/decisions/m2220_en.pdf>). The latter was particularly controversial, with Competition Commissioner Mario Monti releasing a statement denying the 'politicisation' of the *GE/Honeywell* investigation (see Commission Press Release IP/01/855, 18 June 2001).

182 See the various reports by the EC Commission on the operation of the E.C.-U.S. agreements, available at: http://www.europa.eu.int/comm/competition/international/bilateral.htm.

183 Despite some efforts at the formulation of common principles, such as the OECD principles on 'effective action against hard-core cartels' (1998).

184 See Slot (2001) 38 CML Rev. 1573 for discussion, criticism and suggestions for some procedural alignment.

185 For earlier examples, see n. 137, above.

186 This common form applies where a merger falls to be examined in two or more of these three countries. See OFT 526, *Mergers – procedural guidance* (2003), para. 3.26 (available on the internet from: <http://www.oft.gov.uk/Business/Mergers/default.htm>).

187 See the following internet address: <http://www.internationalcompetitionnetwork.org> – it describes the ICN as 'a competition authority forum supported by the competition authorities themselves'.

icant comparative efforts by the I.C.N.'s Mergers Working Group, a set of general principles on mergers was agreed at the I.C.N.'s inaugural conference.[188] While it is acknowledged that the 'Principles are non-binding and it is left to governments and agencies to implement them as appropriate',[189] and even in the absence of detailed agreement upon international, legally binding and harmonised substantive rules, such initiatives are a key means of co-ordinating international competition law enforcement and alleviating the difficulties which can be created by the non-collaborative exercise of potentially extra-territorial jurisdictional claims. In this field, then, the rule of procedures may yet evolve to provide a perfectly acceptable, efficient and tailored way forward to address the difficult legal and economic issues which must be faced by competition law enforcement in an economically interlinked world.

5   Conclusions

The nation state remains a key building block in the international system, but as a notion it is no longer the only type of brick in the wall. This raises the vital question of national *attitudes* (both of the government and its independent agencies – such as competition authorities) toward international influences upon and their consequences for the nation state. The implication is not that states must bow unquestioningly to these forces and accept some of the wide-ranging prescriptions about the need to move the focus to the international level; rather, states should be encouraged to engage in good faith interaction *inter se*, so as to be able to deal with the problems that arise and acknowledge when the benefits of co-operation outweigh the loss of (perceived) national *control* over particular issues. A good current example is the fate of asylum-seekers and other immigrants within the E.U.: Ruud Lubbers, the U.N. High Commissioner for Refugees, has recently urged countries to develop international approaches to the problems that the large increases in migrant population have caused in recent years, rather than seeking to adopt uncoordinated, national 'get-tough' policies in an attempt to discourage such immigrants from attempting to darken *their* particular door. The result of such responses is likely to be to shift the problem to another state in the vicinity.[190] Certain international initiatives have been taken to address these problems (such as the

---

188   For the set of agreed guiding principles on 'Merger Notification and Review', see the following internet address: <http://www.internationalcompetitionnetwork.org/icn_np_working_group_guiding_principles.pdf.> Meanwhile, the I.C.N.'s Mergers Working Group has recently published a set of Recommended Practices for Merger Notification Procedures (see the following internet address for further details: <http://www.internationalcompetitionnetwork.org/2003_practices.pdf>): these recommendations were discussed at the September 2002 conference and have now been reviewed by the Working Group with a view to their adoption at the annual conference in June 2003.
189   See <http://www.internationalcompetitionnetwork.org/wg1_practices_principles.html>.
190   See, e.g., *The Daily Telegraph*, 28 December 2002, p. 9.

Dublin Convention),[191] but have failed to secure significant enforcement resources or cooperation.

It must be acknowledged that the phenomenon of globalisation *has* happened and will *continue* to happen, *with or without* an ideal (or even a fairly effective) global idea of the Rule of Law. Indeed, as we hope has emerged from this paper, the process of globalisation *influences* how we fulfil that goal of the Rule of Law and what the content of that goal ought to be in any given context. A focus on the considerable jurisdictional difficulties has been the basis for developing this analysis here: other fields also need fuller investigation if the viability of these assertions is to be tested more fully.

Shakespeare's Antonio, despite being threatened by Shylock's notorious and deadly claim for a pound of his flesh (the contractually agreed penalty for default under his bond) does not hesitate to refute Solanio's optimistic suggestion that the moneylender's (purported) rights might not be enforced:

> The duke cannot deny the course of law;
> For the commodity that strangers have
> With us in Venice, if it be denied,
> Will much impeach the justice of the state,
> Since that the trade and profit of the city
> Consisteth of all nations.[192]

To read far more into this than (perhaps) one should, the observation that 'the trade and profit of the city consisteth of all nations' has potential to draw welfare circles in terms of regulation and reform that are wide enough to encompass countries beyond the nation state. The problems which we have sought to highlight are, therefore, not new, although the context in which they are now embedded makes their resolution necessarily more complex. The protean nature of jurisdiction in the light of globalisation is demonstrated by the sectoralisation which we have seen: markedly different frameworks and approaches pepper the various fields which we have examined. Co-operation; unresolved conflict; potentially positive competition; strange alchemies of all of these – such phenomena and others are endemic and, increasingly, drive the development of substantive law. Such sectoralisation does not preclude a uni-

---

191   [1997] OJ C254/1. For a brief outline of the Dublin Convention and its operation in the EU, see Peers, *EU Justice and Home Affairs Law* (Pearson Education, Harlow, 2000), Ch. 6, esp. pp. 112-117.

192   The Merchant of Venice, III.III. 28-33. Readers impressed by Antonio's stoicism will doubtless be glad to recall that he is eventually saved by Portia's timely and ingenious construction of the contract: namely that 'This bond doth give thee here not one jot of blood' (i.e., the forfeit flesh would have to be cut out without spilling any blood); and 'if thou [Shylock] tak'st more/ Or less than a just pound – be it but so much/ As makes it light or heavy in the substance,/ Or the division of the twentieth part/ Of one poor scruple; nay, if the scale do turn/ But in the estimation of a hair -/ Thou diest, and all thy goods are confiscate'. It would be churlish to point out that such a precedent would have paralysed the Venetian commodities markets.

fied theory of jurisdiction: but it serves as a forceful indication that any such theory must comprehend far more factors, and greater complexity, than orthodox techniques might suggest. Would this not require some degree of deconstruction of classical international law theory? Yes, inevitably so; but, as we have attempted to demonstrate, the rule(s) of law(s) in this context is a concept which admits of (and, indeed, *requires*) the flexible reinterpretation of otherwise relatively unchallenged axioms.

What has international private law achieved in meeting the challenges posed by globalisation ?

Patrick Wautelet

1   INTRODUCTION

(1) The issue of *jurisdiction* certainly constitutes one of the main challenges of what is commonly called 'globalisation', i.e. the rapid internationalisation of economic (and, to a somewhat lesser extent, of other) activities. Since legal regulation of these human activities is still largely state-based – with the notable exception of the European Union, whose existence and the large body of rules it produces, also raises questions of jurisdiction – rules on jurisdiction are necessary to define which part of these activities can be subject to regulation by a given State.

This paper aims to examine what private international law has achieved to answer the question of jurisdiction.[1] Before doing so, one needs to define what must be understood by 'jurisdiction' in private international law.

(2) Jurisdiction has been defined as 'the State's right under international law to regulate conduct in matters not exclusively of domestic concern'.[2] As classic as Mann's statement is the distinction between different categories of jurisdiction. The right of regulation of a State can be exercised in different ways. It has become commonplace to distinguish between the jurisdiction to *prescribe* (i.e. to make its law applicable to activities and relations, whether by legislation, regulation or determination of a court), jurisdiction to *adjudicate* (i.e. to subject persons or things to process of courts) and, finally, jurisdiction to *enforce* (i.e. to induce or compel compliance, through courts or by use of executive, administrative, etc.).[3]

(3) What has private international law to say on these questions? The question of the relationship between private international law and jurisdiction is a vexed one, as is more generally the issue of the relationship between private

---

1   For recent accounts of the impact of globalisation on transnational litigation, see A. S. Bell, 'Forum Shopping and Venue in Transnational Litigation', *Oxford Private International Law Series* (OUP, Oxford, 2003), pp. 1-5 and H. P. Glenn, Globalization and Dispute Resolution, 19 *Civil Justice Quarterly* 136 (2000).

2   F. A. Mann, *The Doctrine of Jurisdiction in International Law*, Collected Courses of the Hague Academy for International Law 1964-I, at p. 2. Another definition is that of Reisman, who sees jurisdiction as the process of 'allocating to particular states the competence to make or apply law to particular persons, things or events that are, simultaneously or sequentially, claimed by or subject to, the control of two or more states' (W. M. Reisman, *Jurisdiction in International Law* (Ashgate, Dartmouth, 1999), p. xi.

3   See § 401, 3rd Restatement Foreign Relations Law of the United States.

international law and international law.[4] It is tempting to think that the three classic categories of jurisdiction correspond to the three main questions addressed by private international law – that of the law applicable to a transnational relationship, that of the jurisdiction of national courts to rule on a dispute concerning such a relationship and, finally, the question of the enforcement of foreign judgments.

However, a close analysis reveals that the link between 'jurisdiction' as defined in international law and the three issues dealt with by private international lawyers is not obvious, nor always direct. No question exists that private international law rules determining the circumstances in which a national court can rule on a dispute involving elements from different States have a direct link with jurisdiction as understood here. The same goes for those rules dealing with the enforcement of foreign judgments. In these two cases, the rule aims to determine when a court of a given State can address an international situation, i.e. it determines the limits in which a State can exercise its jurisdiction through its courts – or, when a foreign judgment has been rendered, when this judgment can be considered to have been issued by a court which could legitimately exercise jurisdiction over the case.[5] The link between jurisdiction and rules of private international jurisdiction is obvious, since the latter determine the sphere of influence of national courts.

(4) Private international law also contains rules which aim to resolve the question of *legislative diversity* – which law is applicable to a situation with transnational aspects. These rules come in different shapes and models – from the traditional conflict of laws rule, based on the Savignian model, determining indirectly and abstractly which national law is applicable, to a more direct method, which imposes the international application of a given rule of national law.[6]

The link between jurisdiction and these rules (the conflict of laws rules in the *strict sense*) is less obvious. Can it be said that a rule according to which the marriage between persons of different nationalities is subject to the requirements (minimum age, relationship of kin etc.) laid down by the national laws of the future spouses,[7] touches upon the jurisdiction of these States ?

As is known, there has been an *evolution* in the way private international

---

4   See generally J. Verhoeven, 'Droit international public et droit international privé: où est la différence ?' *Archives de Philosophie du droit* (1987) 23-34.

5   This is however contested; for some, rules of recognition and enforcement have no bearing on the issue of jurisdiction as they do not directly invest a foreign court with jurisdiction, see P. Mayer, 'Droit international privé et droit international public sous l'angle de la notion de compétence', *Revue critique de droit international privé* (1979) (1-29, 349-388 and 537-583)18.

6   For an account of this diversity, see e.g. Th. De Boer, 'Een 'zoo doeltreffend en rechtvaardig mogelijke ordening'. Vragen rond de bestaansgrond van het internationaal privaatrecht', *Royal Dutch Academy of Sciences, Communications of the Section on Literature*, New Series 59/1, Amsterdam, Noord-Hollandsche, (1996) 58 p., in particular at pp. 19-37.

7   A rule traditionally found in the laws of Roman-Germanic countries, see e.g. L. Palsson, 'Marriage and Divorces', in: *International Encyclopedia of Comparative Law, Vol. III: Private International Law*, Chap. 16, (J.C.B. Mohr Siebeck, Tübingen (1978)), p.171

lawyers think about this question. During much of the 19th century, rules of conflict of laws – at least those determining the national law applicable to a transnational situation – were said to *delimit* the competence of the States involved. By determining which law was applicable to a relationship, conflict of laws rules were said to describe the territorial sphere of application of national laws, and hence also the limits of each sovereignty.[8] In this approach, the distinction between international law and private international law was blurred, both were considered to be part and province of the 'law of nations'.[9]

It is only gradually that private international lawyers came to accept that conflict of laws rules (in the strict sense) also serve *private* interests and, hence, that the rules determining which law is applicable to a given relationship do not necessarily impact on the sovereignty of the (foreign) State whose law is declared applicable. The function of the conflict of laws rule came to be seen as simply to resolve private international situations, without necessarily passing a judgment on the sovereignty or jurisdiction of foreign States. Under this model, the rule of State X prescribing application of the law of State Y or of State Z, does not in essence deal with jurisdiction of these States. State X simply borrows the law of State Y or Z for application in a given situation, or State X accepts that his own law will apply. At most, these rules tell us in which situations State X accepts that its laws do or do not apply.

The view that conflict of laws rules do not have any bearing on jurisdiction, on the 'power to regulate' of the States concerned, is certainly not uncontested.[10] It should also be qualified: only the most traditional approach focuses exclusively on private interests, and in particular on the so-called 'Sitz' of the relationship at hand, to determine which law applies. One cannot forget that there are other methods of resolving a situation of legislative diversity than the indirect and abstract conflict of laws rule devised by Savigny. It is enough to refer in this respect to the phenomenon of *internationally mandatory rules*, i.e. particular rules of national law that are deemed too important to tolerate application of foreign law.[11] When State X elevates one of its rules to the level of internationally mandatory, this State excludes the application of any foreign law. This decision has a more direct bearing on the issue of jurisdiction, as internationally

---

8   Hence conflict of laws were seen as 'conflits de souverainetés'; and the emphasis put e.g. on *renvoi*. See generally, P. Mayer, 'Le mouvement des idées dans le droit des conflits de lois', *Droits, Revue française de théorie juridique* (1985) 129-143.

9   The epitome of this view is to be found with Bartin's thinking, according to which private international law has as its object to 'délimiter, en fixant les justes limites de chacune d'elles, les différentes souverainetés dans leur double fonction législative et juridictionnelle de droit privé' (*Principes de droit international privé*, vol. I, Paris (1931) p. 55, § 122).

10   The idea that conflict of laws rules are not part of a '*Grenzrecht*' has been challenged, most recently and most brilliantly by P. de Vareilles Sommières, *La compétence internationale de l'Etat en matière de droit privé. Droit international public et droit international privé* (Paris, LGDJ,1997).

11   Also called the '*règles d'application immédiate*', see art. 7 of the 1980 Rome Convention on the Law Applicable to Contractual Obligations.

mandatory rules will almost always go together with a rule reserving jurisdiction to the courts of the State concerned. In this sense, this method has a more direct link with the issue of jurisdiction. Furthermore, internationally mandatory rules are in effect direct translations of particular state policies, whose enforcement the State wants to guarantee even in international cases.

(5) The debate between the 'private' and the 'public' function of the conflict of law rules will certainly go on. Given the uncertainty surrounding the relationship between jurisdiction and rules relating to the applicable law, the following will be exclusively focused on the rules of private international jurisdiction.

Rules of private international jurisdiction have been around for as long as lawyers have thought about cross-border relationships. Before examining whether it is possible to find any *common ground* [12] in the way lawyers of different nations think about jurisdiction (3), it is important to examine who decides on jurisdiction (2).

2   NATIONAL AND INTERNATIONAL RULES OF JURISDICTION

(6) Before attempting to discover if State practices reveal any common on the issue of jurisdiction, it should be made clear that jurisdiction is not primarily, or at least not exclusively, an international issue. Most issues of jurisdiction will be settled at the national level, using national rules. The courts of State A will for instance refer to the rules laid down by State A to decide if they can take up a case brought by a citizen of State A against a citizen of State B. Whatever State B holds on jurisdiction generally speaking, and in the particular matter put to the courts of State A, is of no direct relevance to determine whether the courts of State A have jurisdiction. International law remains largely silent on the consequences of the wrongful exercise of jurisdiction (i.e. excess of jurisdiction). Put differently, there is no direct sanction for what State A decides in terms of jurisdiction. If State B feels State A has overreached its jurisdiction, it cannot *directly* prevent A from taking jurisdiction. At most, B will interfere indirectly with A's claim for jurisdiction. State B can for example refuse to enforce a judgment rendered by the courts of State A. State B can also accept jurisdiction itself as a way of reprisal.[13] State B can finally enjoin the

---

12   A phrase recently used by Prof. R. Brand in a similar context, see his contribution entitled: 'Jurisdictional Common Ground: In Search of a Global Convention', in: J. Nafziger and S. Symeonides (eds.), *Law and Justice in a Multi-State World: Essays in Honor of Arthur Taylor von Mehren* (Ardsley, NY, Transnational Publishers, 2002), pp. 11-32.

13   Several statutes provide that State B has jurisdiction only in so far as courts of State A would assume jurisdiction in a similar dispute, thereby extending national jurisdiction to reciprocate a claim by a foreign state, see for example article 636 of the Belgian Judicial Code, which, combined with Article 638 of the same Code, extends the reach of Belgian courts to disputes over which foreign courts also exercise jurisdiction. See for other examples, P. Lagarde, 'La réciprocité en droit international privé', *Collected Courses* (1977-I) t. 154, (pp. 103-214), at pp. 149-150, n° 47.

plaintiff in State A to cease and desist.[14] In some rare occurrences, jurisdictional overreach will lead to diplomatic protest.[15]

This is because international law of jurisdiction only limited ambitions. It is commonly accepted that customary international law does not contain detailed rules regulating the taking of jurisdiction in private matters by this or that national court. It merely provides for very *general principles* that limit the freedom of States in enacting their rules of jurisdiction.

At most, two basic principles can be deducted from customary international law, i.e. respect for immunities of foreign States [16] and the prohibition of denial of justice. Outside these general principles, the discretion of States seems unfettered. As the Permanent Court of International Justice held in the famous *Lotus*-case,

> Loin de défendre d'une manière générale aux Etats d'étendre leurs lois et leur juridiction à des personnes, des bien et des actes hors du territoire, [le droit international]leur laisse, à cet égard, une large liberté, qui n'est limitée que dans quelques cas par des règles prohibitives; pour les autres cas, chaque Etat reste libre d'adopter les principes qu'il juge les meilleurs ou les plus convenables.[17]

Even though the precise contours of the international law on jurisdiction are subject to debate, one can agree with M. *Akehurst's* conclusion to the effect that:

> In practice, the assumption of jurisdiction by a State does not seem to be subject to any requirement that the defendant or the facts of the case need have any connection with that State; and this practice seems to have met with the acquiescence by other States [...] It is hard to resist the conclusion that [...] customary international law imposes no limits on jurisdiction of municipal courts in civil trials.[18]

---

14   The so-called antisuit injunction, see *Airbus Industrie GIE v. Jaisukh Arjun Bhai Patel and others* [1999] A.C. 119, [1998] 2 All.E.R. 257, [1998] 2 W.L.R. 686, [1998] 1 Lloyd's Rep 631, (1998) 37 I.L.M. 1076 (H.L.). For classic studies of the subject, see T. C. Hartley, 'Comity and the Use of Antisuit Injunctions in International Litigation', *Am. J. Comp. L.*,(1987) 487-511; G. Bermann, 'The Use of Anti-Suit Injunction in International Litigation', *Col. J. Trans. L.* (1990) 589-631; W. Hau, 191-192 and P. B. Carter, 'Anti-suit Injunctions in Private International Law', Vorträge, Reden und Berichte aus dem Europa Institut n° 368, Europa-Institut Universität des Saarlandes (1997), p. 22. The subject of antisuit injunctions fascinates scholars well beyond common law, and has spawned a large literature over the last years, see S. Clavel, *Le pouvoir d'injonction extraterritorial pour le règlement des litiges privés internationaux*, (PhD., Paris I, 1999); M. Requejo Isidro, *Proceso en el extranjero y medidas antiproceso (anti-suit injunctions)*, De conflictu legum – estudios de Derecho internacional privado n° 1, (2000), p. 282; M. Maack, *Englische antisuit injunctions im Europäischen Zivilrechtsverkehr* (Duncker & Humblot, Berlin, 1999), p. 229.

15   On this issue, P. de Vareilles-Sommières, supra, note 10, at pp. 239-240, §§ 387-388.

16   If the principle of immunity for foreign States is generally accepted, the limitations imposed on the immunity privilege vary greatly. For a recent study of the 'common ground' between States, see I. Pingel-Lenuzza, *Les immunités des Etats en droit international public* (Bruylant, Brussels, 1997).

17   PCIJ, case *'Lotus'*, decision of 7 September 1927, *Recueil des arrêts*, n° 9, Publications de la CPJI, Leyden, Sijthoff, pp. 18-19.

18   M. Akehurst, *Jurisdiction in International Law*, British Yearb. Int'l L., 1972-73, (145), 177.

The only limit to the assertion of judicial jurisdiction by a State in private matters seems to be the competing assertions of other States. Fundamental rights, and in particular the right to fair trial, have also recently been invoked to limit the jurisdictional claims of States. Their role is however timid at best and will certainly not confine these claims to well defined limits.[19]

(7) Two important lessons can already be learned from the absence of clear constraints on the taking of jurisdiction by national courts. In the first place, the lack of a well defined international framework for jurisdictional claims inevitably brings about the existence of *competing claims* for jurisdiction. Concurrent jurisdiction will be the norm, rather than the exception. As a rule, jurisdiction is by no means 'exclusive'. When State A claims jurisdiction for a given situation, this does not exclude the jurisdiction of other States, which are free to claim jurisdiction on their own. Jurisdiction is therefore said to be *concurrent*, rather than exclusive. Rules of customary international law granting exclusive jurisdiction to one State are indeed not frequent.[20]

In practice, the only way to achieve *exclusive* jurisdiction is to allocate jurisdiction by agreement between the States concerned. Hence the second lesson, i.e; that the lack of clear constraints imposed by international law creates an impetus and incentive for States to agree on shared rules for jurisdiction. If jurisdiction is primarily a national issue, this does not mean that States cannot agree to define limits within which their courts are allowed to exercise their jurisdiction.

Customary international law has not brought much for the resolution of private disputes. Treaties and conventions on the other hand have existed for long. The first treaties date back to the 18th century.[21] Since these first attempts, the number of treaties and conventions allocating jurisdiction between states has grown exponentially, in all fields of law where human activities is prone to cross national borders. Regional agreements – in Europe [22] or in South

---

19 See the attempt by P. Schlosser, 'Human Rights and Litigation', (1990) *Rivista Diritto Internazionale*, 5 et seq. to define the limits. The same may not be true in the United States, where the due process clause of the Constitution has, since the *International Shoe* ruling of the Supreme Court, dominated all thinking about jurisdiction – both domestic and international. *See* generally, A. Mirandes, *La competence inter-étatique et internationale des tribunaux en droit des Etats-Unis* (Economica, Paris, 2002).

20 As Mann wrote, 'It is no doubt evidence of the rudimentary state of international law and a matter for regret that international jurisdiction is almost always concurrent' (F. A. Mann, supra, note 2, at p. 4);

21 See the first treaties cited by M. Foelix in his *Traité de droit international privé ou du conflit des lois en matière de droit privé* (4th ed., Paris, 1866), vol. 1, 323, n° 154 and in particular Article 7 of the Treaty concluded between France and Russia on 11 January 1757 . See also the treaty between France and Swiss, concluded on 18 July 1823 and between the German States of Bavaria and Wurtemberg on 7 May 1821, on which K. Lipstein, 'Unification of Jurisdiction: An Early German Example', in: *L'unificazione del diritto internazionale privato e processuale. Studi in memoria di Mario Giuliano* (Cedam, Padoue, 1989), p. 543-558.

22 G. A. L. Droz, 'L'harmonisation des règles de conflit de lois et de juridiction dans les groupes régionaux d'Etats', in *Rapports généraux au Vième Congrès international de droit comparé*, (Bruylant, Brussels, 1964) (393) 411-433.

America [23] – have been a resounding success. This has undoubtedly incited more ambitious projects such as the one launched by the United States in the 1990's to negotiate a worldwide jurisdiction convention – although it has proven much more difficult to obtain agreement among the different parts of the world, witness the impasse reached by the Hague Judgments Project.[24]

When it comes to private international jurisdiction, national law still dominates in most parts of the world. It is only in Europe where, thanks to the integrating forces of the common market, national rules have given way to uniform, European rules. If agreement is to be found on a truly international plane, one needs therefore to identify first what separates and what unites the different national traditions. With this general background in mind, we can now turn to the question of what has been achieved by private international law in terms of jurisdiction.

3   COMMON PRINCIPLES OF PRIVATE INTERNATIONAL JURISDICTION ?

(8) The following account has only limited ambitions. It is concerned only with rules of private international jurisdiction, defined as rules dealing with *adjudicative* jurisdiction in what are essentially *private* matters.[25] Tradition distinguished between rules of *direct* jurisdiction, which determine when a court can take jurisdiction and rules of *indirect* jurisdiction, which determine under which circumstances a foreign court could legitimately exercise jurisdiction - 'recognition and enforcement'. In both questions, the issue of jurisdiction is the same: can the court of State X rightly exercise jurisdiction over this piece of litigation? In the second branch of civil jurisdiction, the question is however asked with regard to a *foreign* court.

---

23   In Latin America, see the Treaty of Montevideo of 1899, revised in 1940, in force in Argentina, Urugay, Paraguay, Bolivia and Peru. See also the Bustamente Code of 1928 and generally J. Samtleben, *Internationales Privatrecht in Lateinamerika. Die Codigo Bustamente in Theorie und Praxis*, (Mohr, Tübingen, 1979), 58 e.s. as well as M. A. Vieira, 'Le droit international privé dans le développement de l'intégration latino-américaines', *Recueil des cours* (1970) II, 351-453, spéc. pp. 398-402. More recently, the Buenos Aires Protocol of 1994 (published in ILM (1997) 1263) has followed the earlier examples, J. Samtleben, 'Das internationale Prozeß- und Privatrecht des Mercosur. Ein Überblick', *RabelsZ.* (1999) (1-69), spec. 32-45.

24   See the following two progress reports: A. T. von Mehren, 'La rédaction d'une convention universellement acceptable sur la compétence judiciaire internationale et les effets des jugements étrangers: le projet de la Conférence de La Haye peut-il aboutir?' RCDIP (2001) 85-99 and R. Wagner, 'Die Bemühungen der Haager Konferenz für Internationales Privatrecht um ein Übereinkommen über die gerichtliche Zuständigkeit und ausländische Entscheidungen in Zivil- und Handelssachen. Ein Sachstandsbericht nach dem 1. Teil der Diplomatischen Konferenz', IPRax (2001) 533-547.

25   These are defined as 'civil and commercial issues' in European parlance.

(9) The latter branch of the alternative could provide useful insights on what is acceptable and what is not when it comes to jurisdiction. The enforcement practice of States indeed constitutes the 'acid test' of jurisdiction: if State B accepts to enforce a judgment rendered by State A, then it can be presumed that it finds nothing objectionable in the jurisdiction claim made by State A. The court addressed will indeed almost systematically enquire into the jurisdiction of the court of origin. An enquiry into the enforcement practice of States would therefore produce a detailed picture of the boundaries of jurisdiction.

Such an enquiry goes beyond the limited scope of this paper. Furthermore, the enforcement practice of States depends in the first place on how the court addressed deals with indirect jurisdiction. The test can vary significantly. Under Belgian law for example, the jurisdiction of the court of origin is not part of the enquiry, except in the sole hypothesis where the court of origin asserted jurisdiction based on the nationality of the plaintiff, a clear condemnation of the infamous Article 14 of the French Civil Code.[26]

An enquiry of the Belgian practice would therefore not be very helpful, for it would only reveal that the nationality of the plaintiff is considered not sufficient to justify jurisdiction – a result that is too obvious.[27] Under German law, a foreign judgment will receive recognition only if the foreign jurisdiction rule matches standards of German law (the so-called *Spiegelbildprinzip*).[28] This mirror-image principle does not teach much more than the study of rules of direct jurisdiction. Conversely, French law has developed a rather flexible test, based on the requirement of a nexus between the claim and the court of origin.[29] Unfortunately, the application of this sound principle does not lead to a system of clear and broad rules or statements as every case needs to be studied in its precise factual context.[30]

At most therefore, the enforcement enquiry could serve to validate negative conclusion, i.e. that some claims for jurisdiction are neither accepted nor acceptable. We will turn instead to a study of the practice of jurisdiction.

---

26   See Article 570 of the Belgian Civil Code and our comments in 'Artikel 570 Gerechtelijk Wetboek', in: J. Laenens et al. (eds.), *Gerechtelijk recht: artikelsgewijze commentaar met overzicht van rechtspraak en rechtsleer* (Kluwer, Antwerp, 1997), p. 38.

27   See infra on the prohibited grounds of jurisdiction.

28   See for comments on this method, F. K. Juenger, 'The Recognition of Money Judgments in Civil and Commercial Matters', Am. J. Comp. L. (1988) (1), 15.

29   This approach was pioneered in the *Simitch*-ruling of the French Court of Cassation 6 April 1985, published in the *Revue critique de droit international privé* (1985) at p. 369 and in the *Journal de droit international* (1985) at p. 460.

30   The courts in Canada have adopted a similar approach: *Morguard Investments Ltd. v. De Savoye* (1991) 76 D.L.R. (4th) 256; 282 (according to the Supreme Court, a foreign judgment should be recognised as long as the court of origin 'properly, or appropriately, exercised jurisdiction in the action'. This is the case when the court of origin 'has a real and substantial connection with the action'. See also *Hunt v. T. & N. plc* (1993) 109 D.L.R. (4th) 16 and *United States of America v. Ivey*, (1995) 130 D.L.R. (4th) 674.

(10) Can general principles of private international jurisdiction be found? At most, one can distinguish three (modest) principles, which are likely to receive general assent. We will start with these generally accepted principles and move gradually to the more debatable issues.

3.1   *Territorialism as a sole justification / limitation for jurisdiction has been abandoned*

(11) For a long time, it was thought that territorialism was the key, the sole justification for assertions of jurisdiction by courts. This idea was central to Story's thinking.[31] In his classic *Commentaries on the Conflict of Laws*, the Supreme Court Justice offered the following statement of the territoriality doctrine as applied to judicial jurisdiction:

> Considered in an international point of view, jurisdiction, to be rightfully exercised, must be founded either upon the person being within the territory, or upon the thing being within the territory; for, otherwise, there can be no sovereignty exerted, upon the known maxim Extra territorium jus dicenti impune non paretur... no sovereignty can extend its process beyond its own territorial limits, to subject either persons or property to its judicial decisions.[32]

American courts adhered strictly to these views during much of the 19th century. This culminated with the twin statements issued by the Supreme Court in the *Pennoyer*-case.[33] According to the Court, 'every state possesses exclusive jurisdiction and sovereignty over persons and property within its territory' and 'no State can exercise direct jurisdiction and authority over persons and property without its territory'.[34]

The corollary of this assertion was that 'The foundation of jurisdiction is physical power'.[35]

(12) Most systems have outgrown this narrow, rigid territorialism.[36] No reasonable lawyer will claim today that the courts of State X can only rule upon disputes wholly localised within the borders of State X. This evolution was in-

---

31   On Story's contribution to private international law, see K. H. Nadelmann, 'Observations sur la seconde édition des 'Commentaries ...' de Joseph Story à l'occasion de son bicentenaire' RCDIP (1981) 1-15.

32   J. Story, *Commentaries on the conflict of laws foreign and domestic in regard to contracts, rights and remedies, and especially in regard to marriages, divorces, wills, successions and judgments* (Little & Brown, Boston, 1841, 2nd ed.) § 539.

33   *Pennoyer* v. *Neff*, 95 U.S. 714, 24 L.Ed. 565 (1878).

34   95 U.S. 722.

35   As Justice Holmes held in *McDonald* v. *Mabee*, 23 U.S. 90, 91 (1917).

36   Territorialism is part of what Arthur von Mehren calls the 'power theory' in his 'Adjudicatory Jurisdiction: General Theories Compared and Evaluated,' Boston Univ. L. Rev. (1983) 279 et seq.

evitable, economic changes dictated a more flexible approach to jurisdiction. Territorialism was found to be at once too narrow – for activities conducted outside the State, but with effect inside the State, escaped completely the jurisdiction of that State – and too broad since jurisdiction could also be founded on the temporary presence of the defendant.[37]

In the case law of the United States, the move away from the *Pennoyer* formula evolution was crystallized in the *International Shoe formula*, which still dominates jurisdictional thinking today. As the Supreme Court stated, 'due process requires only that in order to subject a defendant to a judgment in personam, *if he be not present within the territory of the forum*, he have certain minimum contacts with it such that the maintenance of the suit does not offend 'traditional notions of fair play and substantial justice".[38] The message was clear: a court can exercise jurisdiction even if the defendant is not immediately present in the territory under direct supervision by the court. The Court left the definition of these 'minimum contacts' to future rulings, which would be numerous but in many respects insatisfactory.[39]

Today, the idea that jurisdiction is not strictly bound by the national borders, seems trite, if not banal. It is enough to refer to the famous 'long arm

---

37   On the many devices to escape the rigid limits on personal jurisdiction, see A. A. Ehrenzweig, 'The Transient Rule of Jurisdiction: the 'Power' Myth and Forum Conveniens', Yale L.J. (1956) 289-314.

38   *International Shoe* v. *State of Washington*, 326 U.S. 310, 316 (1945), per Chief Justice Stone (italics added).

39   Scholars have not been mild in their criticism of the Supreme Court rulings, see P. J. Borchers, 'Comparing Personal Jurisdiction in the U.S. and the European Community: Lessons for American Reform', Am. J. Comp. L. (1992) (121), 126-127 (according to Borchers, 'In a area in which stability and certainty are at premium, the Court's intervention has produced a haphazard jurisdictional doctrine that has left matters in an unacceptable posture. The Supreme Court has evinced great uncertainty as to, and a great preoccupation with, the theoretical underpinnings of its doctrine, while steering an erratic course that confuses courts, counsels, academicians and often the Justices as well'). In 'A Map out of the Personal Jurisdiction Labyrinth', U. C. Davis L. Rev. (1995) 531-559, at p. 531, R. J. Weintraub explained that the case law of the Supreme Court 'has added layer upon layer of complexity to the due process test for personal jurisdiction and [...] as a result, the threshold determination of in personam jurisdiction has become one of the most litigated issues in state and federal courts [...]'). It is enough to read the title of numerous contributions published by F. K. Juenger to understand that the late author was not very found *International Shoe* and its legacy...: 'American Jurisdiction: A Story of Comparative Neglect', U. Colo. L. Rev. (1993) 1 et seq.; 'A Shoe Unfit for Globetrotting' U. C. Davis L. Rev. (1995) 1027 et seq. and 'Supreme Court Intervention in Jurisdiction and Choice of Law: A Dismal Prospect' U. C. Davis L. Rev. (1981) 907 et seq. Mann was also very critical. In his second Hague Academy lectures, he wrote that the Supreme Court 'has led the lower courts to results which in many cases are unattractive and [...] unsatisfactory [...]. The general impression which [these cases] create [...] is that due process as understood in modern American law cannot provide firm guidance to the doctrine of international civil jurisdiction' (F. A. Mann, o.c., *Recueil des cours*, 1984-III, t. 186, 68).

statutes' that determine at the state level, the limits of jurisdiction of courts.[40] The word 'long arm' already conveys the idea that the state borders are no longer irremediably closed.

The 3rd *Restatement Foreign Relations Law of the United States* states that

> In general, a State's exercise of jurisdiction to adjudicate with respect to a person or a thing is reasonable if, at the time jurisdiction is asserted: [...] (j) the person, whether natural or juridical, had carried on outside the state an activity having a substantial, direct and foreseeable effect within the state, but only in respect of such activity [...] (§ 421 (2)).

European courts can similarly exercise jurisdiction in disputes involving persons or property located outside their national borders. Under Article 5-3 of the 44/2001 Regulation,[41] a defendant domiciled in a EU State can be sued before the courts of another state 'in matters relating to tort, delict or quasi-delict, in the courts for the place where the harmful event occurred or may occur'. According to the Court of Justice, a court of a Member State can, in case of transborder pollution, exercise jurisdiction over the defendant even if the pollution originated in another Member State, provided the direct damage caused is felt in the Member State where the court sits – the effects doctrine applied to private jurisdiction.[42]

(13) In reality it is the very concept of territoriality that has been abandoned, or at least questioned.[43] How else to explain that courts are today no longer hesitant to issue extra-territorial rulings, that directly seek to impose certain effects outside the national borders? It is enough to invoke the long series of Dutch cases pertaining to cross border injunctions in intellectual property lit-

---

40   See for an overview, G. B. Born, *International Civil Litigation in United States Courts. Commentary and Materials* (3rd ed., Kluwer Law International, Boston, 1996), pp. 68-70.

41   Regulation 44/2001 adopted on 22 December 2000 ([2001] OJ, L-12/1of 22) replaces the Brussels Convention of 27 September 1968 and lays down detailed rules on the jurisdiction of courts of EU Member States in civil and commercial matters; It also provides for the European equivalent of the US Full Faith and Credit Clause.

42   E.C.J., 30 November 1976, *Bier* v. *Mines de Potasse d'Alsace*, case 21/76, ECR [1976] 1735.

43   M. Rigaux, reporter of the Ninteenth Commission of the Institut de droit international, dealing with the issue of extra-territorial jurisdiction, refers in this respect to the 'perte de confiance dans le caractère opérationnel des concepts mêmes de territorialité et d'extra-territorialité': « Rapport provisoire sur la compétence extraterritoriale des Etats », *Ann. Institut Droit International*, vol. 68, (1998) (507), 509.

igation to illustrate this new trend.[44] Today, courts of all countries commonly enjoin defendants from committing acts abroad.[45]

The demise of territoriality has been accompanied with proposals to replace this concept with new paradigms, such as the use of a 'reasonable link' – test to assess the exercise of jurisdiction.[46] This raises other questions, which will be dealt with by Dr. Ralf Michaels in his study, *Jurisdiction after Territory*.

(14) This does not mean that the idea of territory has lost all its relevance in delimitating jurisdiction. Many rules of jurisdiction recognise the importance of a direct link between the dispute and the territory under the jurisdiction of the court – witness the continued relevance of the *actor sequitur* principle.[47] In disputes involving *in rem* property, the idea that the court where the property is located should have jurisdiction, is very much alive.[48]

The paradigm of territory is however no longer the only one accepted. With the disappearance of a strict notion of territoriality as all-encompassing principle, the enforcement of judgments has gained increased importance. Since jurisdiction is no longer strictly tied to physical power over the defendant, there will be instances where a judgment cannot be enforced in the State where it was rendered. Hence the development of an important body of case law on enforcement, and the growing importance of international agreements

---

44   See generally M. Pertegás Sender, *Cross-Border Enforcement of Patent Rights: An Analysis of the Interface between Intellectual Property and Private International Law* (Oxford University Press, Oxford, 2002). See also H. Bertrams, 'Das grenzüberschreitende Verletzungsverbot im niederländischen Patentrecht', (1995) GRUR Int., 193-201; J. J. Brinkhof, 'Het grensoverschrijdende verbod in octrooizaken in kort geding', *Molengrafica. Europees privaatrecht 1995* (Lelystad, 1995), 225-261; W. V. Meibom & J. Pitz, 'Cross-Border Injunctions in International Patent Infringement Proceedings' EIPR, (1997) 469-478; D. Stauder, 'Grenzüberschreitende Verletzungsverbote im gewerblichen Rechtsschutz und das EuGVÜ', IPRax (1998) 317-322.

45   As has been observed, '*il serait [...] particulièrement difficile d'invoquer l'existence d'une règle de droit international coutumier interdisant au juge d'ordonner l'accomplissement d'un acte à l'étranger; la pratique est trop répandue*': P. Kinsch, *Le fait du prince étranger*,(LGDJ, Paris, ,1994), 134. See also P. Schlosser, *Der Justizkonflikt zwischen den USA und Europa* (Walter de Gruyter, Berlin, 1985), 17 (the famous German jurist wrote that 'Höchst selten hat man hierzulande Skrupel, zu einer Handlung verurteilen zu lassen, die im Ausland vorzunehmen ist' and at p. 21 'kann es keine Regel des Völkergewohneitsrechts geben, die es gerichten und Behörden eines Staates verböte, auf fremdem Territorium oder aus fremdem Territorium heraus vorzunehmende Handlungen auzuordnen und die Nichtbeachtung solcher Anordnungen zu sanktioneren').

46   See C. Kessedjian, *International Jurisdiction and Foreign Judgments in Civil and Commercial Matters*, Hague Conference on Private International Law, Preliminary Document n° 7, April 1997, 35-37. *See* also the review by H. Muir Watt of A. Bucher's, *Droit international privé suisse. Tome I/1: Partie générale – Conflits de jurisdictions* (Helbing et Lichtenhahn, Basel, 1998) [published in: *Rev. Int'l. Dr. Comp.* (1999) (1157), at pp. 1158-1159].

47   Generally, B. Buchner, *Kläger- und Beklagtenschutz im Recht der internationalen Zuständigkeit*, (Mohr, Siebeck, Tübingen, 1998), p. 170.

48   See Article 22 of the 44/2001 Regulation.

dealing with the issue of enforcement, as reciprocity and mutual trust seems to be the motor of this question.[49]

3.2   *Consent is generally recognised as a satisfactory base for jurisdiction*

(15) While territoriality is no longer the sole defining principle of jurisdictional claim, another general principle has gradually been accepted, which justifies the exercise of jurisdiction by reference to the consent of parties. Legal systems have indeed unmistakeably grown to recognise that parties to a contract or, more generally, to a legal relationship, can determine which court will hear their dispute.

This freedom has not been recognised overnight. There was a time when courts regarded choice of court clauses with distrust. In 1959, the Court of Appeal of the 5th Circuit could still refer to '[...] the universally accepted rule that agreements in advance of controversy whose subject is to oust the jurisdiction of the Courts are contrary to public policy and will not be enforced'.[50] The same could be said of arbitration, which was not always favorably viewed by courts jealous of their prerogatives.

This attitude of distrust has gradually disappeared to give way to a warm embrace. The 'dramatic shift that American jurisprudence has taken from almost universal hostility towards exclusive forum clauses to enthusiastic acceptance'[51] can be explained by the need to give businessmen certainty that what they bargained for will be upheld in court. As the Supreme Court held in the famous *Zapata case* '[t]he expansion of American business and industry will hardly be encouraged if, notwithstanding solemn contracts, we insist on a parochial concept that all disputes must be resolved under our law and in our courts'.[52]

(16) The vast majority of legal systems recognise today the freedom for parties to a contract to decide which court will hear their dispute. It is enough to

---

49   This also goes to show that when dealing with private international jurisdiction, one ought to take into account the parallel issues of enforcement and applicable law. One cannot design rules of jurisdiction without knowing what attitude the courts will take concerning foreign judgments. Inexplicably the Dutch rules of international jurisdiction were recently reformed, and adapted to modern thinking, while at the same time the antiquated Article 431 of the Dutch Code of Civil Procedure, prohibiting almost all extra-territorial effect of foreign judgments, remained in place.

50   *Carbon Black Export, Inc. v. S. S. Monrosa*, 245 F.2d 297 (5th Cir. 1958), *cert. denied* 359 U.S. 1980 (1959).

51   E. F. Scoles, P. Hay, P. J. Borchers & S. C. Symeonides, *Conflict of laws* 3rd ed. (West Publishing Co., St. Paul, 2000), p. 473.

52   *M/S Bremen* v. *Zapata Off-Shore Co.*, 407 U.S. 1, 8 (1972). Some difficulties remain with choice of court clauses found in adhesion contracts, see W. M. Richman, 'Carnival Cruise Lines: Forum Selection Clauses in Adhesion Contracts' Am. J. Comp. L. (1992) 977-984 and L. Mullenix, 'Another Easy Case, Some More Bad Law: Carnival Cruise Lines and Contractual Personal Jurisdiction', Texas Int'l L. J. (1992) 323-370.

refer to the evolution of South American legal systems in this respect to show that the distrust has given way to a more than conciliatory attitude, where parties enjoy a great freedom to shape their contracts also for issues of dispute resolution.[53] It is true that certain legal systems have long resisted the recognition of this freedom. Companies doing business in the Netherlands had to wait until 1985 to see the Dutch Supreme Court upholding a bargained for choice of court.[54]

However, much of the western world today could easily subscribe to the rule enshrined in Article 23 of the 44/2001 Regulation, which provides that

> If the parties, one or more of whom is domiciled in a Member State, have agreed that a court or the courts of a Member State are to have jurisdiction to settle any disputes which have arisen or which may arise in connection with a particular legal relationship, that court or those courts shall have jurisdiction.

Recently, States negotiating at the Hague Conference for Private International Law have singled out choice of forum clauses as the main issue where they could probably find agreement [55] – this in sharp contrast to the ambitious plans with which the negotiations for a worldwide Judgments Convention started in 1996.[56]

---

53   In the past, courts in South America have long been reluctant to give effect to a contractual choice of court or an arbitration agreement. See for arbitration the situation in 1984, as described by A. M. Garro, 'Enforcement of Arbitration Agreements and Jurisdiction of Arbitral Tribunals in Latin America' J. Int'l. Arbitration (1984) 293-321. Today, arbitration is widely recognised as a valid alternative to state court resolution: H. A. Grigera-Naón, 'Overcoming Traditional Hostility Towards Arbitration' in: *International Commercial Arbitration. Recent Developments, Commercial Law & Practice Course Handbook* Series No. 477, II (New York, 1988), pp. 377-447 and B. M. Cremades (ed.), *Enforcement of Arbitration Agreements in Latin America* (Kluwer Law International/IBA, La Haye, 1999), p. 250

54   The famous *Piscator* case decided by the Hoge Raad on 1 Feb. 1985 (NJ, 1985, 698). See also for France, the ruling of the Court of Cassation of 1 December 1985, where the Court held that '[...] les clauses prorogeant la compétence internationales sont en principe licites, lorsqu'il s'agit d'un litige international [...]' (published in the *Revue Critique de Droit international privé*, (1985), p. 537, with comments by H. Gaudemet-Tallon).

55   R. Brand, 'Forum Selection and Forum Rejection in U.S. Courts: One Rationale for a Global Choice of Court Convention', in: J. Fawcett, *Reform and Development of Private International Law – Essays in Honour of Sir Peter North* (Oxford University Press, Oxford, 2002), pp. 51-87.

56   See on the whole project; A. F. Lowenfeld and L. J. Silberman (eds.), *The Hague Convention on Jurisdiction and Judgments. Records of a Conference Held in a New York University School of Law April 30-May 1*, (New York, 1999) Jurispublishing, 2001 mult. pag. and S. Baumgartner, *The Proposed Hague Convention on Jurisdiction and Foreign Judgments. Trans-Atlantic Lawmaking for Transnational Litigation* (Mohr Siebeck, 2003) p. 210.

(18) The rise of arbitration as the preferred – if certainly not flawless – [57] method for resolution of international business disputes also bears testimony to the ever increasing recognition of parties' consent as a general principle of jurisdiction. Most legal systems have sanctioned the possibility for parties to opt out radically of the judicial system and to entrust the resolution of their disputes to a private arbitral tribunal. By entrusting their disputes to a private tribunal, businesses hope to benefit from certainty, privacy, speed, commercial expertise and above all from neutrality.[58]

Even though significant differences remain, international commercial arbitration is today not only universally recognized as a valuable alternative to state justice, it can count on the active support of States who have concluded far-reaching international agreements to ensure the respect for the findings of the arbitrators.[59] What is more, States seem to be engaged in a sort of competition to devise liberal legislations supporting the arbitration process, with a view to attract what is perceived to be a lucrative or at least a prestigious business.[60] Courts have also shown increased willingness to shake off the old judicial hostility to arbitration and in some cases are ready to cede jurisdiction to arbitral tribunals even when the controversy at hand involved special public policy considerations.[61]

---

57 The advantages and drawbacks of party autonomy in the resolution of private international disputes have already been well documented, see e.g. W. W. Park, 'When and Why Arbitration Matters', in: G.M. Beresford Hartwell (ed.), *The Commercial Way to Justice. The 1996 International Conference of the Chartered Institute of Arbitrators* (Kluwer Law International, 1997), pp. 73-99.

58 Mayer argues convincingly that neutrality is the main reason businesses opt for arbitration: 'L'arbitrage est le mode les plus fréquent de résolution des litiges du commerce international. La raison principale du succès qu'il remporte auprès des justiciables est sa neutralité, liée à son caractère privé: les arbitres ne statuant pas au nom d'un Etat, mais uniquement en leur nom propre, ne sont pas soupçonnés de partialité envers l'une ou l'autre partie', P. Mayer, *L'autonomie de l'arbitre international dans l'appréciation de sa propre compétence*, Collected Courses (1989-V), vol. 217, (319), 327.

59 Most notably the New York Convention on the Recognition and Enforcement of Foreign Arbitral Awards, 10 June 1958, 21 U.S.T. 2517, 330 U.N.T.S. 38, in force in more than 100 countries.
    The success of the New York Convention is even more remarkable if one thinks of the absence of a worldwide Judgments Convention. This means that, for a variety of reasons, States have agreed to give more respect to private justice than to each other's justice.

60 There is also a fierce competition between 'different arbitral institutions hawking their wares', as D.F. Vagts, *Dispute-Resolution Mechanisms in International Business*, Collected Courses of the Hague Academy for International Law (987-III), vol. 203, (9), p. 8.

61 See for instance two ground-breaking rulings of the U.S. Supreme Court, *Scherk* v. *Alberto-Culver Co.* 417 U.S. 506 (1974) (the Court held that the fact that the U.S. securities legislation applied to the transaction at hand did not make the dispute non-arbitrable); *Mitsubishi Motors Corp. Soler Chrysler-Plymouth, Inc.*, 105 S. Ct. 3346 (1985) (the Court held that an arbitration clause between a Japanese manufacturer and an American distributor was valid even though the distributor complained of violation of U.S. antitrust legislation). On this last case see J. Robert, 'Une date dans l'extension de l'arbitrage international: l'arrêt Mitsubishi c. Soler' [1986] Rev. Arbitrage 173 and the controversy between T. Carbonneau, 'Mitsubishi: The Folly of Quixotic Internationalism' (1986) 2 Arb. Int'l 116 and A. Lowenfeld, 'The Mitsubishi case: Another View' (1986) 2 Arb. Int'l 178.

In the same line, parties choose more and more today to forgo completely the idea of adjudication of their disputes by a neutral third party and opt for one or the other mechanisms embodying the idea of *informal justice*. Whatever the name, mediation, conciliation, etc, the basic idea remains the same: instead of agreeing to submit to the binding resolution of a dispute according to rules of law, parties choose to work out their differences through negotiation, with or without the help of a third party or of a simulated trial. Characteristic of this approach is that parties are not bound by legal rules and do not await a solution imposed on them. The consequences of this evolution for the concept of jurisdiction have yet to be worked out.

The recognition of consent as a general principle of jurisdiction goes hand in hand with the greater weight given to parties in the selection of the applicable law. Party autonomy also dominates conflict of laws rules, both in Europe [62] and in the United States.[63]

(18) However, choice of court agreements (and choice of law agreements) cannot resolve all issues. For one thing, party autonomy is only recognised in certain fields. Parties involved in divorce proceedings are rarely afforded the freedom to determine which court will hear their claim.[64] On the other hand, the principle of party autonomy 'has been given effect in a number of different ways'.[65] The result is that 'It is by no means the case [...] that [...] jurisdiction (or arbitration) agreements foreclose the possibility of often decisive interlocutory litigation on the question of venue for and or mode of the resolution of disputes arising between parties to such contracts. The law reports record many instances of litigation by parties 'in order to determine where they shall litigate' notwithstanding the existence of a jurisdiction clause or arbitration agreement'.[66]

Litigants can too often wriggle out of jurisdiction agreements, on the basis of convenience arguments or other. It remains that the principle of party autonomy has acquired today a fundamental value and constitutes indisputably an *acquis* of the modern law of jurisdiction.

---

62   See Article 3 of the 1980 Rome Convention: 'A contract shall be governed by the law chosen by the parties. The choice must be expressed or demonstrated with reasonable certainty by the terms of the contract or the circumstances of the case. By their choice the parties can select the law applicable to the whole or a part only of the contract'.

63   See e.g. § 187 *Restatement of the Law, Conflict of Laws* 2nd: 'The law of the state chosen by the parties to govern their contractual rights and duties will be applied if the particular issue is one which the parties could have resolved by an explicit provision in their agreement directed to that issue'.

64   Except maybe when the divorce petition is brought by the two spouses together, see Article 2(1)(a), fourth hypothesis of EU Regulation 1347/2000.

65   C. McLachlan, 'Third Interim Report: Declining and Referring Jurisdiction in International Litigation', *International Law Association. Report of the London Conference (2000)*, 5.

66   A. S. Bell, 'Jurisdiction and Arbitration Agreements in Transnational Contracts', J. Contract L., (1996) (53), 54. See also Chapter 5 of Mr. Bell's recent book, referred to supra note 1, entitled 'Escaping the Bargain' (at pp. 283 – 333).

3.3   Prohibition of 'jurisdictionally improper fora'

(19) Beyond the demise of pure territoriality and the rise of consent, the last general principle that can be singled out is the prohibition of certain grounds of jurisdiction, deemed too self-serving. It has become commonplace to refer in this respect to 'exorbitant' or 'improper'[67] fora.

It is often said that the exercise of jurisdiction should be founded on a 'minimum connection' or a 'genuine link' between the State claiming jurisdiction and the dispute.[68] The only practical translation of this very general principle is in effect that the idea that some rules of jurisdiction are objectionable, in that they do not guarantee that the court will show the desired minimum link with the dispute.

This idea has been taken over in various international agreements. Both the Brussels Convention [69] and the 1971 Hague Enforcement Convention [70] contained a catalogue of grounds of jurisdiction whose exercise is prohibited between Contracting Parties.[71]

The Draft Hague Convention of 2001 goes one step further. Besides the general catalogue of prohibited grounds of jurisdiction, Article 18(1) of the 2001 Draft Hague Judgments Convention also contains a general prohibition of the exercise of any jurisdiction that is not founded on a 'substantial connection' between the State exercising jurisdiction and the dispute.[72] The second

---

67   After the title of Mr. Nadelmann's essay, 'Jurisdictionnally Improper Fora' in: *Legal Essays in Honor of H. E. Yntema*, (Leyden, 1961) p. 321 et seq.

68   F. A. Mann, referred to the concepts of 'genuine link', 'sufficiently strong interest' and 'reasonable relation' (*The Doctrine of Jurisdiction in International Law*, Collected Courses, (1964-I), t. 111, (9-162), 46-47. See also G. Born, 'Reflections on Judicial Jurisdiction in International Cases', Georgia J. Intl. L. (1987), (1), 19 (who sees an 'emerging principle of international law requiring assertion of judicial jurisdiction to be reasonable') and G. van Hecke, *Principes et méthodes de solution des conflits de lois*, Collected Courses (1969-I), t. 126, (399), 418. See more recently, J. Bertele, *Souveränität und Verfahrensrecht. Eine Untersuchung der aus dem Völkerrecht ableitbaren Grenzen staatlicher extraterritorialer Jurisdiktion im Verfahrensrecht* (Mohr Siebeck, Tübingen, 1998), pp. 182-185 ('Genuine Link') and the references quoted by P. de Vareilles-Sommières, oc, 1997, at p. 243, § 394.

69   Originally, the catalogue of prohibited grounds appeared directly in the text of the Convention, even though it did not add anything to the first part of Article 3 of the Convention, which already stated that parties domiciled in a Member State could only be sued on the basis of the grounds of jurisdiction expressly recognised by the Convention. Recently the famous black list was removed to an Annex of the EU 44/2001 Regulation.

70   Article 4 of the Additional Protocol to the 1971 Hague Enforcement Convention.

71   The European 'black' list is drafted with reference to specific provisions of national law, whereas the Hague 'black' list is drafted in abstract terms, with reference to jurisdiction claims that should be prohibited whatever their precise legislative or jurisprudential translations.

72   Article 18, entitled *Prohibited grounds of jurisdiction*, reads as follows:
'(1) Where the defendant is habitually resident in a Contracting State, the application of a rule of jurisdiction provided for under the national law of a Contracting State is prohibited if there is no substantial connection between that State and the dispute'.

part of this provision goes on to single out a series of rules of jurisdiction that are presumed not to satisfy this general test.[73]

(20) The educational value of the black lists of exorbitant fora cannot be underestimated. It must be said, however, that the 'minimum connection' principle they convey is probably much less firmly well established than the first two general principles singled out in this essay.

On the one hand, the prohibition of certain fora only works well when it is the object of a *mutual pact*. It goes without saying that States are much less willing to compromise on their traditional grounds of jurisdiction in the absence of the reciprocity of a bargain, even if it is impossible to ignore the unreasonable nature of certain claims for jurisdiction. Unilateral disarmament is as difficult in the field of jurisdiction as in other fields of human activities...

On the other hand, even rules that are objectionable in principle can be acceptable in certain contexts. This is the case with the infamous *forum actoris*, i.e. a rule that links the exercise of jurisdiction to certain characteristics of the plaintiff, such as his domicile or nationality. This is in principle objectionable, as the European Court of Justice regularly repeats in the framework of the Brussels Regulation. However, the forum actoris may be justified in the field of family law, *e.g.* when it comes to jurisdiction in matters of divorce. How else can the Italian wife of an Belgian man obtain a divorce in her home country when the husband has left the matrimonial home in France and returned to Belgium ? [74] Finally, one should not forget that Article 18 of the Draft Hague Convention was the subject of strong criticism, mainly by U.S. experts who found it too restrictive. There is reason to think that it would not have been accepted as it stood in the 2001 Draft.

---

73   '(2) In particular, jurisdiction shall not be exercised by the courts of a Contracting State on
        the basis solely of one or more of the following:
        – the presence or the seizure in that State of property belonging to the defendant, except
            where the dispute is directly related to that property;
        – the nationality of the plaintiff;
        – the nationality of the defendant;
        – the domicile, habitual or temporary residence, or presence of the plaintiff in that State;
        – the carrying on of commercial or other activities by the defendant in that State, except
            where the dispute is directly related to those activities;
        – the service of a writ upon the defendant in that State;
        – the unilateral designation of the forum by the plaintiff;
        – proceedings in that State for declaration of enforceability or registration or for the en-
            forcement of a judgment, except where the dispute is directly related to such proceed-
            ings;
        – the temporary residence or presence of the defendant in that State;
        – the signing in that State of the contract from which the dispute arises'.
74   See Article 2 of the Brussels II Regulation 1347/2000, which grants jurisdiction to the
        courts of the habitual residence of the plaintiff, provided the plaintiff resides in the Mem-
        ber State for at least 12 months – or 6 months in case the plaintiff is a national of the coun-
        try.

(21) All this considered, we might need to reduce the third principle to a simple prohibition of discrimination against foreigners in assertion of jurisdiction. It is uncertain whether there is enough agreement to go beyond this general prohibition.

The recent evolution of some national laws gives, however, reason to be optimistic. One of the clearest signs of change is the recent revision of the Dutch Code of Civil Procedure. This process has led to the disappearance of the infamous Article 126 of the *Wetboek van Burgerlijke Rechtsvordering*, which embodied one of the crudest forms of *forum actoris*.[75] Similarly, Spanish and Italian rules on jurisdiction were reformed in the last decade to incorporate many of the rules of jurisdiction found in the Brussels Convention, thereby doing away with older rules that were not always free from bias against foreigners and foreign courts. At the same time, the general acceptance of the doctrine of *forum non conveniens* in common law systems has contributed to the refinement of excessively broad traditional rules of jurisdiction.[76] If only France could follow the example of its European neighbors and do away with the Articles 14 and 15 of its Civil Code !

4   AN ATTEMPT TO CONCLUDE: THE DIFFERENCES THAT SEPARATE US

(22) Once upon a time, it was thought that States could easily agree on generally acceptable rules of jurisdiction. The famous Dutch internationalist, Tobias Asser, wrote at the end of the 19th century that

> il ne sera pas difficile, croyons-nous, de déterminer, pour chaque procès, quel en est le juge naturel et d'arriver sur ce point à un accord international.[77]

One cannot but accept that these dreams have not (yet?) been fulfilled.[78] There is no agreement today on a detailed framework for international adjudicative jurisdiction in private matters.

---

75   See for a comment, P. Vlas & F. Ibili, 'De nieuwe commune regels inzake de rechtsmacht van de Nederlandse rechter', WPNR, nr. 652, at pp. 310 ff.

76   On this see recently A. Nuyts, *L'exception de forum non conveniens* (Bruylant-LGDJ, Brussels-Paris, 2003) 973 p., in particular at pp. 161-201.

77   T. M. C. Asser, *Eléments de droit international privé* (Rousseau, Paris, 1884) 154 – it is interesting to note that the only principle Asser put forward to found jurisdiction was what would later be called 'Gleichlauf', i.e. the idea that the court of country A should have jurisdiction when the law of country A applies.

78   This is not for lack of effort by scholars. Some internationalists took up Asser's challenge and drafted model conventions providing uniform rules on international jurisdiction for the courts of all Nations. See the attempts made by H. Sperl, 'Eine internationale Zuständigkeitsordnung in bürgerlichen Rechtssachen', published in *Zeitschrift für Internationales Recht* (NiemZ.) (1925) 19 et seq. and the draft convention elaborated by the Dutch lawyer J. Kosters, *Bijdrage tot internationale regeling der rechtsmacht in burgerlijke en handelszaken* (De Erven F. Bohn, Haarlem, 1914), p. 107.

This essay attempted to draw the lines around three general principles, on the (naïve?) presumption that most jurisdictions would have no difficulty to approve them.

Beyond these basic tenets, disagreements abound. It is difficult to single out other principles of private international jurisdiction that could count on the same general approval. Even the *'forum sequitur actor rei'*-principle – granting general jurisdiction to the courts of the domicile of the defendant – is not wholly uncontested. It has been argued that 'Legal systems agree that natural persons may be sued at their domicile on any claim'.[79] One can, however, doubt whether this rule would in all instances pass the 'due process' test laid down by the US Supreme Court in *International Shoe*. There is certainly disagreement on the importance of the rule: some see it as the most fundamental principle, to which all other rules should be subordinated; other refuse to grant it any special status. On a more theoretical plane, the idea that the defendant deserves special protection is certainly not unchallenged.

(23) Once the solid core of generally accepted principles is identified, one should attempt to single out areas of disagreement. The task is infinite. By way of conclusion, we will outline two of the main problem issues that stand in the way of general agreement on private international jurisdiction.

The first one is an issue of *legal technique*.[80] Careful students of the numerous documents produced by the Hague attempt to draft a worldwide Jurisdiction Convention will soon notice that the process often stumbled on issues of drafting. There is probably a general agreement that a distinction should be made between rules granting *general jurisdiction* (for all disputes) and rules granting *special jurisdiction* (for a specific category of disputes).

Beyond this very general distinction, one can distinguish two models that compete for attention.[81] On the one hand there is the 'Brussels' model, made up of 'hard and fast' rules leaving little room for flexibility, which typically focus on a well-defined category of disputes. This approach, called '*Typisierung*' in the German doctrine, is exemplified by Article 5-1 of the Brussels Regulation, the basic European rule for disputes in contractual matters.

Article 5-1 selects a single element of the contractual relationship, i.e. the place of performance of the obligation in dispute,[82] which is deemed to determine jurisdiction in all contractual disputes, whatever their nature and shape.

---

79   P. Hay, *Flexibility versus Predictability and Uniformity in Choice of Law – Reflections on Current European and United States Conflict of Law*, Collected Courses (1991-I), vol. 226, (281) p. 311.

80   An issue underlined by J. Hill, 'Jurisdiction in Civil and Commercial Matters: Is There a Third Way?', *Current Legal Problems*, OUP (2001), 439-476.

81   See generally on this distinction, T. Pfeiffer, *Internationale Zuständigkeit und Prozessuale Gerechtigkeit. Die internationale Zuständigkeit im Zivilprozess zwischen effektivem Rechtsschutz und nationaler Zuständigkeitspolitik* (Vittorio Klostermann, Frankfurt a.M., 1995), p. 199 et seq.

82   And for some categories of contracts, the characteristic obligation. See on the new Article 5-1, P. Vlas, 'Stoeien met verbintenissen, worstelen met art. 5 sub 1 EEX-Verordening', WPNR (2002) nr. 6485, pp. 301-302.

This certainly provides for a good deal of certainty – even though the drafting of the provision is itself a source of uncertainty and dispute. The certainty comes, however, at the cost of some unwanted results, not the least in determining whether the dispute is concerned with a contract. Other problems abound, most disturbing of all the fact that Article 5-1 fails to give appropriate weight to other connecting factors which may be as relevant as the place of performance of the characteristic obligation. Finally, one is at a loss to locate the place of performance of an obligation to refrain from doing something. It is therefore no surprise that Article 5-1 has given rise, not only to a real cottage industry in the legal literature, spawning commentaries in all languages but invariably critical,[83] but, more troublesome, to a long list of references to the Court of Justice by national courts seeking help in interpreting the European *forum contractus*.

The second model, which can somewhat arbitrarily be called the 'English' model, avoids the pitfalls of Article 5-1 in that it builds on an ad hoc decision making on the basis of flexible criteria. This case-by-case approach – '*individuelle Einzelfallabwägung*' in the German terminology – gives rise to open-ended, open-textured jurisdiction rules, which are qualified by a very broad discretion of the court. This is where the *forum non conveniens* doctrine comes into play, giving the court the power to refuse to exercise jurisdiction when it deems it inappropriate.

This sounds attractive in principle, but is certainly not free from side effects. The most troublesome of these is that the 'English' model leads to speculative litigation on jurisdictional questions and wasteful litigation to determine the place of litigation.

The choice between these regimes, presented here without much nuance, is influenced by the eternal debate between legal certainty on the one hand and the need for flexibility on the other, which is in turn heavily dependent on one's legal upbringing. A common lawyer may think that 'the life of law has not been logic; it has been experience'.[84] A lawyer educated on the old continent will shiver when reading MM North and Fawcett's statement that 'Private international law is no more an exact science than is any other part of the law of England; it is not scientifically founded on the reasoning of jurists, but it is beaten out on the anvil of experience'.[85]

---

83   See e.g. G. A. L. Droz, 'Delendum est forum contractus ?', *D.*, 1997, Chron., 351-356; V. Heuzé, 'De quelques infirmités congénitales du droit uniforme: l'exemple de l'article 5-1 de la Convention de Bruxelles du 27 septembre 1968', *Revue critique de droit international privé*, (2000) 595 et seq.; H. Muir Watt, 'Peut-on sauver le for européen du contrat?', *Revue Générale des procédures* (1998) 371 et seq. and L. Palsson, 'The Unruly Horse of the Brussels and Lugano Conventions: the Forum Solutionis', in: L. L. Andersen (éd.), *Festkrift für Ole Lando*,(Copenhagen, 1997), 259 et seq.

84   O. W. Holmes, *The Common Law* (1881) 1.

85   P. M. North and J. J. Fawcett, *Cheshire and North's Private International Law* (Butterworths, London, 1999), pp. 31-32.

This is not to say that the two models cannot be reconciled. There are ways to bridge the gap and the process of negotiating the Hague Judgments Convention showed the way. Unfortunately, this process has failed, at least in its early, ambitious form.

(24) Beyond mere drafting problems, the search for common ground is also mired by issues of principles. The very first of these is the need to define which objectives should command when defining the limits of jurisdiction. German doctrine speaks in this respect of '*Zuständigkeitsinteressen*'.

An agreement can certainly be found that jurisdiction is not a valueless, abstract process, but also embodies substantive policies. Unlike choice of law rules, rules of jurisdiction have never been thought of as mere conceptual rules, whose sole function would be to allocate power between competing nation-states. The student of jurisdiction will very soon discover that there is more to jurisdiction than neatly 'compartmentalizing' disputes according to their territorial or personal connections.[86]

It should not be too difficult to agree that jurisdiction can be influenced by a variety of principles, such as concerns for *sovereignty* – giving rise to rules founded on the nationality of parties or on the location of real property – and concerns for the need to regulate human activity on a given territory – leading to rules pegging jurisdiction to the effects of certain conducts in a State. Principles of 'fairness' and 'justice' can probably also receive approval, and lead to rules based on the need to protect the defendant or ensure that a dispute is allocated to a court convenient for all parties involved.

Besides these jurisdictional principles, one can probably agree that other objectives also deserve attention, such as the need to avoid parallel litigation, concerns for forum shopping or the idea that jurisdiction should go hand in hand with a well thought of recognition policy. The 'meta-jurisdictional' principles also include the need to further substantive policy objectives, such as concerns for protecting 'weaker' parties.

Identifying general principles is one thing. Determining which principle deserves priority in a given case or reconciling principles which lead to contradicting outcomes, can prove much more difficult. The first question one should address is whether there is a need for some sort of *hierarchy* between competing principles. This is a delicate task, for all principles seem worthy of attention.[87] The US Supreme Court seemed to recognise that it is illusory to

---

86   On this theme see already Ph. Francescakis, 'Review of the 4th edition of Batiffol's Droit international privé', in: *Revue critique de droit international privé* (1967) (435) p. 437. See also T. Pfeiffer, 'Materialisierung und Internationalisierung der internationale Zuständigkeit', in: C.-W. Canaris (ed.), *50 Jahre BGH. Festgabe aus der Wissenschaft* (Beck, München, 2000, III), pp. 617-653.

87   This is the major flaw of Schröder's study (*Internationale Zuständigkeit. Entwurf eines Systems von Zuständigkeitsinteressen im zwischenstaatlichen Privatverfahrensrecht aufgrund rechtshistorischer, rechtsvergleichender und rechtspolitischer Betrachtungen* (Westdeutscher Verlag, Opladen, 1971) 852 p.): although it clearly identifies all relevant principles, it does not offer a key to understand their relationship.

pretend that a single most important concern can be singled out, when it held that

> the burden on the defendant, while always a primary concern, will in an appropriate case be considered in light of the relevant factors, including the forum State's interests in adjudicating the dispute; the plaintiff's interest in obtaining convenient and effective relief [...] at least when that interest is not adequately protected by the plaintiff's power to choose the forum [...]; the interstate judicial system's interest in obtaining the most efficient resolution of controversies and the shared interest of the several States in furthering fundamental substantive social policies.[88]

(24) In the end, theories on jurisdiction may be in a 'transitional' period. General principles have been identified, as have been areas of disagreement. We may safely conclude that jurisdiction is a complex equation,[89] one that requires that the relationship between the various principles be elucidated.

Whatever weight is given to each element of this equation, the drafter of the rule will need to remember that globalization brings about more and more 'pluri-localised' situations, i.e. situations that have substantial connections with more than one State. If one remembers that assertions of jurisdiction must answer to many competing interests, it is easy to accept that the idea of a single natural forum for each dispute is an illusion.[90]

We should therefore start from the premise that several States will be able to claim jurisdiction for the same dispute and move towards the idea of cooperation between States with a substantial interest in solving the dispute. Jurisdiction should not be thought of as a unilateral decision by a single State, but more as an exercise in cooperation between the States involved.

---

88   *Worldwide Volkswagen Corp.* v. *Woodson*, 444 U.S. 286, 292 (1980).
89   A phrase used A. T. von Mehren, *Conflict of Laws: American, Comparative, International, Cases and Materials* (West, St. Paul, 1998), p. 736.
90   See generally H. Gaudemet-Tallon, 'L'introuvable juge naturel', in: C. Bontems (ed.), *Nonagesimo ano. Mélanges en hommage à J. Gaudemet* (PUF, Paris, 1999), pp. 591-612.

European private international law and the challenges of globalisation

Johan Meeusen

1   INTRODUCTION

(1) In his very interesting contribution to this book, P. Wautelet gives his view on what private international law has achieved in meeting the challenges posed by globalisation. Though I agree on many points with Wautelet's theses, I wish to make a few brief comments on that same question, focusing especially on the impact of the europeanization of private international law.

(2) The question of what 'private international law' has achieved, is rather abstract. It risks creating the false impression that an internationally shared private international law approach exists, and that this unique system can be developed in one way or another to manage (the legal effects of) globalisation. Lea Brilmayer's observation that 'the fundamental and unavoidable problem of choice of law is one of perspective'[1] is true in many senses, also in that it indicates that conflicts law cannot be approached in any abstract way. Private international law is to a large degree still national law (or, in the United States, state law), and therefore also in that same degree dependent on national, c.q. state policies. Private international law is no bleak, neutral and coordinating subdiscipline regulating international flows of trade and persons, but a bundle of norms which materialize national or state policies. The concept of a benign legislator pre-eminently concerned with international interests is very theoretical, as Brainerd Currie demonstrated half a century ago.[2]

2   THE BENEFITS OF INTERNATIONAL COOPERATION

(3) One may expect of course that rational market economy States will attempt, through the formulation of adequate private international law rules, to create a safe legal environment in which market participants can trust when engaging in cross-border transactions. Such a conflicts system necessarily rests upon a balance -which is often difficult to find- between the interests of the various parties involved. Therefore, the promotion of international trade,

---

1   L. Brilmayer, *Conflict of Laws. Foundations and Future Directions* (Little, Brown and Company, Boston, 1991), p. 1.

2   B. Currie, *Selected Essays on the Conflict of Laws* (Duke University Press, Durham N.C., 1963).

e.g. through the protection of party autonomy, will not be the sole perspective, but will be combined with the pursuance of other objectives, such as e.g. the protection of consumers and employees. The limitations on party autonomy found in the Rome Convention of 19 June 1980 on the law applicable to contractual obligations provide a good example of this delicate balance between various policy objectives.

(4) Due to the limitations of their jurisdiction however, individual states, even those wishing to adopt an internationalist private international law approach, are necessarily unable to guarantee well-determined legal results to those engaged in international transactions. As international transactions have, by definition, (meaningful) links to more than one legal system, no legal response to the effects of globalisation can be successful if it does not rest upon cooperation between and a shared approach of those systems.

(5) A further question is to what extent public authorities -national or international- still have effective power to intervene in and regulate international trade flows, and to what degree they have not given way to powerful private actors, such as multinationals and, more generally, the markets. Setting up international or regional (e.g. European) systems of shared governance appears to be the only possible way for public authorities to provide some counterweight.

3   EUROPEANIZATION OF PRIVATE INTERNATIONAL LAW

(6) In view of the importance of regional and/or international cooperation, it is no accident that private international law has been considered important in the EC, right from the start in 1957, although it was partly given a peculiar and uncertain status through its incorporation in (current) art. 293 EC Treaty. The reference in art. 293 to 'the simplification of formalities governing recognition and enforcement of judgments of courts or tribunals and of arbitration awards', which is made subject to negotiations between the Member States, demonstrates that private international law was felt to be relevant for the achievement of the Community's goals, but that it was at the same time considered to be of a particular nature. Many years later, the Treaty of Maastricht adopted a similar approach when it referred judicial cooperation in civil matters to the third, intergovernmental pillar of the European Union.

The recognition that private (international) law might have an important impact on the establishment and functioning of the common or internal market has indeed only gradually risen. Yet, in its very first judgment on the interpretation of the Brussels Convention of 27 September 1968 on jurisdiction and the enforcement of judgments in civil and commercial matters, the Court of

Justice characterized the convention as an attempt to facilitate the achievement of the common market[3]. The same is undoubtedly true for the Rome Contracts Convention of 19 June 1980, though it has no formal legal basis in the EC Treaty; in the same vein, the adoption of Community internal market legislation incorporating choice-of-law rules, e.g. on insurance contracts[4], has demonstrated that adequate common private international law measures indeed are felt to contribute or, even more, to be necessary for, the proper functioning of the internal market.[5] At the same time, one observes that the impact of private international law is increasingly examined in the judgments of the Court of Justice.[6]

(7) The recognition of the impact private international law may have on the achievement of the Community's objectives has led to the incorporation, by the Treaty of Amsterdam, of a new provision in the EC Treaty, art. 65, which constitutes a legal basis for Community private international law measures. It is true that the interpretation of this provision, and especially its delimitation with art. 95 c.q. 94, has given rise to much academic controversy, a debate which is to a large degree due to the very inaccurate drafting of art. 65. In my view, which I developed earlier[7], *articles 61c and 65 EC constitute a lex specialis* on which Community measures of private international law with regard to the issues mentioned in art. 65, can and must be based, insofar as they are necessary for the proper functioning of the internal market and which must be

---

3   ECJ, 6 October 1976, case 12/76, *Tessili*, ECR [1976] 1473, §9. See later also ECJ, 10 February 1994, case C-368/92, *Mund & Fester*, ECR [1994] I-467, §11. See also §2 of the Commission communication to the Council and the European Parliament 'towards greater efficiency in obtaining and enforcing judgments in the European Union', [1998] OJ C33/3.

4   See art. 7 of the Second Council Directive 88/357/EEC of 22 June 1988 on the coordination of laws, regulations and administrative provisions relating to direct insurance other than life assurance and laying down provisions to facilitate the effective exercise of freedom to provide services and amending directive 73/239/EEC, [1988] OJ L 172/88 and art. 32 of directive 2002/83/EC of the European Parliament and of the Council of 5 November 2002 concerning life assurance, [2002] OJ L 345/1.

5   Cf. H.U. Jessurun d'Oliveira, 'The EU and a Metamorphosis of Private International Law' in *Reform and Development of Private International law. Essays in Honour of Sir Peter North* (Oxford University Press, 2002), p. 119; P-E. Partsch, *Le droit international privé européen. De Rome à Nice* (Larcier, Brussels, 2003), p. 253 and p. 258; H.J. Sonnenberger, „Das Internationale Privatrecht im dritten Jahrtausend – Rückblick and Ausblick', ZvglRWiss, 2001, p. 116.

6   See e.g., in different fields, ECJ, 27 September 1988, case 81/87, *Daily Mail*, ECR [1988] 5483; ECJ, 24 January 1991, case C-339/89, *Alsthom Atlantique*, ECR [1991] I-107; ECJ [1999] case C-430/97, *Johannes*, ECR [1999] I-3475; ECJ [2000] case C-381/98, Ingmar, ECR [2000] I-9305.

7   See J. Meeusen, 'Institutioneel- en materieelrechtelijke aspecten van het internationaal privaatrecht in de Europese Unie' in: *De invloed van het Europees recht op het Belgisch recht. XXVIIIste Postuniversitaire Cyclus Willy Delva 2001-2002* (Kluwer, Mechelen, 2003), p. 693 et seq.

given preference over art. 95 (and 94) EC.[8] The Community legislator apparently has not doubts in this regard and, soon after the entering into force of the Treaty of Amsterdam, started to use articles 61c and 65 for the adoption of a wide array of measures, ranging from family law issues (Brussels II) over procedural questions (service, taking of evidence, legal aid) to issues related to commercial, economic and civil law (Brussels I, insolvency).[9]

(8) The express recognition, both by the Member States and the Community legislator, of the potential contribution of private international law to the proper functioning of the internal market, is not very surprising. As export and import statistics demonstrate, international trade is, for the EU Member States' market participants, still to a large extent European cross-border trade. Achieving a unified or common approach regarding jurisdiction, recognition and enforcement and also choice of law appears to be no less than a necessity to provide a reliable legal framework for those engaging in international, and especially intra-Community, transactions. Article 65 EC confirms this by linking the adoption of private international law measures expressly to the proper functioning of the internal market.

(9) Further, and in spite of the opt-outs granted to the U.K., Ireland and Denmark, it is clear that the Community initiatives regarding private international law have an impressive reach. With the upcoming enlargement of the European Union with ten new Member States, on 1 May 2004, the scope of application of Community private international law will increase even further. Sec-

---

8   In the same vein: K. Boele-Woelki & R.H. van Ooik, 'The Communitarization of Private International Law' in: *Yearbook of Private International Law – Volume IV – 2002* (Kluwer Law International, The Hague, 2003), p. 17; B. Hess, 'Aktuelle Perspektiven der europäischen Prozessrechtsangleichung', JZ (2001). p. 574; S. Leible & A. Staudinger, 'Article 65 of the EC Treaty in the EC System of Competencies', ELF (2000-2001), p. 232-233; R. Wagner, 'Vom Brüsseler Übereinkommen über die Brüssel I-Verordnung zum Europäischen Vollstreckungstitel', IPRax (2002), p. 85. Of course, private international law provisons can still be incorporated in Community legislation based upon another legal basis, where they are ancillary to the goals pursued by that legislation (e.g. consumer or employee protection), cf. E. Jayme & C. Kohler, 'Europäisches Kollisionsrecht 1997 – Vergemeinschaftung durch 'Saulenwechsel'?', IPRax (1997), p. 386.

9   Council directive 2002/8/EC of 27 January 2003 to improve access to justice in cross-border disputes by establishing minimum common rules relating to legal aid for such disputes, [2003] OJ L 26/41; Council regulation (EC) No 1206/2001 of 28 May 2001 on cooperation between the courts of the Member States in the taking of evidence in civil or commercial matters, [2001] OJ L 174/1; Council regulation (EC) No 44/2001 of 22 December 2000 on jurisdiction and the recognition and enforcement of judgments in civil and commercial matters, [2001] OJ L 12/1; Council regulation (EC) No 1348/2000 of 29 May 2000 on the service in the Member States of judicial and extrajudicial documents in civil or commercial matters, [2000] OJ L 160/37; Council regulation (EC) No 1347/2000 of 29 May 2000 on jurisdiction and the recognition and enforcement of judgments in matriomonial matters and in matters of parental responsibility for children of both spouses, [2000] OJ L160/19; Council regulation (EC) No 1346/2000 of 29 May 2000 on insolvency proceedings, [2000] OJ L 160/1. Together with art. 66, art. 61c EC also constituted the legal basis for the Council decision of 28 May 2001 establishing a European judicial Network in civil and commercial matters, [2001] OJ L 174/25.

ondary Community law on private international law will be binding for 25 (or 24)[10] Member States, which are in this regard subject to judicial control... a result which is likely to make the draftsmen of most international treaties in this field, including the Hague Conventions, rather envious. The Brussels I regulation[11], e.g., will then provide an almost pan-European judicial framework for jurisdiction, recognition and enforcement, and realize at European level what the Hague Conference is hoping to achieve one day at international level.

(10) Not only the Community legislator, but also the Court of Justice, is very much aware of the instrumental function private international law can fulfill for the achievement of the internal market. A major example of this is the Court's judgment in *Ingmar*.[12] In this case, the Court ruled that articles 17 and 18 of the Community's commercial agents directive, which guarantee certain rights to commercial agents after termination of agency contracts, must be applied where the commercial agent carried on his activity in a Member State (i.c. the U.K.), although the principal is established in a non-member country (i.c. the United States) and a clause of the contract stipulates that the contract is governed by the law of that third country. In fact, the Court follows the same approach here as the Community legislator has adopted since the early nineties in a number of consumer law directives in order to guarantee the consumer a minimum protection, irrespective of the chosen law.[13] The Court considered that 'the purpose of the regime established in Articles 17 to 19 of the Directive is thus to protect, for all commercial agents, freedom of establishment and the operation of undistorted competition in the internal market. Those provisions must therefore be observed throughout the Community if those Treaty objectives are to be attained' (§24), which allowed it to subordinate party autonomy to the requirements of the internal market, even in the absence of a directive provision in that sense.

---

10   The U.K. and Ireland have until now systematically adhered to the Community measures on private international and have expressed their intention to continue doing so in the future; Denmark on the other hand has remained absent from all Community initiatives based on article 61c. See with regard to the position of Denmark also SEC (2002), p.483.
11   Council regulation (EC) No 44/2001 of 22 December 2000 on jurisdiction and the recognition and enforcement of judgments in civil and commercial matters, [2001] OJ L 12/1.
12   ECJ [2000] case C-381/98, *Ingmar*, ECR [2000] I-9305.
13   Art. 6,2° of directive 93/13/EEC of the Council of 5 April 1993 on unfair terms in consumer contracts, [1993] OJ L 95/29; Art. 9 of directive 94/47/EC of the European Parliament and the Council of 26 October 1994 on the protection of purchasers in respect of certain aspects of contracts relating to purchase of the right to use immovable properties on a timeshare basis, [1994] OJ L 280/83; Art. 12,2° of directive 97/7/EC of the European Parliament and the Council of 20 May 1997 on the protection of consumers in respect of distance contracts, [1997] OJ L 144/19; Art. 7,2° of directive 1999/44/EC of the European Parliament and the Council of 25 May 1999 on certain aspects of the sale of consumer goods and associated guarantees,[1999] OJ L 171/12; Art. 12,2° of directive 2002/65/EC of the European Parliament and of the Council of 23 September 2002 concerning the distance marketing of consumer financial services and amending Council directive 90/619/EEC and directives 97/7/EC and 98/27/EC, [2002] OJ L 271/16.

A further example is found in the Court's recent judgments relating to freedom of establishment for companies. The Court is not interested in abstract private international law theory on the choice between the incorporation and real-seat theories, but makes clear, most recently in *Überseering*[14] *and Inspire Art*[15], that Member States must adapt their conflicts approach to ensure that companies enjoy the full freedom of establishment guaranteed by the EC Treaty. While it has not condemned the real-seat theory as such, the Court's striking down in *Überseering* of particular aspects of German international company law will certainly again be invoked by those pleading in favour of the incorporation theory. And not without reason: the incorporation theory fits better in a legal climate of trust and mutual recognition than the traditional real-seat theory, aimed at protecting the interests of the State of that seat.

4   MUTUAL RECOGNITION IN THE EUROPEAN UNION AND ITS EFFECTS ON
           PRIVATE INTERNATIONAL LAW

(11) This instrumental approach of private international law in the internal market has in recent years led to the repeated recognition of the specific connection which appears to exist between conflicts law and the well-known Community law principle of mutual recognition. It is remarkable how much emphasis has been laid upon this principle during the last few years. While it is not even mentioned in the pertinent Treaty provisions currently in force nor in the Vienna Action Plan[16], the European Council, at its Tampere summit of 15-16 October 1999, destined the principle of mutual recognition to become 'the cornerstone of judicial co-operation in both civil and criminal matters' (§33). Tampere became a crucial turning point. One year later, and at the request of the European Council, the Council adopted a programme of measures for implementation of the principle of mutual recognition of decisions in civil and commercial matters (further: Mutual Recognition Programme).[17] The draft Treaty establishing a Constitution for Europe, adopted by the European Convention on the future of Europe in June 2003 (further: draft Constitutional Treaty), continues along the same lines when it states that 'The Union shall constitute an area of freedom, security and justice by promoting mutual confidence between the competent authorities of the Member States, in particular on the basis of mutual recognition of judicial and extrajudicial decisions' (art. I-41,1°) and that judicial cooperation in civil matters is 'based on the principle of mutual recognition of judgments and decisions in extrajudicial cases' (art. III-170,1°).

---

14   ECJ, 5 November 2002, case C-208/00, *Überseering*, ECR [2002] I-9919.
15   ECJ, 30 September 2003, case C-176/01, *Inspire Art*, n.y.r.
16   Action Plan of the Council and the Commission on how best to implement the provisions
      of the Treaty of Amsterdam on an area of freedom, security and justice, [1999] OJ C 19/1.
17   [2001] OJ C 12/1.

(12) The Community legislator and the Court of Justice also give increasing weight to mutual recognition. A major, recent example of its impact on choice of law can be found in the e-commerce directive, where the introduction of the country-of-origin principle replaces far-reaching substantive harmonization as well as the detailed elaboration of choice-of-law rules.[18] It also inspired the Commission's recent proposals for a Council regulation creating a European enforcement order for uncontested claims[19] and for a Rome II regulation[20], and also of course the proposal for a new Brussels II regulation.[21] The Court of Justice introduced mutual recognition as a basic concept of EC free movement law in *Cassis de Dijon*[22] and later extended it from the free movement of goods to the other freedoms protected by the EC Treaty.[23] Recent decisions of the Court have demonstrated to what extent the Court relies on it as a basic principle of Community law: in *Überseering*, mentioned before, the Court of Justice restated its approach on the establishment of companies and, fundamentally relying on mutual recognition, dealt a serious blow to the traditional real-seat theory.[24] In *Gözütok and Brügge*, its first preliminary ruling regarding the third pillar, the Court emphasised that the Member States must 'have mutual trust in their criminal justice systems and that each of them [must recognize] the criminal law in force in the other Member States even when the outcome would be different if its own national law were applied'.[25]

(13) As the Court emphasizes in *Gözütok and Brügge*, and as had become evident earlier with *Cassis de Dijon*, the main contribution of the principle of mutual recognition, is to bridge disparities in the laws of the Member States. Taking into account the often difficult process of harmonization, mutual recognition functions as a substitute mechanism which allows persistent disparities in Member States' laws to combine with the requirements of an internal market (the 'level playing field') and of the so-called 'area of freedom, security and justice' (art. 61 EC). Viewed in this light, the draft Constitutional Treaty's emphasis on the 'different legal traditions and systems of the Member States' (art. III-158,1°) may gain a new sense: diverging approaches of the Member States need not necessarily be harmonized as the concept of mutual recognition can help to overcome them without hurting the essence of the area of freedom, se-

---

18   Directive 2000/31/EC of the European Parliament and of the Council of 8 June 2000 on certain legal aspects of information society services, in particular electronic commerce, in the Internal Market ('Directive on electronic commerce'), [2000] OJ L 178, 1. See about its impact on choice of law: M. Fallon & J. Meeusen, 'Le commerce électronique, la directive 2000/31/CE et le droit international privé', RCDIP (2002) p. 435 et seq.
19   COM(2002) 159 final.
20   COM(2003) 427 final.
21   COM(2002) 222 final.
22   ECJ, 20 February 1979, case 120/78, *Rewe-Zentral*, ECR [1979] 649, §15.
23   See e.g. ECJ, 30 November 1995, case C-55/94, *Gebhard*, ECR [1995] I-4165, §37-38.
24   ECJ, 5 November 2002, case C-208/00, *Überseering*, ECR, [2002] I-9919.
25   ECJ, 11 February 2003, joined cases C-187/01 and C-385/01, *Criminal proceedings against Gözütok and Brügge*, ECR [2003], I-1345, §33.

curity and justice. Choice of law is taken to the background and the divergent contents of judgments within the EU are accepted in order to allow their free movement, which is considered an important value as such: form goes above substance.[26] And when choice-of-law unification or approximation is undertaken, it is also placed in the perspective of improving the foreseeability of solutions.[27]

(14) The emphasis on mutual recognition undeniably influences the development of a proper European private international law approach. The Council's Mutual Recognition Programme focused on the recognition and enforcement in one Member State of a decision taken in another Member State, which for the Council implied that harmonized jurisdiction rules should be adopted. The Council observed that this approach in no way prejudged work to be undertaken in other areas of judicial cooperation in civil matters, particularly with regard to conflict of laws, but then twice mentioned the harmonization of choice-of-law rules as a (mere) instrument to facilitate the mutual recognition of judgments. Even more conspicuous is the absence of the harmonization of choice-of-law rules in the Tampere conclusions: the European Council expressly invited the Council and the Commission to prepare new procedural legislation in cross-border cases and further requested an overall study on the approximation of the Member States' substantive law (par. 38-39), but did not mention any activities relating to choice of law.

This procedural emphasis is of course not new and is in fact incorporated in the EC Treaty itself. Art. 293 calls for the simplification of the reciprocal recognition and enforcement of judgments, but is silent on choice of law. The unification of the choice-of-law rules on contracts followed only twelve years after the Brussels Convention, without legal basis in the EC Treaty and put in the perspective of unification of jurisdiction and enforcement rules. With the exception of some aspects of the insolvency regulation, all measures adopted to date on the basis of art. 61c have a procedural subject-matter; the Commission only recently adopted a proposal for a choice-of-law regulation ('Rome II').[28]

(15) Some may consider the attribution of a mere 'facilitating function' to the harmonization of the choice-of-law-rules a 'give-it-up attitude', inspired by the political difficulties involved with such harmonization. It might be easier indeed to agree on jurisdictional issues (especially when access to the courts is

---

26 E. Jayme & C. Kohler, 'Europäisches Kollisionsrecht 2001: Anerkennungsprinzip statt IPR?', IPRax, (2001) p. 501; H.U. Jessurun d'Oliveira, *l.c.*, 130-131; C. Kohler, 'Systemwechsel im europäischen Anerkennungsrecht: Von der EuGVVO zur Abschaffung des Exequaturs' in: *Systemwechsel im europäischen Kollisionsrecht* (C.H. Beck, München, 2002), p.158.

27 Explanatory memorandum of the Commission's Rome II-proposal, §2.1 (COM(2003) 427 final).

28 COM(2003) 427 final.

not exclusive) and on the recognition and enforcement of judgments delivered in other Member States, than on common choice-of-law rules.[29] Still, one shouldn't underestimate the persistence of major differences between the substantive laws of the Member States, which might threaten the success of a procedural approach.[30]

Nevertheless, the course taken in the EU compensates to a certain degree the long underestimation, also in private international law, of 'procedural' issues. Mutual recognition indeed has the advantage that it allows the avoidance of complete harmonization without this leading to internal market barriers. As it appears to be impossible to have complete international, or even European, consensus on choice-of-law rules, or even the proper choice-of-law method, shifting the focus to jurisdiction and recognition may create a proper and more efficient framework for private international dispute solving. The many references by the Commission in its Rome II-proposal to mutual recognition further demonstrate that the emphasis on this concept does not make the harmonization and unification of choice-of-law rules completely superfluous. The Community legislator considers that unification of conflicts rules improves the foreseeability of solutions and reinforces the mutual trust in judicial decisions given in other Member States and that this constitutes a vital element in attaining the longer-term objective of the free movement of judgments without intermediate review.[31]

5   PRIVATE INTERNATIONAL LAW MUST NOT BE DETACHED FROM ITS SUBSTANTIVE LAW ENVIRONMENT

(16) This emphasis on mutual recognition and the evolution it brings in the European approach to private international law give evidence of the circumstances under which private international law can best flourish and contribute to the internationalisation of trade. Although it is often considered to be a rather formal set of rules, designed merely to coordinate the reach of divergent legal systems, private international law must not be detached from its substantive law environment. As was stated above, private international law is a bundle of norms materializing substantive policies. In a national legal system, one might of course expect private international law to be compatible and coordinated with the goals set in substantive law. Private international law thus can add an additional 'layer' to the substantive law approach adopted. Within the EC, private international law can give an important stimulus to

---

29   Cf. Th.M. de Boer, 'Prospects for European Conflicts Law in the Twenty-First Century' in *International Conflict of Laws for the third Millennium. Essays in honor of Friedrich K. Juenger* (Transnational Publishers, New York, 2001), p. 207-210.

30   Cf. C. Kohler, 'Europäisches Kollisionsrecht zwischen Amsterdam und Nizza', ZEuS (2001) p. 590.

31   Explanatory memorandum of the Commission's Rome II-proposal, §1.1 and 2.1 (COM(2003) 427 final).

the achievement of the internal market. As mutual recognition cannot be separated from mutual trust, which in its turn rests upon confidence in the substantive legislation of the other States involved, the swift implementation of
art. 65 and the interpretation of conflicts law by the Court of Justice must not
be looked at in isolation. The Court's case law on freedom of establishment for
companies, e.g., must be understood in the perspective of the harmonization
of company law for which art. 44,2°g EC grants competence to the EC. For example, one might very well accept the idea that a real-seat State would replace
this approach by the incorporation theory, but only with regard to intra-Community relations; for extra-Community activities, the real-seat theory could
then be maintained and fulfill its protective function. In the same vein, it appears to be a sound approach to relax the requirements for the recognition and
enforcement of European judgments and to maintain a stricter approach for
third countries. In an international framework, where a common substantive
approach is most often lacking, such coordination of substantive and conflicts
law is often much more difficult to achieve. The very close relation which un-
avoidably exists between substantive and conflicts policy concerns provides
one explanation for, on the one hand, the success of the Vienna Sales Convention[32] and numerous transport conventions (e.g. Air Carriage, C.M.R.)[33],
which combine conflicts provisions with substantive rules, and, on the other
hand, the many difficulties met when drafting, without support by any substantive unification, a world-wide 'Convention on international jurisdiction
and foreign judgments in civil and commercial matters' (Hague Conference
on Private International Law).

(17) The prospects for a true contribution of private international law to the
challenges of globalisation are therefore not so good. Even though the
Hague Conference now has 62 Member States all over the world and would
therefore seem to be an ideal forum for international unification, world-wide
success of conflicts conventions is rare. Chances would be even less when, as
one can often observe, conflicts unification would continue to be considered
as no more than a substitute, in fact a second-best solution to substantive law
harmonization. Any effort to truly contribute to the challenges of globalisation should combine both a substantive and conflicts approach. Within the
European Union, this conclusion calls for a well-balanced approach where
private international law harmonization is not considered to be a goal in itself.

---

32   UN Convention on Contracts for the International Sale of Goods (Vienna, 11 April 1980).
33   E.g. the Warsaw Convention of 12 October 1929 relating to the Unification of certain Rules
     relating to International Air Carriage and the CMR Convention on road transport (Gene-
     va, 19 May 1956).

6   REGIONAL OR INTERNATIONAL UNIFICATION?

(18) Pertinent for the European Union is further that, while its harmonization efforts in principle deserve support, it must not let itself be blinded by the advantages of swift conflicts unification, irrespective of international efforts. While the extent of the Community's external competences concerning private international law is still uncertain, it is interesting to refer to the recent decisions of the Council to authorise the Member States to sign, ratify or accede to the so-called HNS and Bunkers Conventions, both concluded in the context of the International Maritime Organization.[34] Both conventions contain rules on jurisdiction, recognition and enforcement, over which the EC claims exclusive competence after the adoption of the Brussels I regulation. According to the Council, the Member States should declare that judgments given by Member State courts on matters of concern to the conventions, shall be recognized and enforced in the other Member States according to the rules of Brussels I. The Commission stated that the suggested reservation 'would ensure unity in the Community judicial area and the free 'movement' of court rulings within the Community, without involving repercussions on the effective implementation of the Convention nor fundamental implications on non-EU States Parties to it'.[35/36]

Community initiatives such as those on the HNS and Bunkers Conventions, inspired by the so-called disconnection clauses in other international treaties[37], attempt to balance and combine the advantages of international unification with the aim of creating European unity. But at the same time they show the dilemma which the Community faces when it wishes the Member States to participate in international unifying initiatives, but fears that such initiatives will threaten the internal (regional) uniformity created by Brussels I or other Community legislation. The Council decisions cited make it very probable that the Community would, in such circumstances, prefer internal, regional unity over international unification and harmony. Of course, unification between 25 Member States is in itself a tremendous achievement, to which a characterization as 'regional unification' might be detracting. Still, as

---

34   Council decision 2002/762/EC of 19 September 2002 authorising the Member States, in the interest of the Community, to sign, ratify or accede to the International Convention on Civil Liability for Bunker Oil Pollution Damage, 2001 (the Bunkers Convention), [2002] OJ L 256/7; Council decision 2002/971/EC of 18 November 2002 authorising the Member States, in the interest of the Community, to ratify or accede to the International Convention on Liability and Compensation for Damage in Connection with the Carriage of Hazardous and Noxious Substances by Sea, 1996 (the HNS Convention), [2002] OJ L 337/55.

35   Commission Explanatory Memorandum, COM/2001/674 (HNS Convention) and COM/2001/675 (Bunkers Convention).

36   Compare also art. 3 of Council decision 2003/93/EC of 19 December 2002 authorising the Member States, in the interest of the Community, to sign the 1996 Hague Convention on jurisdiction, applicable law, recognition, enforcement and cooperation in respect of parental responsibility and measures for the protection of children, [2003] OJ L 48/1.

37   Cf. B. de Witte, 'Internationale verdragen gesloten tussen lidstaten van de Europese Unie', Preadvies voor NVIR (T.M.C. Asser Press, The Hague, 2001), p. 121.

the system of the Community's external competences makes clear, it is very difficult to separate internal from international action. Due to its subject-matter, this observation has peculiar force for matters of private international law. Community private international law which would be inward-looking only, is therefore doomed to fail. One can wonder e.g. about the long term negative effects of maintaining a controversial clause such as art. 4,2° of the Brussels I regulation.

(19) One solution, which tries to combine Community self-interest with an international orientation, is to have the Community priorities included in the international agreement itself. This way, the Commission managed to safeguard the application of Brussels I in the 2002 Protocol to the Athens Convention Relating to the Carriage of Passengers and their Luggage by Sea. This recent IMO instrument allows, for the first time, regional economic integration organisations, such as the Community, to become contracting parties and allows parties to the Protocol to apply, as between themselves, other rules on the recognition and enforcement of judgments, thus paving the way for the continued application of Brussels I. As to jurisdiction, the Commission managed to have removed, in the Protocol's final version, a ground of jurisdiction deemed incompatible with the Brussels I regulation.[38]

Of course, such compromise will not be possible that often. In that case, the best way out appears to be moderation and self-restraint. Pursuing international cooperation, even if the negotiations do not allow the achievement of all the objectives put forward, is beneficial for all those wishing to engage in international commerce and necessarily rests upon step-by-step progress.

---

38   See the Commission's proposal for a Council decision concerning the conclusion by the European Community of the Protocol of 2002 to the Athens Convention Relating to the Carriage of Passengers and their Luggage by Sea, 1974, COM(2003) 375 final.

The common law rules of jurisdiction of the English courts over companies' foreign activities

Pippa Rogerson

1   INTRODUCTION: MULTINATIONAL CORPORATIONS AND FOREIGN ACTIVITIES[1]

Multinational corporations, by definition, carry on business in many countries. Often there will be a head office in one country which controls the activities abroad, although the head office may not be in the place of incorporation of the multinational. To effect its foreign activities, company may use many different forms – a branch office or agency, a locally incorporated subsidiary, or a joint venture vehicle with a local business, to name a few. Claimants who wish to seek redress from the multinational for the activities in the foreign country often face a number of difficulties. There may be a problem of obtaining jurisdiction over the multinational, rather than merely over the local agent or subsidiary. Enforcing any local judgment against the multinational where it has assets can be problematic. The locally incorporated subsidiary may be inadequately capitalised to meet the liability and become insolvent. The multinational may then hide behind the veil of incorporation to avoid being liable for the debts of its local subsidiary. Damage caused by the activities of the multinational in the foreign country often affects large numbers of local people. The local courts may not have well developed legal procedures to deal with complex tortious actions. In recent years, there have been moves towards making multinationals incorporated in England subject to the jurisdiction of the English courts for activities which the multinational carries on abroad. This movement is contrary to the established principle of forum conveniens, which would usually suggest that the most appropriate forum in which to pursue such claims would be the foreign court. It is in that country that the damage was suffered, and the activity carried on, so that country's courts are best positioned to decide matters of evidence. Often the foreign country's rules will apply as a matter of choice of law and it is, in principle, better and more efficient for the courts of that country to determine its own law. Indeed, both parties might reasonably have expected that the foreign court would determine their rights and liabilities according to that law. However, where the claim is being made against a multinational which has been controlling the ac-

---

1   See too Muchlinski, 'Corporations in international litigation: problems of jurisdiction and the United Kingdom asbestos cases' (2001) ICLQ 1; P. Nygh , 'The Liability of Multinational Corporations for the Torts of their Subsidiaries' (2002) *European Business Organization Law Review* 51.

tivities of the foreign subsidiary (via control of the board or shareholding) and has been taking profits made by the foreign business out of the subsidiary, there is some argument that the parent company should be subject to the jurisdiction of its local courts. This paper will argue that the English courts' approach is unprincipled and its reasoning flawed. This has resulted in cases in which the English courts have encouraged inappropriate forum shopping. There is an alternative explanation to justify the use of the English courts' jurisdiction, which is also more consistent with the Brussels 1 Regulation.

Jurisdiction over defendant companies which are domiciled in a Member State of the EU is determined by the Brussels 1 Regulation.[2] The primary rule is that a defendant should be sued in the courts in which it is domiciled. For a company, its domicile is its statutory seat or the place of its central management and control.[3] Thus companies incorporated in England have their statutory seat in England and should be sued there. There is an interesting question, presently before the ECJ, whether the English court retains the power to stay proceedings commenced against defendants domiciled in England in favour of the courts of non-Member States of the EU.[4] If this is answered in the negative, multinational holding companies incorporated in England will be sued there for liability arising out of their activities abroad. However, even if the court were to take jurisdiction, the applicable law in these cases will then be determinative of the substance of the case.

The ECJ may, on the other hand, decide that Member States' courts can retain some power to stay proceedings brought against defendants domiciled in that Member State, in which case the common law rules on jurisdiction will continue to operate. Jurisdiction at common law against both English and foreign incorporated companies is decided by service within the jurisdiction under the traditional rules (or service out of the jurisdiction with permission of the court). The rules on service within the jurisdiction over companies which have a place of business here or which are incorporated here are extremely wide. Mere service is enough to commence proceedings; there is no requirement at this stage for the proceedings to have any substantial connection with England. Nevertheless, the forum conveniens doctrine controls access to the English courts. It was developed as a counterweight to prevent inappropriate forum shopping in England by claimants who took advantage of the rules which give the English court jurisdiction by virtue of the mere presence of the defendant within the jurisdiction at the time the claim form is served.[5] The English proceedings can be stayed in favour of another available

---

2   Regulation EU 2001/44.
3   Article 60.
4   *Owusu* v. *Jackson* (2002) EWCA Civ 877, (2002) ILPr 45.
5   The highpoint of this came with *Maharanee of Baroda* v. *Wildenstein* (1972) 2 QB 282, where the Court of Appeal refused to stay proceedings in England concerning a painting, allegedly by Boucher, which had been sold in France by a French/US dealer to a French woman. The case had nothing to do with England at all apart from the defendant having been served at the Ascot races.

court in which the English court considers that justice can be done. This depends on identification of the 'natural forum' for the dispute to be decided. If the natural forum is abroad generally English proceedings will be stayed.[6] The 'natural forum' is determined via a number of factors: the location of the evidence and the witnesses, the likely applicable law, the domicile of the parties, the nature of their relationship, and so on. In these cases concerned with mass torts done abroad, the natural forum – by virtue of the claimant's residence, the facts giving rise to the damage and the damage itself all suggest that the natural forum is abroad.

The doctrine also takes into account efficiency arguments: where can justice most efficiently be done? These can be particularly powerful where there are a number of defendants. For example, it is relatively easy to obtain a stay in favour of foreign court where all defendants can be sued[7] or to continue in England where all defendants can be sued. [8] However, even if the foreign forum is the natural and most appropriate forum identified by the factors outlined in the previous paragraph, the claimant may resist a stay and continue in the English courts if the claimant is deprived of a 'legitimate advantage' available in the English courts. These advantages are only legitimate if claimant by being deprived of them cannot achieve substantial justice in the natural forum.[9] It can be difficult to predict what 'substantial justice' will amount to. For example, is it 'substantially just' to force a claimant to a court in which his action will not be practically possible due to a lack of local attorneys prepared to take the case on a contingency or conditional fee basis? One might argue that whether a country permits or refuses these arrangements for enabling litigation is a local matter, not for the English court to pass judgment on as 'unjust'.[10]

Many of the cases turn on these advantages: both for companies incorporated in England[11] and for foreign companies.[12] The decided cases arose out of claims in tort, where the activity giving rise to the alleged tortious damage, many of the relevant events and the damage suffered, all occurred outside England. The appropriate forum for deciding the matters were in all these cases accepted by the court to be abroad. Nevertheless, the advantages to the claimant of pursuing the defendant in England outweighed the appropriate forum. The cases were therefore allowed to proceed on the merits in England. However, this was only after several appeals to determine the 'legitimacy' or weight to be attached to various advantages the claimants were seeking here.

---

6   *Spiliada Maritime Corpn v. Cansulex Ltd, The Spiliada* (1987) AC 460 at 476.
7   *Owusu v. Jackson* supra.
8   *CitiMarch v. Neptune* (1997) 1 LLR 72.
9   *The Spiliada* supra.
10   It was not so long ago that the English court avoided all such arrangements as champertous.
11   *Lubbe v. Cape Plc* (2000) 1 WLR 1545, *Connelly v. RTZ Corp Plc (No 2)* (1998) AC 854.
12   *Domansa v. Derin Shipping* (2001) 1 LLR 362.

2   ADVANTAGES OF THE ENGLISH COURTS?

The English court has many advantages to claimants, both procedural and substantive. For example, there are very wide rules of basic jurisdiction over defendants; either by physical presence, if an individual, or by having established a place of business in England, if a company. There are broad rules allowing joinder of defendants to one set of proceedings, even when many of the defendants are foreign.[13] Often defendants hold liquid assets in London against which judgments can be enforced. Once a judgment has been obtained the enforcement rules enable a judgment creditor to obtain disclosure of the defendants' assets and enforcement directly against third parties (such as banks).[14] The English court and the lawyers who practice in it have a well-developed expertise in complex, multiparty cases both with respect to experts, lawyers and courts. In addition, conditional fee arrangements and even contingency fee arrangements enable poorer claimants to bring actions against well-financed defendants, particularly when coupled with a class action. The party driven rules of discovery of evidence, though not as wide as some other common law jurisdictions such as the United States, are wider than many civilian jurisdictions. The adversarial system allows parties to make their own case to their own advantage, fairly free from judicial interference. The standard and independence of the judiciary is generally observed as a great benefit to both parties. Also, the substantive rules of domestic law (if applied) can be attractive to foreign claimants. For example, the high standard of duty of care to employees and others, the generous rules on causation,[15] and the rules which make it possible that one tortfeasor among many will be made wholly liable. Of course, ultimately the lure of higher levels of damages (as the quantum of damage is a matter for the *lex fori* even if the substantive law is foreign) must be taken into account as an advantage.

Is it unacceptable forum shopping to allow claimants from other countries where activities took place to continue actions in the English courts to seek these advantages? Our forum conveniens doctrine is founded on the overriding principle of doing justice between claimant and defendant, but this encompasses a number of competing policy objectives: preventing defendants from being sued in an inappropriate court while allowing claimants access to appropriate courts; ensuring all matters between all parties are dealt with efficiently (more cheaply, more quickly, keeping uncertainty of outcome to a minimum); reducing *lis pendens*; enforcing parties' agreements (via jurisdiction or arbitration clauses); and respect for the different methods of determination of other courts.

---

13   See *Canada Trust* v. *Stolzenberg (No 2)* (2002) 1 AC 1.
14   Although very recently this has been limited to bank accounts held at branches of banks in England many defendants use branches of banks in London to make their international payments (*Société Eram Shipping Co Ltd* v. *Compagnie Internationale de Navigation* (2003) 3 WLR 21).
15   See the recent House of Lords case on causation in mesothelioma, *Fairchild* v. *Glenhaven Funeral Services* (2003) 1 AC 32.

3　　RESPONSE OF ENGLISH COURTS

The House of Lords in *Connelly* v. *RTZ Corp Plc* and *Lubbe* v. *Cape Plc*[16] has indicated that the English court views the efficiency of justice objective extremely highly, more important even than the case continuing in the appropriate forum. The fact that the claimants were unlikely to be able to bring this type of case in the foreign court because certain procedural advantages[17] were unavailable abroad meant no stay of the English proceedings. This was despite the finding at the Court of Appeal that the foreign forum was the more appropriate forum for the decision of these cases. That finding was not challenged on the appeal to the House of Lords, so the cases turned entirely on justifying the continued proceedings in England as the claimants would be deprived of substantial justice by being forced to litigate abroad. First in time was *Connelly* v. *RTZ Corp Plc* in which the claimant, who had emigrated from Scotland to South Africa, had been employed by a subsidiary of RTZ to work in Namibia on a uranium mine. He returned to England where he was diagnosed, some years later, with cancer of the throat. The likely cause of his cancer was the uranium inhaled while mining activities were carried on, but it could have been due to some other cause such as 'passive smoking'. The claimant did not want to sue RTZ in Namibia. This was partly because RTZ was not subject to the jurisdiction of the Namibian courts (though it later agreed to submit to those courts) and therefore any Namibian judgment would have been unenforceable in England. Also, practically, he was too ill to go to Namibia to instruct local lawyers, he was unable to fund the litigation and legal aid was available in England.[18] Probably he would also have obtained a lower judgment in Namibia. At this stage of proceedings, the English court was not considering the merits of the action against RTZ[19] but merely the question of whether the case could go ahead to be heard on the merits. The House of Lords decided that it could. The claimant would have been deprived of substantial justice by being forced to continue proceedings in Namibia rather than England: as a matter of practical reality, he would have been unable to recover anything there. The Namibian lawyers would not have acted as the claimant was unable to pay them, and the medical expertise in Namibia was less advanced than in England.

　　In *Lubbe* v. *Cape Plc*, *Connelly* was taken further. Here the claimants were around three thousand mostly South African citizens and residents who came to the English courts to pursue the multinational mining company Cape Plc in respect of activities carried out in South Africa by its South African sub-

---

16　　There are other cases, but these have the highest authority.

17　　Notably contingency fees, medical expertise and class actions.

18　　Legal aid (public provision of legal fees for personal injury) has now been largely abolished but this issue was a large part of the court's decision.

19　　Under the procedural rules the claimant must have an 'arguable' case to prevent it being struck out as an abuse of process, but no more than that.

sidiaries which had allegedly caused the claimants' damage. The claimants were gathered into a class action by some London based solicitors who were prepared to act in return for a conditional fee. Importantly, the claimants were arguing that the multinational head office was responsible directly for failures in imposing suitable health and safety procedures in accordance with English standards on their South African subsidiary. This, as a matter of the merits, was not in issue at the jurisdictional stage, but raised some interesting and important questions on choice of law.[20] The fact that the claimants were almost all foreign raised the spectre of forum shopping. Why should these foreign claimants have access to the English courts to seek all these advantages when their injuries occurred entirely in the place of their residence? Were the South African courts not better placed to decide such issues? The defendant company had been prepared to submit to South African jurisdiction for this case. The House of Lords here too refused to grant a stay of the English proceedings. This large class action could be better dealt with in England. It was more efficient, cost-effective and speedier for the matters between all the claimants and the defendant to be determined in a court experienced in such class actions with lawyers who were prepared to act on a contingency basis and good medical and other experts. To force these claimants to pursue their claims in South Africa would amount to a denial of justice.

In both cases, their Lordships followed a very traditional forum conveniens plus exception analysis. The defendants were subject to suit in England by virtue of the claim form having been served within the jurisdiction. This then placed the onus on the defendants to show that it was clearly more appropriate for the case to be heard in another available forum, the natural forum, in which case a stay of the English proceedings would have been granted. Even once that test was satisfied, the claimants could still continue in England if 'substantial justice' would not be done abroad.

It might be argued that both these cases involved particular facts and could be limited thereto. In *Connelly* v. *RTZ Corp Plc* the claimant was Scottish originally and returned to live in England where the cancer was discovered and treated. He no longer had any connection with Namibia and was practically unable to return there to instruct lawyers to take on his case. In *Lubbe* v. *Cape Plc* the claimants were represented by some London based solicitors. Their ultimate substantive claim was dependent on the application of English law. Under South African law, it was likely that damages would be so limited as to be worthless. At that time the South African legal system had only recently accepted the possibility of a class action and neither lawyers nor experts were experienced in these matters. This argument is, in reality, a criticism of the quality of justice which the claimant can obtain abroad. It offends comity between courts and has been expressly disapproved of in many cases. As Lord Goff opined, the plaintiff must take the appropriate foreign court as he finds

---

20   The case has since settled with the defendant company agreeing to make payments to the claimants.

it.[21] Nevertheless, the overwhelming interest of justice to all the parties, through the efficiency of being able to deal with all these cases in one court, justified the English court retaining jurisdiction.

The analysis followed by the English courts would therefore allow proceedings to continue in England merely because of these advantages being available here, without any careful justification for the exercise of jurisdiction. Lord Hoffmann's dissent in *Connelly* v. *RTZ Corp Plc* raised some important issues. He argued strongly that the proceedings should be stayed in England in favour of proceedings in Namibia, the appropriate forum. The claimant had been employed via the South African office of the company to work for a different subsidiary in Namibia, all the evidence of working conditions was to be found there and, especially, neither of the parties could have contemplated litigation between them on the claimant's employment in any country other than Namibia. Merely because the claimant had returned to the United Kingdom to live and the cancer allegedly caused by the defendant's activity discovered in England, did not make England an appropriate forum as these were post event factors. Lord Hoffmann saw that it was unacceptable forum shopping by the claimant to seek the advantages of the English courts which could not have been foreseen as an available forum at the time of the employment. Much of this is persuasive. However, the connections of these defendants to England which could objectively justify the English courts' jurisdiction were completely obscured in the analysis.

Paradoxically, the reasoning also means that foreign-incorporated defendants with little or no connection with England can therefore be subject to proceedings in the English courts, where the claimants seek procedural and substantive advantages here. The forum conveniens doctrine is insufficient to protect such defendants from claimants seeking the advantages of the English courts. For example, in *Domansa* v. *Derin Shipping & Trading*[22] three Polish seamen were killed in an explosion aboard a Liberian registered vessel in Cuban waters. It was owned by a one-ship company, incorporated in Liberia but managed by a company operating in Cyprus. The employment contracts between the owners of the vessel and the seamen were subject to an exclusive Cyprus jurisdiction agreement.[23] The company had given a c/o address in England to Lloyds Shipping Register. It was that address at which it was served with notice of the Polish seamen's claims. These claims arose in England under the Fatal Accidents Act, which is an English law remedy giving

---

21 '(The) general principle . . . is that, if a clearly more appropriate forum overseas has been identified, generally speaking the plaintiff will have to take that forum as he finds it, even if it is in certain respects less advantageous to him than the English forum. He may, for example, have to accept lower damages, or do without the more generous English system of discovery', *Connelly* v. *RTZ Corp Plc* (1998) AC 854 at 872.

22 (2001) 1 LLR 362.

23 This would normally have been observed and the English court stayed the proceedings. However, at common law the English court has a discretion not to stay, which it exercised in this case.

damages for loss of a breadwinner to the Polish dependants, the claimants. The English court continued with these proceedings finding that the shipowners, the Liberian company, had established a place of business here. This place of business was no more than a mailbox address notified to Lloyds. The court held that the jurisdiction agreement did not operate as it only covered small contractual claims and not claims of the nature in dispute. In particular, and unsurprisingly, the court held that the claims under the Fatal Accidents Act could only be determined in England making England the most appropriate forum for these claims. All this despite the clear lack of connections with England other than a possible address for a one-ship company. Perhaps this is an unusual case, in that there were rather few clear connections to any single jurisdiction. However, either Poland or Cyprus appeared objectively to be better connected with the events and the parties than England.

A distinction must be drawn in these cases of jurisdiction over a foreign incorporated company, however, between establishing a place of business (which is necessary in order to effect service) and merely 'doing business' (which is insufficient). It is possible to do business in England but not be liable to be served within the jurisdiction unless there is also a place at which the foreign company's business is established. Note that in those cases, if there is a sufficient connection with England to make England the appropriate forum, the court may grant permission for the claim form to be served on the defendant out of the jurisdiction and for proceedings to go ahead in England. However, the burden is here placed on the claimant to show that England is clearly the most appropriate forum in order to persuade the English court to exercise jurisdiction it does not otherwise have. Compare with the stays cases in which the English court exercises a discretion not to use jurisdiction it considers it has as of right so it is the defendant that has to show another clearly more appropriate forum. The place of business established in England by the foreign company could be a branch office, an agency (either conducted via a legal or natural person), a subsidiary company or via a joint venture. But, in each case, the English court will consider the detailed arrangements to determine whether or not the particular foreign company has established a place of business where itself is carrying on business or whether the agent or subsidiary is carrying on his or its own business, albeit connected to the foreign company. This line can be difficult to draw, especially with subsidiary companies, many of which are set up in order *not* to establish the parent's place of business in England. So, in comparison to *Domansa* v. *Derin Shipping & Trading*, one might look to *Rakusens Ltd* v. *Baser Ambulaj Plastik* [24] in which the activities of an agent in England did not amount to a doing of business here by the foreign company. The agent had been able to produce cards identifying him as the 'agent' of the defendant foreign company but there was no evidence that he was able to contract on behalf of the company to bind it. This lack of authority to contract was critical in finding that the foreign company had established no

---

24   (2001) EWCA Civ 1820, (2001) 1 BCLC 204.

place of business in England. However, it is only one element in a number that the English court will take into account in determining whether the parent has established a place of business in England.

Other factors, such as the parent renting office space for the subsidiary, the parent reimbursing expenses of the agent, the control exercised by the parent of the agent and putting up the parent's nameplate are also important. The list comes from a case on the recognition of foreign judgments, *Adams* v. *Cape Industries*.[25] This case is the source of many of the consequent difficulties including the central theme of this article. Cape Industries escaped enforcement being levied against its English assets in respect of a judgment obtained against it and its local subsidiary in the United States. The English court upheld the traditional, and rigid, English view of separation of personality of a parent company from its subsidiary. The court refused to see a group of companies as one entity and declined to hold that the subsidiary was an agent of the parent. It did not do the parent's business but its own. Likewise, in the recent case of *Harrods Ltd* v. *Dow Jones & Co Inc*[26] the 'agent' was a subsidiary company which had been established to sell advertising space in the parent company's journals, gathering financial news for the parent and handling and supervising accounts. Although the parent reimbursed some of the expenses of the office, it did not control the business of the subsidiary, nor could the subsidiary contract on behalf of the parent. Dow Jones Inc was not therefore liable to suit in England. Careful parent multinationals can make use of these criteria to ensure that the local agent or subsidiary does not establish a place of business for the parent so that the parent is not liable to suit in the local jurisdiction nor is the parent likely to be the subject of an enforceable foreign judgment from that jurisdiction.

The analysis used in *Lubbe* v. *Cape Plc* and *Connelly* v. *RTZ Corp Plc* can be criticised too, for uncertainty and concomitant expense merely to decide issues of jurisdiction.[27] Both these cases involved lengthy appeals to the Court of Appeal and House of Lords, the costs involved in defending these actions merely as to jurisdiction were extensive. In order to avoid the possible expense, time and trouble in challenging the jurisdiction, many defendants might be forced to settle weak cases. Lord Hoffmann identified this risk in *Connelly* v. *RTZ Corp Plc* and later events in that case proved him entirely correct.[28] On the other hand, wealthy defendants should not be permitted to waste a claimant's time and expense on preliminary jurisdictional skirmishes in order to avoid the real issues on the merits. It might be regretted that *Lubbe* v. *Cape Plc* has settled so that the difficult questions of choice of law rules to determine these substantive claims have not been answered. It must be a serious criticism of the application of the forum conveniens doctrine if it allows tacti-

---

25   (1990) Ch 433.

26   (2003) EWHC 1162.

27   See Reed (2001) NLJ 177.

28   The claimant lost at first instance on the substantive case (1999) CLC, 533.

cal jurisdictional litigation to take up so much time and expense, leaving little for the substance of the issues.

4   ALTERNATIVE ANALYSIS FOR SUCH CASES

A far better analysis would be to give sufficient weight to the fact that these particular multinational companies are incorporated in England, have their head offices here, control the activities of their subsidiaries from England and are listed on the London stock exchange. These factors point to England being an appropriate and justifiable forum for this type of case. It was no postbox incorporation. Companies which have taken advantage of a stable political environment, well developed commercial law and access to the capital markets in London are properly sued here irrespective of the claimants' connections or lack thereof. They cannot complain that the claimants' use of the English courts was unexpected as the English courts are the defendants' 'home' courts. In contrast, where the jurisdiction of the English courts is established merely by a foreign company having a place of business here then little weight should be given to this factor unless there are other significant factors linking the cause of action to that business here, making England a natural forum. Such a significant factor might be that English law will apply as a matter of substantive law, but that is only likely where the accident has occurred here[29] or there are other overwhelming substantial connections to England. There should not be all that much argument that the claimants' choice of the English courts in which to sue English incorporated defendants is unacceptable forum shopping, given the structure which these multinationals adopted which prevented them being sued in the foreign country except at the defendant's option. In *Lubbe* v. *Cape Plc*, Cape Plc in the event were prepared to undertake to submit to the South African courts' jurisdiction as a *quid pro quo* for the stay of the English action. However, this undertaking of submission was not achieved until after the case had commenced here. Although the Court of Appeal regarded the undertaking as acceptable as a price to pay for a stay of English proceedings, this could be an unfair advantage to the defendant. The parent multinational can wait until proceedings are commenced to weigh up whether it is worth being sued abroad or in England. It is also an unnecessary burden on the claimant who will not know until after proceedings are commenced whether they will be stayed.

Of course, in a case in which the Brussels 1 Regulation operates, Article 2 would make England the primary place in which such defendants could be sued. The court heard argument in *Lubbe* v. *Cape Plc* that Article 2 required the English court to take jurisdiction as the defendant was domiciled in England and left no discretion to stay the proceedings. The House of Lords, *obiter*, agreed that this question (if it arose) would have to be referred to the ECJ for

---

29   Private International Law (Miscellaneous Provisions) Act 1995, s11.

determination but decided that it did not arise as the court refused to grant a stay of the English proceedings. The interesting question of the relationship between the allocation of jurisdiction under the Brussels 1 Regulation and non Member State courts has now been referred to the ECJ in *Owusu* v. *Jackson*.[30]

5   SUBSTANTIVE MATTERS – CHOICE OF LAW

The criticism of inappropriate forum shopping in England against defendants incorporated here alluded to by Lord Hoffmann in *Connelly* v. *RTZ Corp* could be largely overcome by appropriate choice of law rules. Merely suing defendants in England does not, of itself, lead to English law. If the substantive law to be applied were to be foreign then the benefits to the claimant of suing in England would be limited to the procedural advantages. These are not insubstantial, as they include the rules of assessment of damage and on discovery of evidence. Nevertheless, a defendant company cannot really complain about foreign claimants making recourse to the company's local courts together with the advantages and disadvantages of those courts. The defendants have chosen to take advantage of the benefits of incorporating in England, such as access to liquid capital, an independent judiciary, a stable political regime and so on. Therefore the possible disadvantages should also be taken. Indeed, the major issue for defendants should be that of substantive liability for the type of activity undertaken by the defendants.

The usual English choice of law rule in tort would refer liability to the substantive law of the place where the injury occurred.[31] On the other hand, one could well argue that the direct claim being made against the parent company for failure to impose or maintain proper standards in its subsidiaries resulted in the claimants' damage. This argument could lead to an application of English law by virtue of it being 'substantially more appropriate' that English law applies.[32] This is a very open question and it is by no means certain that the general rule would be disapplied. Regrettably, the outcome of the substantive matters in these cases is presently particularly difficult to decide or predict. In *Connelly* v. *RTZ Corp Plc* the claimant lost on a limitation point. In *Lubbe* v. *Cape Plc*, the parties settled without the merits being decided. In both, the defendants complained that the claimants' use of the expensive English court was forcing them to settle weak cases. However, the high cost of defending proceedings in England arises at present largely out of the uncertainty of the jurisdictional issues. The court rarely decides the substantive issues. If the jurisdictional rules were less opaque the merits of such claims could be focused upon more clearly. The relative strength or weakness of the claims could then be determined on the merits. In particular, the difficult matter of under which

---

30   (2002) EWCA Civ 877, (2002) ILPr 45.
31   Private International Law (Miscellaneous Provisions) Act 1995, s11.
32   Private International Law (Miscellaneous Provisions) Act 1995, s12.

system of law a parent company is to be liable (or not) for the activities of its subsidiary company abroad could be answered.

There are two ways of characterising this question. First, whether a parent company is liable for its subsidiary's activities could be a matter of company law. Just as a company incorporated and operating in England should be subject to the English courts' jurisdiction so as a company law matter it is only subject to English company law. Unfortunately for these claimants, English law is extremely generous to parent companies in allowing the separate legal personality doctrine to prevent liability for a subsidiary's activities.[33] The fons et origo is *Salomon* v. *Salomon & Co Ltd*[34], but *Adams* v. *Cape Industries* is a more appropriate and recent authority in this context. This separation applies equally to tortious claims as contractual ones[35] and has few exceptions. The major one is 'fraud' but this is not as wide as it might appear. First, it is not fraud on the part of the parent to set up a subsidiary suspecting that it might be unable to meet its liabilities in the future. It is not fraud to use debt rather than equity finance, i.e. to leave the creditors (both contractual and tortious) with the liability rather than the shareholder parent company. It is not fraud to set up a foreign local subsidiary in such a way as to protect the parent's assets from enforcement of the foreign judgment. It is therefore not fraud to make use of the corporate form, and indeed, the English court has regarded the possibility of 'cutting off the runt of the litter' to save the rest of the group as a benefit of modern corporate personality. Characterising the issue as one of company law is very advantageous to the parent company in such a system. One might speculate why the liability of the parent shareholder for the subsidiary's debts should be necessarily referred to the parent company's law. There seems no especially convincing argument why that question could not alternatively be referred to the foreign subsidiary company's law as a question of the liability of *its* shareholders for its debts.

A company law characterisation can be contrasted with the characterisation in tort between the parent company as tortfeasor owing a direct duty to the employees of the subsidiary. That question would be referred to the law of the place where the events giving rise to the injury occurred under the general rule in the Private International Law (Miscellaneous Provisions) Act 1995. In such cases, the claimants seek to rely on the exception to the general rule in s 12 to argue for English law as the law under which the parent company operates.

It is up to the claimant to characterise the claim. The availability of different characterisation of the issue and the flexibility of the choice of law rule make the outcome on the substantive matters very uncertain. Nevertheless, the application of a domestic law to determine liability will depend on the outcome of a choice of law process which in turn requires significant connections with the law to be applied.

---

33   See the discussion above.
34   (1897) AC 22.
35   The distinction was rejected in *Adams* v. *Cape Industries* supra. The case is authority for most of the following statements.

6   ENFORCEMENT AND RECOGNITION OF JUDGMENTS

Much of the reason why claimants from abroad have to seek direct access to the English courts lies in the fact that their home courts' judgments would not be recognised in England. The traditional recognition and enforcement of judgments rules require the judgment debtor (parent company) to be subject to the foreign court's jurisdiction in a particular way. A judgment debtor which is a company must have been doing business from a fixed and reasonably permanent place in the foreign state either itself or through an agent, representative or subsidiary. There is no further requirement for any connection between the subject-matter of the dispute and the foreign state.[36] Mere presence of the defendant at the time of commencement of proceedings is sufficient. Therefore, by establishing a place of business abroad *any* judgment of the foreign court against an English incorporated defendant would be enforceable in England. However, the point has not been taken in the modern cases, in which some connection has always been apparent. The corollary is that despite close connections with the subject-matter, if the defendant is not present in the foreign country the judgment cannot be enforced. As we have seen, it is very easy for a multinational company to structure its business to ensure that the agent, representative or subsidiary is doing their own business and not that of the company. The company is then not bound by the foreign judgment. Allowing powerful multinational companies to pick and choose the jurisdictions in which they wish to risk their assets could be unfair on claimants. The recent jurisdictional cases have redressed the balance somewhat, even if the reasoning is flawed.

---

36   *Sirdar Gurdyal Singh v. Rajah of Faridkote* (1894) AC 670.

Territorial jurisdiction after territoriality*

Ralf Michaels

Territory has long shaped our thinking about adjudicative jurisdiction of state and national courts.[1] Choice of law may have overcome territoriality – at least in the United States,[2] and at least in theory[3] – but the law of jurisdiction has not, it seems, yet taken a similar step. Still we speak of territorial jurisdiction.[4] Indeed, jurisdiction is still entangled in the dichotomy of (legitimate) territorial jurisdiction and (problematic) extraterritorial jurisdiction.[5] The latter is

---

■   This paper, finished early in 2003, is part of a bigger project devoted to the impact of globalization on the conflict of laws. See also Ralf Michaels, 'Globalizing Savigny? The State in Savigny's Private International Law, and the Challenge of Europeanization and Globalization', in: *European and International Regulation after the Nation State: Different Scopes and Multiple Levels* (M. Stolleis & A. Héritier, eds., forthcoming). I thank participants at the Leiden workshop, as well as Arthur T. von Mehren, for valuable suggestions, and Daniel Zimmer, LL.M. candidate (LL.M. '03, Duke) for excellent research assistance. Insufficiencies are of course my own responsibility, and I am aware of several of them.

1   On the history cf. J. Weinstein, 'The Early American Origins of Territoriality in Judicial Jurisdiction', 37 St. Louis U. L.J. 1 (1992); R. T. Ford, 'Law's Territory (A History of Jurisdiction)', 97 Mich. L. Rev. 843 (1999). This paper is not concerned with another important basis of jurisdiction, namely nationality. See Art. 14, 15 French Code Civil (Jurisdiction of French courts for certain actions brought by, and against, French nationals); secs. 606a (1) (i) No. 1; 640a (2) (i) No. 1; 661 (3) German Code of Civil Procedure (jurisdiction based on nationality in family law); E. Pataut, *Principe de souveraineté et conflits de jurisdictions* (LGDJ, 1999), p. 69-132.

2   In Europe, the goal of choice of law norms is still to determine the 'spatially best law' ('das räumlich beste ... Recht'): G. Kegel & K. Schurig, *Internationales Privatrecht* (8th ed. 2000), p. 114. The concept reflects Savigny's search for the seat („Sitz') of a legal relation; see F.C. von Savigny, *System des heutigen römischen Rechts VIII* (1849), p. 108; for criticism already M. Gutzwiller, *Der Einfluss Savignys auf die Entwicklung des Internationalprivatrechts* (1923), p. 45-46.

3   There is talk of a return of 'principled territorialism'. See, e.g., *Cipolla v. Shaposka*, 267 A.2d 854, 439 Pa. 563 (Pa. 1970). Territorial thought still underlies much post-territorial choice of law theory, mainly because the concept of 'governmental interests' points to a state's interest, and as the state is defined by territorial boundaries, so are, at least to a point, its interests.

4   'Territorial jurisdiction' is still sometimes used as a category distinct from 'subject-matter jurisdiction', see, e.g., W. M. Richman & W. L. Reynolds, *Understanding Conflict of Laws*, (Matthew Bender, 3rd ed. 2002), p. 14.

5   See only, K. Meessen ed., *Extraterritorial Jurisdiction in Theory and Practice* (1996); A. V. Lowe, *Extraterritorial jurisdiction: an annotated collection of legal materials* (1983); E. Y. Wu, 'Evolutionary trends in the United States application of extraterritorial jurisdiction', 10 Transnat'l Law (1997) 1-37.

thought to violate norms of international and/or constitutional law,[6] or at least to require special legitimation. Consequently, jurisdiction is only legitimate if it is 'intraterritorial' (a term not usually used), i.e. when a court confines itself to regulating things, persons, and conduct within its territory. This presupposes that a conception of jurisdiction based on a distinction between intra- and extraterritoriality is both intelligible (i.e. any case can be placed in either of the two groups), and legitimate.

The connection between jurisdiction and territoriality is no coincidence. Territoriality has always been one defining characteristic of the state;[7] its function was to provide safety and prosperity on the one hand,[8] to affect and control people on the other.[9] Adjudicative jurisdiction is an emanation of state sovereignty, so it should come as no surprise to find that it follows the same criteria. Now if, as it is claimed, globalization leads to an 'unbundling of territoriality'[10] and challenges both the legitimacy and the intelligibility of traditional concepts of territoriality,[11] then such a conception of jurisdiction must run into problems. If such problems challenge the very fundaments on which our contemporary approach is grounded, then they cannot be answered adequately by this approach itself. They then require a re-conceptualization of jurisdiction.[12] This is, indeed, what I want to argue.

---

6   See generally, S.S. Lotus, 1927 P.C.I.J. (ser. A) No. 10 (Sept. 7), Restatement (Third) of For-
       eign Relations Law §§ 402-403 (1987); P. R. Trimble, 'The Supreme Court and Internation-
       al Law: The Demise of Restatement Section 403', 89 Am. J. Int'l L. 53 (1995); for restrictions
       by international law on extraterritoriality in civil actions against foreigners see, C. Focarel-
       li, 'The Right of Aliens Not to Be Subject to So-Called 'Excessive' Civil Jurisdiction', in: B.
       Conforti & F. Francioni, eds., *Enforcing International Human Rights in Domestic Courts*
       (1997), p. 441-447. In recent decisions regarding extraterritoriality the U.S. Supreme Court
       has suggested that international law might impose no limits in this area. See, e.g., *Hartford
       Fire Ins. Co.* v. *California*, 509 US 764, 113 S. Ct. 2891; 125 L. Ed. 2d 612 (1993), *United States*
       v. *Alvarez Machain*, 504 US 655, 112 S.Ct. 2188, 119 L.Ed.2d 441 (1992).
7   See P. J. Taylor, 'The State as Container: Territoriality in the Modern World System', 18
       Progress in Human Geography (1994) 151-162.
8   J. Gottmann, *The Significance of Territory* (1973).
9   M. Mann, 'The Autonomous Power of the State: Its Origins, Mechanisms and Results', 25
       Archives européennes de sociologie (1984), 185-213; R. D. Sack, *Human Territoriality: Its Theory
       and History* (1986).
10   John G. Ruggie, 'Territoriality and Beyond: Problematizing Modernity in International Re-
       lations', 47 *Int'l Organization* (1993), 139-174. Others speak of a 'territorial trap', see J.
       Agnew, 'The Territorial Trap: The Geographical Assumptions of International Relations
       Theory', 1 Rev. of Int'l Pol. Economy (1994) 53-80.
11   See, from the abundant literature, e.g., A. Hudson, 'Beyond the Borders: Globalisation,
       Sovereignty and Extraterritoriality', 3 *Geopolitics* (1998) 89-105; N. Brenner, 'Beyond State-
       Centrism? Space, Territoriality, and Geographical Scale in Globalization Studies', 28 *Theo-
       ry and Society* (1999) 39-78; S. Sassen, 'Territory and Territoriality in the Global Economy',
       15 Int'l Sociology (2000) 372-393; Y. H. Ferguson & R.J. Barry Jones (eds.), *Political Space*
       (SUNY Press, 2002).
12   See, for an excellent new study in accordance with many findings of this text, P. Schiff
       Berman, 'The Globalization of Jurisdiction', 151 U. Pa. L. Rev. (2002) 311-529.

1   TERRITORY AS BASIS FOR JURISDICTION

1.1   Territory as a basis for classical jurisdiction

'The foundation of jurisdiction is physical power', Justice Holmes said famously in 1917.[13] If this is true, and if the state's power is confined to the state territory, then we should find jurisdiction to be largely territorial. Indeed, a look at typical bases for jurisdiction confirms this expectation.

The most obvious connection between territory and jurisdiction exists for in rem jurisdiction. Both US-American[14] and European jurisdictional laws[15] base such jurisdiction on the presence of the asset within the jurisdiction. This is true both for chattels[16] and land.[17] Such jurisdiction, based on presence within the territory is, of course, a territorial concept.

It may be more relevant to see that the same is true, by and large, for in personam jurisdiction – it is usually based on territorial considerations. The most important basis for general jurisdiction under the common law, namely service within the territory,[18] is a territorial concept. Originally it was a direct emanation of territorial power: the defendant was actually arrested so that his appearance before the court could be guaranteed. While now service is a mere symbolic reference to this seizure, it still reveals the same territorial foundation. Yet territoriality is not confined to tag jurisdiction. Outside this, general in personam jurisdiction is based either on (habitual) residence[19] or on domi-

---

13   *McDonald v. Mabee*, 243 US 90, 91, 37 S.Ct. 343, 343, 61 L.Ed. 608, 609 (1917).
14   See, in general, Rest. 2nd (Conflict of Laws) ch. 3, topic 2, intro. note (1971); Fraser, 'Actions in Rem', 34 *Cornell L. Q.* (1948), 29; Smit, 'The Enduring Utility of In Rem Rules: A Lasting Legacy of Pennoyer v. Neff', 43 *Brook. L. Rev.* (1977) 600; R. J. Weintraub, *Commentary on the Conflict of Laws* (4th ed. 2001), p. 246-252 with further references.
15   Art. 22 No. 1 Brussels Regulation; Sec. 24 ZPO (Ger.).
16   Rest. 2nd (Conflict of Laws) § 60.
17   *Freeman v. Alderson*, 119 US 185, 7 S.Ct. 165, 30 L.Ed. 372 (1886); *In re Estate of Reed*, 233 Kan. 531, 664 P.2d 824, *cert. denied*, 464 US 978, 104 S.Ct. 417, 78 L.Ed.2d 354 (1983).
18   Or „tag' jurisdiction. On presence at the time of service as a sufficient condition of jurisdiction see B. Currie, 1963 *U. Ill. L. Forum* (1963), 533, 583; *Burnham v. Superior Court*, 495 US 604, 110 S.Ct. 2105, 109 L.Ed.2d 631 (1990). For England see Dicey & Morris, *The Conflict of Laws*, no. 11-003 (13th ed., Sweet and Maxwell 2000, author: Lawrence Collins). The basis is unavailable under the Brussels Regulation; see its Art. 3 with Appendix I.
19   Zivilprozessordnung [ZPO] § 13 (F.R.G.) (German Code of Civil Procedure); Bundesgesetz über das Internationale Privatrecht [IPRG] art. 2, 20(1) (Switz.) (Swiss Code of Conflict of Laws); Code civil art. 102 (Fr.), Code de procédure civile art. 42, 43 (Fr.) (French Code of Civil Procedure); Jurisdiktionnorm §§ 65, 66 (Aus.) (Austrian Code of Jurisdiction). Under Art. 2, 59 Council Regulation (EC) No 44/2001 of 22 December 2000 on jurisdiction and the recognition and enforcement of judgments in civil and commercial matters, 2001 OJ (L 12) 1-23, 'Wohnsitz' or domicile must be determined according to the law of the member state seized. See Kaye, 'The Meaning of Domicile under United Kingdom Law for the Purposes of the 1968 Brussels Convention on Jurisdiction and the Enforcement of Judgments in Civil and Commercial Matters', Neth. Int'l L. Rev. (1988) 181.

cile.[20] Domicile is of course a tricky concept[21] that may not easily fit into the territoriality box, a strange mix between facts and norms, between territorial concepts of 'home' and imaginative concepts of belonging.[22] Residence, on the other hand, is a strictly territorial concept; it refers to a place. Thus, a defendant can be sued at his or her (territorial) home. We see here an emanation of the state's control over citizens on its territory[23] – jurisdiction over a resident is an emanation of sovereign control over him or her.

Finally, territory plays a great role also for a third connection: conduct. Almost all conduct-connected bases of jurisdiction under the Brussels regulation are based on territorial concepts[24]. Thus, jurisdiction lies at the *place* of contract performance[25] (Art. 5 (1)), the *place* where a tort was committed (Art. 5 (3)). Likewise, such territorial connections play a predominant role as relevant factors in the minimum contacts test in U.S. jurisdictional thinking.

1.2   Problems of the concept

Actual territorial presence or the place of conduct have been considered unattractive as bases of jurisdiction for some time, because they appeared too narrow and too broad at the same time.

On the one hand they appeared too narrow. Modern communication methods as well as industrial progress made it more frequent for an individual to have an impact on circumstances within a state without ever entering that state. Thus a defamatory statement could be uttered on the phone in one state and hurt an individual in another.[26] Companies may engage in anticom-

---

20   *Miliken* v. *Meyer*, 311 U.S. 457, 61 S.Ct. 339, 85 L.Ed. 278 (1940). See also Art. 5(5) Brussels
        Regulation (jurisdiction at place of branch, agency or other establishment).
21   W. L. M. Reese, 'Does Domicile Bear a Single Meaning?', 55 Colum. L. Rev. (1955) 589. Res-
        idence may have different meanings as well, though, see W. L. M. Reese & R. S. Green,
        'That Elusive Word, 'Residence', 6 Vand. L. Rev. (1953) 561; D. Cavers, 'Habitual Resi-
        dence: A Useful Concept?', 21 Am. U. L. Rev. (1972) 475.
22   See only Rest. 2nd (Conflict of Laws) ch. 1; Dicey & Morris (supra n. 19), ch. 6 (author: J.D.
        McClean).
23   See supra n. 10.
24   See, in more detail, Ralf Michaels, 'De-Placing Brussels', in: *Civil judicial Cooperation in the
        Relations Between European and Third States* (A. Nuyts, ed., Bruylant, forthcoming).
25   Art. 5 (1) Brussels Regulation. The most erudite study on jurisdiction based on the place
        of performance is still Haimo Schack, *Der Erfüllungsort im deutschen, ausländischen und in-
        ternationalen Privat- und Zivilprozeßrecht* (1985).
26   *Cantor Fitzgerald, L.P*, v. *Peaslee*, 88 F.3d 152 (2nd Cir. 1996); *Ticketmaster-New York, Inc.* v.
        Alioto, 26 F.3d 201 (1st Cir. 1994); *Wilson* v. *Belin*, 20 F.3d 644 (5th Cir. 1994); *De Prins* v. *Van
        Damme*, 953 S.W.2d 7 (Tex. Ct. App. 1997) (all denying personal jurisdiction over defen-
        dant who had placed allegedly defamatory telephone calls into the state of the forum); but
        see *Brown* v. *Flowers Industries, Inc.*, 688 F.2d 328, 332- 33 (5th Cir.1982) (holding that a sin-
        gle defamatory telephone call to a person in Mississippi was sufficient for a Mississippi
        court to invoke personal jurisdiction because injury occurred in Mississippi and the de-
        fendant knew that the call was to Mississippi). See also S. Kubis, *Internationale
        Zuständigkeit bei Persönlichkeits- und Immaterialgüterrechtsverletzungen* (1999).

petitive behavior with regard to a specific market miles away from the place where they themselves act.[27] On a conduct-based territoriality concept the interested market state is unable to assume jurisdiction over such conduct.[28] A factory in one state could pollute a river and thereby cause injuries in another state. The states where the damage occurs have an interest in assuming jurisdiction over the tortfeasor, yet cannot do so on the basis of traditional concepts of territorial jurisdiction over the person and his or her actions.

On the other hand, a territorial conception of jurisdiction might often be too broad. It may be questionable whether the place where an act takes place, or where a defendant is served with process, should really determine jurisdiction *vel non*, even if it appears otherwise accidental. The example from antitrust shows this with regard to conduct: Why should a state assume jurisdiction over anti-competitive agreements directed entirely to markets outside the state? The problem is more obvious for jurisdiction based on service of process where territorial presence may be accidental. This problem becomes more urgent in a more mobile society. For example, in 1870 a Massachusetts court was entitled to assume jurisdiction over a defendant who, en route with a ship from Halifax, Nova Scotia, to his home town in New York, was served with process while his ship was docked in Boston.[29] The decision found a renactment in the even more bizarre 1959 decision in *Grace* v. *MacArthur*.[30] Here, the defendant was served aboard a plane on a non-stop flight from Memphis, Tenn., to Dallas, Texas, while the plane was above Pine Bluff, Arkansas. The Arkansas court considered this sufficient to establish jurisdiction and only hinted at the possibility that 'a time may come, and may not be far distant, when commercial aircraft will fly at altitudes so high that it would be unrealistic to consider them as being within the territorial limits of the United States or of any particular State while flying at such altitudes',[31] without a real suggestion how high that was and why that height had not been reached in the case.

An additional problem is determinability. Territoriality may long have looked like a sensible basis for jurisdiction because presence of persons or things could easily be established. Yet with modern technology even localization, necessary to establish jurisdiction, is difficult to accomplish in many areas. For example, the location of a person talking into a telephone, or even articulating something over the internet, may be relevant but hard to establish.[32] Likewise, where the place of the injury is relevant, this place is not always easy to establish.

27　See infra III.3.
28　*American Banana Co.* v. *United Fruit Co.*, 213 US 347, 356, 29 S. Ct. 511, 512; 53 L. Ed. 826 (1909): 'the general and almost universal rule ... that the character of an act as lawful or unlawful must be determined wholly by the law of the country where the act is done'.
29　*Peabody* v. *Hamilton*, 106 Mass. 217 (1870).
30　*Grace* v. *MacArthur*, 170 F. Supp. 442 (E.D. Ark. 1959).
31　Idem at 447.
32　See, for an example from choice of law, *Linn* v. *Employers Reinsurance Corp.*, 153 A.2d 483, 397 Pa. 153, (Pa. 1959).

Finally, territoriality occasionally needs to resort to fictitious locations. Corporations are artificial persons which are not physically present anywhere. One may focus on the place of incorporation and / or the place of the headquarters,[33] but both these localizations are necessarily fictitious presences of a fictitious entity. The same problem arises with regard to the localization of immaterial assets like debts. U.S. courts held, for a long time, that debts were situated in a debtor's body and that thus quasi in rem jurisdiction could be assumed over the creditor at the place of the debtor, even if the creditor had no other relation to that place.[34] Likewise, under sec. 23 of the German Code of Civil Procedure courts can establish jurisdiction over a defendant at the place of his assets, even if these assets are only debts and their territorial location thus purely fictitious.[35] It is interesting to note that it seems necessary to territorialize immaterial things like corporations and debts in order to determine whether a court has jurisdiction. Apparently, without territorialization this thought process would be impossible.

1.3   Insufficient solutions

How have jurisdictional law and theories dealt with these problems? By and large by tinkering with the established territorial concepts. Territoriality is not given up as basis for jurisdiction but made flexible. On the one hand it alone is not sufficient. On the other it is not necessary – at least in the original sense.

Thus the place of conduct has long been considered insufficient for jurisdiction in torts and antitrust law. It gave rise to jurisdiction based on effects, instead of the place of conduct – now the dominant approach both to antitrust[36] and torts[37] actions. Likewise in defamation cases courts now focus on the place

---

33   See, e.g., 28 U.S.C. § 1332(c)(1) (providing for both the place of incorporation and of principal place of business for jurisdictional purposes); Art. 60 Brussels Regulation (providing for both the statutory seat and the principal place of business); ZPO § 17 (F.R.G.) (German Code of Civil Procedure) (providing for the principal place of business).

34   *Harris v. Balk*, 198 US 215, 25 S.Ct. 625, 49 L.Ed. 1023 (1905); see also *Seider v. Roth*, 17 N.Y.2d 111, 216 N.E.2d 312, 269 N.Y.S.2d 99 (1966) (jurisdiction over a car driver at the place of his insurer's office).

35   It has been characterized as an exorbitant ground for the exertion of jurisdiction, see only T. Pfeiffer, *Internationale Zuständigkeit und prozessuale Gerechtigkeit* (1995), p. 620-650 (but cf. H. Schack, *Internationales Zivilverfahrensrecht* no. 330). The basis is therefore excluded between the Member States of the E.U. pursuant to Art. 3 (2) Brussels Regulation with Annex I; see J. Kropholler, *Europäisches Zivilprozeßrecht*, Art. 3 no. 4 (7th ed., 2002).

36   See, for the US, *Hartford Fire Ins. Co. v. California*, 509 US 764, 113 S. Ct. 2891; 125 L. Ed. 2d 612 (1993); for the E.U. joined cases C-89/85, C-104/85, C-114/85, C-116/85, C-117/85 and C-125/85 to C-129/85, *Ahlstroem Osakeyhtioe and Others v. Commission*, [1993] ECR I-1307, (1993) 4 CMLR 407 ('Woodpulp'); for Germany Gesetz gegen Wettbewerbsbeschränkungen [GWB] § 130(2) (F.R.G.) (German Antitrust Law).

37   Art. 5 (3) Brussels Regulation. For the US, see E. Scoles et al., *Conflict of Laws*, ch. 7 (West, 3rd ed. 2000). Case law from transborder pollution shows this neatly Cf. Case 21/76, *Bier v. Mines de Potasse d'Alsace*, [1976] ECR 1735 (pollution of the Rhine in France caused damages in the Netherlands); Cour de Cassation 3 April 1978, JCP 1978.Jur.185 = 1980 Foro it. IV.405

of the injury, albeit with limitations. Thus the U.S. Supreme Court has held that, for jurisdiction in defamation cases, the plaintiff's domicile alone is insufficient for jurisdiction, unless an additional factor is present – either a territorial factor (e.g. the slanderous statement was made in the forum state),[38] or, more importantly, a non-territorial factor like intent.[39] European law does not require such additional showings, but limits the jurisdiction of a member state other than that of the defendant's domicile to damages incurred within that state[40] (the so-called 'mosaic principle') – a radical consequence of the territoriality principle. Indeed, replacing conduct by effect is only replacing one territorial concept by a different one: the place of effects is just as territorial as the place of conduct.

The way to deal with the inherent danger of overreaching has been to require additional elements to be present before jurisdiction can be established. One is the requirement of 'minimum contacts', introduced into U.S. jurisdictional law in 1945 by the Supreme Court decision in *International Shoe*.[41] According to the test, power over the defendant is not enough in order to establish jurisdiction. In addition a court requires enough 'contacts ... as [to] make it reasonable ... to require the [defendant] to defend [himself]'.[42] Quasi in rem jurisdiction in the U.S., just like jurisdiction based on sec. 23 of the German Code of Civil Procedure, now requires some kind of minimum contacts as a limit to the most exorbitant cases.[43] Thus the fictitious presence of debts alone

(Fr.) (French jurisdiction for damages in France caused by pollutions in the Mediterranean caused from Italy); Entscheidungen des österreichischen Obersten Gerichtshofes in Zivilsachen (supreme court) 24 Feb 1998, SZ 71/31 (Aus.). See also, on the countervailing principle of exclusive jurisdiction at the polluter's domicile, T. Pfeiffer, 'Der Umweltgerichtsstand als zuständigkeitsrechtlicher Störfall – Bermerkungen zu § 32a ZPOl', 106 *Zeitschrift für Zivilprocess* (1993) 159-179.

38   *Burt v. Board of Regents of the Univ. of Nebraska*, 757 F.2d 242, 245 (1th Cir. 1985) (Seth, J, diss.).

39   *Calder v. Jones*, 465 U.S. 783, 104 S.Ct. 1482, 79 L.Ed.2d. 790 (1984).

40   Case C-68/93, *Shevill v. Presse Alliance*, (1995) ECR I-415; for an extension to copyright claims see Cour de Cassation 16 July 1995, report Clunet 1998, 136 (*Huet*), [1999] I.L.Pr. 379 (Fr.).

41   *International Shoe Co. v. Washington*, 326 U.S. 310, 66 S.Ct. 154, 90 L.Ed. 95 (1945). On the history of the case see Cameron & Johnson, 'Death of a Salesman? Forum Shopping and Outcome Determination Under International Shoe', 28 U.C. Davis L. Rev. (1995), 769.

42   326 U.S. at 317, 66 S.Ct. at 158, 90 L.Ed. at 102.

43   For U.S. law see *Shaffer v. Heitner*, 433 U.S. 186, 97 S.Ct. 2569, 53 L.Ed.2d 683 (1977). For Germany see Entscheidungen des Bundesgerichtshofes in Zivilsachen [BGHZ] [Supreme Court] 115, 90 (F.R.G.) and for background information on the decision Oskar Hartwieg, 'Forum Shopping zwischen Forum Non Conveniens und 'hinreichendem Inlandsbezug'?', 51 *Juristenzeitung* (1992), 109-118; cf. also, 'Entscheidungen des Bundesverfassungsgerichtes' [BVerfGE] [Constitutional Court] 61, 1 (F.R.G.). A similar restriction exists in Austrian law, see, Jurisdiktionsnorm § 99(1), 2nd sentence (Aus.) (Austrian Code of Jurisdiction). See also, for comparative analyses, Kleinstück, *Due Process-Beschränkungen des Vermögensgerichtsstandes durch hinreichenden Inlandsbezug und Minimum Contacts* (1994); Arthur. T. von Mehren, *Theory and Practice of Adjudicatory Authority in Private International Law: A Comparative Study of the Doctrine, Policies and Practices of Common- and Civil Law Systems ch. 3* (Kluwer, 2003).

should not be sufficient. However, the minimum contacts test has proved unpredictable both in its scope and its application and has given rise to numerous, not always consistent, decisions.[44] In addition, at least according to a plurality in the Supreme Court, it is unavailable, where it might be needed most, namely in jurisdiction based on service.[45]

The other important restriction is the doctrine of forum non conveniens,[46] according to which a court can decline to exercise its jurisdiction with regard to a more appropriate forum. Thus, the English courts could assume jurisdiction over the Baroness Wilderstein, who had been served on a brief visit from her home in Paris to the Ascot derby,[47] but could decline to exercise it on the basis of forum non conveniens.[48] U.S. courts can stay proceedings even at the defendant's U.S. home court if they consider the place of the accident better equipped to deal with the litigation.[49] Because both the minimum contacts test and the forum non conveniens doctrine serve largely similar purposes, their interrelation is not entirely clear.[50]

Thus, while jurisdiction based on territory is at the same time extended and limited, it is not itself questioned as a concept. There seems to be little concern with the legitimacy of territory as such as a basis for jurisdiction. This may explain why, for example, the question of jurisdiction regarding the internet is still often resolved through location – of the server,[51] of the users,[52] al-

---

44   For an early account of decisions see H. Schack, *Jurisdictional Minimum Contacts Scrutinized* (1983).

45   *Burnham* v. *Superior Court* (supra n. 19).

46   For recent comparative analyses see Ronald A. Brand, 'Comparative Forum Non Conveniens and the Hague Jurisdiction and Judgments Convention', 37 Tex. Int'l L.J. 467 (2002); A. Nuyts, L'exception de forum non conveniens (Bruylant, 2003).

47   *Maharanee of Baroda* v. *Wildenstein* (1972) 2 QB 283 (Eng. C.A.).

48   The most recent important English case on forum non conveniens is *Lubbe and Others* v. *Cape plc*, 2 Lloyd's Rep. 383, (2001) I.L.Pr 12 HL.

49   *Piper Aircraft* v. *Reyno*, 454 U.S. 235 (1981).

50   Allan R. Stein, *Forum Non Conveniens and the Redundancy of Court-Access Doctrine*, 133 U. Pa. L. Rev. 781 (1985); M. G. Stewart, 'Forum Non Conveniens: A Doctrine in Search of a Role', 74 Cal. L. Rev. 1251 (1986); A.W. Albright, 'In Personam Jurisdiction: A Confused and Inapproproate Substitute for Forum non Conveniens', 71 Tex. L. Rev. 351 (1992).

51   See, *Intercon, Inc.* v. *Bell Atlantic Internet Solutions, Inc.*, 205 F.3d 1244, (10th Cir. 2000) (exercising personal jurisdiction over non resident provider of a dial-up Internet service when routing its customer's e-mail through an Oklahoma mail server causing problems for an Oklahoma-based company); but see, e.g., *Nam Tai Electronics, Inc.* v. *Titzer*, 113 Cal. Rptr. 2d 769, 93 Cal. App. 4th 1301 (2001) (finding location of server of Yahoo! in forum state on which allegedly libelous bulletin board messages were posted to be insufficient to exercise personal jurisdiction).

52   To exert jurisdiction in the forum where the user acted, U.S. courts distinguish between a defendant company that 'clearly does business over the internet' and 'purely passive websites' on a sliding scale with interactive websites falling between these two ends of the spectrum. *Zippo Mfg. Co.* v. *Zippo Dot Com, Inc.*, 952 F. Supp. 1119 (W.D. Pa. 1997). Passive websites are generally held insufficient to justify personal jurisdiction, see, e.g., *ALS Scan Inc.* v. *Digital Serv. Consultants, Inc.*, 293 F.3d 707 (4th Cir. 2002); *Mink* v. *AAAA Development LLC*, 190 F.3d 333 (5th Cir. 1999); *Bensusan Restaurant Corp.* v. *King*, 126 F.3d 25 (2d Cir.

though these are usually unknown to the parties at the time of their actions and bear little relation to the facts underlying litigation.

Why is territoriality still such a central concept for jurisdiction? The reason lies in its close connection with the state. As the state is territorially defined, so jurisdiction must be territorially defined. It may be true that additional factors, contacts and fairness, have become more relevant in more recent years,[53] yet they have been unable to replace the territoriality paradigm. In many instances they look like no more than a test in addition to territory.[54] Yet even if we were to accept that fairness is not an afterthought but the very basis for the assumption of jurisdiction, we would not be able to leave territoriality behind. If we want to justify the assertion of state power, and if this state power is, essentially, territorial in nature, then all fairness factors must necessarily have a more or less strong territorial component. In other words, state jurisdiction must be territorial as long as the state is territorial.

2   THE TRANSMUTATION OF TERRITORIALITY

2.2   *Globalization and territoriality*

How does globalization influence territoriality? Territoriality is made up of several factors: space, boundaries, and distance. Simply speaking, the classical image of territoriality is that of an unalterable, objective topological geography, an objective conception of 'space' with clear boundaries. Persons, events, things, everything has a clear location within this space. Boundaries delimit one space from the other and make it possible to localize every person, thing, and event within one space and thus outside all others. Finally, distances between these locations are objectively defined, inalterable, and context-independent.

Globalization challenges this concept in various ways. The first is what one might call a transmutation of distance. Distances still exist in the real world, and they can be measured, but they play a vastly reduced role in many situations. Progress in transportation has made it possible to travel from Bangkok to London quicker than from Bangkok to some provinces of Thailand. Some points on the maps are connected so neatly that no distance on earth is insurmountable any longer or even poses a great barrier. This has ram-

---

1997); but see, *Inset Systems Inc.* v. *Instruction Set, Inc.*, 937 F. Supp. 161 (D. Conn. 1996). Interactive websites can support a finding of personal jurisdiction, see, e.g., *CompuServe Inc.* v. *Patterson*, 89 F.3d 1257 (6th Cir. 1996); *Zippo Manufacturing Company* v. *Zippo Dot Com, Inc.*, 952 F. Supp. 1119 (W.D. Pa. 1997) (both for online contracting); but increasingly courts require more than mere interactivity to justify the exercise of personal jurisdiction, see, e.g., *Response Reward Systems, L.C.* v. *Meijer, Inc.*, 189 F. Supp. 2d 1332 (M.D. Fla. 2002); *GTE New Media Servs., Inc.* v. *BellSouth Corp.*, 199 F.3d 1343 (D.C. Cir. 2000).

53   See von Mehren (supra n. 44) ch. III.A. (describing a move from a power theory to a litigational-justice theory of jurisdiction).

54   See, e.g., infra n. 7.

ifications in the law of jurisdiction. Thus, in *Burnham* Justice Brennan reasoned that the burdens on a transient defendant were minimal, because traveling from Florida to California was not prohibitively inconvenient.[55] He did not draw the radical, although possible conclusion, that therefore territory should not matter at all.[56]

Along with the transmutation of distance comes that of borders.[57] Territorial jurisdiction, as far as it is based on the state's power over that territory, rests on the assumption that the state has power to contain persons and events within its borders, and keep others outside – in short, is able to control its borders. This idea has never been applicable in the United States, where the borders between the states provide no control at all; the same is true more and more for the member states of the European Union. It is even inapplicable where borders still exist, to the extent these cannot be controlled. Thus, it fails with regard to environmental pollution – rivers transgress borders, so do clouds of toxic gas. Finally, borders are challenged in a more fundamental way: they can be transgressed virtually by modern means of communication. As long as telecommunication and internet communication are not censored, communication and actions across borders are possible, while no individual and no thing actually crosses those borders.

A related problem of territoriality concerns the potential overlap of territorial spaces. Territorial jurisdiction is based on a premise of a map where every place is located in one and only one territory, a map without gaps or overlaps.

---

55 *Burnham v. Superior Court of California, County of Marin*, 405 U.S. 604, 638-639 (1990), *citing, Burger King Corp.* v. *Rudzewicz*, 471 U.S. 462, 474, 105 S.Ct., 2174, 2183, 85 L.Ed.2d 528 (1985), and *McGee* v. *International Life Ins. Co.*, 355 U.S. 220, 223, 78 S.Ct. 199, 201, 2 L.Ed.2d 223 (1957) (where, however, inconvenience was denied because the defendant traveled to the forum state to do business there). It has been argued that this argument is weaker for international cases, because it is more inconvenient for aliens to travel. See P. Hay, *Transient Jurisdiction, Especially over International Defendants: Critical Comments on Burnham* v. *Superior Court of California*, 1990 U. Ill. L. Rev. 593. The U.S. Supreme Court used a similar distinction three years before *Burnham* in *Asahi Metal Industry Co. Ltd.* v. *Superior Court*, 480 U.S. 102, 114, 107 S.Ct. 1026, 1033, 94 L.Ed.2d 92 (1987): 'Asahi has been commanded by the Supreme Court of California not only to traverse the distance between Asahi's headquarters in Japan and the Superior Court of California in and for the County of Solano, but also to submit its dispute with Cheng Shin to a foreign nation's judicial system. The unique burdens placed upon one who must defend oneself in a foreign legal system should have significant weight in assessing the reasonableness of stretching the long arm of personal jurisdiction over national borders'. The quotation does not make clear whether physical distance (a territorial factor) or inconvenience of foreign laws and procedures (a non-territorial factor) are decisive.

56 J. Scalia hinted at this in his rejoinder (*Burnham* v. *Superior Court of California, County of Marin*, 495 U.S. at 624, 110 S.Ct. at 2117-2118): 'The problem with these assertions is that they justify the exercise of jurisdiction over *everyone, whether or not* he ever comes to California' (emphasis in original).

57 See, e.g., J. Anderson & L. O'Dowd, 'Borders, Border Regions and Territoriality: Contradictory Meanings, Changing Significance', 33 *Regional Studies* (1999) 593-604; J.C. Myers, 'Politics Without Borders: Internationalist Political Thought', 24 *New Political Science* (2002) 395-410.

Such a map fails with regard to objects that cannot be located in just one place, as well as to objects with altogether fictitious locations. Thus markets were originally local places: places in towns where seller and buyer got together. Markets today look very different; they transcend not only city boundaries, but also state boundaries. It is a goal of the European Union as well as of the WTO to create such transnational markets. In a real sense, therefore, markets cannot be localized within one territory – at best they cover more than one state's territory, at worst (for territoriality) they cannot be localized anywhere.

The final and biggest challenge comes from the concept of virtual spaces and thus virtual territories. The prime example is, or course, the internet. The notion itself of 'cyberspace' signifies a conception of the internet as a space beyond 'real' space, as a space of its own.[58] This space shares borders with the real world, namely computer screens and keyboards all over the world. At the same time it has, arguably, its own virtual territory with its own virtual reality and its own events. It is possible to say that things happen 'in cyberspace', and that relations between persons exist 'in cyberspace', in other words, to localize these events and relations in cyberspace. Yet cyberspace is not the only conceivable virtual space. Sociologists have long spoken of social spaces, bringing certain people close together and at the same time distancing them from others.[59] Here, proximity and distance, apparently territorial concepts, have nothing to do with (topological) territoriality but in fact signify an alternative, community-based way of setting up territories.

2.2   Why should we bother?

The question remains, of course, whether all this is relevant – both in general and specifically for the law of jurisdiction. Critics have long held globalization either to be nothing new or not to exist at all,[60] and have defended the intelligibility of territoriality, because they consider the concept sufficiently flexible to take in new developments. They point to the fact that the impact of events in cyberspace is still felt in the real world – people lose real money; they are insulted as real, not virtual persons. Therefore, they deem the conception of a cyberspace, detached from real space, unnecessary.[61] Territories may overlap, but it may still be possi-

---

58   For legal ramifications of this see, e.g., A. Gaitenby, 'A Law's Mapping of Cyberspace: The Shape of New Social Space', 52 *Technological Forecasting and Social Change* (1996) 135-145; M. A. Lemley, 'Place and Cyberspace', 91 Cal. L. Rev. (2003) with further references.

59   M. Davies & M. Niemann, 'The Everyday Spaces of Global Politics: Work, Leisure, Family', 24 *New Political Science* (2002) 557-577.

60   See, e.g., M. Veseth, *Selling Globalization: The Myth of the Global Economy* (1996).

61   See, from a legal point of view, J. L. Goldsmith, 'Against Cyberanarchy', 65 U. Chi. L. Rev. (1998) 1199; P. Mankowski, 'Das Internet im Internationalen Vertrags- und Deliktsrecht', 63 RabelsZ (1999) 203; 'The Abiding Significance of Territorial Sovereignty', 5 Ind. J. Global Legal Stud. (1998) 475; J. H. Sommer, 'Against Cyberlaw', 15:2 Berkeley Tech. L. J. (2000); A. R. Stein, 'The Unexceptional Problem of Jurisdiction in Cyberspace', 32 Int'l Law (1998) 1167

ble to find some 'center of gravity', to localize persons and events in the territory most affected by them. Borders may have little real importance and may not make a substantive difference in many aspects of real life, but they still serve their formal role as clear-cut delimitations. Finally, real distances may not be the only relevant distances in life, but unlike many other concepts of distance they are objectively measurable and thus perfectly useful for legal purposes.

These critics may be missing the point. It is certainly true that traditional concepts of territoriality still give us a picture of the world. Likewise it is true that a jurisdictional theory based on territorial concepts still 'works', in the sense that it yields results. Fuzziness at the borders between territoriality and extraterritoriality can be remedied by invoking additional factors, and ultimately through rules allocating burden of proof. But the problem is not whether territoriality gives us *a* picture of the world but whether it gives us an *adequate* picture of the world. We cannot be satisfied with a theory of jurisdiction that yields *any* results; we need a theory which yields *legitimate* results. The claim is that territoriality may no longer give us an adequate picture of the world, in which case it could no longer serve as fundament for a law of jurisdiction supposed to yield legitimate results. A jurisdictional theory founded upon a faulty concept must in itself be faulty.

Any such claim must seem sterile in the abstract. Its ramifications shall be shown in three short case studies.

3   THREE CASE STUDIES

3.1   *Free speech and the internet*

The first example involves the by now famous *Yahoo!* case. France, like many European countries,[62] has a statute prohibiting the exhibition and sale of Nazi memorabilia,[63] while such actions are legal in the United States and protected by the First Amendment. Such Nazi memorabilia were offered for sale on the auction site of Yahoo!'s U.S. site, www.yahoo.com. Yahoo!'s French site,

---

62   See now Council of Europe, Additional Protocol to the Convention on Cybercrime Concerning the Criminalisation of Acts of a Racist and Xenophobic Nature Committed through Computer Systems (7 Nov 2002), Doc. PC-RX (2002) 24 (provisional version); special reference is made to Holocaust denial in the Explanatory Report no. 39.

63   Sec. R 645-1 French Criminal Code ('Du port ou de l'exhibition d'uniformes, insignes ou emblèmes rappelant ceux d'organisations ou de personnes responsables de crimes contre l'humanité'): 'Est puni de l'amende prévue pour les contraventions de la 5e classe le fait, sauf pour les besoins d'un film, d'un spectacle ou d'une exposition comportant une évocation historique, de porter ou d'exhiber en public un uniforme, un insigne ou un emblème rappelant les uniformes, les insignes ou les emblèmes qui ont été portés ou exhibés soit par les membres d'une organisation déclarée criminelle en application de l'article 9 du statut militaire international annexé à l'accord de Londres du 8 août 1945, soit par une personne reconnue coupable par une juridiction française ou internationale d'un ou plusieurs crimes contre l'humanité prévus par les articles 211 à 212-3 ou mentionnés par la loi n.64-1326 du 26 décembre 1964'.

www.yahoo.fr, did not offer a similar service, but provided a link to the American site. The Tribunal de Grande Instance Paris, at the request of a French organization, ordered Yahoo! to prevent the sale of such items to citizens on French territory.[64] This caused vehement protests from both free speech supporters and internet companies in the United States,[65] not only as a violation of the First Amendment and an intrusion into the internet's (imaginary) total freedom, but because, so the argument went, the French court was trying to bind the whole world.[66] Sure, the judge had carefully restricted his order to sales on French territory. But Yahoo! argued that no software existed to restrict access to their website territorially,[67] and that therefore its only way to comply with the order was to ban the sales worldwide. Thus, effectively, a French court was ordering Yahoo! what to do worldwide.

Of the many interesting aspects of the case, only territoriality shall be of concern here. Of course, the decision had no direct effect of its own outside the French borders – this would be true even if the French judge had not restricted his order to sales in France. The French cannot enforce it outside France (because such action would be extraterritorial), and other nations are under no obligation to enforce foreign decisions automatically. In fact Yahoo! asked for, and received, a declaratory judgment from a court in California saying that the French decision was unenforceable in the United States.[68] However, this may have been little more than a public relations victory.[69] In all likelihood the plaintiffs never intended to have their judgment enforced in California, it was enough to gain their public relations victory in France, and to be able to enforce the judgment in France.[70]

---

64 Président du Tribunal de Grande Instance de Paris, 22 May 2000 and 11 Aug 2000, <www.juriscom.net/txt/jurisfr/cti/tgiparis20000522-asg.htm>. In separate proceedings, the president of Yahoo, Tim Koogle, was indicted for propaganda. He has since been acquitted by the tribunal correctionnel de Paris, though not on jurisdictional but on substantive grounds: he was held not to have condoned or praised Nazism. See 'L'ex-patron de Yahoo relaxé', *La Tribune*, Feb 12, 2003; 'French Court Clears Yahoo! in Nazi Case', *New York Times*, Feb 13, 2003.

65 C. L. Kaplan, 'French Decision Prompts Questions About Free Speech and Cyberspace', *New York Times*, Feb 11, 2002, with further quotes. For a friendlier analysis see M. S. Kende, 'Yahoo!: National Borders in Cyberspace and their Impact on International Lawyers', 32 N.M. L. Rev. (2002) 1. See also 'Can You Yahoo!? The Internet's Digital Fences', 2001 Duke L. & Tech. Rev. 0012.

66 Cf. *Buchanan* v. *Rucker*, 9 East 192: 'Can the island of Tobago pass a law to bind the rights of the whole world? Would the world submit to such a jurisdiction?' (*Lord Ellsborough*). Analytically, of course, these are two separate questions – the answer may well be yes to the first, no to the second question.

67 But see infra sub IV.4.

68 *Yahoo! Inc.* v. *La Ligue Contre le Racisme et l'Antisémitisme*, 169 F. Supp. 2d 1181 (N.D. Cal. 2001), also published in 2002 Gewerblicher Rechtsschutz und Urheberrecht International (GRUR Int) 960.

69 J. R. Reidenberg, 'Yahoo and Democracy on the Internet', 42 Jurimetrics J. (2002) 261, 269.

70 See 'Yahoo estime avoir eu un procès inéquitable en France', 10/01/2001, <www.legalis.net/cgi-iddn/french/affiche-jnet.cgi?droite=decisions/responsabilite-/ord_tgi-paris_110800.htm.>

The real question seems to be whether France should really be able to bind the world by forcing an American company to forego its rights under the first amendment. The obvious answer seems to be no, but things are not this one-sided. What Americans happily ignore is that the alternative is equally troublesome. If a French court cannot give such a decision, even territorially restricted, because it would be violating U.S. law and interests, then in return the United States are effectively binding the world, and the first amendment becomes directly binding on the French court! Either French or U.S. law seems to govern universally. The problem, of course, is that the internet does not fit territorial concepts. The French court's confinement to internet users situated in France is just as territorial and inadequate as Yahoo!'s argument that the company is situated in the U.S and should therefore only be held to U.S. standards. If the internet transcends boundaries and is not territorial, then every regulation of the internet is potentially global (and thus, if performed by a state, extraterritorial). But likewise, prohibiting such regulation potentially has global effects and is therefore extraterritorial.

The friction with traditional concepts of jurisdiction has become obvious in another recent case. The Australian High Court has held that a court in Victoria has jurisdiction to decide the defamation suit of an Australian citizen against American company Dow Jones, because it published a defamatory article about Joseph Gutnick, a businessman living in Melbourne, on its web publication Barron's Online.[71].

Australia's territories have strict defamation laws, and therefore the outcry in the United States both against restriction of free speech and legal hegemony was enormous again.[72] Unlike the French decision, however, this Australian decision appears to be, at least in its result, largely in accordance with US principles of jurisdiction. Defamation is an intentional tort, the journalist knew that Gutnick lived in Australia, and thus, under the *Calder* test,[73] jurisdiction at the place where the intentional message was directed is not completely unusual.[74]

Again, the practical problem is that worldwide internet publication runs the risk of jurisdiction in every country with internet access.[75] There may be

---

71   *Dow Jones & Company Inc* v. *Gutnick* (2002) HCA 56 (2002); available at <www.austlii.edu.au/au/cases/cth/high_ct/2002/56.html>.

72   See, e.g., 'Down (Under) with the Internet', *Wall Street Journal* 11 Dec 2002. (Of course, the Wall Street Journal is not likely to be sympathetic to the High Court, as it is owned by the defendant).

73   Supra n. 39.

74   *But cf. Young* v. *New Haven Advocate* (4th Cir. 2002), 2002 WL 31780988: The warden of a Virginia prison sued two Connecticut newspapers in Virginia, alleging that the newspapers defamed him in articles posted on Internet. The Court of Appeals held that newspapers did not post materials on their Internet sites with manifest intent of targeting readers in Virginia, as required to establish sufficient minimum contacts with Virginia.

75   See 'How Diamond Joe's libel case could change the future of the internet', *The Guardian* (U.K.), 11 Dec 2002:'[T]he ruling has thrown internet publishers into disarray and left them facing a choice between two equally costly and undesirable options: restricting access to their websites to prevent people in potentially difficult legal jurisdictions reading them; or employing international legal teams to vet all content to ensure that it complies with the libel laws in each of the countries it is likely to be read'.

ways to deal with this problem.[76] Yet as long as discussions remain within a territorial paradigm, they are likely to be inadequate. Such a territorial approach appears to be precisely what the Australian High Court has in mind when it says: that '[t]he principal issue ... was where was the material of which Mr Gutnick complained published?'.[77] This may already be the wrong question. It leads to technical discussions on whether the server 'sends' information to Australia, or whether a user from Australia 'picks' that information up at the server in the U.S. Such arguments are not only riddled with complex analogies, because they accept the requirement to situate publication of a web text somewhere territorially. Moreover, they rely on technical niceties entirely unknown, and irrelevant, to the actors and their interaction. The case makes clear how inadequate such an approach is. If the internet is characterized by its ubiquity and virtuality, then 'publication' takes place everywhere, and at the same time nowhere – at least in 'real' space. Localization, territorialization appear inadequate. The author of the article has since appealed to the United Nations High Commissioner for Human Rights, arguing that Australia's libel laws violate Art. 19 of the International Covenant on Civil and Political Rights.[78] This is an interesting attempt to find a global solution to a globalization problem, but it would be surprising if the High Commissioner should find that Art.19 is essentially similar to the first Amendment of the U.S. Constitution, rendering the laws of many other countries problematic.

The focus on intent, following the *Calder* case law,[79] is more attractive only at first sight. Giving a state jurisdiction only if an allegedly defamatory statement was intentionally aimed at this state looks like a welcome restriction of worldwide jurisdiction.[80] However, it may only help in a limited number of cases. Thus, it may make sense to say that the online version of the New Haven Advocate, just like its printed twin, is aimed at readers only in Connecticut.[81] But it makes little sense to say that a worldwide online information service like Barron's online, reporting about world markets, is aimed at a locally confined audience.[82] The problem of using intent as a factor is that this in-

---

76   See, e.g., American Bar Association, 'Achieving Legal and Business Order in Cyberspace: A Report on Global Jurisdiction Issues Created by the Internet', 55 Bus. Law. (2000), 1801

77   *Dow Jones & Company Inc* v. *Gutnick* (2002) HCA 56 at no. 4 (per Gleeson CJ, McHugh, Gummow and Hayne JJ).

78   Australian laws challenged at UN, ww.smh.com.au/articles/2003/04/18/1050172745955.html>.

79   Supra n. 40.

80   See, e.g., M. Traynor & L. Pirri, 'Personal Jurisdiction and the Internet: Emerging Trends and Future Directions', 712 PLI/Pat 93 (2002) 135-147.

81   Cf. supra n. 75. The site has an explicitly localizing headline: 'news, arts and entertainment weekly for the New Haven area'. In general, however, it may even be doubtful whether local papers, once online, remain truly local. People may move away from a place and find the local newspaper's online version a welcome link to their former home place, the newspaper in return may be interested in reaching a broader audience precisely by catering to these relocated people as well.

82   Barron's had about 1700 subscribers in Australia, a small fraction of subscribers worldwide (and far less than in the US), but a significant number taken by itself.

tent in itself must be defined territorially: jurisdiction lies in the territory at
which a message was aimed. The approach clearly fails when a message is not
aimed at a particular territory at all, which will often be the case on the internet. After all, messages are aimed at people, not at territories. Ultimately, intent may look like an alternative to territory, but it is hampered by its own
foundation in territoriality.

3.2   Problems of e-commerce

A second internet-related example shows a slightly different problem. In the
course of the negotiations for a Hague Judgments Convention,[83] one highly
disputed issue was whether there should be a special basis of jurisdiction for
consumers[84]. Europeans supported such a basis, invoking the need to protect
consumers, while Americans opposed it,[85] arguing that Internet companies
were unable to internalize the costs caused by such protection. These positions
certainly reflect countries' respective experiences – European law has long allowed for ample consumer protection in Art. 13-15 Brussels Convention (now
Art. 15-17 Brussels Regulation),[86] while U.S. law provides rather little consumer protection through the law of jurisdiction, at least in the realm of contract law[87]. One might also suspect that the positions reflect interest groups –
perhaps most internet sellers are situated in the United States, while Europe
might have more consumers. At least the last hypothesis was put into question by New Zealand's position in the negotiations. New Zealand opposed

---

83   Convention on Jurisdiction and Foreign Judgments in Civil and Commercial Matters,
      <http://www.hcch.net/e/workprog/jdgm.html>. For an analysis of the different posi-
      tions from which Europeans and Americans argued, see A. T. von Mehren & R. Michaels,
      'Pragmatismus und Realismus für die Haager Verhandlungen zu einem weltweiten
      Gerichtsstands- und Vollstreckungsübereinkommen', 25 DAJV-Newsletter (2000) 124-128.
      At present, chances are that the negotiating countries will, at best, agree on a convention
      regarding forum choice clauses, which excludes consumer contracts. See *Report on the Sec-
      ond Meeting of the Informal Working Group of the Judgments Project* – January 6-9, 2003, pre-
      pared by Andrea Schulz, First Secretary- Preliminary Document No 21 of January 2003
      (available at the aforementioned website).
84   See N. Reich & A. P. Gambogi Carvalho, 'Gerichtsstand bei internationalen Ver-
      brauchervertragsstreitigkeiten im e-commerce', *Verbraucher und Recht* (2001) 269-280.
85   In- and outside the negotiations. See, for example, P. Hofheinz, 'Cross-Border E-Com-
      merce Continues to Raise Concerns', *Wall Street Journal*, Aug 16, 2001.
86   De Bra, *Verbraucherschutz durch Gerichtsstandsregelungen im deutschen und europäischen
      Zivilprozessrecht* (1996); see also the contributions in 108 *Droit et Patrimoine* (Sep 2002).
87   See *Carnival Cruise Lines, Inc* v. *Shute*, 499 U.S. 585, 111 S.Ct. 1552, 113 L.Ed.2d 622 (1991)
      (enforcing a choice of forum clause embedded in Standard terms printed on a cruise tick-
      et against a consumer). The decision has been criticized in the U.S. See P. Borchers, 'Forum
      Selection Agreements in the Federal Courts After Carnival Cruise: A Proposal for Con-
      gressional Reform', 67 Wash. L. Rev. (1992) 55; L. S. Mullenix, 'Another Easy Case, Some
      More Bad Law: Carnival Cruise Lines and Contractual Personal Jurisdiction', 27 Tex. Int'l
      L.J. (1992) 323. For a contrasting European decision (albeit on venue) see *Océano Grupo Ed-
      itorial SA* v. *Rocio Murciano Quintero*, Cases C-240/98 – 244/298, [2000] ECR I-494.

consumer protection in the Convention in the interest not of its sellers but of its consumers. It feared that New Zealanders would never be able to profit from the internet, because no foreign company would take the risk of selling to New Zealand and then face litigation so far from home[88].

The debate over the costs of consumer protection is not new, but it has been grossly enhanced by the advent of the internet. The reason is that e-commerce promises a vast reduction of transaction costs. Seller and buyer may be situated on different ends of the world, but because communication between them is practically costless, they can enter into negotiations and transactions with almost as few expenses as if they were in the same city (essentially the only additional cost comes from higher shipping costs). This gives consumers a dramatically larger choice of potential sellers to buy from, and at the same time it enables especially small sellers with no large budgets to compete with bigger companies. Big companies like Amazon.com, although they complain about consumer protection as well, should be better suited to shoulder additional costs and finance them through their income from new markets. Smaller sellers, on the other side, are unlikely to make enough profits from such new markets to defend themselves in various jurisdictions.

Why is this a problem of globalization and territoriality? The internet came with the implicit promise of overcoming territoriality by doing away with distance. In the global village, everyone, big or small, would be able to sell to everyone as though they were territorial neighbors. Introducing consumer protection jurisdiction, the argument goes, resituates the consumer at his or her home place. It thereby re-territorializes an aspect of life that was thought to transcend territoriality,[89] because, in case of litigation, it forces the seller to travel to the consumer's domicile. The argument is prima facie convincing, but cuts both ways. Actually, it is not just the introduction of consumer jurisdiction bases, but the availability of any court assuming jurisdiction, the mere possibility of litigation in general, which re-territorializes e-commerce (and adds prohibitive transaction costs). Just as a small company cannot be expected to litigate at any place in the world, nor can a consumer be expected to litigate in a faraway country against a shop that is a neighbor on the web, but is situated far away for matters of jurisdiction and litigation. As long as litigation happens at a place in the real world, re-territorialization seems unavoidable. The choice seems to be between e-commerce without consumer protection (because the consumer will never sue at the seller's home place), and consumer protection without e-commerce (because the seller will not even sell to consumers in other countries). Having both at once seems to be no option.

---

88 See David Goddard, *Rethinking the Hague Judgments Convention: A Pacific Perspective*, 3 Yearbook of Priv. Int'l L. 27, 35, 45-48 (2001).

89 See Buchner, 2000 EWS 147, 152 (seller and buyer meet in a 'virtuellen Niemandsland' – virtual no-man's-land).

3.3   World markets and international antitrust[90]

Not all problems of globalization are internet-related. This can be seen from
Kruman v. Christie's, a 'real world' case[91] currently pending for cert. before the
U.S. Supreme Court. It involves anticompetitive behavior by the world's
largest auction houses, Sotheby's and Christie's. When their price fixing became public, plaintiffs in the United States started a class action, the class consisting of all sellers and buyers at U.S. auctions. This litigation was eventually settled.[92] The problem in Kruman arises from a different litigation: Eight
participants of auctions held in England brought an independent action in
the U.S., relying on U.S. antitrust law with its sweet promise of multiple damages. In similar cases, U.S. courts had decided that they did not have jurisdiction. Thus, for example, *Statoil v. HeereMac*[93] involved two non-American
companies disputing over a price-fixing scheme regarding the provision of
heavy-lift barge services for oil exploitation in the North Sea. The court saw
no impact on the US markets, although, allegedly, the price-fixing also raised
prices for platforms in the Gulf of Mexico.[94] On the other hand, in the most recent decision by a U.S. court of appeals, the court assumed jurisdiction over
the action brought by foreign purchasers of vitamins against manufacturers,
because their price fixing agreement had a substantial impact on the U.S.
market.[95]

Again, there are arguments on both sides. On the one hand it appears
bizarre that US courts and US law should be available to English plaintiffs,
suing an English company because of damages suffered in an auction that
took place in England. On the other hand there may well be an interest in
bundling antitrust litigation in order to both minimize costs and put maximum deterrence pressure on companies that violate global standards of an-

90   See also the article by W. T. Miller and D. I. Baker in this volume.
91   *Kruman v. Christie's International plc*, 284 F.3d 384 (2nd Cir. 2002), *petition for certiorari filed*,
      71 U.S.L.W. 3169 (U.S. Sep 03, 2002) (No. 02-340). The parties have since settled, see Brooks
      Barnes, 'Sotheby's, Christie's to Settle Claims by Overseas Customers', *Wall Street Journal*,
      March 12, 2003, B2.
92   The modified settlement was approved in *In re Auction Houses Antitrust Litigation*, 42
      Fed.Appx. 511 (2nd Cir. 2002). See, in general, <http://www.auctionsettlement.com>.
93   *Den Norske Stats Oljeselskap As v. HeereMac v.o.f.*, 241 F.3d 420 (5th Cir. 2001), *cert. denied sub
      nom. Statoil ASA v. HeereMac v.o.f.*, 122 S.Ct. 1059 (2002), *reh'g denied*, 122 S.Ct. 1597 (2002).
94   See also, *In re Microsoft Corp. Antitrust Litig.*, 127 F. Supp. 2d 702, 715 (D. Md. 2001) (dis-
      missing the claims by foreign plaintiffs against Microsoft's licensing monopoly that al-
      legedly deprived them of the benefits of competition including, inter alia, technological
      innovation, market choice, and product variety, because they had not 'participated in any
      way in the U.S. market' and thus had no right to institute a Sherman Act claim); *BHP New
      Zealand, Ltd. v. UCAR International, Inc.*, 153 F. Supp. 2d 700 (E.D. Pa. 2001) (limiting the
      claims of foreign purchasers from an alleged international graphite electrode cartel only
      to those sales invoiced from the United States, but denying jurisdiction over – the far
      greater number of – purchases made outside the United States, even though the members
      of the cartel were U.S.-based companies).
95   *Empagran S.A. v. F. Hoffman-Laroche, Ltd*. (D.C. Cir. 2003), 2003 WL 131805.

titrust.[96] Private party interests may advocate a denial of jurisdiction (because plaintiffs lack contact to the United States and have a more appropriate forum at home), public interests in law enforcement may advocate giving every private plaintiff the chance to bring suit.

The trouble is that the courts, bound in traditional modes of thought, appear unable to even conceptualize such questions, because they focus entirely on territorial concepts, here the effects doctrine. Thus, the lack of any contacts between the plaintiffs and the United States was no problem for the court in *Kruman*, because the price-fixing clearly had an effect on the US market. Almost the whole decision deals with issues of statutory interpretation, namely whether the illegal behaviour gave rise to 'a' claim or 'the' plaintiff's claim. On the other hand, *Statoil* was decided against the plaintiffs because the plaintiffs' injury did not arise from the anticompetitive effect in the United States Both decisions seem to agree that effects occurred *inside*, and the injury to the plaintiffs *outside*, the territory of the United States. This presupposes that the effect in the United States can somehow be distinguished from the effect on the plaintiffs elsewhere, that the market in the U.S. is somehow different from that of the plaintiffs.

The effects doctrine appears inadequate for this particular kind of problem for two reasons, both stemming from territorial conceptions. First, many markets are no longer local. There is now a worldwide art market in which both buyers and sellers will go to those places in the world where the circumstances for buying and selling are best for them. In this sense, the market in New York is not different from the one in London except for the venue (and, perhaps, some procedures), because all participants are the same: buyers, sellers, and auctioneer. If the rates in New York are higher, then buyers and sellers are likely to go to London. Similarly, it is artificial to distinguish one market for heavy-lift barge services to be used in the Gulf of Mexico, and another for those to be used in the North Sea. Ultimately there is one world market with a very small number of players, and any localization appears arbitrary.

There is a second problem with the effects doctrine. In a globalized economy, everything has an effect on everything.[97] Thus, even if markets are separate, they are still interconnected, so any anticompetitive behavior will ultimately, indirectly, affect the U.S. market. What courts then have to do under the effects test is to distinguish direct from indirect, stronger from weaker effects – all very fuzzy concepts necessary for highly political decisions. The globalization of markets – its independence from territories as well as its interconnectedness – makes the effects doctrine almost unworkable.

---

96 See S. K. Mehra, 'Deterrence: The Private Remedy and International Antitrust Cases', 40 Colum. J. Transnat'l L. (2002) 275.

97 This is by no means a new insight. Judge Learned Hand, in establishing the 'effects doctrine' had already recognized that 'almost any limitation of the supply of goods in Europe, for example, or in South America, may have repercussions in the United States if there is trade between the two', *U.S. v. Aluminum Co. of America ('Alcoa')*, 148 F.2d 416, 443 (2nd Cir. 1945).

4   JURISDICTIONAL PRINCIPLES AFTER TERRITORIALITY

What can be done? Six possible answers can be sketched in the abstract. None is fully satisfactory alone, each has its own problems, but their combination may provide a guideline.

4.1   Anarchy

The failure of territorial jurisdiction reflects a failure of the territorial concept of the state. One approach would be to accept that jurisdiction cannot deal adequately with problems of globalization, with the loss of territoriality. One consequence would be to go on as before and simply accept that the results are unsatisfactory. Another possible consequence is for courts to accept their limited power and legitimacy, to restrain themselves altogether, and to let the forces of the market perform the regulation which used to be the courts' task. This approach looks attractive to those fearful of state power. If states restrain liberty, then less state power is a good thing, and if courts as emanations of state power fail their task, then this is good for liberty. Also, if there is competition between courts, this may avoid monopolies and create benefits for 'consumers' of justice – hence everybody.

  Yet this position is doubtful. First, one task of courts is to control states, thus less court power may mean more, not less unbounded state power. Second, competition between courts may undermine the ability of courts (and states) to stand up combined against powerful non-state actors – especially if those form cartels. States provide liberty just as they restrain it. The restraint of courts has allocative and distributive effects just as their intervention does.[98] Therefore, if courts should fail in their task of bringing about justice, we would need a very good and trustworthy alternative to replace them in this task, unless we are convinced that global governance is possible without institutions.

4.2   Universalization

On the opposite end of the spectrum stands the universalization of jurisdiction – the idea of world courts (and world law). No territory, can transcend the globe and its population. Thus, universal jurisdiction by world courts seems to provide a solution. Problems of extraterritorial jurisdiction would disappear, because there would (seem to) be no extraterritoriality. Yet, while it may be difficult to judges the pros and cons of legal unification in the abstract, some concerns must be mentioned.

---

98   Cf. R. L. Hale, 'Coercion and Distribution in a Supposedly Non-Coercive State', 38 *Political Science Quarterly* (1923) 470.

There are two variants of this approach. The typical one sets its hope in supranational institutions like the International Criminal Court (ICC,[99] or a global antitrust law.[100] The hope for world courts has been with us for a long time,[101] but it may be both unrealistic and unattractive. First, the present problems with the ICC[102] show how difficult it is to establish such courts even for universally condemned crimes. It should be difficult to reach a consensus on matters where different states differ, like the condemnation of hate speech versus the protection of free speech. Equally, a global antitrust law is hard to establish as long as there are not only concerns of (territorial) sovereignty, but also disagreements on the content of such law.[103] The 19th century dream of worldwide unification has become doubtful, and the values of pluralism come into light.[104] World courts could prove less attractive than one might have expected – they would monopolize powers and likely become immune to influences from outside.

According to the other variant of world courts, such courts already exist – in the form of US courts. Other countries complain about what they perceive as an exaggerated willingness of US courts to adjudicate cases with minimal relations to the United States.[105] The step to their official status as world courts is perhaps not that big, and has been proposed. Fore example, Judge Weinstein, after exposing the insufficiencies of traditional jurisdiction under globalization, has proposed that in mass tort actions with victims all over the world, New York would provide a good forum for these plaintiffs, and New

---

99   The ICC was established pursuant to the Rome Statute of the International Criminal Court, July 17, 1998, U.N. Doc. A/CONF. 183/9, on July 1, 2002 in accordance with article 126, available at <http://www.un.org/law/icc/statute/romefra.htm>.

100   J. Basedow, *Weltkartellrecht* (1998); cf. J. Basedow, 'International Antitrust: From Extraterritorial Application to Harmonization', 60 La. L. Rev. (2000) 1037-1052.

101   P. de Auer, 'A Permanent Court in Civil Matters', *Reports of the 33d Conference of the ILA in Stockholm* (1925) 366-381; Andre-Prudhomme, 'De la nécessité d'une juridiction internationale compétente à l'égard des litiges d'ordre privé mettant en jeu l'application des futures Traités de Paix', 1945 *Journal de droit international privé* 725-729; Ch. Carabiber, *Les juridictions internationales de droit privé* (1947); René David, II-5 Int. Enc. of Comp. L. – 'The International Unification of Private Law', 115-120 (1971). See Patrick Wautelet, *Les Conflits de Procédure, section 'Une juridiction internationale de droit privé* ?' (forthcoming).

102   See only M. H. Morris, 'High Crimes and Misconceptions: The ICC and Non-Party States', 64 Law & Contemp. Probs. (2001) 13.

103   Basedow himself has doubts whether such a development is likely in the near future; see J. Basedow, 'The Effects of Globalization on Private International Law', in: *Legal Aspects of Globalization* (J. Basedow & T. Kono eds., 2000), 1, 10.

104   See only R. Michaels, 'Im Westen nichts Neues?', 66 RabelsZ (2002) 97-115; see also, on different paradigms and how they alone are inconclusive for the pros and cons of legal unification, R. Michaels, 'Three Paradigms of Legal Unification: National, International, Transnational', *Proceedings of the 96th Annual Meeting of the American Society of International Law* (2002) 333-336.

105   For a recent, very sharp attack on tendencies in the U.S. to use domestic law for the regulation of international relations see N. Krisch, 'More Equal than the Rest? Hierarchy, Equality and US Predominance in International Law', in: M. Byers & G. Nolte eds., *United States Hegemony and the Foundations of International Law* 135 (M.Byers & G.Nolte eds. 2003).

York law a good law to govern their claims.[106] Indeed some might argue that it is still unclear whether US courts systematically disadvantage foreigners, and that unlike global courts at least U.S. courts have sufficient experience and pedigree to be predictable and reasonably trustworthy. In any event the *Yahoo!* case has shown that the advent of globalization has suddenly enabled other courts to act as world courts, too. Just as US courts may set out to be 'a forum for the world, in return 'all the world's a forum'[107] over US actors and corporations. The criticism of the French court as setting out to 'bind the world'[108] mirrors the criticism otherwise directed against the U.S: the arrogation of a position as a world court. U.S. courts may become world courts, but they are unlikely to be the only ones.

4.3   Collaboration

If conflicts between courts look unattractive and world courts cannot be established, the alternative might be to support collaboration between courts. Several legal instruments are already in place to enable such collaboration.[109] In addition, academics like Annemarie Slaughter support the idea of a freestanding collaboration of courts around the world,[110] perhaps in the hope of bringing about some kind of world common law. Such collaboration may hold promise for some areas, but it is unlikely to avoid the perils of territoriality – first because collaborating courts will still be territorial, and second because collaboration alone will not overcome disagreements. The *Yahoo!* case reveals a difference between the United States and France over the relative weight of free speech on the one hand and the fight against racism on the other. Better communication between U.S. and French courts would not, in all likelihood, have helped here.

---

106   Jack B. Weinstein, 'Mass Tort Jurisdiction and Choice of Law in a Multinational World Communicating by Extraterrestrial Satellites', 37 Willamette L. Rev. (2000), 145. *Cf.* the criticism by A. T. von Mehren, 'American Conflicts Law at the Dawn of the 21st Century', 37 Willamette L. Rev. (2000) 133, 139 et seq.
107   The National Law Forum, Feb 11, 2002.
108   Supra n. 67.
109   See D. McClean, *International Co-Operation in Civil and Criminal Matters* (Oxford University Press, 2002). However, their importance may be diminishing; see, e.g., P. J. Borchers, 'The Incredible Shrinking Hague Evidence Convention', 38 Tex. Int'l L. J (2003) 73-85.
110   A. Slaughter, 'Court to Court', 92 Am. J. Int'l L. (1998) 708-712; A. Slaughter, 'Judicial Globalization', 40 Va. J. Int'l L. (2000) 1103-1124; see also Basedow (supra n.101) for collaboration on antitrust matters.

4.4   Re-territorialization

A fourth possibility is gaining more and more prominence: re-territorialization[111]. Globalization and with it the transmutation of territoriality is not an unalterable development. If globalization makes our concepts of jurisdiction look old-fashioned, maybe we should not alter jurisdiction but do away with globalization. The Yahoo! litigation provides a good example: Yahoo argued that there was no software which allowed them effectively to restrict access to their websites. Yet China for example controls web access of its citizens by controlling the servers and is thus able to filter out any unwanted content.[112] Moreover, software exists for private users like corporations which may help limit access territorially.[113] The long-term effect of judgments like the one by the Paris court might be that they serve as strong incentives for the development of such software.

If such software is indeed developed, the internet could be compartmentalized, re-territorialized – it would no longer be ubiquitous but would be bound to traditional concepts of territory.[114] Indeed, Lawrence Lessig, among others, has long argued that the internet is by no means anarchical by nature, but instead structured by its code which functions like an architecture.[115] He claims in a recent book that much of the early freedom and innovation of the internet is indeed in danger from a restructuring of the internet, although he blames not states but corporations.[116]

Indeed, the problem with re-territorialization is perhaps no longer whether it is possible – it might well be – but whether it is desirable.[117] The internet is attractive, to a large extent, precisely because it can transcend nation-

---

111   Jonathan Zittrain, 'Be Careful What You Ask For: Reconciling a Global Internet and Local Law', in: *Who Rules the Net?*, 13 (Adam Thierer and Wayne Crews, eds., 2003).

112   See Jonathan Zittrain & Benjamin G. Edelman, *Internet Filtering in China*, Harvard Law School, Public Law Working Paper No. 62 (2003).

113   One company developing such software is InfoSplit. See <http://www.infosplit.com> (advertising 'We know where your customers are'). Liquid Audio, a music distribution company, alleges to hold a patent titled 'Territorial Determination of Remote Computer Location in a Wide Area Network for Conditional Delivery of Digitized Products' and has sued Infosplit for patent violation in the U.S. District Court for the Northern District of California; see *Liquid Audio sues over tracking patent violation*, <http://news.com.com/2100-1023-941272.html>.

114   See 'The Revenge of Geography', *The Economist*, March 15, 2003. A similar re-compartmentalization of world markets into national markets is imaginable (although perhaps less likely).

115   Lawrence Lessig, *Code and other Laws in Cyberspace* (1999).

116   Lawrence Lessig, *The Future of Ideas* (2001); see already James Boyle, 'Foucault in Cyberspace: Surveillance, Sovereignty, and Hard-Wired Censors', 66 U. Cin. L. Rev. (1997) 177, also at <http://www.law.duke.edu/boylesite/foucault.htm>.

117   Another question is, of course, to what extent the internet still conforms to some extent to national borders anyway. A recent empirical study claims that it does, based on the finding that most web sites only link to other websites hosted in the same country. See Alexander Halavais, 'National Borders on the World Wide Web', 2 *New Media & Society* (2000) 7-28.

al boundaries. Re-territorializing software would take away this advantage and thereby disappoint some of the biggest hopes set in the internet. Similarly, there is a strong interest in international trade now, which would be seriously hampered by re-territorialization. Control of both the internet and of world market will likely take place. It remains to be seen if such control is possible under traditional territorial concepts without destroying the very object of control.

4.5   Re-conceptualizing territory

A fifth possible answer is the re-conceptualization of territory. It was said earlier that topological space is only one of several kinds of space, that non-topological spaces shape human interactions in often more important ways. Jurisdiction could utilize these concepts of space and enrich its own territorial concepts with them. Jurisdiction would no longer (only) be based on location within topological space, but on location within a social space, within certain patterns of interactions, certain communities.[118] Such jurisdiction would not even have to be state jurisdiction – arbitration within specific business communities is, arguably, a kind of non-territorial (in the classical sense) jurisdiction.

In addition virtual space could be accepted as a territory with its own jurisdiction and its own law.[119] In fact such a conception might provide a solution for both the Yahoo case and the e-commerce problem. One could conceive of particular rules of speech for the internet, enforceable through its technological filtering features – or through the internet community. Likewise, it is conceivable to establish some kind of internet jurisdiction to deal with problems of e-commerce, so that neither seller nor buyer would have to travel to meet the other. Online arbitration is one possibility, another is the uses of credit card companies as de facto arbitrators through credit card charge back mechanisms.[120] Non-state solutions are harder imaginable to deal with questions of market domination: they would lack powers of direct enforcement.

Such approaches show that creativity may lead away not only from territoriality, but also from state courts for the decision of disputes in globalization. Some such solutions may be promising. Others may be too idealistic. (Neti-

---

118   Such a community-based approach is proposed by *Berman* (supra n. 13).

119   See David R. Johnson & David G. Post, 'Law and Borders – The Rise of Law in Cyberspace', 48 Stan. L. Rev. 1367(1996); D. G. Post, 'Against "Against Cyberanarchy"-<http://www.law.berkeley.edu/journals/btlj/articles/vol17/Post.stripped.pdf>, also in: Who rules the Net 71 (supra n.111) responding to Goldsmith (supra n. 62).

120   E.g. J. Arsic, 'International Commercial Arbitration on the Internet: Has the Future Come too Early?', 14 J. of Int'l Arb. (1997) 209-221; A.E. Almaguer & W. Baggott III, 'Shaping New Legal Frontiers: Dispute Resolution for the Internet', 13 Ohio St. J. on Disp. Resol. (1998) 711; J. Rothchild,'Protecting the digital consumer: the limits of cyberspace utopianism', 74 Ind. LJ (1999) 893; K. Stewart, 'Online Arbitration of Cross-Border, Business to Consumer Disputes', 56 U. Miami L. Rev. (2002), 1111, all with further references.

quette as a substitute for law on the web has proved to be an illusion). What gives reason for concern, however, is that they are still based on conceptions of territory, or of community. Jurisdiction in virtual space may make sense for fact-patterns confined to this space, but it does not take care of cases arising on the borderline between territories (real or virtual). There are conflicts that are not situated within one community or the other, but which take place between communities. It is hard to see how jurisdiction based on any conception of territory can deal with such places. Re-conceptualizing territory does not abolish conflicts; at best it can make some situations easier to deal with in.

4.6   *Doing away with territory*

The last solution may sound the most radical. If territory bothers us in jurisdiction, maybe we should just do away with it and base jurisdiction on other, non-territorial, considerations. Such considerations already permeate the law as additional factors. The requirement of intent for jurisdiction in defamation could be a move in this direction[121], as long as intent is stripped from territorial direction and instead serves as an independent justification why it is fair to establish jurisdiction over the defendant. The fairness prong of the 'minimum contacts'[122] test is another example, insofar as it focuses on fairness to the defendant, a concept much broader than territory. In fact it might be possible to establish fairness not just as a limitation of territorial jurisdiction, but instead as an independent basis of jurisdiction, where territory – inconvenience of travel, etc. – only appears as one of several factors relevant for fairness. State interests could enter the considerations as well, but perhaps they could be stripped of territorial overtones as well. Ultimately, such a concept of jurisdiction could account for territorial consideration where they still play a role, but it would no longer have to be based on territory as its foundation.

Indeed, some claim that fairness has already supplanted territory as the basis for jurisdiction. However, it is unlikely that it is possible, at least for state and national courts, to do away with territory altogether. The reason lies in what was said in the beginning: Courts, as emanations of state power, are inseparably linked to territory, just as the state is necessarily defined through its territory. Completely non-territorial bases for jurisdiction may be possible for non-state jurisdiction (and in fact situations with little or no territorial basis may be better dealt with in such non-state courts). Jurisdiction by state courts without a territorial basis, however, seems inconceivable.

---

121   Supra n. 40.
122   Supra n. 42.

5   CONCLUSION

It is, of course, too early to tell how theory and practice of jurisdiction will develop. The responses to the transmutation of territoriality proposed here are still rough and abstract, and some may prove unworkable in practice. In addition, whether the problems of contemporary jurisdictional thought are really so fundamental as to require a rethinking of basic concepts may also be put into question. Perhaps territoriality is more resistant than is argued here; perhaps it will carry the day. But it seems unlikely that we can take our traditional concepts of territorial jurisdiction for granted as before. We must challenge the very foundations of our thinking about jurisdictions before we can assess whether those foundations are still appropriate for our era of globalization, and we should think seriously about radical alternatives before we feel safe either to return to what we know, or to rebuild it to face the future.

Globalisation and antitrust litigation: Are the U.S. jurisdictional boundaries sensible, mercantilist or just random?

W. Todd Miller and Donald I. Baker

1   INTRODUCTION

Global business activities flow across national borders swiftly and on an increasing scale, generating consequences that may be injurious or controversial in several (or many) different jurisdictions, each with its own sets of legal rules and judicial systems. Increasingly, this reality has caused national sovereigns to assert jurisdiction over foreign activities that produced domestic effects.

This trend gathered momentum during the 20th century, as the international economy became more interdependent and complex. A hundred years ago the general assumption was that jurisdiction was based entirely on the situs of the wrongful conduct. This view was reflected in a landmark antitrust decision by the U.S. Supreme Court written by that celebrated American jurist, Oliver Wendell Holmes, who wrote: '[t]he general and almost universal rule is that the character of an act is lawful or unlawful must be determined wholly by the law of the country where the act is done.' *American Banana Co* v. *United Fruit Co.*, 213 U.S. 347 (1909). Because Costa Rica had no law against monopolies, there would be no legal remedy against monopolistic acts in Costa Rica that allegedly restricted the supply of bananas flowing into the U.S. market and thereby injuring U.S. consumers. See also *Laker Airways, Ltd.* v. *Sabena, Belgian World Airlines*, 731 F.2d 909, 921 (D.C. Cir. 1984) ('the territorial base of jurisdiction is universally recognized. It is the most pervasive and basic principle underlying the exercise by nations of prescriptive regulatory power').

This result proved unsatisfactory to the U.S. government and ultimately to the U.S. courts. Thus, the U.S. Department of Justice ('DOJ') brought a series of cases that were to dispatch the 'territorial' rule of *American Banana* to the dustbin and substitute the initially-controversial 'effects' doctrine in its place. See especially *United States* v. *Sisal Sales Corp.*, 274 U.S. 268 (1927); *United States* v. *Aluminum Co. of America* 148 F.2d 416, 444 (2nd Cir. 1945) ('*Alcoa*'). These decisions authorized U.S. courts to apply U.S. antitrust law and exercise jurisdiction over offshore activities by foreign parties that produced adverse competitive effects within the United States. This 'effects' doctrine produced decades of acrimonious controversy with foreign sovereigns that clung to 'territorial' principles and insisted that the U.S. was interfering with their sovereign prerogatives to regulate their nationals in their domestic markets. The controversies were particularly acute with the leading common-law countries – the U.K., Canada, and Australia – but were not confined to them.[1]

It is perhaps not surprising that competition law should have been the focal point of so much jurisdictional controversy. First, antitrust involves a system on how markets should be regulated – an intensely political subject – and for much of the 20th century most other countries did not share the American enthusiasm for letting free-market principles and courts police the operation of the markets, rather than entrusting these matters to bureaucrats, politicians, and administrators. Second, the U.S. applied the criminal law and its secretive grand jury system to many antitrust violations, including agreements by foreign enterprises not to compete in the U.S. market.

The U.S. also authorized private parties (and state attorneys general) to enforce the antitrust laws based on competitive injury to themselves (or their constituents); and these diverse plaintiffs often proved much more aggressive in challenging activities by national champions, and foreign enterprises generally. See, e.g., *Hartford Fire Insurance Co.* v. *California.* 509 U.S. 764 (1993) (*'Hartford Fire'*), *Laker Airways*, 731 F.2d 909, *In re Uranium Antitrust Litigation*, 617 F.2d 1248 (7th Cir. 1980); and *National Bank of Canada* v. *Interbank Card Assn.*, 666 F.2d 6 (2d Cir. 1981). Foreign plaintiffs have been entirely willing to use the more favorable U.S. antitrust rules and private remedies against their foreign rivals back home (as in *Laker Airways, National Bank of Canada*, and *Consolidated Gold Fields* v. *Minorco, S.A.*, 871 F.2d 252 (2d Cir. 1989)). Some of these private cases in the U.S. have generated serious political and diplomatic controversies and, in response, various foreign parliaments enacted 'blocking statutes' in the 1970s and 1980s to prevent discovery and enforcement of private antitrust judgments without consent of the foreign government. See, e.g., Protection of Trading Interests Act of 1980 (1980 ch.11, U.K.). The U.K., Canada, and Australia were in the forefront of this obstructionist movement.

Criminal sanctions against cartels and private remedies against antitrust wrongdoing have become increasingly common (as illustrated by recent legislation in the U.K. and Ireland). Jurisdiction based on an 'effects' test is now widely accepted in principle, although particular applications may prove controversial (as well illustrated by the EU rejection of the GE-Honeywell merger involving two U.S. companies with global operations).

At the same time, greater harmonization in substantive principles, jurisdiction, and private enforcement has not put the whole subject of antitrust jurisdiction to rest. At one time, the question was 'can the U.S. exercise jurisdiction over this foreign activity?' Today, the question is much more *'where should antitrust jurisdiction be exercised*, given the increasing exercise of jurisdiction by various nations over competition law violations?' Or 'how do we avoid extensive *duplicative litigation* in the competition law area?' This whole issue is in fact highlighted by the recently enacted European Union Modernization Reg-

---

1   See generally Joseph P. Griffin, 'Foreign Governmental Reactions to U.S. Assertions of Extraterritorial Jurisidiction', 6 Geo. Mason L. Rev. 505 (1998).

ulation, which will generate a lot of competition law litigation – and potential duplication – in the national courts of the European Union, and the just-enacted U.K. Enterprise Act which has created new private remedies for competition law violations in a major member state.

The United States continues to do its bit to generate controversy and confusion in this whole area – which we propose to explore in this paper. The confusion results from the practical consequences of some fairly obvious political and practical factors. *Firstly,* the basic idea of 'effects' based jurisdiction is politically attractive, because it involves a sovereign protecting its consumers (and maybe its enterprises) against offshore misdeeds that are allegedly injuring them. *Secondly,* the U.S. business community has long felt that U.S.-based enterprises were placed at a competitive disadvantage vis-a-vis foreign competitors because they were subject to a more vigorous antitrust system than existed in most foreign countries – which has generated some less-than-clear U.S. legislation to exclude some overseas activities from the U.S. antitrust laws. *Thirdly,* the U.S. is overwhelmingly the forum of choice for any antitrust plaintiff who thinks he might be able to satisfy whatever jurisdictional nexus is required to bring a case in the U.S. courts under the U.S. antitrust laws; this occurs because the U.S. (a) awards mandatory treble damages and attorneys fees as bounties to encourage suits, (b) allows class actions, (c) imposes joint and several liability on the defendants (without rights of contribution), (d) provides for certain evidentiary shortcuts where the U.S. government has obtained a judgment or plea against the defendant, (e) permits wide-ranging and disruptive discovery, and (f) has a huge cadre of experienced plaintiffs' antitrust lawyers ready, willing and able to leap promptly on any promising litigation opportunity, often on a contingency basis. This combination of factors is producing a rising tide of private antitrust cases testing when, where and whether the U.S. 'effects' doctrine is to be applied in particular circumstances involving overseas activities.

Our principal focus is on the application of the 'effects test' in 'non-import' cases. Where the conduct was part of a scheme to limit imports into the United States in any fashion, the jurisdictional issues seem somewhat clearer. Where, however, the plaintiffs are not suing for 'foreign commerce' antitrust violations concerning imports, the jurisdictional approach becomes cloudier and the policy questions broader. Numerous works analyze the extraterritorial application of U.S. jurisdiction in the antitrust field.[2] Rather than simply repeat and update these works, and in an effort to develop on the Europa Instituut's work in Palo Alto in 2001, we thought it might be useful to break down the cases and to analyze the policy implications of the exercise of jurisdiction by examining a handful of key factors that are and/or should be part of the analysis.

---

2   See, e.g., Andreas F. Lowenfeld, 'Conflict, Balancing of Interests, and the Exercise of Jurisdiction to Prescribe: Reflections on the Insurance Antitrust Case', 89 Am. J. Int'l L. 42, 52 (1995).

2   THE TERRITORIAL DILEMMA

Territory has been an important factor in determining jurisdiction to regulate economic activities, and a territorial nexus was easier to define and analyze in the traditional commercial world in which goods and physical documents were transported from place to place. The main bases for territorial jurisdiction rested on (i) where the challenged conduct was perpetrated and (ii) where it had a significant effect. U.S. antitrust jurisprudence has embraced both approaches – indeed it pioneered the 'effects' doctrine – generating both controversy and some confusion in the process.

Today, in a globalized economy, there are many more faraway (and often intangible) activities that have some *causal connection* with the U.S. domestic market or the interests of U.S.-based enterprises. Where that connection includes some adverse effect on competition, then quite varied issues of antitrust jurisdiction come into play. Some of these issues are quite old, some relatively new.

Before turning to them, we first look at how the U.S. has developed its approach to extra-territorial jurisdiction.

2.1   *Effects on the U.S. domestic market: Local cases and import cases*

When a case involves purely domestic commerce (*e.g.*, a price-fixing case involving U.S. companies directed at U.S. consumers), the jurisdictional standard is relatively straightforward – there simply must be an 'effect on interstate commerce' in order to satisfy the jurisdictional requirements that create a controversy under federal law. See, *e.g.*, *McLain* v. *Real Estate Bd. of New Orleans*, 444 U.S. 232 (1980).[3]

Given the statutory language of the Sherman Act (the principal competition law statute), there is no reason to think that the jurisdictional requirements for international cases should be different.[4] Nonetheless, there have been varied interpretations about what constituted 'trade or commerce . . . with foreign nations' sufficient to invoke the Act when the allegedly illegal activity has taken place outside of the United States. See *Dee-K Enterprises, Inc.* v. *Heveafil Sdn. Bhd*, 299 F.3d 281 (4th Cir 2002), *cert. denied*, 123 S.Ct. 2638 (2003).

---

3   Even so, the *McLain* case has generated considerable confusion over the precise dimensions of the test. See, e.g., *Summit Health* v. *Pinhas* 500 U.S. 332 (1990).

4   Section 1 of the Sherman Act, for example, declares illegal 'every contract, combination . . . or conspiracy, in restraint of trade or commerce among the several States, or with foreign nations'. 15 U.S.C. § 1.

Indeed, it is not an unimportant question to wonder why such different jurisdictional standards have evolved.[5]

As might be expected, the different standards evolved because of early discomfort with an assertion of jurisdiction on anything other than a strict territorial basis. See, *e.g.*, *American Banana*, 213 U.S. 347 (1909). While subsequent cases eroded this 'territoriality' rule (*e.g.*, *United States* v. *American Tobacco Co.*, 221 U.S. 106 (1911); *United States* v. *Pacific & Arctic Ry. & Navigation Co.*, 228 U.S. 87 (1913); *United States* v. *Sisal Sales Corp.*, 274 U.S. 268 (1927)), the legal damage was done – even *per se* illegal agreements to restrain trade directed at the United States were treated differently if conceived and implemented outside the U.S. than if inside the U.S.

Judge Hand's famous decision in *Alcoa* holding that the Sherman Act reaches actions abroad by foreign companies 'if they were intended to affect imports and did affect them' did not reconcile the divergent paths. See *Alcoa*, 148 F.2d at 444. Nor was this difference addressed when the Supreme Court reiterated the *Alcoa* effects test in the *Hartford Fire* decision and explained that the 'Sherman Act applies to foreign conduct that was meant to produce and did in fact produce some *substantial* effect in the United States.' See *Hartford Fire*, 509 U.S. at 796 (emphasis added). *Hartford Fire* involved domestic U.S. insurance coverages written at Lloyds and with other foreign insurers and reinsurers, and the case focused on an alleged agreement – clearly directed at the United States – not to provide reinsurance for certain kinds of liability risks. It is thus essentially an 'import' case involving a market in which entirely-foreign enterprises were and are important players.

We therefore essentially have three jurisdictional standards to contend with in any given case. First is the standard for domestic commerce (discussed above). Plaintiffs in international antitrust cases will often contend that their particular case should be governed by those standards because they are easier to meet. See, *e.g.*, *Kruman* v. *Christie's International PLC*, 284 F.3d 384 (2ⁿᵈ Cir. 2001). Second is the standard applied to import commerce which has been laid out by *Alcoa* and refined in *Hartford Fire*. See also U.S. Dept. of Justice & Federal Trade Comm., Guidelines for International Operations (1995) (hereinafter, *'International Guidelines'*), at 3.11; *Turicentro, S.A.* v. *American Airlines, Inc.*, 303 F.3d 293, 303 (3d Cir. 2002) (law distinguishes between conduct that 'involves' import commerce and conduct that 'affects' such commerce). Putting aside the philosophical question about why have a different standard for 'foreign

---

5   Why, for example, treat a price-fixing agreement that admittedly was not implemented or had no effect (see, e.g., *United States* v. *Socony-Vacuum Oil Co.*, 310 U.S. 150, 224 n.59 (1940) ('agreement' to fix price is illegal; effect not relevant to legality) as a Sherman Act violation, but not an agreement that clearly limits competition but has a less than 'substantial effect' on the U.S. domestic market? Cf. Restatement (Third) of Foreign Relations Law § 415(a) (1987) (for subject-matter jurisdiction in antitrust cases, requiring only 'principal purpose to effect the U.S. market' rather than having a substantial effect on the U.S. market).

commerce' at all, the issues that the *Hartford Fire* standard raises, while varied, seem relatively straightforward. Does the case involve 'import' commerce? Was the conduct meant to produce an adverse effect in the U.S.? Was that effect substantial? See *Dee-K Enterprises*, 299 F.3d at 287. Third, what is the standard for 'foreign commerce' that involves neither 'import' nor 'domestic' commerce? This is a subject that we now turn to in some detail.

2.2   *Effects on 'foreign commerce' that is not import or domestic commerce*

The open-ended language of the Sherman Act about 'restraint of trade or commerce...with foreign nations' certainly was broad enough to cover various restraints involving *U.S. export commerce*. Despite a perception that U.S. companies were disadvantaged by countries that failed to prosecute local cartels that could boycott U.S. goods, there were no export cases to be found. The U.S. cases that involved exports were cartel market division cases in which the U.S. enterprise agreed not to export to a foreign country in return for that country's enterprise(s) agreeing not to export to the U.S. See, e.g., *Timken Roller Bearing Co v. United States*, 341 U.S. 593 (1951). The only 'non-domestic/non-import' case that showed up was *Pacific Seafarers, Inc. v. Pacific Far East Line*, 404 F.2d. 804 (D.C. Cir. 1968), *cert. denied*, 393 U.S. 1093 (1969). At the same time, non-U.S. plaintiffs appeared to be using the U.S. courts to address injuries caused outside the U.S. to their home markets. See, e.g., *National Bank of Canada*, 666 F.2d 6.

It was all the debate about export and overseas restraints that Congress set out to fix when they passed the Foreign Trade Antitrust Improvements Act of 1982 ('FTAIA'), 15 U.S.C. § 6a. This Act was passed to reduce uncertainty and risks that U.S. firms said that they faced competing abroad. As reflected in the House of Representatives Report on the legislation, the FTAIA was designed to 'establish that restraints on export trade only violate the Sherman Act if they have a direct and substantial effect on commerce within the United States or on a domestic firm competing for foreign trade.' H.R. Comm. on the Judiciary, H.R. Rep. No. 686, 97th Cong., 2d Sess. 7-8 (1982). The Act itself provides, in relevant part:

> The [Sherman Act] shall not apply to conduct involving trade or commerce (other than import trade or import commerce) with foreign nations unless:
> (1) such conduct has a direct, substantial, and reasonably foreseeable effect:
>
> (A) on trade or commerce which is not trade or commerce with foreign nations, or on import trade or import commerce with foreign nations; or
> (B) on export trade or export commerce with foreign nations, of a person engaged in such trade or commerce in the United States; and
>
> (2) such effect gives rise to a claim under the provisions of [Section 1 or 2 of the Sherman Act] other than this section.

> If this Act applies to such conduct only because of the operations of paragraph (1)(B), then this Act shall apply to such conduct only for injury to export business in the United States.[6]

The FTAIA has justified limits on U.S. jurisdiction in cases involving predominantly foreign activities. In one of the early cases interpreting the Act, *Eurim-Pharm* v. *Pfizer, Inc.*, 593 F. Supp. 1102 (S.D.N.Y. 1984), the court held that the plaintiff had failed to establish that defendant Pfizer's foreign price-fixing and market allocation scheme had resulted in a sufficient effect on U.S. commerce to justify jurisdiction. There, Pfizer had issued exclusive licenses to foreign drug manufacturers for an antibiotic. The licensees agreed to engage in what was tantamount to resale price maintenance and other restrictive practices with respect to distributors outside the United States. Because the plaintiff had failed to (and could not) allege any effect on U.S. commerce arising from this conduct, the court declined to accept jurisdiction. Id. at 1106.[7]

The FTAIA was helpful (as in *Pfizer*) in eliminating risks to U.S. enterprises of being charged with Sherman Act violations where it was reasonably clear that the alleged restraint was not directed and did not effect the U.S. These matters would be left to the foreign antitrust authorities and courts.

At the same time, the Act left open a serious collection of questions where the facts were mixed – these have tended to involve *horizontal restraint and cartel cases* where there is at least some activity and general effect in the U.S.:

(1) Can a foreign purchaser from a participant in a global cartel that affected the U.S. market sue on a purchase that was executed entirely abroad? If so, does it make any difference whether the seller or buyer acting abroad was a U.S. enterprise?

(2) If members of an international cartel hold illegal meetings in the U.S. is that sufficient to support U.S. jurisdiction over all transactions affected by those meetings?

(3) Can a U.S. purchaser sue a foreign company that had never sold in the U.S. on proof of an agreement between this company and U.S. sellers that it would stay out of the U.S. market? If so, would the plaintiff have to show that the foreign company would have made sufficient U.S. sales to affect U.S. market prices?

(4) Can the participants in a largely foreign cartel directed at foreign domestic markets be sued for Sherman Act violations if a U.S. plaintiff can only show a less than substantial effect on the U.S. market?

---

6   15 U.S.C. § 6a. See also 15 U.S.C. § 45(a)(3) (for the FTAIA's similar limitation on FTC jurisdiction under Section5 of the Federal Trade Commission Act).

7   See also *McGlinchy* v. *Shell Chemical Co.*, 845 F.2d 802 (9th Cir. 1988); *McElderry* v. *Cathay Pacific Airways, Ltd.*, 678 F. Supp. 1071 (S.D.N.Y. 1988); *The In Porters, S.A.* v. *Hanes Printables, Inc.*, 663 F. Supp. 494 (M.D.N.C. 1987); *Liamuiga Tours* v. *Travel Impressions, Ltd.*, 617 F. Supp. 920 (E.D.N.Y. 1985). This approach was recently confirmed in *Turicentro*, 303 F.3d 293, where the Third Circuit declined jurisdiction over an alleged price-fixing agreement implemented in the U.S. to lower the commissions earned by travel agents in certain countries outside the U.S.

(5) Can a U.S.-based exporter sue a group of foreign wholesalers who agree
     not to handle imports?

These are not fanciful examples. Number 1 is very much like the *Kruman* case
from the Second Circuit and the *Empagran* case from the D.C. Circuit. Number
3 is similar to *Statoil* from the Fifth Circuit, while Number 4 resembles somewhat *Dee-K Enterprises* from the Fourth Circuit. Example 5 sounds a lot like
some of the allegations made by Eastman Kodak in the *Japanese Film Case* that
was brought before the U.S. Trade Representative and the WTO. We shall discuss these in Part C below. As we shall see, the courts are having a difficult
time drawing clear and principled lines through this maze, and the U.S.
Supreme Court has now agreed to review this area by accepting *certioriari* in
the *Empagran* case.

3   Sorting through the confusion

One thing is absolutely clear: the lower courts are having a very difficult time
sorting their way through the FTAIA and conflicts among different courts of
appeals are clear. Congress clearly intended to spare U.S. firms from antitrust
suits for their overseas activities that did not affect the U.S. market, while also
preserving a remedy against those restraining U.S. exporters – but leaving foreign governments to protect their consumers. However, the words and concepts that Congress selected for these limited purposes have generated a lot of
confusion in other circumstances, often involving rather large stakes.
      We propose here to review briefly some of the circumstances giving rise to
litigation and confusion and then, in Part VI to try to suggest some ordering
principles.

3.1   *Foreign purchasers from member of a global cartel*

Where there is a global cartel to fix prices or allocate customers, the foreign
purchasers would generally prefer to sue the cartel members in the U.S. rather
than in their home courts, even where private remedies are available at home.
They thus get the benefit of automatic treble damages, joint and several liability, and a one-way rule on attorneys' fees. Whether the FTAIA prevents such
plaintiffs from suing is a rather large question, given the high proportion of
foreign sales in such international cartel cases as *Vitamins, Lysine,* and *Art Auctions.*
      The issue had been squarely raised by the *Art Auction* cartel, but a settle-
ment left the ultimate legal outcome uncertain. *Kruman* v. *Christie's International plc* involved a class action by plaintiffs who purchased and sold art outside
the United States. Four of the plaintiffs were U.S. nationals and four were foreign. They alleged that defendants, Sotheby's and Christie's auction houses,
agreed to fix their buyer's premiums and seller's commissions on sales out-

side of the United States.[8] The lower court had dismissed this claim on the ground that the FTAIA required the plaintiffs to show that their injury was a result of the effect on U.S. commerce.

The Second Circuit reversed. It found that the FTAIA did not change prior case law, which required a showing of injury to U.S. commerce,[9] but did not add to the Sherman Act a requirement that plaintiff's injury stem from the injury to U.S. commerce. The essence of the Second Circuit's holding was that, if there were a conspiracy that injured both U.S. and foreign purchasers, then the foreign purchasers could sue in the U.S. courts despite their own lack of injury in the U.S. The court brushed aside concerns that its decision would allow foreign plaintiffs to bring cases based on injury outside the U.S.: plaintiffs still must show that the alleged violation of the U.S. antitrust laws causes an injury to U.S. commerce through an anticompetitive effect or by making possible anticompetitive acts directed at domestic commerce. The court added that the FTAIA itself severely limits the reach of the antitrust laws because in such cases, the 'effect' on the U.S. of the conduct still must be 'direct, substantial, and reasonably foreseeable'.

The same issue has arisen even more recently in the massive *Vitamins* litigation. On January 17, 2003, the Court of Appeals for the District of Columbia Circuit overturned the District Court's rejection of a class action on behalf of foreign vitamins purchasers. *Empagran S.A.* v. *F. Hoffman-LaRoche, Ltd.*, 2003 WL 131804 (D.C.Cir. 2003)('*Empagran*'). As in *Kruman*, the panel split 2-1. The majority said:

> ...the question is whether FTAIA precludes actions under the Sherman Act unless a plaintiff shows that the injuries it seeks to remedy arise from the anticompetitive effects of the defendant's conduct on U.S. commerce; or, alternatively, is it enough for a plaintiff to show that anticompetitive effects of the defendant's conduct on U.S. commerce give rise to an antitrust claim under the Sherman Act by *someone*, even if not the plaintiff who is before the court. (emphasis added)

The court concluded that the latter approach (not requiring plaintiffs to show that their injury was in U.S. commerce) was the better approach. After extensive review of the legislative history in an effort to parse the language of the statute, the court's holding was largely based on policy grounds related to deterrence. In the court's view, the members of a global cartel were more likely to be deterred if they knew that private plaintiffs could recover treble damages for both domestic and foreign sales. Quoting *Kruman*, the majority concluded that in these circumstances: '[o]ur markets can benefit from the additional deterrence of conduct affecting foreign markets.' This case has been accepted by review by the U.S. Supreme Court and therefore a decision is expected by Summer 2004.

Equally interesting, but somewhat different, is the situation where the for-

---

8   A class action by domestic users of the auction services in the U.S. had been settled.
9   See *National Bank of Canada*, discussed below.

eign purchaser is suing a foreign cartel participant which did not sell in the U.S. market. This was the situation in *Dense Norske Stats Oljeselskap AS* v. *HeereMac*, 241 F.3d 420 (5th Cir.2002) (*'Statoil'*), where the Fifth Circuit (also by a 2-1 vote) held that the FTAIA barred the lawsuit by the foreign purchaser. The defendant, a foreign supplier of offshore oilfield services, had agreed as part of the cartel not to compete in the U.S. in return for the U.S. firms not competing in its home markets in the North Sea. The plaintiff, a Norwegian oil producer, sued, apparently claiming that the absence of U.S. bidders resulted in it paying higher prices to the defendant. So far as the Court of Appeals was concerned, plaintiff's injury was neither in the U.S. 'domestic' market nor a U.S. 'import' market and hence plaintiff lacked standing under the FTAIA. The plaintiff appealed to the U.S. Supreme Court, which then asked the U.S. Department of Justice for its views on the issues presented. The Department endorsed the analysis of the Fifth Circuit and the Supreme Court declined to hear the appeal.

If *Statoil* had involved a U.S. domestic purchaser of oilfield services, the result would almost certainly have been different. The domestic purchaser would argue that the cartel was depriving it of the benefit of competitive bidding by the foreign defendant. Its injury would be in U.S. 'import' commerce and hence not limited by the FTAIA. Since under U.S. law, each member of the illegal agreement can be held liable for the harm caused by all cartel members collectively, the foreign non-seller in the U.S. could be held liable for all the cartel overcharges in the U.S. 'domestic' market. Meanwhile, if *Statoil* is correct, foreign purchasers victimized by such a market allocation scheme would have to look to whatever redress their own domestic laws provide.

There seems to be a fairly clear conflict between the treatment of foreign purchasers as between *Kruman* and *Empagran* on one hand and *Statoil* on the other. In *Kruman* and *Empagran* the foreign purchasers purchased from the same sellers that were selling in the U.S. market, while in *Statoil* the foreign purchasers were purchasing from foreign enterprises that had agreed to stay out of the U.S. market as part of the cartel. It seems less than obvious that the FTAIA dictates opposite results in the two types of case. The Justice Department has endorsed the *Statoil* approach of denying foreign purchasers standing in the U.S., and apparently will do so in the *Empagran* case currently on the Supreme Court's docket.

3.2   *Domestic purchases from a foreign cartel*

Where the main impact of a foreign cartel is felt in foreign markets, the question arises whether a domestic U.S. purchaser must show a 'substantial effect' on the U.S. domestic market in order to assert jurisdiction over cartel members. This issue is raised both by the 'direct, substantial, and reasonably foreseeable effect' language in the FTAIA and the 'some substantial effect' language in *Hartford Fire*. Stated another way, does the domestic purchaser of $10 million in goods from members of a large foreign cartel face a different jurisdictional threshold than the $10 million purchaser from some local price fixers? The answer seems to be 'yes'.

As evidenced by the Fourth Circuit's decision in *Dee-K Enterprises*, the question whether a conspiracy should be treated as 'domestic' or 'foreign' can be a more difficult task than it might appear. *Dee-K Enterprises* involved a suit by two United States purchasers of rubber thread who alleged a price-fixing conspiracy by Southeast Asian thread producers. Plaintiffs' purchases were about $50 million during the conspiracy. A jury found that, although there (a) had been a conspiracy to fix rubber thread prices, which (b) was intended to affect United States commerce, (c) the conspiracy did not have a 'substantial effect' on U.S. commerce. The court thus entered judgment for defendants, and plaintiffs appealed.

On appeal to the Fourth Circuit, the plaintiffs asserted that the standard applied in domestic commerce cases was the correct jurisdictional standard because there were allegations and evidence to show that the price-fixed goods were sold directly into the U.S. The defendants sold rubber thread into the U.S. in three ways: (i) through a U.S.-based division of a defendant, (ii) directly from abroad to large customers and (iii) to smaller customers through wholly-owned subsidiaries incorporated in the United States. Notwithstanding these facts, the court suggested that there was little guidance on how to define 'foreign conduct' in this type of 'mixed fact' case for purposes of deciding which jurisdictional test to apply. It therefore reasoned that:

> a court should properly engage in a more flexible and subtle inquiry. In determining which jurisdictional test (*Hartford Fire* or *McLain*) applies, a court should consider whether the participants, acts, targets, and effects involved in an asserted antitrust violation are primarily foreign or primarily domestic

Id. at 294.

After analyzing those factors, it concluded that the rubber thread conspiracy was largely foreign, notwithstanding some U.S. activities, and that this meant that the proper test was *Hartford Fire*'s 'some substantial effect.' The Fourth Circuit specifically rejected plaintiffs' notion that sales into and among the U.S. make it a 'domestic' case as well as defendants' argument that the only relevant conduct to examine to determine whether it was 'foreign' or 'domestic' were conspiratorial meetings.[10] It therefore upheld (a) the application of the *Hartford Fire* as requiring a showing of both an intent to affect U.S. commerce and a substantial effect on that commerce and hence (b) the jury's verdict.

While the outcome seems quite strange, the court made clear that the plaintiffs 'had their day in court and it was over.' They simply failed to con-

---

10   Compare *Carpet Group Int'l* v. *Oriental Rug Importers Ass'n, Inc.*, 227 F.3d 62 (3d Cir. 2002) (finding that conspiracy was not subject to FTAIA because conduct was principally in the U.S. and was designed to limit competition from imports, but was ultimately subject to test under *McLain*; this position was supported by amicus brief from U.S. Dept. of Justice).

vince the jury of an effect that perhaps should have been obvious. The key issue that seems unclear in the *Dee-K Enterprises* case is what the 'no substantial injury' finding by the jury really means. Does it mean that no price increase in the U.S. actually occurred, or that whatever increase did occur was caused by other factors (*e.g.*, dumping orders or threats)? Or does it mean that whatever happened in the U.S. was not substantial in relation to the consequences outside the U.S.? If the answer is the former, then it means that the plaintiff simply failed to prove a necessary element of standing for private damage recovery. If it means the latter, then the decision would suggest that even the DOJ could not bring a case in the same circumstances. The latter would be a somewhat startling conclusion given what would be clearly a different result in a domestic commerce case where the Government does not have to prove that the conspiracy was effective in order to prevail. See note 3, *supra*. But see *International Guidelines* at n.16.

In any event, as the court in *Dee-K Enterprises* recognizes, the decision over how to characterize conduct (as 'foreign' or 'domestic'), which in turn determines which jurisdictional test will apply, requires a weighing of a variety of factors. This teaches that any attempt to analyze various potential jurisdictional approaches and to propose any new (perhaps simpler) approach is fraught with a strong potential to be undermined in the 'characterization' process. Given a chance to apply discretion, a court can simply characterize the conduct in a way that suits the court's belief as to the just result.

What is interesting is that all this weighing and balancing has been imported into the *jurisdictional threshold* stage of these antitrust cases rather than the *damage* phase. If, for example, the Asian rubber thread conspiracy in *Dee-K Enterprises* had no significant impact on prices in any relevant U.S. domestic market, then the plaintiffs did not pay more for rubber thread or its close substitutes than it would have absent the conspiracy and accordingly plaintiffs did not suffer antitrust injury and should not be awarded any significant damages. Instead the courts held that they lacked jurisdiction to hear plaintiffs' claim. Whether this is an important difference or not might be more important in a government criminal or injunctive case, where proof of damages is not an issue.

At the same time, it is at least interesting to note both how often courts have been unwilling to determine whether conduct would be subject to the FTAIA[11] and the types of cases that the U.S. antitrust enforcement agencies appear to characterize as 'non-domestic, non-import' commerce cases. Of the latter, the U.S. government treats a sale through a foreign intermediary as such a case. See *International Guidelines*, 3.121 Example B.

---

11   See, e.g., *Hartford Fire*, 509 U.S. 764; *Kruman*, 284 F.3d 384.

4   TRYING TO DEVELOP SOME ORDERING PRINCIPLES

The FTAIA has substantial potential to enhance the uncertainty and confusion in a world that is becoming increasingly interconnected and interdependent economically. In the Internet Age, the line between 'exports' and 'imports' is becoming ever more blurred, as is the line between 'foreign' and 'domestic' transactions and effects. The 'direct, substantial, and reasonably foreseeable effects' test is potentially useful in restraining forum shopping by those whose injuries are well-removed from the U.S.- but it only works if some reasonably clear boundaries and concepts can be defined. Finally, the 'export opportunities' provision in the Act is both novel and vague and, without reasonably defined boundaries, is likely to generate recurring conflicts with foreign governments.

This leads us to consider the factors that are important, or should be important, to any decision on the exercise of extraterritorial jurisdiction in non-import commerce cases. These factors are reflected in Table A where many of the recent cases are briefly summarized. It is worth repeating that the exercise today is less about where one can and should theoretically exercise jurisdiction. Instead, in a world where many fora may have a claim of jurisdiction over a set of conduct, the relevant question is what jurisdiction(s) is (are) the appropriate forum (fora) against relief for any particular injury to competition. In any event, one can suggest that only a couple of factors should truly matter for these purposes: obviously where the plaintiff suffered harm is far and away the most important. Beyond that, perhaps the only other factor that should receive serious attention is the location of the defendant – particularly when the alleged wrongful acts have been committed where the defendant is located. Justice dictates that where there are difficulties in obtaining personal jurisdiction over a defendant in the forum in which the plaintiff has been injured, the defendant should not be able to avoid liability simply because it is not subject to suit in that forum. In the global trading system, and as discussed below, however, such a situation should be rare.

In approaching these difficult issues, we focus here on private litigation because it is the private cases that continue to raise the hard jurisdictional issues. This occurs because the government enforcement agencies have every incentive to cooperate with each other and to defer to each other when jurisdictional issues are difficult. See, e.g., *International Guidelines* at 3.2 ('The Agencies will consider whether the objectives sought to be obtained by the assertion of U.S. law would be achieved in a particular instance by foreign enforcement'). Private plaintiffs ('private attorneys general' as they are sometimes called in the U.S. decisions) have no such incentives for restraint and will tend to push the jurisdictional envelope to the limit in order to recover in what they regard as the most advantageous forum (which, in a majority of instances, means the United States). Still, the Justice Department and the Federal Trade Commission do have a significant stake in how these private cases actually come out – because the jurisdictional limits created in such cases as *Hartford Fire* or *Dee-K Enterprises* will apply equally to government criminal or civil prosecutions. Moreover, the aggressive assertion of jurisdiction in private cases may affect (a) public policy choices made by other sovereign nations and (b) undermine efforts to bring governmental enforcement actions outside the U.S. because of concerns with being subject to suit (and hence discovery) in the United States.

With this background, let us turn to some analytical factors that appear useful.

4.1 Location of plaintiff's injury

Placing the situs of the plaintiff's injury at the center of the jurisdictional inquiry forces, at a minimum, consideration of two separate questions: relationship between the plaintiff's injury and market injury and the directness of plaintiff's injury.

4.1.1 Relation of plaintiff's injury to market injury

Under the FTAIA, it is clear that there must be an anticompetitive effect in the United States in order for any plaintiff to have a right to recover. Adverse effects on competition within foreign markets do not trigger United States antitrust jurisdiction, unless there is also some direct impact on U.S. import or export commerce or on price levels in the U.S. internal market. See, *e.g.*, *Eurim-Pharm* v. *Pfizer, Inc.*, 593 F. Supp. 1102 (S.D.N.Y. 1984).

The legislative history of the FTAIA suggests that the Act was intended to embrace the Second Circuit's analysis in *Nat'l Bank of Canada* v. *Interbank Card Ass'n*, 666 F.2d 6 (2d Cir. 1981), on this point. In that case, National Bank sued a competing Canadian bank and the U.S. Master Charge (now MasterCard) association, alleging a Sherman Act violation for refusing to license National Bank as a Master Charge issuer in Canada because it was also a Visa issuer. The Second Circuit (reversing the lower court on the law, but upholding the judgment) found that jurisdiction was lacking: '[W]e think the inquiry should be directed primarily toward whether the challenged restraint has, or is intended to have, any anticompetitive effect upon United States commerce, either commerce within the United States or export commerce from the United States.' Id. at 8 (citing Areeda and Turner, Antitrust Law (1978)). The challenged restraint concerned the membership rules of the 'MasterCharge' network in Canada. '[W]e do not see that enforcement of the agreement posed a foreseeable threat to United States commerce of a type sufficient to justify assertion of [U.S.] jurisdiction.' Id. at 9. The court applied the concept of antitrust injury[12], and held that there was no anticompetitive effect on U.S. commerce or exports. This was true because: (1) increased fees to Canadian merchants were not of direct concern to the U.S., and (2) there was no showing that U.S.

---

12   See, e.g., *Brunswick Corp.* v. *Pueblo Bowl-O-Mat, Inc.*, 429 U.S. 477, 489 (1977); and *Cargill, Inc.* v. *Monfort of Colorado, Inc.*, 479 U.S. 104 (1986).

merchants depended on Canadian banks to clear 'MasterCharge' transactions.

In adopting the FTAIA, Congress appeared to agree: 'the 'domestic effect' that may serve as the predicate for antitrust jurisdiction . . . must be of the type that the antitrust laws prohibit.' H.R. Rep. 686, at 11. This view appears to have been adopted by courts interpreting the Act. See *Liamuiga Tours*, 617 F. Supp. 920, 924 (E.D.N.Y. 1985) (act 'adopts the stricter effects test of National Bank of Canada'). But see *Hartford Fire*, 509 U.S. at 796 n.23 (with regard to FTAIA, it is unclear whether the 'direct, substantial and reasonably foreseeable effect' was a new limitation on jurisdiction or simply codified pre-existing law).

This still leaves a variety of critical questions concerning the injury requirement under the FTAIA. First is the question of whether the plaintiff's injury must stem from the adverse consequences in the United States. At present, there is a split among the U.S. courts on how to approach this question. *Kruman* and *Empagran*, allowed the plaintiffs to proceed with the litigation even though they admittedly utilized the price-fixed auction services and purchased vitamins, respectively, outside the United States on the theory that allowing such recovery would deter price fixing within the United States; but other courts have held that the plaintiff's injury must be derived from and part of the overall injury to the U.S. market. See *Statoil* and *Sniado. v. Bank of Aus. AG*, 174 F. Supp. 2d 829 (E.D. Pa. 2001). Yet another case has adopted *Kruman* to allow subject-matter jurisdiction, but denied the particular plaintiff standing because it could not show that it was either a competitor or purchaser in the U.S. market. See *Galavan Supplements v. Archer Daniels Midland Co.*, 1997 U.S. Dist. LEXIS 18585 ('herinafter '*Galavan*').

Kruman, *Empagran* and *Galavan* each involved single conspiracies with the same defendants selling to both domestic and foreign purchasers. The situation becomes more complex and tenuous where there is an international market or customer allocation that leaves the foreign purchaser suing its foreign supplier which did not make sales to customers in the U.S. This, it appears, was the situation in *Statoil*, where the Fifth Circuit had said the foreign plaintiffs lacked standing to bring an antitrust case by virtue of the FTAIA. The foreign plaintiffs sought Supreme Court review, the U.S. Solicitor General advised the Court that the Fifth Circuit decision was correct, and the Supreme Court declined to hear the case.

At the end of the day, and despite some ambiguous legislative history cited by the Second Circuit in *Kruman* and the D.C. Circuit in *Empagran*, such cases do not seem appropriate. They allow one country's litigation system to take control of the redress for harms felt in another. For those victims fortunate enough to be able to show a nexus between the illegal conduct and general harm in United States, compensation is perhaps likely. The courts of appeals in *Kruman* and *Empagran* suggest that this is desirable because it increases the deterrence of illegal cartels. Yet such a rule leaves uncompensated other antitrust violations, even where the defendants themselves are U.S. companies, if the effect in the United States is not apparent, indirect, or insignificant. This potential compensation disparity highlights a potential problem in devising a subject-matter jurisdiction rule that makes universal sense – the need to obtain personal jurisdiction over any potential defendant (discussed briefly below).

4.1.2   Directness of injury

Even putting aside the issue of the relationship between the plaintiff's injury and the effect on U.S. commerce, the plaintiff still must show either that its injury or the U.S. injury more generally is a direct result of defendant's anticompetitive activities. In non-import commerce cases, the 'directness' of injury is not assured. On the one extreme are the global conspiracy cases (like *Kruman* and *Empagran*) where there is already a clear effect in the United States and the foreign purchasers were apparently treated the same way outside the U.S. as the domestic purchasers were treated in the U.S. At the other extreme are the 'conspiracy on exports' cases, where any effect on consumers in the United States is secondary to the effect in the targeted export market. While this latter injury was addressed as one aspect of *National Bank of Canada* analysis, and thus is likely part of the jurisdictional coverage of the FTAIA, it leaves much to be desired. There is substantial room for subjective application of the statute because what one person considers 'direct' in such an ambiguous area may be considered 'indirect' by another.

The market allocation cases (such as *Statoil*) also raise a clear 'directness' issue. If the claim is based on the theory that the foreign plaintiff suffered injury in its home market because U.S. competitors agreed not to sell there, then should not the foreign plaintiff be required to show that the U.S. competitor(s) would have been likely to compete in the foreign market and on a sufficient basis to make a difference in prices and terms? The same is of course true in reverse: a U.S.-based purchaser would have to show that a market allocation scheme that obliged foreign competitors to stay out of the U.S. market was actually effective – i.e., that those who were excluded would have otherwise been likely to be significant competitors in the U.S. market. Otherwise there would be no 'direct, substantial, and reasonably foreseeable effect' on the domestic or import markets. Obviously, such a showing would be much more easily made where the market allocation agreement obliged parties to withdraw from each other's home markets.

To the extent that the U.S. antitrust agencies have focused on the 'directness' issue, their emphasis has been on foreign sales through unaffiliated intermediaries. See, e.g., *International Guidelines* at 3.121 Example B (foreign cartel members sell price-fixed products to 'an intermediary outside the United States, which they know will resell the product in the United States. The intermediary is not part of the cartel'). They have also focused on foreign cartels where there is no agreement as to members' sales into the U.S., but sales of 'excess' production at low prices affect pricing in the U.S. market. See *Ibid.*, Example C. Needless to say, these are somewhat esoteric issues.

4.1.3   The export cases

The other side of the 'effects' test is the exporter. An exporter may be 'affected' by an anticompetitive scheme to deprive it of market access to a particular country (or group of countries). Yet the 'true' victims of such an effort are the consumers in that particular country because they are denied the benefits of free and open competition. Yet when one combines traditional notions of antitrust standing and injury to most antitrust violations that an exporter may encounter,[13] there should be few situations where an exporter would be entitled to sue regardless of subject-matter jurisdiction. Such situations should be limited to group boycott or other exclusionary behavior. See, e.g., *Zenith Radio Corp.* v. *Hazeltine Research, Inc.*, 395 U.S. 100 (1969) (Canadian patent pool as foreclosing export competition from U.S. firm); *International Guidelines* at 3.122 and Examples D and E (including organization of distribution boycotts in import market); *Coors Brewing Co.* v. *Miller Brewing Co.*, 889 F. Supp. 1394 (D. Colo. 1995) (challenge to alliance between Miller and Molson which allegedly affected Coors' Canadian export opportunities sufficiently to meet FTAIA). Nonetheless, most other types of antitrust violations (including price-fixing or mergers by competitors) would not give rise to traditional antitrust standing. See, *e.g.*, *Cargill*, 479 U.S. 104 (1986).

Nonetheless, the pursuit of an antitrust lawsuit by a U.S. exporter is a difficult concept to implement appropriately – especially in circumstances where those restraining the U.S. exports are foreign companies engaged in business outside the United States. Even if personal jurisdiction can be obtained over any relevant foreign enterprises, the issue of conducting litigation and obtaining the necessary discovery and then obtaining effective relief for activities carried out by persons outside the U.S. in their own countries or elsewhere abroad is a serious challenge.[14] Perhaps for this reason, there have been few true 'export foreclosure' cases.

At the same time, an exporter may be faced with the same issue addressed in *Kruman* and *Empagran*. By ensuring that the U.S. exporter had a cause of action under the U.S. antitrust laws, Congress surely could not have meant to require the exporter to also show that the relevant U.S. market as a whole had been substantially injured. Such a requirement does not find support in the specific language of the FTAIA and indeed would not make sense since, as noted, the principal harm of a restraint on U.S. exports will be in the market(s) where the restraint exists. Imposing such a requirement would make the U.S. exporters' rights illusory. This is hardly the politically attractive solution that Congress undoubtedly had in mind in crafting the FTAIA section addressing U.S. exporters.

---

13   See discussion above.

14   It is in recognition of these practical problems that the U.S. and the EC supplemented their 1991 Cooperation Agreement to allow the use of 'positive comity'. The cases which are covered by the 'positive comity' agreement clearly include export restraint matters.

The U.S. agencies approach this issue very gingerly in the *International Guidelines*. They seem to look to 'a direct, substantial, and reasonably foreseeable effect on the exports of U.S. companies'. See 3.122 Example E. This seems to suggest some form of 'U.S. exports' market that is used for analysis. The agencies then add: 'Only if exclusion from [country] Alpha as a quantitative matter were so *de minimis* in terms of actual volume of trade that there would not be a substantial effect on U.S. export commerce would jurisdiction be lacking' under FTAIA. *Ibid*. They also emphasize that this whole area is one where the U.S. agencies are prepared to work with the appropriate foreign agency, 'if the conduct is unlawful under the importing country's antitrust law...that country's authorities...are better situated to remedy the conduct, and...they are prepared to take action that will address U.S. concerns, pursuant to their antitrust laws.' At 3.122

4.2   Nature of alleged violation

One potentially unsolvable problem stems from the differences in law around the world on the underlying substantive violation. Just as private litigants seek out the U.S. courts for access to treble damages, attorneys' fees, liberal discovery, etc., there is substantial 'arbitrage' in seeking out the most favorable substantive rules for a particular position. It is therefore no great secret that opponents of the General Electric/Honeywell transaction quickly made their way to the European Commission, where they expected and were pleased to have confirmed that the Commission would apply a somewhat different analysis to the transaction that was more likely to result in either a prohibition of the deal (which is what happened) or a more severe restructuring (which would have been achieved had GE's offer been accepted).

In those areas of the law – mergers, monopolization, vertical restraints – where there are meaningful differences in the analysis in finding a violation, is it appropriate to allow a defendant to avoid liability where the victim's country would not recognize a violation but the defendant's home country would? The Supreme Court has made clear that federal antitrust laws do not extend to protect foreign markets from anticompetitive effects and 'do not regulate the competitive conditions of other nations' economies.' *Matsushita Elec. Indus. Co. v. Zenith Radio Corp.*, 475 U.S. 574, 582, 106 S.Ct. 1348, 89 L.Ed.2d 538 (1986) (citations omitted). Hence, the stricter requirements of U.S. antitrust law generally cannot be used to impose liability unless there is an appropriate nexus with the U.S. But what about the reverse situation, where the home country would not find a violation, but the victim's country would? This latter situation is of course the essence of the history of extraterritorial jurisdiction with the U.S. both asserting jurisdiction and alleging violations where the home countries of the targets either did not recognize a violation or decided as a matter of prosecutorial discretion to ignore it. See, e.g., *United States v. Watchmakers of Switzerland Information Center, Inc.*, 133 F. Supp. 40 (S.D.N.Y. 1955) (agreement to control watch exports from Switzerland, not focused on U.S., and subject to monitoring and support of Swiss government subject to challenge in U.S.).

But such is the nature of trading around the world. Indeed, a tight focus on the location of plaintiff's injury would align rights of recovery with general compliance with the law in the jurisdiction where the putative defendant is doing business. Stated another way, when a multinational enterprise decides to do business in a particular jurisdiction (either directly or indirectly), it has the reasonable expectation that it will be subject to suit there for the harm caused in that jurisdiction. Cf. *World-Wide Volkswagen Corp.* v. *Woodson*, 444 U.S. 286, 297 (1980). An important corollary of this is that companies do not expect to be haled into courts in far-off jurisdictions where the plaintiffs have not suffered injury there. The critical question in such circumstances might be viewed as the reasonable expectation of the parties. Where the trading in a jurisdiction is indirect (i.e., through some form of intermediary), one can question whether a company reasonably expected to be subject to litigation in the jurisdiction for harm caused within that jurisdiction. This is of course ultimately a factual determination that has been often made in other contexts (e.g., assertion of personal jurisdiction) as well as under the FTAIA (which limits jurisdiction of U.S. court unless there is, among other things, a 'direct' effect on U.S. commerce). See, e.g., *United States* v. *Nippon Paper Indus. Co.*, 109 F.3d 1 (1st Cir. 1997) (applying criminal sanction of U.S. antitrust laws to cartel that sold to U.S. through intermediaries).

There seems little reason to depart from the basic focus on the situs of the plaintiff's harm even in those cases where the violation is clear and almost universally recognized, as in the cartel area. Indeed, most of the cases raising the issue of who should have access to U.S. courts have involved cartels. It is these cases where the potential for overly obvious and aggressive 'forum-shopping' is likely to take place. Many countries prohibit cartels, but not many provide the same generous relief as the United States. Hence, the U.S. is the forum of choice for plaintiffs regardless of where their harm was suffered. See discussion above regarding *Kruman*.

4.3   The personal jurisdiction problem

The somewhat ignored wild card in all of the subject-matter jurisdiction debate is personal jurisdiction.[15] It is fundamental that a putative defendant must be subject to personal jurisdiction of the court for the litigation to proceed in a common law country. See e.g., *International Shoe Co.* v. *Washington*, 326 U.S. 310 (1945). It seems well and good to limit cases to the jurisdiction(s) where the true (consumer) victims reside or engaged in the relevant transaction. But what if personal jurisdiction cannot be obtained over the defendant

---

15   In the *International Guidelines*, the U.S. government agencies simply assume that personal jurisdiction can be obtained.

in that jurisdiction? One can fairly ask why one country would want to subject its citizens to lawsuits by non-residents. But one can also ask why an antitrust violation should go unpunished simply because the perpetrator is not subject to the jurisdiction of the court.

The answer lies, of course, in the difference between the jurisdiction to prescribe versus the jurisdiction to adjudicate. But this begs the question: should the jurisdiction to prescribe differ depending on the amenability of the perpetrator to punishment elsewhere? Isn't it appropriate to allow the country in the best position to adjudicate a case to proceed?

4.4   Possible role of comity

This leads us to the notion of comity. Many of the cases at the margin (such as *Kruman*) would have, in a different time, been disposed of by the invocation of judicial comity. The most famous U.S. antitrust case on comity remains *Timberlane Lumber Co. v. Bank of America N.T.&S.A.*, 549 F.2d 597 (9th Cir. 1976), which established a set of balancing factors (the so-called '*Timberlane* factors') for exercising U.S. antitrust jurisdiction based on causation and comity considerations. This occurred in the context of an overseas production market (in Honduras) for a product which was regularly exported to the United States.[16] Since *Hartford Insurance*, however, the doctrine of comity as a basis for determining jurisdiction in the United States is severely wounded.[17] More importantly, if the focus becomes centered on situs of the plaintiff's injury, there should be little, if any, need to invoke comity – it is essentially adopted into the initial jurisdictional analysis.

5   CONCLUSION

Unless the Supreme Court clarifies this area in *Empagran* or something else is done, we will continue to faced a hodge-podge of confusing rules and different approaches to what in the end (as illustrated by Exhibit A) are similar cases in terms of key elements. But perhaps all can agree on a few key points. First,

---

16   In *Timberlane*, the Ninth Circuit ordered the trial court to conduct a balancing test to see whether, '[a]s a matter of international comity and fairness', the U.S. interest in the alleged anticompetitive conduct was sufficiently strong to justify extraterritorial jurisdiction. Prior to *Hartford Insurance*, the Tenth Circuit had also held that comity was a jurisdictional limitation on the extraterritorial scope of U.S. antitrust laws. *Montreal Trading Ltd. v. Amax Inc.*, 661 F.2d 864 (10th Cir. 1981), cert. denied, 455 U.S. 1001 (1982). Some courts accepted the *Timberlane* comity factors as a discretionary standard. *Mannington Mills, Inc. v. Congoleum Corp.*, 595 F.2d 1287 (3rd Cir. 1979); *In re Uranium Antitrust Litigation*, 617 F.2d 1248 (7th Cir. 1980); *Industrial Inv. Dev. Corp. v. Mitsui & Co.*, 671 F.2d 876 (5th Cir. 1982), vacated, 460 U.S. 1007 (1983), on remand, 704 F.2d 785 (5th Cir.), cert. denied, 464 U.S. 961 (1983).

17   *Crompton Corp. v. Clariant Corp.*, 220 F. Supp. 2d 569 (M.D. La. 2002).

the FTAIA has clearly set forth a sensible basic rule – there is no role for U.S. courts where there is no effect in the United States. Second, the effect – or at least the potential effect – in the U.S. must be 'substantial', i.e., not *de minumis*. Third, there is nothing inherently wrong with giving exporters (i.e., competitors) a cause of action when they have been excluded from a market, particularly where they may have a difficult time litigating abroad.

There are serious problems, however, as illustrated by *Dee-K, Kruman, Empagran* and *Gallavan*. There needs to be a uniform, or at least more clearly articulated, approach to decide (a) which jurisdictional standard should apply and when; and (b) the relationship of plaintiff's injury to injury in the U.S. *Dee-K* ultimately seems quite right in its application of current law. Again, it is the jury's finding that there was no substantial effect within the U.S. that seems so troubling in light of direct imports to customers and direct sales to customers through U.S. subsidiaries. On the other hand, *Kruman* seems wrong on the ultimate outcome, but *Gallavan* does not, although the court's reasoning in *Gallavan* is subject to serious question because it may be unique in finding that the standing requirements for purchasers under the Clayton Act may be limited when the purchases were not made in the U.S.

At the same time, governments are increasingly cooperating on antitrust enforcement; and there is no conceptual problem in having several government agencies bringing criminal or other penal actions against the members of a global cartel (as indeed has happened in *Lysine, Vitamins* and other recent cases). The DOJ, which had done so much to generate the historic conflicts over the 'effects' doctrine, has clearly been working hard to cooperate and coordinate with the overseas enforcers who are becoming ever more powerful and important as stronger competition laws spread in the world.

It is therefore the rise of private antitrust actions that generates much more of the intriguing problems and conflicts – and doubly so, as the DOJ's major international cartel cases have generated an expanding flow of follow-on actions involving transactions and parties from around the world and the threat of U.S. antitrust litigation may have a severe chilling effect on non-U.S. leniency programs. The U.S. Congress clearly wanted to limit the magnet of treble damages and intrusive U.S. discovery when it enacted the 'direct, substantial, and reasonably foreseeable' requirement for bringing international wrongs to U.S. courts – but it was less than clear as to the precise boundaries of what it intended. The Supreme Court somewhat (but not completely) clarified a few of the issues in *Hartford Fire* and the U.S. is thus left with a confusing body of jurisprudence as innovative plaintiffs try to squeeze through the doors of U.S. courthouses in search of the golden fleece of mandatory treble damages. Because foreign countries are increasingly offering private remedies for competition law wrongs, the case for judicial restrain by the U.S. over essentially foreign cases is becoming stronger and there is greater reason for clear and focused subject-matter jurisdiction rules.

APPENDIX – Selected FTAIA Cases

Case	Situs of Conduct	Situs of Harm	Situs of Plaintiff(s)	Situs of Defendant(s)	Situs of Plaintiff's Harm	Type of Case	Result	Status
Caribbean Broadcasting System, Inc. v. Cable & Wireless PLC, 148 F.3d 1080 (D.C. Cir. 1998)	OUS (but court found US purchasers were the targeted victims)	OUS/US	OUS	OUS	OUS	Exclusionary conduct (radio advertising)	Court found that jurisdiction appropriate because harm to plaintiff meant harm to US purchasers	No subsequent appellate history
Crompton Corp. v. Clariant Corp., 220 F. Supp. 2d 569 (MD LA 2002)	OUS	OUS/US	US	OUS	OUS/US	Cartel (monochloroacetic acid- MCAA)	It would be inappropriate to dismiss the claims for lack of subject matter jurisdiction when more jurisdictional discovery was warranted.	
Dee-K Enters. v. Heveafil Sdn. Bhd., 299 F.3d	OUS(but direct sales into US)	Intended for US, but jury found insuf-	US	OUS	OUS	Cartel (rubber thread)	No jurisdiction because the conspiracy involved pri-	*cert. denied*, 2003 U.S. LEXIS 5188

Case	Situs of Conduct	Situs of Harm	Situs of Plaintiff(s)	Situs of Defendant(s)	Situs of Plaintiff's Harm	Type of Case	Result	Status
281 (4th Cir. 2002)		ficient effect)					marily 'foreign conduct' and the conduct had no 'substantial effect' on the United States' commerce (question of which test to apply – *Hartford* or domestic case?)	(June27,2003)
Ferromin Int'l Trade Corp. v. UCAR Int'l, Inc., 153 F. Supp. 2d 700 (ED Pa 2001)	Global	Global	OUS	US/OUS	OUS/US	Cartel (graphite electrode)	No jurisdiction unless invoiced from US: Injury needed to result from US market. The motions to dismiss were granted in part (with respect to those not invoiced from US) and denied in part (with	No subsequent appellate history.

Case	Situs of Conduct	Situs of Harm	Situs of Plaintiff(s)	Situs of Defendant(s)	Situs of Plaintiff's Harm	Type of Case	Result	Status
							respect to those invoiced from US).	
Galavan Supplements v. Archer Daniels Midland Co., 1997 U.S. Dist. LEXIS 18585 (ND Cal.1997)	Global	Global	OUS (Ireland)	US	OUS	Cartel (citric acid)	Court has jurisdiction, but plaintiff lacked standing because it wasn't a competitor or consumer in US market	No subsequent appellate history.
Kruman v. Christie's Int'l Plc, 284 F.3d 384 (2d Cir. 2002)	Global	OUS	OUS	US/UK	OUS	Cartel (auction commissions)	Court has jurisdiction because there is no need to show that the 'effect' on US domestic commerce was the basis for the claim (exact opposition of *Sniado* and *statoil*)	Cert. granted; case withdrawn after settlement.
Den Norske Stats Oljesel-	Global	Global	OUS (Nor-	OUS/US	OUS (North-	Cartel (market al-	No jurisdiction because injury did	*cert. denied,* 534 U.S. 1127

Case	Situs of Conduct	Situs of Harm	Situs of Plaintiff(s)	Situs of Defendant(s)	Situs of Plaintiff's Harm	Type of Case	Result	Status
skap As v. HeereMac v.o.f., 241 F.3d 420 (5th Cir. 2001)			wegian oil co.)		sea)	location for heavy barge services)	not arise from effect on US domestic commerce	(2002)
Empagran S.A. v. F. Hoffman-Laroche, 315 F.3d 338 (DC Cir. 2003)	Global	Global	OUS	US/OUS	US/OUS	Cartel (vitamins)	Court has jurisdiction and plaintiffs have standing to sue because the conduct had requisite harm on US domestic commerce; FTAIA permits suits by foreign plaintiffs who were injured solely by that conduct's effect on foreign commerce (similar with *Kruman*)	*cert. granted,* Dkt. No. 03-724 (2003).

Case	Situs of Conduct	Situs of Harm	Situs of Plaintiff(s)	Situs of Defendant(s)	Situs of Plaintiff's Harm	Type of Case	Result	Status
Metallgesellschaft AG v. Sumitomo Corp. of Am., 325 F.3d 836 (7th Cir. 2003)	Global	Global	OUS	US/OUS	OUS	Cartel (physical copper)	Court has jurisdiction because the conduct had requisite effects in US domestic commerce and plaintiffs suffered injury as a result of physical copper transaction that took place within US of copper futures on a US exchange	Rehearing denied by, rehearing *en banc* denied by: *Metallgesellschaft AG v. Sumitomo Corp. of Am.*, 2003 U.S. App. LEXIS 10892 (7th Cir. Wis. May 28, 2003)
Turicentro, S.A. v. Am. Airlines, Inc., 303 F.3d 293 (3d Cir.,2002)	OUS	OUS	OUS	US	OUS	Cartel (airlines sales commissions)	No jurisdiction because defendants were only involved in unlawfully setting extraterritorial commission rates	No subsequent appellate history.

The treatment of the evidentiary sources of international law in U.S. Alien Tort Statute cases

Pieter H.F. Bekker[*]

1   INTRODUCTION

Public international law is perhaps nowhere more prominently featured in the modern domestic context than before U.S. courts through the application of the 'Alien Tort Statute' or 'ATS'.[1] This age-old statute vests U.S. district courts with 'original jurisdiction of any civil action by an alien for a tort only, committed in violation of the law of nations or a treaty of the United States'.[2] The Statute has been interpreted to allow non-U.S. citizens to seek civil damages in U.S. courts from defendants who commit gross violations of international law world-wide. In its application in the U.S. to the overseas conduct of mostly foreign defendants *vis-à-vis* non-U.S. plaintiffs, the Alien Tort Statute is at the apex of the phenomenon of 'globalization and jurisdiction.' As the case law that has developed under the Alien Tort Statute demonstrates, this application does not come without problems. Perhaps the most fundamental problem underlying many Alien Tort Statute complaints and rulings, especially in cases involving corporate defendants, is that they lack a complete and consistent discussion or understanding of the sources and evidence of international law, especially in connection with 'soft-law' such as United Nations resolutions. It is this problem with which this article is concerned.

We will first address the fundamental question of whether the Alien Tort Statute is a statute creating a private right of action on which aliens may rely in alleging a variety of breaches of international law before U.S. courts. After giving a brief summary of the historical background of and case law under the Alien Tort Statute pertaining to this question, we will then examine the problem of the evidence of international law, in particular that of defining violations of international law and determining whether such violations are actionable under the Alien Tort Statute. We will do so by analyzing a recent complaint and U.S. case law addressing the definition and evidentiary weight of the sources of international law. It will be shown that various complaints and decisions are fundamentally flawed in their approach to the sources of international law, thereby resulting in disturbing rulings especially in connection with suits against private companies. At the same time, there are encouraging signs that the U.S. Judiciary may finally be on track to conform to international standards for proving the status and content of international law.

[*]   The author wishes to thank Owen C. Pell of White & Case LLP for his comments and suggestions. The views expressed here are solely those of the author.
1   28 U.S.C. § 1350.
2   Idem.

2   THE HISTORY AND NATURE OF THE ALIEN TORT STATUTE: JURISDICTIONAL
           STATUTE OR PRIVATE CAUSE OF ACTION?

Although the Alien Tort Statute is often referred to as the 'Alien Tort Claims
Act,' or 'ATCA', that nomenclature is misleading because, as discussed below,
the statute only defines a jurisdictional class of cases that U.S. federal courts
may hear. It does not on its face create or imply a private right of action for violations of international law. Commentators have noted that use of the term
'ATCA' is part of a concerted effort by the plaintiffs' bar to characterize the
Alien Tort Statute as conferring a claim or private right of action.[3]

     In its first 190 years, the Alien Tort Statute was relied upon only a couple
of times. This situation changed dramatically in 1980, when the U.S. Court of
Appeals for the Second Circuit (comprising, inter alia, New York State) re-
vived the long-dormant statute by holding that jurisdiction under the Statute
should be assessed in terms of *evolving* standards of international law and
that in that particular case, deliberate torture perpetrated under the color of
law violated universally accepted rules of international law.[4] It is, however,
questionable whether the Alien Tort Statute creates federal jurisdiction over
claims that arise under international law as it has evolved since 1789, when
the Statute was passed as part of the first Judiciary Act.

     The landmark *Filartiga* decision has resulted in an explosive use of the
Alien Tort Statute in relation to a wide variety of allegations. Cases have
featured, inter alia, state-sponsored violence (especially torture),[5] religious
or ethnic persecution,[6] labor standards,[7] expropriation,[8] environmental

---

3   See C. A. Bradley, 'The Alien Tort Statute and Article III', 42 Va. J. Int'l L. 587, 587, 592
     (2002). See also *Argentine Republic* v. *Amerada Hess Shipping Corp.*, 488 U.S. 428, 432-37
     (1989) (using 'Alien Tort Statute'); *Flores* v. *Southern Peru Copper Corporation*, (2d Cir. Sept.
     2, 2003), No. 02-9008, 2003 WL 22038598 at *2 n.1 (*'Flores'*). (References to *'Flores* at * refer
     to the star-pagination of the decision available on Westlaw).
4   *Filártiga* v. *Pena-Irala*, 630 F.2d 876 (2d Cir. 1980) (*'Filártiga'*). The case arose from the death
     of the Paraguayan-Plaintiffs' son which was alleged to have resulted from his kidnapping
     and torture by the Paraguayan police. The Defendant-Paraguayan police inspector-gener-
     al, a state official, was served with notice when he visited the U.S. Reversing the lower
     court's dismissal of the case on narrow grounds, the Second Circuit held that the 'official
     torture' committed by the Paraguayan-Defendant official violated international law.
5   See, e.g., *In re Estate of Ferdinand Marcos Human Rights Litigation* 978 F.2d 493 (9th Cir. 1992)
     (*'Marcos I'*); *In re Estate of Ferdinand Marcos Human Rights Litigation* 25 F.3d 1467 (9th Cir. 1994);
     (*'Marcos II'*); *Xuncax* v. *Gramajo*, 886 F.Supp. 162 (D. Mass. 1995); *Tachiona et al.* v. *Mugabe et al.*,
     169 F.Supp.2d 259 (S.D.N.Y. 2001); idem, 2002 WL 230860 (S.D.N.Y. Feb. 14, 2002); *Wiwa* v.
     Royal Dutch Shell Petroleum Corp., 226 F.3d. 88 (2d Cir. 2001), *cert. denied*, 532 U.S. 941 (2001).
6   See, e.g., *Kadic* v. *Karadzic*, 70 F.3d 232 (2d Cir. 1995) (*'Kadic'*), *cert. denied*, 518 U.S. 1004
     (1996) (holding that Alien Tort Statute claims may be brought against private actors under
     certain circumstances).
7   See, e.g., *Deutsch* v. *Turner Corp.*, 317 F.3d 1005 (9th Cir. 2003).
8   See, e.g., *Bigio* v. *Coca-Cola Co.*, 239 F.3d 440 (2d Cir. 2001).

abuse,[9] and terrorism.[10] Scores of cases increasingly target U.S. and foreign companies in an attempt to hold them accountable under a theory of accessorial liability for wrongs allegedly committed by sovereign entities with which they do or did business. Recent complaints argue that corporate defendants must, in effect, police the activities of foreign sovereigns with whom they do business. A prominent example of the latter category are the *Apartheid* Cases before the Southern District of New York, discussed in detail below (see 4 infra).

A recent U.S. Supreme Court decision has called into question the reasoning of *Filartiga* and suggests that the scope of Alien Tort Statute jurisdiction should be limited to torts under the law of nations as it stood in 1789, when the Statute was enacted, and not as it has evolved since 1789.

In *Grupo Mexicano*,[11] the Supreme Court addressed the parameters of the equitable jurisdiction of the district courts, as originally granted by section 11 of the Judiciary Act of 1789.[12] The question arose after a district court granted, under its equitable powers, a prejudgment injunction restraining defendants from transferring certain assets so as to secure plaintiffs' potential damages in a breach of contract action.[13] The Second Circuit affirmed, holding that equity jurisprudence had evolved to the point where this type of injunction could issue.[14]

The Supreme Court reversed, however, finding that 'the substantive prerequisites for obtaining an equitable remedy as well as the general availability of injunctive relief are not altered by [U.S. Federal Rules of Civil Procedure, Rule 65] and depend on traditional principles of equity jurisdiction.'[15] In analyzing whether the injunction was a proper exercise of federal equity jurisdiction under the Judiciary Act of 1789, the high court rejected the rationale that the district courts could look to evolving principles of equity. Rather, it held that the injunction granted was beyond the equitable jurisdiction of the dis-

---

9   See, e.g., *Jota v. Texaco, Inc.*, 157 F.3d 153 (2d Cir. 1998); *Aguinda v. Texaco, Inc.*, 303 F.3d 470 (2d Cir. 2002); *Beanal v. Freeport-McMoran, Inc.*, 197 F.3d 161 (5th Cir. 1999); *Flores*, supra n. 3; *Sarei v. Rio Tinto PLC*, 221 F.Supp. 2d 1116 (C.D. Cal. 2002), *appeal pending*, Nos. 02-56256, 02-56390 (9th Cir. oral arg. Sept 8, 2003). For an overview of the pertinent case law, see, e.g., R. L. Herz, 'Litigating Environmental Abuses Under the Alien Tort Claims Act: A Practical Assessment', 40 Va. J.Int'l L. 545 (2000) (referring to additional literature at 550 n. 22).

10 See, e.g., *Tel-Oren v. Libyan Arab Republic*, 726 F.2d 774 (D.C. Cir. 1984), *cert. denied*, 470 U.S. 1003 (1985) ('*Tel-Oren*').

11 *Grupo Mexicano de Desarrollo, S.A. v. Alliance Bond Fund, Inc.*, 527 U.S. 308 (1999).

12 Judiciary Act of 1789. § 11, 1 Stat. 73, 78 (federal courts 'shall have original cognizance, concurrent with the courts of the several States, of all suits of a civil nature at common law or in equity'). The Judiciary Act of 1789, 'in vesting jurisdiction in the District Courts, does not create causes of action, but only confers jurisdiction to adjudicate those arising from other sources which satisfy its limiting provisions'. *Montana-Dakota Utils. Co. v. Northwestern Pub. Serv. Co.*, 341 U.S. 246, 249 (1951).

13 527 U.S. 308, at 312-13.

14 *Alliance Bond Fund, Inc.* v. *Grupo Mexicano de Desarrollo, S.A.*, 143 F.3d 688, 695 (2d Cir. 1998).

15 527 U.S. 308, at 318-19.

trict court because an action for this type of injunction was not available in 1789 when the Judiciary Act, which granted the district courts their equity jurisdiction, was passed.[16] As the Supreme Court further explained:

> We do not decide which side has the better of [the arguments on the merits of such a remedy]. We set them forth only to demonstrate that resolving them in this forum is incompatible with the democratic and self-deprecating judgment we have long since made: that the equitable powers conferred by the Judiciary Act of 1789 did not include the power to create remedies previously unknown to equity jurisprudence. Even when sitting as a court in equity, we have no authority to craft a 'nuclear weapon' of the law like the one advocated here.

>   * * *

> The debate concerning this formidable power over debtors should be conducted and resolved where such issues belong in our democracy: in the Congress.[17]

> The jurisdictional grant of the Alien Tort Statute is found in Section 9 of the same Judiciary Act of 1789, which stated:

> The district courts . . . shall . . . have cognizance, concurrent with the courts of the several States, or the circuit courts, as the case may be, of all causes where an alien sues for a tort only in violation of the law of nations or a treaty of the United States.[18]

Grupo Mexicano is significant because it mandates a temporal limit on a federal court's ability to interpret the scope of its jurisdictional grant from the U.S. Congress. 'Equity' was limited to its parameters under the original jurisdictional grant – because Congress had never altered that grant. Similarly, it could be argued that lower federal courts may not look to evolving standards of the 'law of nations' to determine the scope of its own Alien Tort Statute jurisdiction.[19] Rather, the argument goes, the jurisdiction of federal courts is limited to tort claims in violation of international law as it stood in 1789, when the First Congress made this jurisdictional grant-to hold otherwise would allow federal courts to reset the boundaries of their own jurisdiction based on varied and shifting interpretations of international law.[20]

---

16   Idem at 319-21.
17   Idem at 332-33.
18   1 Stat. 73, 76-77.
19   This limitation would not apply to a plaintiff properly relying on a violation of a treaty of the United States that created a cause of action for tort. The U.S. Congress must ratify treaties and thereby, by definition, may expand the jurisdiction of the federal courts by creating causes of action under them. See *Tel-Oren*, 726 F.2d at 822 (Bork, J. concurring) ('[O]nly . . . a treaty negotiated by the President and ratified by the Senate could create a cause of action that would direct courts to entertain cases like this one'.); cf. *Argentine Republic* v. *Amerada Hess Shipping Corp.*, 488 U.S. 428, 437-39 (1989) (holding that Congress implicitly limited jurisdiction under the Alien Tort Statute when it enacted the U.S. Foreign Sovereign Immunities Act).
20   See *Great-West Life & Annuity Ins. Co.* v. *Knudson*, 534 U.S. 204, 217 (2002) (citing *Grupo Mexicano* and stating that what will 'introduce a high degree of confusion' into the use of statutory terms is the 'rolling revision of [a statute's] content').

Under the original jurisdictional grant of the Alien Tort Statute in 1789, federal courts arguably do not have jurisdiction over the clams asserted in most Alien Tort Statute cases.[21] Rather, in 1789, as Blackstone states, 'the principal offences against the laws of nations . . . [were] of three kinds: 1. Violation of safe-conducts; 2. Infringement of the rights of embassadors; and 3. Piracy.'[22] It could be said that *Grupo Mexicano* compels limiting the Alien Tort Statute to its original grant unless further enlarged by Congress.

In sum, before one can address whether certain conduct constitutes a violation of international law and is actionable under the Alien Tort Statute, one must first deal with the question whether this statute creates a private cause of action. A panel of the U.S. Court of Appeals for the Ninth Circuit based in San Francisco held in September 2002 that the Alien Tort Statute creates a private right of action 'as long as 'plaintiffs . . . allege a violation of 'specific, universal, and obligatory' international norms".[23] The prior decisions of the Ninth Circuit on that issue have conflicted. For example, *Marcos II*[24] held that the Alien Tort Statute creates a private right of action.[25] Previously, *Marcos I*[26] held that

---

21   After 1789, Congress re-enacted the Alien Tort Statute three times as part of codifications, each time placing the Statute in the chapter addressing the jurisdiction of the district courts. Rev. Stat. § 563, Sixteenth (2d ed. 1878) (see ch. 3, 'District Court Jurisdiction'); Judicial Code of 1911, § 24, Seventeenth, 36 Stat. 1087, 1091 (1911) (see ch. 2, 'District Court Jurisdiction'); 28 U.S.C. § 1350, 62 Stat. 869, 934 (1948) (see ch. 85, 'District Court Jurisdiction'). See *Marcus II*, 25 F.3d at 1467, 1475.

22   4 W. Blackstone *Commentaries* 68, 72 (1854). Safe conduct relates to a party holding a passport, visa or similar assurance from a sovereign allowing that party's passage through the sovereign's territory without interference. For example, one sovereign might agree to allow entry of merchants from a particular nation. '[A]ny violation of either the person or property of such foreigner may be punished by indictment in the name of the king, whose honor is more particularly engaged in supporting his own safe-conduct'. Idem 68.

23   *Doe v. Unocal Corp.*, Nos. 00-56603, 00-57197, 00-56628, 00-57195, 2002 WL 31063976 (9th Cir. Sept. 18, 2002) (the 'Panel Decision' or '*Unocal*') at *8 (citation omitted). (References to 'Panel Decision at *__' refer to the star-pagination of the Panel Decision available on Westlaw). The *Unocal* case involves a suit brought by Burmese citizens alleging that Unocal, a Californian oil company, had aided and abetted the Burmese military junta's use of forced labor and other human rights abuses during the construction of a gas pipeline in Burma. At the time of writing, the case was awaiting an 'en banc' decision of the Ninth Circuit Court of Appeals (upon a re-hearing of the Panel Decision).

24   *Marcos II*, 25 F.3d at 1475.

25   *Accord Alvarez-Machain v. United States*, 266 F.3d 1045, 1054 (9th Cir. 2001). With respect to the potential existence of a private right of action under the Alien Tort Statute, *Marcos II* also relied on a committee report on the Torture Victim Protection Act, which stated that the Alien Tort Statute 'should remain intact to *permit suits* based on other norms that already exist or may ripen in the future into the rules of customary international law'. H.R. Rep. No. 102-367, pt. 1 at 4 (1991) (emphasis added). As another court observed, however, 'the statement of one congressional committee is by no means a statement of 'Congress,' as some have supposed; the wish expressed in the committee's statement is reflected in no language Congress enacted; it does not purport to rest on an interpretation of § 1350; and the statement is legislative dictum'. *Al-Odah v. United States*, 321 F.3d 1134, 1145 (D.C.Cir. 2003) (Randolph, J., concurring), *pet. for cert. pending*, Nos. 03-334 & 03-343 (filed Sept. 2, 2003) ('*Al-Odah*').

26   *Marcos I*, 978 F.2d at 503.

'§ 1350 is simply a jurisdictional statute and creates no cause of action itself.' The significance of *Marcos II* is that it recognizes private rights of action that have not been recognized as such under the law of nations or in any act of Congress.

Importantly, the U.S. Supreme Court has never held that the Alien Tort Statute creates a private right of action.[27] In fact, the Supreme Court has only once dealt with a case involving the Alien Tort Statute, without pronouncing itself on the statute.[28] Only two Circuit Courts have held that the Alien Tort Statute creates a private right of action,[29] while one has suggested that it does not.[30] The Second Circuit has not squarely ruled on this point. Contrary to *Marcos II, Filartiga* did not rule that the Alien Tort Statute created rights of action.[31] Moreover, in the 1976 *Dreyfus* case,[32] the Second Circuit stated that no right of action was created by the Alien Tort Statute. However, two more recent Second Circuit cases, which do not analyze the question, appear to have recognized certain circumstances where the Alien Tort Statute may create rights of action.[33] Thus, the state of U.S. law is such that it is unsettled whether

---

27   Contrary to *Marcos II*, 25 F.3d at 1473, in *The Paquete Habana*, 175 U.S. 677 (1900), the U.S. Supreme Court did not hold that federal common law incorporates any and all *rights of action* created under international law. In *The Paquete Habana*, several vessels were seized as prizes during the Spanish-American War. As such, the right of action arose under recognized principles of U.S. admiralty law and the case fell within federal court admiralty jurisdiction. Accordingly, in noting that '[i]nternational law is part of our law,' the Supreme Court was not creating a private right of action. It was only looking to and 'incorporating' international law for a *rule of decision* that was not otherwise supplied by federal common law. 175 U.S. at 700; *cf. Tel-Oren*, 726 F.2d at 816 n. 24.

28   See *Argentine Republic v. Amerada Hess Shipping Corp.*, 488 U.S. 428 (1989) (dismissing plaintiffs' claims on sovereign immunity grounds and holding that the U.S. Foreign Sovereign Immunities Act, 28 U.S.C. §§ 1330, 1602-11, bars most suits against foreign sovereigns, including those relying on the Alien Tort Statute). A recent case presents the threshold question whether the Alien Tort Statute is a grant of subject matter jurisdiction or, instead, also creates a private cause of action. See *Sosa v. Alvarez-Machain, et al.*, 331 F.3d 604 (9th Cir. 2001), *pet. for cert. pending*, No. 03-339 (filed Sept. 2003).

29   See *Marcos II*, 25 F.3d at 1474-75; *Abebe-Jira v. Negewo*, 72 F.3d 844, 847 (11th Cir. 1996) (holding that the Alien Tort Statute 'establishes a federal forum where courts may fashion domestic common law remedies to give effect to violations of customary international law').

30   *Tel-Oren*, 726 F.2d at 798, 811 (Bork, J. concurring); *Al-Odah*, 321 F.3d 1134, 1145-47 (Randolph, J., concurring); *cf. Goldstar (Panama) S.A. v. United States*, 967 F.2d 965, 968 (4th Cir. 1992) ('[T]he Alien Tort Statute has been interpreted as a jurisdictional statute only'.).

31   Compare *Marcos II*, 25 F.3d at 1475-76, *with* Bradley, supra n. 3, 42 Va. J. Int'l L. at 592 & nn. 20, 21. The *Filártiga* court did not identify the Alien Tort Statute as the source of a private right of action for aliens seeking to remedy violations of international law, but stated that 'it is sufficient ... to construe the [Alien Tort Statute] ... simply as opening the federal courts for adjudication of the rights already recognized by international law'. 630 F.2d at 887; see also *Flores*, supra n. 3, at *13, n.17 ('*Filártiga* did not identify the ATCA as the source of such rights').

32   *Dreyfus v. von Finck*, 534 F.2d 24, 28 (2d Cir. 1976) ('*Dreyfus*').

33   See *Wiwa v. Royal Dutch Petroleum Co.*, 226 F.3d 88, 103-05 (2d Cir. 2000), *cert. denied*, 532 U.S. 941 (2001); *Kadic*, 70 F.3d at 238.

the Alien Tort Statute creates a private right of action and if so, to what extent, with the situation differing from Circuit to Circuit[34] and depending on what violation is alleged.

Based on the nature of the Alien Tort Statute and the settled law relating to the creation of private rights of action under treaties, there are good grounds for U.S. courts to be careful in fashioning private causes of action unsupported by general international law. As noted above, the Alien Tort Statute was part of the First Judiciary Act in 1789, which, 'in vesting jurisdiction in the District Courts, does not create causes of action, but only confers jurisdiction to adjudicate those arising from other sources'.[35] Given the jurisdictional nature of the statute (indeed, it was part of a collection of laws that related solely to delineating the jurisdiction of the federal courts), there is no textual basis for inferring that the Alien Tort Statute creates any private rights of action.[36]

It also must be kept in mind that treaties are not presumed to create private rights of action unless they are self-executing (i.e., supplying an independent right of action absent some act by the U.S. Congress to domesticate that right of action or explicit language in a treaty[37]) or are accompanied by some express act of Congress creating such rights of action.[38] As such, the annals of international law are littered with dozens of conventions and treaties adopted by hundreds of countries – sometimes including the United States, and sometimes not

---

34   The Second Circuit explicitly acknowledged in a recent decision under the Alien Tort Statute that 'the law of the District of Columbia Circuit stands in contrast to that of our Circuit and of the other Circuits that have followed our holding in Filártiga'. *Flores*, supra n. 3, at *16. The *Flores* court also admitted that 'neither Congress nor the Supreme Court has definitively resolved the complex and controversial questions regarding the meaning and scope of the ATCA' and pointed out that the differing perspectives among jurists and scholars 'ultimately can be resolved only by Congress or the Supreme Court'. Idem at *19.

35   *Montana-Dakota Utils. Co. v. Northwestern Pub. Serv. Co.*, 341 U.S. 246, 249 (1951).

36   It also is telling that for two centuries 'nobody understood [the Alien Tort Statute] to empower courts to entertain cases like this'. *Tel-Oren*, 726 F.2d at 812 (Bork, J., concurring). Indeed, there is no evidence of what Congress intended in enacting the Alien Tort Statute. See *IIT v. Vencap, Ltd.*, 519 F.2d 1001, 1015 (2d Cir. 1975) ('This old but little used section [the Alien Tort Statute] is a kind of legal Lohengrin; although it has been with us since the first Judiciary Act, § 9, 1 Stat. 73, 77 (1789), no one seems to know whence it came'.) (Friendly, J.); *Tel-Oren*, 726 F.2d at 812 ('I have discovered no direct evidence of what Congress had in mind when enacting the [Alien Tort Statute]. The debates over the Judiciary Act in the House – the Senate debates were not recorded – nowhere mention the provision, not even, so far as we are aware, indirectly'.) (Bork, J., concurring).

37   See *Foster v. Neilson*, 27 U.S. (2 Pet.) 253, 314 (1829) (treaties not self-executing); *Head Money Cases*, 112 U.S. 580, 598-99 (1884) (same); *Dreyfus v. Von Finck*, 534 F.2d 24, 29-30 (2d Cir. 1976) (law of nations has been held to be non-self-executing); *Banco Nacional de Cuba v. Sabbatino*, 376 U.S. 398, 422-23 (1964) (law of nations cannot dictate domestic law). See also *Flores*, supra n. 3, at *24 n.24, and *34 n.34 (citing relevant cases and literature).

38   See *Head Money Cases*, 112 U.S. at 598-99; *Man Hing Ivory & Imports, Inc., v. Deukmejian*, 702 F.2d 760, 762 (9th Cir. 1983).

– all without domestic remedies under U.S. law.[39] If the Alien Tort Statute creates rights of action under both general international law and treaties of the United States, then all treaties (as sources of international law), whether or not ratified by Congress and whether or not Congress has created a private right of action under U.S. law in so ratifying, could be used to create private rights of action under the Alien Tort Statute.[40] This would run directly counter to the law on when and how treaties create rights of action under U.S. law.

The possibility of this inconsistent result was borne out recently in *Al-Odah* v. *United States*.[41] There, non-U.S. citizens captured in Afghanistan and held at Guantanamo Bay Naval Base sued under the Alien Tort Statute for, inter alia, alleged violations of the Geneva Convention, a treaty ratified by Congress. While it did not address any issues concerning the nature or scope of the Alien Tort Statute, the District of Columbia Circuit unanimously held that the plaintiffs had no right to sue in U.S. courts regarding their detention under any jurisdictional theory. If the Alien Tort Statute creates a private right of action, then presumably non-U.S. citizens should have a right to sue for violations of the Geneva Convention. However, it is settled law that the Geneva Conventions are not self-executing and do not afford a private right of action in U.S. courts.[42]

Finally, another reason mandating particular care in reading the Alien Tort Statute as creating private rights of action is that to do so would force the courts to define the parameters of these actions, none of which are then derived from any act of Congress.[43] The Alien Tort Statute provides no guidance

---

39   *Dreyfus*, 534 F.2d at 30-31; see *Foster* v. *Neilson*, 27 U.S. (2 Pet.) 253, 314 (1829) ('[W]hen the terms of the stipulation import a contract . . . the treaty addresses itself to the political, not the judicial department; and the legislature must execute the contract, before it can become a rule for the Court'.); *Islamic Republic of Iran* v. *Boeing Co.*, 771 F.2d 1279, 1283 (9th Cir. 1985) (treaty language and intent must show that treaty is self-executing).

40   For example, with respect to a right of action for forced labor, the Panel Decision in *Unocal* relied on the Universal Declaration of Human Rights, G.A. Res. 217(A)III, U.N. Doc. A/810 (1948). *Panel Decision* at *8. That instrument is not self-executing – it creates no right of action under U.S. law because it does not 'prescribe[] rules by which private rights may be determined, [such that they] may be relied upon for the enforcement of such rights'. *Dreyfus*, 534 F.2d at 30; *accord Dickens* v. *Lewis*, 750 F.2d 1251, 1254 (5th Cir. 1984). There are many other treaties that have been ratified, but which are not self-executing. See, e.g., *Dreyfus*, 534 F.2d at 30 (U.N. Charter); *United States* v. *Duarte-Acero*, 296 F.3d 1277, 1282-83 (11th Cir. 2002) (International Covenant on Civil and Political Rights); *Flores*, supra n. 3, at *24 n.24, and *34 nn.34-35.

41   321 F.3d 1134 (D.C. Cir. 2003).

42   *Al-Odah*, 321 F.3d at 1146-47 (Randolph, J., concurring) (*citing Tel-Oren*, 726 F.2d at 808-09 (Bork, J. concurring)); *Hamdi* v. *Rumsfeld*, 316 F.3d 450, 468-69 (4th Cir. 2003).

43   See *Al-Odah*, 321 F.3d at 1146-47. To have federal courts – instead of Congress by express act – 'discovering' private rights of action under customary international law based on the writings of those considered experts in the field and in treaties the Senate may or may not have ratified also raises serious separation of powers issues, given Congress' power to designate offenses under the law of nations and to ratify treaties. U.S. Const., art. I, § 8, cl. 10; art. II, § 2, cl. 2. The Second Circuit has acknowledged that Congress has not 'wholly clarified the scope and meaning of the ATCA'. *Flores*, supra n.3, at *18.

on the scope of or limits on rights of action deemed created under international law. As such, courts repeatedly have been 'forced to invent limiting principles' out of thin air.[44]

In light of recent developments, especially the dramatic increase in cases against corporate defendants, the U.S. Government has begun to express its profound concern in relation to litigation under the Alien Tort Statute. For example, on October 27, 2003, the Legal Adviser to the U.S. Department of State wrote to the U.S. Department of Justice in connection with the *Apartheid* Cases (discussed below) expressing the views and concerns of the U.S. Government.[45] According to the letter, 'continued adjudication [of the *Apartheid* Cases] risks potentially serious consequences for significant interests of the United States,' both from a foreign policy and an economic (investment and development) perspective. In the Government's view, 'it has a substantial interest in the proper interpretation and application of [the Alien Tort Statute] because it implicates profound separation of powers concerns and serious consequences for both the development and expression of the nation's foreign policy'. The letter confirms the U.S. Government's position that 'the Alien Tort Statute is a jurisdictional provision only and does not itself create any private causes of action'. This letter is remarkable in that it is rare for the U.S. Government to intervene in pending cases and indicate its official views.[46]

Notwithstanding the strong arguments militating against interpreting the Alien Tort Statute as directly creating private rights or causes of action, it will be assumed in the remainder of this article, for the purposes of discussion only, that it does create such rights. The next question to be addressed then becomes what the evidentiary standards are for proving violations of international law, i.e., whether a certain violation of international law is actionable under the Alien Tort Statute. In this context, we will examine how plaintiffs and courts sitting in Alien Tort Statute cases have approached this delicate issue.

---

44   *Tel-Oren*, 726 F.2d at 820 (Bork, J., concurring).
45   Letter dated October 27, 2003 from William H. Taft, IV, The Legal Adviser, U.S. Department of State, to Shannen W. Coffin, Deputy Assistant Attorney General, Civil Division, U.S. Department of Justice. The letter refers to 28 U.S.C. § 1350 as 'the Alien Tort Statute,' as does the letter dated August 7, 2003 from U.S. District Judge John E. Sprizzo inviting the Department of State to indicate its opinion. (Both letters are on file with the author.)
46   For another example, see Letter dated July 29, 2002 from William H. Taft, IV, The Legal Adviser, U.S. Department of State, to Hon. Louis F. Oberdorfer, U.S. District Court for the District of Columbia, filed Aug. 1, 2002, in *Doe, et al.* v. *ExxonMobil, et al.*, No. 01-CV-1357 (D.D.C.) (on file with the author). *ExxonMobil* involves claims alleging that the world's biggest energy company was complicit in the torture, rape and murder of villagers residing in the vicinity of the company's natural-gas operations in Indonesia. The letter in *ExxonMobil* is restricted to a discussion of the U.S. Government's concerns regarding the potential impact of Alien Tort Statute litigation on U.S. foreign policy interests and, unlike the letter in the *Apartheid* Cases, does not address legal issues pertaining to the Alien Tort Statute.

3   THE TREATMENT OF INTERNATIONAL LAW BY U.S. COURTS IN ALIEN TORT
           STATUTE CASES

As U.S. courts have recognized, without international agreements and other
indicia of a concrete and substantial consensus, no right of action can be found
under international law, the law expressly made applicable in the Alien Tort
Statute.[47] Such indicia must necessarily lie in the sources of international law.
Although Article 38 of the Statute of the International Court of Justice (ICJ),
which forms an integral part of the UN Charter, does not state in so many
words that it contains the formal sources of international law, this is generally
recognized to be the case.[48] Article 38 identifies three primary sources of international law: (a) international conventions (treaty law); (b) international custom, as evidence of a general state practice accepted as law; and (c) the general principles of law recognized by civilized nations.[49] In addition, Article 38
sub (*d*) refers to judicial decisions as *subsidiary* means for determining rules of
international law. In other words, while these subsidiary means do not themselves qualify as sources of international law, they may be *evidence of* primary
sources or rules of international law. U.S. court decisions under the Alien Tort
Statute belong to this latter category, as do the teachings of the most highly
qualified publicists and resolutions of intergovernmental organizations such
as the United Nations, as will be explained below.

In most Alien Tort Statute cases, the courts are called upon to determine
customary international law in the absence of applicable treaties. The ICJ has
stated that evidence of customary international law can be found in two elements, namely, (1) the uniformity of state practice and (2) *opinio juris sive neces-
sitatis*, i.e., the conviction by states that, in following a certain practice, they are
conforming to what amounts to a legal obligation.[50] This rigorous standard for
ascertaining custom has been applied consistently by the ICJ, and also by the
U.S. Supreme Court.[51] However, many Alien Tort Statute rulings do not include a thorough and systematic analysis of international law based on Article 38 of the ICJ Statute. What could be the reason for this failure?

In a recent statement, U.S. Supreme Court Justice Sandra Day O'Connor
commented that 'American judges are becoming more aware of their responsibilities to respect not only domestic law but also the law of nations',[52] noting

---

47   See, e.g., *Marcos II*, 25 F.3d at 1475 ('Actionable violations of international law must be of a
      norm that is specific, universal, and obligatory'.).
48   See *Flores*, supra n.3, at *24 ('Article 38 embodies the understanding of States as to what
      sources offer competent proof of the content' of international law). See also *United States*
      v. *Yousef*, 327 F.3d 56, 100 (2d Cir. 2003) ('*Yousef*'); *Oppenheim's International Law* at 24 (9th
      ed., R. Jennings & A. Watts eds., 1996).
49   *Accord Flores*, supra n.3, at *46.
50   See *North Sea Continental Shelf*, Judgment, *I.C.J. Reports 1969*, 3, 44, §77 (Feb. 20).
51   See, e.g., *The Paquete Habana*, 175 U.S. 677 (1900) (containing over 20 pages of analysis on
      custom).
52   Justice Sandra Day O'Connor, Keynote Address, American Society of International Law
      Annual Meeting, April 2000, available at <www.asil.org/newsletter/news.pdf> (last
      visited May 28, 2003).

at the same time that '[m]ore is needed.' In response, the American Society of International Law has launched a 'Judicial Outreach' program aimed to educate U.S. judges in international law.[53] One may recall in this context the astute observations made in a popular British textbook on international law:

> Most English barristers and judges know very little about international law, and therefore tend to overlook much of the available evidence of customary international law. They usually seek evidence of customary international law only in the sources which are most familiar to them – in judicial decisions of English courts or of the courts in other common law countries; if such judicial decisions provide no answers, they look at textbooks. Textbooks are not a bad place to look for evidence of customary international law, provided they are reliable and up to date; it is the heavy reliance on judicial decisions which is dangerous, because the most recent judicial decision may have been decided a long time ago, and customary international law may have changed since then. There is thus a danger that English courts may apply obsolete rules of international law instead of modern international law. Moreover, if there are no relevant judicial decisions, English courts may wrongly assume that there is no rule of customary law, and may invent a new rule which conflicts with customary international law.[54]

It may be added that, apart from judges missing the evidence to find customary international law, the gap in knowledge identified in the above excerpt might also result in domestic courts fashioning causes of action under international law that are not supported by the sources of international law. A prominent example of this latter, and potentially more dangerous, problem is found in a recent U.S. case. In its decision in the *Talisman* case,[55] a U.S. district court made the following remarkable statement:

> [T]his Court, as an inferior court, is obligated to accept the law as it has been interpreted by the Supreme Court and Second Circuit [Court of Appeals]. This is no less true with respect to questions of international law than any other question of law. Therefore, in addition to the sources of international law listed [in Article 38 of the Statute of the International Court of Justice], another must be added-interpretations of international law of superior courts.[56]

---

53   See 2002 Annual Report, American Society of International Law, available at <www.asil.org/annual.pdf> (last visited Nov. 14, 2003). As part of this program, the Society has prepared a publication entitled *'International Law: A Handbook for Judges'* that has been disseminated to more than 1,600 federal judges, according to information received from the Society. Justice O'Connor states in the Foreword that the handbook is a 'clear and readable introduction to some basic concepts of international law for the benefit of both the bench and the bar'.

54   M. Akehurst, *A Modern Introduction to International Law* 45 (6th ed. 1987).

55   See *Presbyterian Church of Sudan et al.* v. *Talisman Energy, Inc. and the Republic of the Sudan*, No. 01 Civ. 9882 (AGS), 2003 WL 1339181, *19 n.27 (S.D.N.Y. Mar. 19, 2003) (Schwartz, J.) ('*Talisman*'). (References to '*Talisman*' at *__' refer to the star-pagination of the decision available on Westlaw). Judge Schwartz died five days after handing down his decision denying Talisman's motion to dismiss for lack of subject-matter jurisdiction. The plaintiffs in this case, who are current and former residents of the Republic of the Sudan, are alleging violations of international law (including genocide, war crimes, torture, and enslavement) stemming from oil exploration activities conducted in the Sudan by Talisman Energy, Canada's largest independent oil producer.

56   *Talisman*, supra n. 55, at *18-19.

The danger in this proposition lies in its underlying assumption, namely, that superior domestic courts interpret international law correctly. The U.S. Supreme Court's decision in the *Breard* case,[57] refusing to give effect to an order indicating provisional measures issued by the International Court of Justice,[58] demonstrates, however, that this assumption is flawed.[59] In this respect, a New York federal court erred in recently stating that '[i]n the international system, there is no supreme court to reconcile conflicting interpretations and provide authoritative guidance on customary international law.'[60] This statement flatly ignores the existence of the International Court of Justice, which in its capacity as the principal judicial organ of the United Nations without question is the most authoritative source of interpretation of international law.[61]

The *Talisman* court went on to state:

> Talisman fails to cite a single Supreme Court, Second Circuit, or even Southern District case holding that a corporation is 'legally incapable of violating the law of nations.' ... Similarly, [Talisman's expert witnesses] Messrs. Crawford and Greenwood, while citing a variety of international law sources, fail to cite a single United States case upholding their position [namely, that corporations cannot be held liable under general international law].[62]

Notwithstanding the lack of evidence of corporate aiding and abetting or conspiracy liability *de lege lata*, the *Talisman* court found that private companies may be liable under general international law and denied the corporate defendant's motion to dismiss the case. In support of its finding, the court cited Nuremberg Tribunal cases that were directed against individual directors and officers with respect to wrongs committed by companies,[63] and a limited number of treaties relating to oil and nuclear pollution.[64] None of the Nuremberg cases, however, ever held that private companies could be liable under general international law, and none of the cited treaties has been ratified by the U.S. Congress or been held to be self-executing (at most, they appear to allow states to pursue certain remedies). This undercuts the notion that there is a universal

---

57   *Breard* v. *Greene*, 523 U.S. 371 (1998).

58   See *Vienna Convention on Consular Relations (Paraguay* v. *U.S.)*, Order of April 9, 1998, *I.C.J. Reports 1998*, at 248. For a description of this case, see P.H.F. Bekker, *World Court Decisions at the Turn of the Millennium (1997-2001)* at 93 (2001). The ICJ confirmed in a later, unrelated case that its orders indicating provisional measures of protection are binding. See *La-Grand Case (Germany* v. *U.S.)*, Judgment of June 27, 2001, available at <www.icj-cij.org>. For a description of this case, see Bekker, op. cit., at 313.

59   For a scholarly discussion of the relationship between these decisions, see 'Agora: *Breard*,' 92 Am. J. Int'l L. 666 (1998).

60   *Torres* v. *Southern Peru Copper Corp.*, 2002 WL 1587224, *11 (S.D.N.Y. July 16, 2002) (Haight, J.).

61   On the ICJ's role as 'guardian of international law,' see the statement of ICJ President Shi to the UN General Assembly delivered in New York on October 31, 2003. See ICJ Communiqué 2003/36 (Oct. 31, 2003), available at <www.icj-cij.org>.

62   *Talisman*, supra n. 55, at *24.

63   Idem. at *13, *20.

64   Idem at *21-23.

and obligatory norm supporting corporate liability and underscores that there is a troubling evidentiary deficit in Alien Tort Statute cases, especially those involving private companies as defendants.[65]

Another problem identified by Akehurst and encountered in a number of Alien Tort Statute decisions is that they rely almost exclusively on a textbook or law review article for support under international law, even though these are subsidiary 'sources' at best.[66]

There are encouraging signs, however, that the tide may be turning in favor of a more systemic and thorough analysis of the sources of international law by U.S. superior courts sitting in Alien Tort Statute cases. On August 29, 2003, the Second Circuit, an important forum for complaints relying on the Alien Tort Statute, affirmed the lower court's dismissal of a case involving claims that the U.S. Defendant's conduct (allegedly consisting of pollution from copper mining, refining, and smelting operations in Peru) violated customary international law by infringing upon Peruvian-Plaintiffs' 'right to life,' 'right to health,' and 'right to sustainable development'.[67] These claims were found not to be actionable under the Alien Tort Statute. The Second Circuit reached this result based on a remarkably thorough analysis of the sources of international law.

At the outset, the *Flores* court acknowledged that the determination of what offenses violate customary international law 'is no simple task' given that 'the relevant evidence of customary international law is widely dispersed and generally unfamiliar to United States lawyers and judges'.[68] In the court's view, 'in determining what offenses violate customary international law, courts must proceed with extraordinary care and restraint'.[69] Proceeding with such care and restraint, the court concluded that 'in order for a principle to be-

---

65   The *Talisman* court refused to dismiss the case because the foreign corporate defendant 'fails to cite a single Supreme Court, Second Circuit, or even Southern District case holding that a corporation is 'legally incapable of violating the law of nations."' Idem at *24. At the same time, the *Talisman* court acknowledged that 'the Second Circuit [which is superior to the *Talisman* court] has not explicitly held that corporations are potentially liable for violations of the law of nations'. Idem at *34.

66   See, e.g., *Talisman*, supra n. 55, at*19 n.27, citing Steven Ratner, *Corporations and Human Rights: A Theory of Legal Responsibility*, 111 Yale L.J. 443 (2001); *Beanal v. Freeport-McMoran, Inc.*, 197 F.3d 161 (5th Cir. 1999) (affirming dismissal) citing P. Sands (ed.), *Principles of International Environmental Law I: Frameworks, Standards and Implementation* (1995). See also *Yousef*, 327 F.3d at 56, 101-03 (explaining that scholarly works are not true sources of international law).

67   *Flores*, supra n.3. For the lower court's dismissal of plaintiffs' complaint for lack of jurisdiction and failure to state a claim under the Alien Tort Statute, see 253 F.Supp. 2d 510 (S.D.N.Y. 2002) (holding that plaintiffs had not 'demonstrated that high levels of environmental pollution within a nation's borders, causing harm to human life, health, and development, violate well-established, universally recognized norms of international law').

68   Idem at *19-20. See also idem at *46 ('the primary evidence of customary international law is widely dispersed and generally unfamiliar to United States lawyers and judges'). This statement echoes the above comment made by Justice O'Connor. The *Tel-Oren* court acknowledged that determining the governing standard of liability under international law involves a 'formidable research task'. *Tel-Oren*, 726 F.2d at 782.

69   *Flores*, supra n.3, at *20.

come part of customary international law, States must *universally* abide by it'.[70] Specifically, the principle 'must be more than merely professed or aspirational'.[71] The latter holding is particularly important in that it calls into question the validity of complaints and rulings that rely, in whole or in part, on 'soft-law' sources that are of an aspirational nature only.

The *Flores* court relied directly on an ICJ precedent in describing the elements of customary international law and referred to the ICJ Statute as a guide for determining the proper sources of international law.[72] It confirmed that it is only where the nations of the world have demonstrated that a wrong is of mutual, and not merely several, concern, by means of express international accords, that a wrong generally recognized or accepted rises to the level of an international law violation within the meaning of the Alien Tort Statute.[73]

The *Flores* court explicitly dismissed judicial decisions, including those of international courts and tribunals, as primary sources of customary international law.[74] The court also clarified that 'brief'-like affidavits of law professors, non-binding conventions, and resolutions and declarations of multinational organizations are insufficient evidence of customary international law.[75]

---

70   Idem (citing earlier Second Circuit decisions in *Filártiga*, 630 F.2d at 888, and *Kadic*, 70 F.3d at 239, 243 n.8) (emphasis added).

71   Idem. The court characterized particular provisions of the International Covenant on Economic, Social and Cultural Rights and the UN Convention on the Rights of the Child-both of which have not been ratified by the U.S.-, as vague and aspirational. See also *Yousef*, 327 F.3d at 56, 104 (referring to 'treatises or other scholarly works consisting of aspirational propositions that are not themselves good evidence of customary international law').

72   *Flores*, supra n.3, at *21, *23 (citing *North Sea Continental Shelf*, Judgment, *I.C.J. Reports 1969*, at 3, 44 (Feb. 20). The court's reliance on ICJ sources is remarkable, as it is rare for U.S. courts to invoke anything having to do with the ICJ.

73   Idem at *22 (citing *Filártiga*, 630 F.2d at 888), *26-27 ('where the customs and practices of States demonstrate that they do not universally follow a particular practice out of a sense of legal obligation and mutual concern, that practice cannot give rise to a rule of customary international law').

74   Idem at *23, *43-44 (referring to Art. 38 of the ICJ Statute as 'listing judicial decisions as 'subsidiary,' rather than primary, sources of customary international law'). As regards the evidentiary weight of ATS rulings by U.S. courts, the Second Circuit has pointed out in another case outside the ATS context that 'it is not possible to claim that the practice or policies of any one country, including the United States, has such authority that the contours of customary international law may be determined by reference only to that country ... '. *Yousef*, 327 F.3d at 56, 92, n.25.

75   According to the court, 'we look ... only secondarily to the works of scholars as evidence of the established practice of States'. Idem at *23 (citing *United States* v. *Yousef*, 327 F.3d 56, 103 (2d Cir. 2003). In its words, 'Article 38 of the ICJ Statute does *not* recognize the writings of scholars as primary or independent sources of customary international law'. Idem. at *45. The court pointed out that '[n]otably absent from Article 38's enumeration of the sources of international law are conventions that set forth broad principles without setting forth specific rules'. Idem at *25. Specifically, it found that the principles set out in Articles 3 and 25 of the Universal Declaration of Human Rights, the International Covenant on Economic, Social and Cultural Rights (not ratified by the U.S.), and the Rio Declaration on Environment and Development are 'boundless and indeterminate'. Idem at *30, *43. The decision also includes important statements on the evidentiary weight to be afforded to a treaty in the context of customary international law. See idem at *32-34. The *Flores* court's statements regarding the evidentiary value of UN resolutions are addressed in the section below discussing the treatment of international law by complaints relying on the Alien Tort Statute.

The *Flores* court's statement of the proper sources and evidences of international law undoubtedly sets a new standard, one which other U.S. courts, and the plaintiffs' bar, should follow rigorously in future Alien Tort Statute cases. The court's decision indeed 'established the proper framework for analyzing ATCA claims'.[76]

4   THE TREATMENT OF INTERNATIONAL LAW IN COMPLAINTS RELYING ON THE ALIEN TORT STATUTE: A CASE STUDY

The root of the problem identified above lies in the attempt by the plaintiffs' bar to bring cases under the Alien Tort Statute that are manifestly unsupported by the sources of international law. The Statute is increasingly employed as a policy instrument. As a result, U.S. courts are confronted with complaints that are fundamentally flawed from the perspective of international law. Given the general reluctance of U.S. courts to find the absence of a cause of action, such flawed complaints run the risk of being turned into bad law, especially if courts resort to teleological reasoning, use judicial analogy as a tool, or engage in judicial activism.[77] The *Talisman* decision referred to above constitutes a prominent example.[78]

The plaintiffs' bar also increasingly employs the Alien Tort Statute as an instrument to mount a public relations campaign against 'deep-pocket' corporate defendants in hopes of forcing such companies to make the case go away quickly by settling under favorable terms.[79] The only real disincentive for the plaintiffs' bar to engage in this conduct lies in Rule 11 of the U.S. Federal Rules of Civil Procedure, which provides in pertinent part:

> [b]y presenting to the court ... a pleading, written motion, or other paper, an attorney or unrepresented party is certifying that to the best of the person's knowledge, information, and belief, formed after an inquiry reasonable under the circumstances, ... *the claims, defenses, and other legal contention therein are warranted by existing law* or by a nonfrivolous argument for the extension, modification, or reversal of existing law or the establishment of new law.[80]

---

76   Idem at *29.
77   The Second Circuit has recognized that 'the incorrect use of [non-primary] sources [of international law] can easily lead to an incorrect conclusion about the content of customary international law'. *Yousef*, 327 F.3d at 56, 99.
78   It seems unlikely that the *Talisman* decision will withstand the scrutiny of *Flores* on appeal before the Second Circuit.
79   A recent example is *Sinaltrainal et al.* v. *The Coca-Cola Company et al.*, Nos. 01-3208, 02-20258, 02-20259, 02-20260 Civ.-Martinez/Dubé (S.D.Fl. Mar. 28, 2003). This case involves a complaint by members of a Colombian labor union against, inter alia, The Coca-Cola Company and its Colombian subsidiary alleging that these corporate defendants had conspired with and aided and abetted Colombian right-wing paramilitary groups in violation of international law under the Alien Tort Statute. The district court granted the motion to dismiss in favor of the Coca-Cola entities, but allowed the case to proceed against another corporate defendant under the U.S. Torture Victim Protection Act.
80   Fed. R. Civ. P. 11(b)(2) (emphasis added).

One possible sanction for a violation of Rule 11 is an order that a party or its counsel pay the other party's legal fees and costs. It is doubtful, however, that Rule 11 will be easily enforced in connection with complaints relying on the Alien Tort Statute, especially in light of the unsettled nature of international law.

The remainder of this section addresses the relative evidentiary weight of international law sources in the context of a number of class-action lawsuits filed in the Southern District of New York in June 2002 and styled *In re South African Apartheid Litigation*.[81] In this class action, involving over 80 U.S. and foreign companies (including some of the world's largest banks, oil, automotive, and computer companies), plaintiffs allege that by doing business in or with South Africa while the South African government maintained the apartheid system, the defendant-companies, while not having committed the alleged crimes against humanity themselves, violated international law by 'aiding and abetting' those crimes so as to be liable to all South Africans who suffered injuries at the hands of the South African government during the apartheid era (1948-1993). Plaintiffs are seeking over $50 billion in damages.

The complaint in the *Apartheid* Cases ('Complaint') relies exclusively on seven UN resolutions – four of the General Assembly and three of the Security Council – for the assertion that apartheid is a crime against humanity and that the named corporate defendants are liable for aiding and abetting, or conspiring to commit, crimes under international law. Given that the plaintiffs in *Flores* also relied on several UN resolutions, albeit not exclusively, the pertinent statements of the *Flores* court are directly relevant to the *Apartheid* Cases, which also are pending before a court within the Second Circuit. These cases signal a trend according to which complaints rely mainly or exclusively on so-called 'soft-law' in alleging violations of international law. In light of this trend, we will address below the evidentiary weight of 'soft' international law, in particular UN resolutions, in the light of the proof required to show a violation of customary international law under the Alien Tort Statute.

4.1   The text of the UN resolutions

First, the Complaint in the *Apartheid* Cases relies on General Assembly resolutions 395 (1950), 1761 (1962), 1978 (1963), and 2923 (1972). An examination of the actual text of each of these resolutions is instructive.

Resolution 395 'considered' (not 'declared') that 'a policy of 'racial segregation' (*Apartheid*) is necessarily based on doctrines of racial discrimination'. It 'recommends' that 'the Governments of India, Pakistan and the Union of

---

81   These and similar cases from other districts were consolidated for pre-trial purposes before the U.S. District Court for the Southern District of New York. See MDL No. 1499 (S.D.N.Y. filed Sept. 11, 2003). Oral argument on defendants' joint motion to dismiss was heard in November 2003. The author's law firm represents one of the corporate defendants in these cases.

South Africa' hold a round table conference and negotiate the treatment of people of Indian origin in South Africa and calls upon them to refrain from taking any steps that would prejudice the success of their negotiations.

Resolution 1761 'recalls' that 'the Security Council in its resolution of 1 April 1960 [134] recognized that the situation in South Africa was one that had led to international friction and, if continued, might endanger international peace and security' and that the Council's resolution 'called upon the Government of South Africa to initiate measures aimed at bringing about racial harmony based on equality'. Resolution 1761 goes on to 'regret' that 'the actions of some *Member States* indirectly provide encouragement to the Government of South Africa to perpetuate its policy of racial segregation'. (Emphasis added).

Resolution 1978 merely 'appeals' to 'all States' to 'take appropriate measures and intensify their efforts, separately and collectively, with a view to dissuading the Government of South Africa from pursuing its policies of *apartheid*'.

Resolution 2923 consists of six parts. Part A 'calls upon' the Government of South Africa 'immediately to put an end to all forms of physical and mental torture and other acts of terror against opponents of *apartheid* under detention or imprisonment and to punish the perpetrators of such criminal acts'. It is not addressed to UN member states or other entities. In Part E, the General Assembly is '[*f*]*urther reaffirming* that the practice of apartheid constitutes a crime against humanity.' It also 'condemns' the 'racist Government of South Africa for continuing and intensifying the implementation of its inhuman policy of *apartheid*'. Paragraph 5 of Part E '[*c*]*ondemns* the continued and increasing co-operation of certain States and foreign economic interests with South Africa in the military, economic, political and other fields, as such co-operation encourages the South African regime in the pursuit of *apartheid* in defiance of the United Nations'.[82]

Second, the Complaint cites three Security Council resolutions relating to the issue of apartheid: 181 (1963), 182 (1963), and 311 (1972). Resolution 181, which was adopted by nine votes to none, with two abstentions (France and

---

82   Resolution 2923 does not specify what is meant by 'foreign economic interests'. However, if the Assembly had wanted to address or target 'juridical persons,' or private companies, it presumably would have used those words, similar to its practice in resolutions pertaining to other questions. Thus, resolution 2749 (XXV) of December 17, 1970, declares that the seabed and ocean floor beyond the limits of national jurisdiction 'shall not be subject to appropriation by any means by States or persons, natural or juridical' and that '[n]o State or person, natural or juridical, shall claim, exercise or acquire rights with respect to the area or its resources incompatible with the international regime to be established and the principles of this Declaration'. Even more instructive is paragraph 7 of Security Council resolution 283 (1970) on the illegal presence of South Africa in Namibia, which '[*c*]*alls upon* all States to discourage their nationals or companies of their nationality not under direct governmental control from investing or obtaining concessions in Namibia'. Paragraph 7 speaks to states, not to nationals or companies of states. None of the resolutions cited in the Complaint contains a clause similar to paragraph 7 of resolution 283.

the UK), expresses 'regret' that 'some states are indirectly providing encouragement in various ways to the Government of South Africa to perpetuate, by force, its policy of *apartheid*'. It goes on to 'strongly deprecate' the 'policies of South Africa in its perpetuation of racial discrimination as being inconsistent with the principles contained in the Charter of the United Nations and contrary to its obligations as a Member of the United Nations,' and it 'calls upon' the South African Government 'to abandon the policies of apartheid and racial discrimination, as called for in Security Council resolution 134 (1960)'.[83] Finally, resolution 181 '[s]*olemnly calls upon* all States to cease forthwith the sale and shipment of arms, ammunition of all types and military vehicles to South Africa'.

Resolution 182, adopted unanimously, characterizes South Africa's policies of apartheid and racial discrimination as 'abhorrent to the conscience of mankind,' 'contrary to the principles and purposes of the Charter' and 'in violation of its obligations as a Member of the United Nations and of the provisions of the Universal Declaration of Human Rights'. It '[a]*ppeals* to all States to comply with the provisions of Security Council resolution 181'. It also '[s]*olemnly calls upon* all States to cease forthwith the sale and shipment of equipment and materials for the manufacture of arms and ammunition in South Africa'.

In Resolution 311, adopted by 14 votes to none (France abstaining), the Council states that it is 'gravely concerned' that the situation in South Africa seriously disturbs international peace and security. It '[c]*ondemns* the Government of South Africa for continuing its policies of *apartheid* in violation of its obligations under the Charter of the United Nations'. It '[c]*alls upon* all States to observe strictly the arms embargo against South Africa' and '[u]*rges* Governments and individuals to contribute generously and regularly to the United Nations funds which are used for humanitarian and training purposes to assist the victims of *apartheid*'.

In sum, the text of none of the above resolutions addresses directly the conduct of non-state entities (such as companies or individual corporate officers) with regard to the problem of apartheid and refers nowhere to the possibility of accessorial liability of corporations doing business with South Africa's apartheid regime. As such, these resolutions, which are largely aspirational in nature, do not purport to create a private cause of action for plaintiffs in cases under the Alien Tort Statute.

---

83   Resolution 134 of April 1, 1960, which was adopted by nine votes to none, with two abstentions (France and the UK), refers to 'the continued disregard by [the South African] Government of the resolutions of the General Assembly calling upon it to revise its policies and bring them into conformity with its obligations and responsibilities under the Charter of the United Nations'. Note the frequent reference to 'it' and 'its'. The resolution further '[d]*eplores* the policies and actions of the Government of the Union of South Africa which have given rise to the present situation'. It also '[c]*alls upon* the Government of the Union of South Africa to initiate measures aimed at bringing about racial harmony based on equality in order to ensure that the present situation does not continue or recur, and to abandon its policies of *apartheid* and racial discrimination'.

4.2   *The evidentiary weight of UN resolutions*

The Complaint's exclusive reliance on UN resolutions fails to recognize that they are not a direct or primary source of international law and thus could never give rise, standing alone, to a private right or cause of action under the Alien Tort Statute. At best, such resolutions constitute secondary *evidence of* a source of international law. For example, as to customary law, they may constitute proof of the element of *opinio juris*, which is one of the two elements constituting custom, the other being state practice.[84] In its exclusive reliance on 'soft' law, the Complaint in the *Apartheid* Cases example highlights the evidentiary deficit in Alien Tort Statute cases from the perspective of the introductory complaint on which courts sitting in these cases must rule in their decisions on jurisdiction and admissibility.

The Restatement (Third), which has been cited favorably by U.S. courts sitting in Alien Tort Statute cases,[85] includes as evidence of international law rules the pronouncements by states that undertake to state a rule of international law, including through 'declaratory resolutions of international organizations'.[86] The Restatement recognizes, however, that UN resolutions, referred to in Comment (*c*) to §103[87] are not a direct or primary *source* of international law set forth in §102.

Thus, the Restatement (Third) distinguishes between *sources* of international law (§102) and *evidence of* international law (§103). Within the latter category, a further distinction is made between primary and secondary evidence of international law. According to the Restatement, 'for customary law the 'best evidence' is proof of state practice, ordinarily by reference to official documents'.[88] In other words, state practice constitutes primary evidence of customary international law (together with *opinio juris*).

At best, UN resolutions constitute secondary (not primary) *evidence of* a source of international law. For example, as to customary law (a primary source), UN resolutions may provide proof of the element of *opinio juris*, which is one of the two elements of *primary* evidence for establishing custom (the other being state practice). UN resolutions are but a first step in the formation of custom, but they do not constitute customary rules by themselves. As

---

84   As correctly phrased in a recent Second Circuit decision: 'Because General Assembly documents are at best merely advisory, they do not, on their own and without proof of uniform state practice, ..., evidence an intent by member States to be legally bound by their principles, and thus cannot give rise to rules of customary international law'. *Flores*, supra n. 3, at *40.

85   See, e.g., *Kadic*, 70 F.3d at 240; *Torres* v. *Southern Peru Copper Corp.*, 965 F. Supp. 899, 908 (S.D.Tex. 1996), *aff'd* 113 F.3d 540 (5th Cir. 1997); *Flores* v. *Southern Peru Copper Corp.*, 2002 WL 1587224 (S.D.N.Y. July 16, 2002); *but see* *Yousef*, 327 F.3d at 56, 99 ('The Restatement (Third), a kind of treatise or commentary, is not a *primary* source of authority upon which, standing alone, courts may rely for propositions of customary international law').

86   See *Restatement (Third) of the Foreign Relations Law of the United States* 37 (1987), Comment (*c*), §103 ('*Restatement (Third)*').

87   Significantly, UN resolutions are not referred to in §103 itself.

88   *Restatement (Third)*, at 36.

the current British member of the ICJ has pointed out, 'resolutions cannot be a *substitute* for ascertaining custom: this task will continue to require that other evidences of State practice be examined alongside those collective acts evidences in General Assembly resolutions'.[89]

Comment (*c*) of the Restatement (Third) states the following about 'declaratory' resolutions of international organizations (i.e., resolutions that purport to be declaratory of contemporary international law):

> International organizations generally have no authority to make law, and their determinations of law ordinarily have no special weight, but their declaratory pronouncements provide some evidence of what the states voting for it regard the law to be. The evidentiary value of such resolutions is variable. Resolutions of universal international organizations, if not controversial and if adopted by consensus or virtual unanimity, are given substantial weight.[90]

Only a few resolutions of the General Assembly purport to be 'declaratory'.[91] Whatever the evidentiary weight of such resolutions, none of the apartheid-related resolutions cited in the Complaint qualify as 'declaratory,' as their text makes clear. Moreover, the Restatement's use of the words 'given substantial

---

89   R. Higgins, The Role of Resolutions of International Organizations in the Process of Creating Norms in the International System in: *International Law and the International System* 21, 27 (W.E. Butler ed. 1987). See also S. M. Schwebel, 'The Effect of Resolutions of the U.N. General Assembly in Customary International Law', 73 ASIL Proc. 301 (1979).

90   *Restatement (Third)*, at 37.

91   The Office of Legal Affairs of the UN Secretariat explained in a 1962 memorandum: 'In United Nations practice, a 'declaration' is a formal and solemn instrument, suitable for rare occasions when principles of great and lasting importance are being enunciated, such as the Declaration on Human Rights. A recommendation is less formal. Apart from the distinction just indicated there is probably no difference between a 'recommendation' and a 'declaration' in United Nations practice as far as strict legal principle is concerned. A 'declaration' or a 'recommendation' is adopted by resolution of a United Nations organ. As such it cannot be made binding upon the parties to it, purely by the device of terming it a 'declaration' rather than a 'recommendation.'' UN Commission on Human Rights, 34 ECOSOC O.R. Supp. No. 8, UN Doc. E/CN.4/L.610, p. 15 (1962). The Second Circuit in *Filártiga* relied on two such resolutions, namely, General Assembly resolutions 217(III)(A) (Universal Declaration of Human Rights) and 3452 (Declaration on the Protection of All Persons from Being Subjected to Torture), in finding that torture by government officials violates international law. See *Filártiga*, 630 F.2d at 882. The Second Circuit's recent decision in *Flores* addresses the overall evidentiary weight of resolution 217. The *Flores* court dismissed the principles expressed in Articles 3 (recognizing the right to life) and 25 of resolution 217 (recognizing 'the right of everyone to the enjoyment of the highest attainable standard of physical and mental health') as 'boundless and indeterminate' and non-binding. *Flores*, supra n. 3, at *30, *37. The lower court in *Talisman* thus erred seven months earlier by finding that the UN Declaration of Human Rights '[b]y its terms, ... is binding on states as well as corporations'. *Talisman*, supra n. 55, at *41. The *Flores* court explicitly addressed the *Filártiga* court's reliance on resolution 217. See *Flores*, supra n. 3, at *40 n. 38 ('These statements are consistent with *Filártiga*, which recognized that the Universal Declaration constitutes evidence of customary international law only insofar as States have universally abided by its principles out of a sense of legal obligation and mutual concern'), *41. In the view of another Circuit Court, the Universal Declaration is 'merely a non-binding resolution'. *Haitian Refugee Ctr.* v. *Gracey*, 809 F.2d 794, 816 n.17 (D.C. Cir. 1987).

weight' is critical. Substantial weight of what? As indicated by the Restatement (Third) and the case law of the ICJ, UN resolutions may be given substantial weight for one of the two elements of primary evidence of customary international law, namely, *opinio juris*. In other words, UN resolutions may not be given substantial weight as a source of international law (custom) themselves, for to do so would be to ignore the other element of primary evidence required to prove custom, namely, state practice. As the Second Circuit has recently recognized with regard to both resolutions and declarations of the UN General Assembly, '[t]hese documents are not proper sources of customary international law because they are merely aspirational and were never intended to be binding on member States of the United Nations'.[92] The same court has also explained that it does not suffice for General Assembly resolutions to describe the actual customs and practices of states; in addition, the proclamation of rights in those resolutions must be sufficiently clear and definite in order to constitute rules of customary international law.[93]

As the above indicates, the recognition by states of norms included in recommendatory resolutions as legally binding is a separate process that is wholly independent of the resolution adoption process (including voting). As one author has pointed out:

> there are many instances when for political reasons a State votes for a resolution with which its practice is inconsistent and has no intention of changing its practice. The votes by some States for a number of U.N. General Assembly resolutions on disarmament, colonialism, apartheid, etc., are vivid examples.[94]

---

92   *Flores*, supra n. 3, at *37 ('The General Assembly ... is not a law-making body. ... . General Assembly resolutions and declarations do not have the power to bind member States because the member States specifically denied the General Assembly that power after extensively considering the issue'). See also *Banco Nacional de Cuba* v. *Chase Manhattan Bank*, 658 F.2d 875, 889 (2d Cir. 1981) (noting that General Assembly resolutions on the question of expropriation 'are of considerable interest' but 'do not have the force of law'); Gregory J. Kerwin, *The Role of United Nations General Assembly Resolutions in Determining Principles of International Law in United States Courts*, Duke L.J. 876 (1983) (citing U.S. case law). According to Art. 10 of the UN Charter, the General Assembly may make 'recommendations' only 'to the Members of the United Nations or to the Security Council or to both' on any question or matter that the Assembly may discuss within the scope of the Charter. Arts. 11(1)-(2) and 13(1) again refer to 'recommendations'. Art. 12(1) employs the term 'recommendation'. Art. 14 uses the word 'recommend'. The *travaux préparatoires* of the UN Charter leave beyond doubt that the drafters of the Charter deliberately rejected the idea to give the General Assembly legislative authority. The Philippines proposed to give such authority to the Assembly, but this proposal was rejected by a vote of 26 to 1. See *United Nations Conference on International Organization* (1945), Vol. IX, p. 70, 466-467. See also Leland M. Goodrich & Edvard Hambro, *The Charter of the United Nations – Commentary and Documents* at 94-95, 103-04 (1946). Thus, there is no basis under UN law for characterizing General Assembly resolutions as creating directly binding obligations under international law for states, let alone private rights of action against private companies.

93   *Flores*, supra n. 3, at *41 n.40.

94   G.I. Tunkin, 'The Role of Resolutions of International Organisations in Creating Norms of International Law' in: *International Law and the International System* at 5, 12 (W.E. Butler ed., 1987).

The same author has explained that 'States vote for a resolution in the conviction that what they adopt is not legally binding (with the exception of resolutions on internal matters which, according to the constitutive instrument of an international organisation, are legally binding)'.[95]

U.S. State Department practice supports the above observation. The official U.S. position is that 'General Assembly resolutions are regarded as recommendations to Member States of the United Nations'.[96] In 1970, Ambassador Elliot L. Richardson voiced the United States' strong reservation with respect to the legal character of General Assembly resolution 2749 (XXV) entitled 'Declaration of Principles Governing the Seabed and the Ocean Floor, and the Subsoil Thereof, beyond the Limits of National Jurisdiction'. Arguably, resolution 2749 could be characterized as a 'declaratory resolution'. He explained that the United States had voted for the resolution merely in recognition of the fact that the principles embodied in it constituted a basis for subsequent negotiation of a definitive agreement containing an internationally agreed upon regime. However, he said that the U.S. could not accept the suggestion that other states, without its consent, could deny or alter its rights under international law 'by resolutions, statements, and the like'.[97] Ambassador Richardson pointed out that '[t]he prohibition which the draft resolution contains is without binding legal effect; that is the case with almost any General Assembly resolution, and it is certainly the case for any General Assembly resolution purporting to prescribe standards of conduct for states in the oceans'.[98] This example demonstrates that the U.S. does not consider every 'declaratory' resolution (the kind referred to in Comment (*c*) of the Restatement (Third)) to carry equal evidentiary weight.

The ICJ has stated that General Assembly resolutions may assist in identifying *opinio juris*:

> This *opinio juris* may, though *with all due caution*, be deduced from, *inter alia*, the attitude of the Parties and the attitude of States towards certain General Assembly resolutions (...). The effect of consent to the text of such resolutions cannot be understood as merely that of a 'reiteration or elucidation' of the treaty commitment undertaken in the [UN] Charter. On the contrary, it may be understood as an acceptance of the validity of the rule or set of rules declared by the resolution by themselves. The principle of non-use of force, for example, may thus be regarded as a principle of customary international law, not as such conditioned by provisions relating to collective security, or to the facilities or armed con-

---

95   Idem at 13. At the same time, Tunkin accepts apartheid as one of 'many instances when certain norms of United Nations General Assembly resolutions have become or are becoming customary norms of international law'. Idem at 14. But this is different from recognizing conspiracy to commit apartheid on the part of private companies, which constitutes one of the claims set forth in the Complaint.

96   See *Digest of United States Practice in International Law* at 85 (1975) (statement by S. M. Schwebel, Deputy Legal Adviser to the U.S. Department of State).

97   Idem at 160-61 (1978) (*reprinting* Dept. of State File No. P80 0012-1442).

98   Idem at 161.

tingents to be provided under Article 43 of the Charter. It would therefore seem apparent that the attitude referred to expresses an *opinio juris* respecting such rule (or set of rules), to be thenceforth treated separately from the provisions, especially those of an institutional kind, to which it is subject on the treaty-law plane of the Charter.[99]

The Court's emphasis on caution must be stressed.[100]

Ten years later, the ICJ opined:

> The Court notes that General Assembly resolutions, even if they are not binding, may sometimes have normative value. They can, in certain circumstances, provide evidence important for establishing the existence of a rule or the emergence of an *opinio juris*. To establish whether this is true of a given General Assembly resolution, it is necessary to look at its content and the conditions of its adoption; it is also necessary to see whether an *opinio juris* exists as to its normative character. Or a series of resolutions may show the gradual evolution of the *opinio juris* required for the establishment of a new rule.[101]

Thus, the ICJ's most recent pronouncement on the legal character of General Assembly resolutions is that they 'are not binding' and may only serve as *evidence of* the *opinio juris* element required to prove the existence of a rule of customary international law. Proof of a customary rule requires both widespread state practice and *opinio juris*.

Another example demonstrates that the official position of the U.S. is that UN resolutions leave unaffected the requirement to prove widespread state practice as a necessary element of customary international law. In 1977, Robert Rosenstock, the U.S. representative to the Sixth (Legal) Committee of the UN General Assembly, gave expression to the U.S. Government's strong opposition to the suggestion, made in a UN document, that a 'declaratory' resolution of the Assembly had 'developed' the principle of permanent sovereignty over natural resources. He stated:

> My government finds this statement startling because it is open to the interpretation that this General Assembly, by its adoption of controverted resolutions, 'develops' principles which arguably are of a legal character. That is an interpretation of the powers and practice of this Assembly which is not accepted by my government, and which does not conform to the United Nations Charter or to international law.
>
> This Assembly is not a lawmaking body. Its resolutions, in the ordinary course, do not enact, formulate or alter international law, progressively or regressively. In the exceptional cases in which a General Assembly resolution may contribute to the development of in-

---

99   *Military and Paramilitary Activities in and against Nicaragua (Nicaragua v. United States)*, Judgment, Merits, *I.C.J. Reports 1986*, at 14, 100, §188 (June 27) (emphasis added).

100 This cautious attitude was displayed by the U.S. Supreme Court in 1900. See *The Paquete Habana*, 175 U.S. 677 (1900). See also *Filártiga*, 630 F.2d at 881 ('The requirement that a rule command 'general assent of civilized nations' to become binding upon them all is a stringent one'.); *Beanal v. Freeport-McMoRan, Inc.*, 197 F.3d 161, 167 (5th Cir. 1999).

101 *Legality of the Threat or Use of Nuclear Weapons*, Advisory Opinion, *I.C.J. Reports 1996*, at 226, 254, §70 (July 8).

ternational law, it can do so only if the resolution gains virtually universal support, if the
Members of the General Assembly share a lawmaking or law-declaring intent-and if the
content of that resolution is reflected in general state practice.[102]

The final words of this official statement ('and if the content of that resolution
is reflected in general state practice') are in accord with ICJ jurisprudence requiring proof of state practice alongside *opinio juris*.

For purposes of the Alien Tort Statute, the situation is similar with regard
to resolutions of the UN Security Council. Not all Security Council resolutions
are binding.[103] Even those binding resolutions that the Security Council
adopts pursuant to its powers under Chapter VII of the UN Charter do not
give rise, in and of themselves, to private rights of action under the Alien Tort
Statute. This is especially the case if the proclamations of rights in such resolutions are insufficiently clear and definite to constitute rules of customary international law.[104] As demonstrated above, none of the Security Council resolutions on which the Complaint relies are addressed to corporate entities and
none of them refer to the possible accessorial liability of corporations in connection with the crime of apartheid.[105]

In sum, the Complaint cannot rely exclusively on these seven UN resolutions, standing alone, to show that the nations of the world universally prohibit the sort of conduct that is alleged in the Complaint and, specifically, to
prove the existence of a rule of customary international law holding juridical
persons (including banks and other companies) liable for conspiracy to commit the crime of apartheid or to violate the UN weapons embargo against the
South African apartheid regime by doing business with such regime. There is
no primary source of international law that supports such accessorial liability
as a rule of general international law. Corporate conspiracy to commit crimes

102   *Digest of United States Practice in International Law* at 54 (1977) (*reprinting* Press Release
      USUN-122(77), Nov. 11, 1977, pp. 16-18).
103   See Leland M. Goodrich & E. Hambro, *The Charter of the United Nations – Commentary and
      Documents* at 122 (1946); but see *Legal Consequences for States of the Continued Presence of South
      Africa in Namibia (South West Africa) notwithstanding Security Council Resolution 276 (1970),*
      Advisory Opinion, *I.C.J. Reports 1971*, at 16, 52-53, §§113-14 (June 21). The official position of
      the U.S. Department of State is that the 'United States has never accepted the proposition
      that all Security Council decisions are legally binding on U.N. members by reason of Article
      25'. *Digest of United States Practice in International Law* at 88 (1975). In the U.S. view, a Securi-
      ty Council resolution, in order to be legally binding, must either invoke the Council's
      mandatory authority under Chapter VII or indicate an intention to be legally binding. See
      Idem at 89. For U.S. court decisions, see G. J. Kerwin, *The Role of United Nations General As-
      sembly Resolutions in Determining Principles of International Law in United States Courts*, Duke
      L.J. 876, 881 (1983); *Digest of United States Practice of International Law* at 163-67 (1978).
104   Cf. *Flores*, supra n. 3, at *41 n.40.
105   Resolution 181 (1963) binds 'all States' immediately to cease 'the sale and shipment of
      arms, ammunition of all types and military vehicles to South Africa'. It '[c]alls upon the
      Government of South Africa to abandon the policies of *apartheid* and discrimination, as
      called for in Security Council resolution 134 (1960)'. Resolution 182 (1963) directs 'all
      States' immediately to cease 'the sale and shipment of equipment and materials for the
      manufacture and maintenance of arms and ammunition in South Africa'. Resolution 311
      (1972) calls on 'all States to observe strictly the arms embargo against South Africa'.

against humanity has not been universally accepted as a discrete violation of general international law and, therefore, is not part of the contemporary body of customary international law.[106] Still, the *Apartheid* Cases remain on the docket and the named corporate defendants are forced to spend millions of dollars in legal fees to defend themselves.[107]

5   CONCLUSION

Claims by non-U.S. citizens seeking relief for international law violations by foreign actors under the U.S. Alien Tort Statute have seen a marked proliferation since the 1980 *Filartiga* decision. Such claims are at the apex of the phenomenon of 'globalisation and jurisdiction.' Ever since *Filartiga*, U.S. courts have been in disagreement over whether the Alien Tort Statute is merely a jurisdiction-vesting statute or, instead, not only confers jurisdiction but also creates a private cause of action. In addition, it is unsettled what violations of international law are actionable under the Alien Tort Statute. There are good grounds for questioning whether the Alien Tort Statute provides a private cause of action for international law violations and, if so, does so for violations other than genocide, war crimes, crimes against humanity, slavery, torture and similar breaches committed by natural persons that truly shock the conscience of mankind and are based either on binding treaties or on universally accepted and clearly articulated and discernable rules of customary international law-as opposed to non-binding expressions of international law that are merely aspirational or insufficiently clear and definite.[108]

The Alien Tort Statute has provided an effective remedy for non-U.S. plaintiffs seeking redress in U.S. court for egregious breaches of international law committed by foreign natural persons outside U.S. territory. As such, it may provide a welcome means of redress especially in cases of torture committed by state actors and private perpetrators alike.[109] In this sense, the Alien

---

106 See P.H.F. Bekker, *Corporate Aiding & Abetting and Conspiracy Liability Under International Law* in *Proceedings of the 6*[th] *Hague Joint Conference on Contemporary Issues of International Law* (forthcoming, 2004).

107 One should not underestimate the nuisance value of a claim. It is an irritant amounting to an inconvenience to the corporate defendant to have to acknowledge an unresolved dispute and to make accounting provision each fiscal year for considerable amounts of potential liability.

108 See *Flores* v. *Southern Peru Copper Corporation*, No. 02-9008, 2003 WL 22038598 (2d Cir. Sept. 2, 2003), at *41, n.40, 42, 43, n.41; *United States* v. *Yousef*, 327 F.3d 56, 104 (2d Cir. 2003).

109 See, e.g., *Xuncax* v. *Gramajo*, 886 F.Supp. 162 (D. Mass. 1995); *Kadic* v. *Karadzic*, 70 F.3d 232 (2d Cir. 1995); *Estate of Winston Cabello, et al.* v. *Armando Fernandez Larios*, Case No. 99-0528-CIV-LENARD/TURNOFF, decision of Oct. 15, 2003 (S.D.Fl.) (awarding $4 million in compensatory and punitive damages to the U.S.-based Chilean beneficiaries for the torture and murder of their brother, a Chilean economist, by a member of former Chilean dictator Augusto Pinochet's 'Caravan of Death' military squad in 1973, based on a finding of liability for torture, crimes against humanity, and extra-judicial killing; this is the first jury verdict for crimes against humanity in the U.S.).

Tort Statute unquestionably has been an important instrument in the fight against impunity on the part of natural offenders.

The Alien Tort Statute should not be allowed, however, for use in disregard of the system of international law and in an attempt to fashion causes of action that manifestly are unsupported by the sources of contemporary international law. This is especially so in cases in which non-U.S. citizens seek to enforce in U.S. courts alleged extra-territorial violations of non-binding UN resolutions and other 'soft-law' against juridical persons, including through unsupported theories of accessorial liability.[110] As one lower court rightly pointed out in a recent decision:

> Plaintiffs' eloquence alone does not equate to law. Nor, regrettably, is the law always as eloquent as we may wish it to be, especially when its outcomes may not comport with our own conception of the ideal.[111]

There is indeed a high degree of idealism and wishful thinking involved in litigation under the Alien Tort Statute. The contemporary body of international law may be imperfect, but that is no justification for judicial law-making or rulings based merely on judicial analogy.[112]

U.S. courts which accept that the Alien Tort Statute provides non-U.S. citizens with a private cause of action should protect the system of international law in assessing whether alleged violations of international law are actionable under the Alien Tort Statute. Such protection should be ensured through a thorough and systematic analysis of the sources of international law and by carefully distinguishing between primary and secondary (or subsidiary) sources or evidence. The fact that none of the recent Alien Tort Statute cases against private companies have yet resulted in a final judgment is no argument for less caution and concern, especially in light of the substantial litigation costs involved and the potential impact of these cases on the fledgling system of international law.

---

110   The recent case law of the Second Circuit pointing to a strict approach to the controversial doctrine of universal jurisdiction, permitting a state to prosecute an offender of any nationality for an offense committed outside of the prosecuting state and without contacts to that state, would seem to undercut civil cases against private companies under the Alien Tort Statute. See *United States* v. *Yousef*, 327 F.3d 56, 97-108 (2d Cir. 2003) (holding that universal jurisdiction arises under customary international law only where crimes (1) are universally condemned by the community of nations, and (2) by their nature occur either outside of a state or where there is no state capable of punishing the crime, and restricting such jurisdiction to piracy, genocide, war crimes, and crimes against humanity). There is a correlation between Alien Tort Statute cases involving a determination of customary international law and universal jurisdiction cases in that 'the universality principle permits jurisdiction over only a limited set of crimes *that cannot be expanded judicially*'. Idem at 103.
111   *Tachiona et al.* v. *Mugabe et al.*, 169 F.Supp.2d 259, *316 (S.D.N.Y. 2001) (Marrero, J.).
112   See, e.g., *Yousef*, 327 F.3d at 56, 99.

Tort claims against multinational companies for foreign human rights violations committed abroad: Lessons from the Alien Tort Claims Act?

Jan Wouters, Leen de Smet and Cedric Ryngaert

1 INTRODUCTION

In the last few decades, methods have been explored to hold non-state actors such as individuals and multinational companies (MNCs) accountable for gross violations of international human rights and humanitarian law. Until now, this effort has focused primarily on a criminal approach, both internationally and domestically. Only in rare cases is a sanctions mechanism civil in nature. Probably the best-known example of such a mechanism is the American *Alien Tort Claims Act* (ATCA).

The recent debacle of Belgium's 'Genocide Act',[1] which so painfully exposed the problems and limitations of a (domestic) criminal approach based on universal jurisdiction, prompted a renewed interest in civil law mechanisms such as the ATCA.[2] The aim of a criminal procedure is obviously to punish, whereas a civil or torts procedure serves a compensatory purpose.[3] Accordingly, the nature of sanctions differs considerably. Deploying criminal law in combating crimes against international humanitarian law almost inevitably entails imprisonment when the accused is found guilty, given the gravity of these crimes. Torts procedures, on the other hand, can only give rise to damages when defendants are found liable, regardless of the gravity of their act. Damages, no matter how severe, are, at a psychological level, considered to be a lesser sanction than imprisonment.[4] In addition, the exercise of civil extrater-

---

1   Former Act of 16 June 1993 concerning grave breaches of international humanitarian law (*Moniteur Belge*, 5 August 1993). The Act was amended by the Act of 10 February 1999 (*Moniteur Belge*, 23 March 1999) and by the Act of 23 April 2003 (*Moniteur Belge*, 7 May 2003). Eventually, the Act was repealed by the Act of 5 August 2003 (*Moniteur Belge*, 7 August 2003). The latter Act incorporated the Genocide Act's incriminations into the Criminal Code, and the procedural and jurisdictional procedures into the Code of Criminal Procedure. See on the Genocide Act and the controversies arisen from it: J. Wouters & H. Panken (eds.), *De Genocidewet in internationaal perspectief [The Genocide Act in International Perspective]* (Ghent, Larcier, 2002), p. xi + 377 p.
2   See for example in Belgium: J.-L. Van Boxstael, 'A la recherche d'une justice universelle: l'Alien Tort Statute et la réparation des crimes contre l'humanité', in: J. Verhoeven (ed.), *La loyauté. Mélanges offerts à Etienne Cerexhe* (Brussels, De Boeck & Larcier, 1997), p. 375-406.
3   Some legal systems, such as the American system, however, provide for so-called 'punitive' damages. See infra.
4   For the sake of efficiency, damages are often granted by the criminal court, once criminal guilt has been established. If national procedural law provides for it, however, civil action can be brought before a civil court. Then, the plaintiff has to prove damage, guilt and the causal connection between guilt and damage. When the prosecutor is unable or unwilling to initiate proceedings, a civil action may be the only way to obtain compensation.

ritorial jurisdiction is held to be less contentious, since the course of the procedure is steered by the parties, while criminal procedure is a public law procedure in which government representatives such as prosecutors and judges
have the primary role. The so-called 'civil parties' are often denied any substantial rights. Although, in theory, the separation of powers avoids interference from the executive branch in the judiciary, a criminal procedure against
foreign citizens raises suspicion, in that political manipulation may be seen as
inherent in the prosecution monopoly of the government. Both the heavier
punishment and the greater government involvement contributed to the
demise of the Belgian Genocide Act, even though it was the very granting of
rights to the civil parties under the Belgian Code of Criminal Procedure (the
so-called *'plainte avec constitution de partie civile'*) that proved to be the key factor in its abuse and ultimate repeal.

Whether, and to what extent, a torts instrument, such as the ATCA, might
respond to objections such as those raised against Belgium's Genocide Act –
and might serve as a model – is the core question of this paper. After briefly
outlining the practical application of the ATCA to date (2), its specific characteristics (3) and the controversies it has entailed (4), we aim to respond to this
question.

2   THE ALIEN TORT CLAIMS ACT IN PRACTICE

As early as 1789, the US Congress adopted the ATCA as part of the Judiciary
Act, regulating the judicial organisation of the United States.[5] This act grants
the district courts competence to hear tort claims from non-Americans who
have been a victim of a violation of a norm of 'the law of nations' or a treaty to
which the United States is party, no matter where the violation has occurred.[6]
The precise intention of the legislature and the exact circumstances under
which this brief and opaque act was adopted, can only be surmised in the absence of any *travaux préparatoires*.[7] It is certain, however, that the ATCA lay
dormant for nearly 200 years, having been invoked successfully only five
times.[8] As late as 1975, a federal judge referred to it as an 'old but little-used

---

5   Alien Tort Claims Act (ATCA), 28 U.S.C. §1350. The Judiciary Act is founded upon Article
       III, Section 1 of the U.S. Constitution.
6   'The district courts shall have original jurisdiction of any civil action by an alien for a tort
       only, committed in violation of the law of nations or a treaty of the United State'. Idem.
7   Unlike the Belgian Genocide Act, the enactment of which was prompted both by obliga-
       tions under international treaties (especially the 1949 Geneva Conventions and their 1977
       Additional Protocols) and by ethical motives, the ATCA might, initially at least, have been
       a response to national security concerns. See C. Shaw, 'Uncertain justice: liability of multi-
       nationals under the Alien Tort Claims Act', 54 *Stanford Law Review* (2002), (1359), 1364.
8   See C. Shaw, l.c., 1365.

section', a 'kind of legal Lohengrin ... no one seems to know whence it came'.[9] However, in recent decades, after several high-profile legal suits, the ATCA has emerged as an important instrument in the fight against international human rights violations.

A first breakthrough came about in 1980 in *Filártiga* v. *Peña-Irala*. In *Filártiga*, the family of a Paraguayan boy had filed a tort claim on the basis of the ATCA against a Paraguayan policeman who had tortured the boy to death and was residing in New York at the time of the suit. Unlike the District Court, which had dismissed the claim invoking a lack of jurisdiction *ratione materiae*, the Court of Appeals ruled that deliberate torture by an official authority constituted a violation of the law of nations, which the US courts had jurisdiction over on the basis of the ATCA.[10] Inspired by this successful precedent, the number of ATCA procedures has been increasing steadily, testing the possibilities and redrawing the limits of the ATCA, both *ratione personae* and *ratione materiae*.

Especially regarding the scope of application *ratione personae*, a clear evolution is discernible. Whereas in *Filártiga* the ATCA was applied to a person having an official capacity, ensuing cases addressed the question of whether the ATCA's scope of application *ratione personae* would, apart from States that traditionally had been the addressees of international law, also encompass non-state, i.e. private actors. While, initially, courts found that this was not the case,[11] eventually, they decided to steer another, more progressive course. The

---

9   See Judge Henry Friendly in *IIT* v. *Vencap Ltd.*, 519F.2d 1001, 1015 (2d Cir. 1975). See also B. Kieserman, 'Profits and Principles: Promoting Multinational Corporate Responsibility by Amending the Alien Tort Claims Act', 48 *Catholic University Law Review* (1999) 889-896; C. Shaw, l.c., 54 *Stanford Law Review* (2002) p. 1364; K. Randall, 'Federal Jurisdiction Over International Law Claims: Inquiries into the Alien Tort Statute', 18 *New York University Journal of International Law and Politics*, (1985) 11-19.

10   *Filártiga* v. *Peña-Irala*, United States Court of Appeals Second Circuit, 30 June 1980 (630 F.2d 876). See for comments: P. Claude, 'The case of Joelito Filártiga and the clinic of hope', 5 *Human Rights Quarterly*, (1983) 275-295; D.E. Ovaska, 'Internal deed of foreign official actionable in United States Court, Filártiga v. Peña-Irala', 5 *Suffolk Transnational Law Journal* (1981) 297-310; D.S.D., 'Enforcement of international human rights in the federal courts after Filártiga v. Peña-Irala', 67 *Virgina Law Review* (1981) 1379-1393; 'Federal jurisdiction, human rights, and the Law of Nations: essays on Filártiga v. Peña-Irala: symposium', 11 *Georgia Journal of International and Comparative Law* (1981) 305-341.

11   *Tel-Oren* v. *Libyan Arab Republic*, United States Court of Appeals District of Columbia Circuit, 3 February 1984 (726 F.2d 774); *Doe* v. *Karadzic*, United States District Court, S.D. New York, 7 September 1994 (866 F. Supp. 734).

Kadic v. *Karadzic* judgment (1995)[12], which was recently confirmed by *Doe I* v. *Unocal Corp.* (2002)[13], elucidated that the ATCA cannot only be invoked against state actors, state officials and private actors for acts *'under color of law'*, but also against private actors for purely private acts. The courts *inter alia* accept this for crimes such as genocide, war crimes, piracy and slavery, for which international law provides individual responsibility, regardless of whether they were committed by state or non-state actors. With respect to non-state actors, however, the courts do not accept jurisdiction under the ATCA for murder, rape and torture.[14]

In the wake of these cases, a few test cases have been filed, first against American, and later against non-American MNCs for violations of international rules committed by their subsidiaries, branches and subcontractors abroad. Often, these claims are based on alleged complicity in violations committed by the government of the State in which the MNC is active. In this context the most advanced case is *Doe* v. *Unocal*. The case concerns a torts claim for human rights violations (forced labour and slavery among others) that took place during the construction of the so-called 'Yadana' gas pipeline from Myanmar to Thailand, by a joint venture of the California-based MNC Unocal, the French MNC Total and the gas company MOGE, controlled by the

---

12   *Kadic* v. *Karadzic*, United States Court of Appeals Second Circuit, 13 October 1995 (70 F. 3d 232). In this case, a number of Croats and Muslims filed a claim against the Serbian leader Karadzic on the basis of the ATCA, alleging violations committed under his command. They accused him of, *inter alia*, committing genocide and war crimes. The District Court dismissed the case because 'the current Bosnian-Serb warring military faction does not constitute a recognized state (...) Accordingly this Court finds that the members of Karadzic's faction do not act under the color of any recognized state law. (...) This Court declines to extend § 1350 to redress acts of torture engaged in by private individuals.' (*Doe* v. *Karadzic*, United States District Court S.D. New York, 7 September 1994 (866 F. Supp. 734)). On appeal however, the Court of Appeals decided that the ATCA could be invoked against private actors when the claim concerns a violation punishable by international law, regardless of whether it was committed by private or state actors: 'We do not agree that the law of nations, as understood in the modern era, confines its reach to state action. Instead, we hold that certain forms of conduct violate the law of nations whether undertaken by those acting under the auspices of a state or only as private individuals'. See also B. Stephens, 'Corporate accountability: international human rights litigation against corporations in US Courts', in: M.T. Kamminga & S. Zia-Zarifi (eds.), *Liability of multinational corporations under international law* (Kluwer Law International, The Hague 2000) (209), p. 214-215; S. Zia-Zarifi, 'Suing multinational corporations in the U.S. for violating international law', 4 *UCLA Journal of International Law and Foreign Affairs* (1999) (81), 92.
13   *Doe I* v. *Unocal Corp.*, United States Court of Appeals Ninth Circuit, 18 September 2002, II. A.3, available on <http://www.ca9.uscourts.gov/>
14   See inter alia *Kadic* v. *Karadzic*, United States Court of Appeals Second Circuit, 13 October 1995 (70 F. 3d 232); *Doe I* v. *Unocal Corp.*, United States Court of Appeals Ninth Circuit, 18 September 2002, II. A.3. These crimes, however, could form the basis for an ATCA claim against a private person, provided that they also meet the criteria of a crime such as genocide, piracy for which international law also provides for individual responsibility with respect to private persons. Furthermore, the 1991 Torture Victim Prevention Act, 28 U.S.C. §1350 App., creates liability under U.S. law, where under 'color of law, of any foreign nation' an individual is subject to torture or extra-judicial killing.

Government of Myanmar (more specifically the State Law and Order Restoration Council or 'SLORC'). A claim was also filed against two Unocal directors. In 1997, the California District Court confirmed its jurisdiction in this case, but, citing State immunity, it dismissed the claims against the Government of Myanmar and the gas company MOGE.[15] In 2000, the Court ruled in favour of Unocal: it followed Unocal's argument that ATCA requires direct participation in the violations concerned, a condition that was not met in the case. Interestingly, the District Court applied the 28 U.S.C. Section 1983 test. Section 1983, a domestic law, limits liability for civil rights violations committed by private entities to acts 'under the color' of government authority. Since Unocal did not 'control' the SLORC's decision to violate human rights, under Section 1983's 'State action' analysis, it could not be held liable.[16] The applicants appealed this decision successfully. On 18 September 2002, the Court of Appeals for the 9th Circuit found that there was sufficient evidence supporting the applicants' claim that Unocal could be held responsible under the ATCA for aiding and abetting murder, rape and forced labour, but not torture. Unlike the District Court, the Court of Appeals considered Section 1983 to be immaterial in the case and applied the 'aiding and abetting' test, borrowed from international law, thereby referring to *Tel-Oren* v. *Libyan Arab Republic* and *Kadic* v. *Karadzic*. As international law attributes individual liability to a number of crimes, regardless of State action, Unocal could be held liable for 'aiding and abetting' international crimes. [17] The Court of Appeals referred the case to the District Court for further investigation.

A second well-known and advanced case is *Wiwa* v. *Royal Dutch Petroleum*. In this case, certain members of the indigenous Nigerian Ogoni tribe alleged complicity of the Royal Dutch Shell Group in acts by the Nigerian Government, notably gross human rights violations (torture and hanging of Ken Saro-Wiwa and John Kpuinen, two leaders of the Movement for the Survival of the Ogoni People), forced occupation of land without compensation and inflicting serious environmental damage to the Nigerian Ogoni territory. In 2002, the Court of Appeals for the 2nd Circuit quashed the circuit judgment, which had dismissed the case on grounds of 'forum non conveniens'.[18] A new attempt by Shell to have the case dismissed on grounds of lack of jurisdiction *ratione materiae* failed.[19]

---

15   *Doe I.* v. *Unocal*, 963 F. Supp. 880 (C.D. Cal. 1997).

16   *Doe I.* v. *Unocal Corp.*, 110 F. Supp. 2d 1294, 1305-1310 (C.D. Cal. 2000), cited in T. Collingsworth, 'Recent ILRF cases to enforce human rights under the ACTA', *International Civil Liberties Report* 2001, available on <http://www.aclu.org/library/iclr/2001/>

17   *Doe I* v. *Unocal Corp.*, United States Court of Appeals Ninth Circuit, 18 September 2002, II. A.15, available on <http://www.ca9.uscourts.gov/> See on the ATCA and the interpretation of Section 1983: S.A. Khalil, 'The Alien Tort Claims Act and Section 1983: the Improper Use of Domestic Laws to 'Create' and 'Define' International Liability for Multinational Corporations', 31 *Hofstra Law Review* (2002) 207-239.

18   *Ken Wiwa* v. *Royal Dutch Petroleum Company*, United States Court of Appeals Second Circuit, 14 September 2000 (226 F. 3d. 88).

19   *Ken Wiwa* v. *Royal Dutch Petroleum Company*, United States District Court for the Southern District of New York, 22 February 2002, (2002 U.S. Sist. Lexis 3293).

More recently, a first decision was handed down in the case brought under the ATCA by the Presbyterian Church of Sudan against the Canadian energy giant Talisman Energy. The Church alleged collaboration with the Sudanese Government in the ethnic cleansing of Christians and other non-Muslim minorities in southern Sudan. Talisman Energy's request to declare the case inadmissible, was dismissed.[20] Other ATCA procedures against MNCs included the case against Coca Cola for deploying paramilitary troops against trade-unionists in Colombia,[21] the recent ExxonMobil case, in which 11 Indonesian peasants claimed damages from ExxonMobil for complicity in human rights violations by Indonesian army units hired to guard gas fields, and the claims against dozens of MNCs and banks for their role in the South African apartheid regime.[22]

Finally, the American judiciary had to address the ATCA's precise scope of application *ratione materiae*. Although the text of the ATCA refers to violations of international law ('law of nations'), it was not clear how this concept was to be understood.[23] At present, it seems that the courts require the international law rules to be 'specific', 'universal' and 'obligatory'.[24] According to case law, this category includes, as mentioned before, piracy, genocide, war crimes, crimes against humanity and slavery.[25] It is less certain whether cultural geno-

---

20   *Presbyterian church of Sudan, et al.,* v. *Talisman Energy, Inc. and the Republic of Sudan,* 01-Civ. 9882 (AGS) (S.D.N.Y.), 19 March 2003, U.S. Dist. Lexis 4085.

21   'Coke sued over death squad claims', *BBC News,* 20 July 2001, available on <http://news.bbc.co.uk/1/hi/business/1448962.stm>; 'La compétence universelle version américaine', *La Libre Belgique,* 17 July 2002 ; 'Coca-Cola schendt mensenrechten in Colombia' [Coca Cola violates human rights in Colombia], *De Financieel-Economische Tijd,* 23 July 2002.

22   *Khulumani et al.* v. *Barcleya National Bank Ltd. et al.,* 11 November 2002, United States District Court Eastern District of New York, complaint available on <http://www.nyed.uscourts.gov/02cv5952cmp.pdf>. See 'Europese en Amerikaanse bedrijven aangeklaagd voor rol in apartheid' [European and American companies sued for their apartheid role], *De Financieel-Economische Tijd,* 13 November 2002.

23   See for example W.S. Dodge, 'Which torts in violation of the Law of Nations', 24 *Hastings International and Comparative Law Review* (2001) 351-360.

24   See *Filártiga* v. *Peña-Irala,* United States Court of Appeals Second Circuit, 30 June 1980 (630 F.2d 876); *Forti* v. *Suarez-Mason,* United States District Court, N.D. California, 6 October 1987 (672 F. Supp. 1531); *In re Estate of Ferdinand Marcos, Human Rights Litigation* v. *Estate of Ferdinand Marcos,* United States Court of Appeals Ninth Circuit, 16 June 1994 (25 F. 3d 1467); *Kadic* v. *Karadzic,* United States Court of Appeals Second Circuit, 13 October 1995 (70 F. 3d 232); *Beanal* v. *Freeport-McMoran Inc.,* United States District Court, Louisiana, 10 April 1997 (969F. Supp. 362); *Papa* v. *U.S.,* United States Court of Appeals Ninth Circuit, 25 February 2002 (281 F. 3d 1004); *Flores* v. *Southern Peru Copper Corporation,* United States District Court, S.D. New York, 16 July 2002 (253 F. Supp.2d 510); *Doe I* v. *Unocal Corp.,* United States Court of Appeals Ninth Circuit, 18 September 2002, II. A.1; *Presbyterian Church of Sudan, et al.,* v. *Talisman Energy, Inc. and the Republic of Sudan,* United States District Court Southern District of New York, 01-Civ. 9882 (AGS) (S.D.N.Y.), 19 March 2003, U.S. Dist. Lexis 4085.

25   See supra, note 15.

cide and international environmental norms also meet these strict conditions, especially after the *Flores* decision (2003).[26]

3   UNIVERSAL JURISDICTION AND AMERICAN CIVIL PROCEDURE

The rise of the ATCA as an instrument in the fight against violations of international human rights and humanitarian norms might in part be attributable to a combination of two factors: universal jurisdiction and some peculiarities of American civil procedure.[27]

As the foregoing cases have already suggested, the ATCA grants U.S. federal courts a form of universal jurisdiction. In order to have such jurisdiction, it is not necessary for the facts to have occurred in the U.S., or for the author or the victim to have been a U.S. national. Precisely this circumstance, namely that cases having no link with the U.S. can be brought before U.S. courts, has

---

26   The Fifth Circuit ruled that the prohibition of cultural genocide is not universally accepted (*Beanal* v. *Freeport-McMoran Inc.*, United States Court of Appeals Fifth Circuit, 29 November 1999 (197 F. 3d 161). ATCA claims for violations of international environmental norms are mostly dismissed on grounds of *forum non conveniens* (see for example *Bano* v. *Union Carbide Corp.*, United States Court of Appeals Second Circuit, 15 November 2001 (273 F.3d 120)) or on the basis of the *'non-justiciability doctrine'* (see for example *Sarei* v. *Rio Tinto*, United States District Court, C.D. California, 9 July 2002 (221 F.Supp.2d 1116)). In a few other cases, the judge ruled that the principles of international environmental law, as invoked by the parties, did not meet the aforementioned test. The District Court of New York, for instance, found a violation of Principle 21 of the Stockholm Declaration to be no violation of the law of nations in the context of ATCA (*Amlon Metals* v. *FMC Corporation*, United States District Court, S.D. New York, 13 December 1991 (775 F. Supp. 668)). In another famous case, the Court of Appeals for the 5th Circuit confirmed the District Court's judgment, holding that the necessary universal consensus on the precise content and legal status of the principle 'the polluter pays', the precautionary principle and the proximity principle, lacks; the court also held that U.S. courts ought to be cautious not to intervene in the environmental policy of other states (*Beanal* v. *Freeport-McMoran Inc.*, United States Court of Appeals for the Fifth Circuit, 29 November 1999 (197 F. 3d 161)). More recently, the District Court of New York dismissed the argument that serious environmental pollution could lead to a lawful complaint on the basis of the ATCA for serious violations of the right to life, the right to health and the principle of sustainable development. The judge ruled that these abstract and undefined human rights do not constitute norms that are enforceable against the MNC. Furthermore, the applicants failed to prove that such environmental pollution belonged to 'those clear and unambiguous rules by which States universally abide, or to which they accede, out of a sense of legal obligation and mutual concern' (*Flores* v. *Southern Peru Copper Corporation*, United States District Court, S.D. New York, 16 July 2002 (253 F. Supp. 2d 510)). See also A. Khokhryakova, 'Beanal v. Freeport-McMoran Inc.: Liability of a Private Actor for International Environmental Tort under the Alien Tort Claims Act', 9 *Colorado Journal of International Environmental Law* (1998) 463-492; R. Herz, 'Litigating Environmental Abuses Under the Alien Tort Claims Act: a Practical Assessment', 40 *Virginia Journal of International Law* (2000) 545-638; M. Hamblett, 'Environmental Suit Disallowed under U.S. Statute. Court Sees Limits to Alien Tort Claims Act', 26 *National Law Journal*, Nr. 3 (2003) 15 September 2003.

27   See B. Stephens, 'Corporate liability: enforcing human rights through domestic litigation', 24 *Hastings International and Comparative Law Review* (2001) 401-413.

met with criticism, both from the international and national enterprise community[28] and the current U.S. administration[29] (infra, 4). Yet the ATCA does not seem to grant 'absolute' universal jurisdiction, as was previously the case with the Belgian Genocide Act. American case law has indeed developed a number of doctrines making the practical application of ATCA dependent on a certain link with the American legal order, thereby filtering a possible flow of cases. On the basis of the 'minimum contacts'-doctrine for instance, federal courts can only deal with procedures against defendants that have minimum contacts with the forum State.[30] To establish minimum contacts, the criterion of 'presence' or 'continuous and systematic business' is considered. On the basis of this criterion, a claim against a Total subsidiary for complicity in human rights violations in Myanmar was declared inadmissible.[31] Second, a federal court can dismiss a case on the grounds of the 'forum non conveniens' doctrine, when it identifies an alternative forum that is more closely linked with the case.[32] Third, the 'non-justiciability' doctrine complicates the application of the ATCA in practice.[33] On the basis of this doctrine, a defendant may request the judge to dismiss jurisdiction because a case involves a 'political' question that encroaches upon the domain of foreign policy. Fourth, the Foreign Sovereignty Act and the 'Act of State' doctrine foreclose ATCA procedures against a foreign State or involving the legality of acts of foreign States.[34]

---

28   See the rather strongly formulated declaration of the presidency of the *International Chamber of Commerce* on 5 December 2002 concerning 'Extra-territorial application of national laws': 'US urged to halt extraterritorial abuse of its national law', available on <http://www.iccwbo.org/home/news_archives/2002/stories/appl-nat_law.asp>. This declaration states: 'The practice of suing companies in the US, whether domestic or foreign, for alleged events occurring in third countries is an unacceptable extraterritorial extension of US jurisdiction.'

29   See the point of view of the U.S. federal government in *Doe v. Unocal*, on appeal from the United States District Court or the Central District of California, Brief for the United States of America as amicus curiae, II, in which the extraterritorial character of the ATCA is denounced.

30   In *International Shoe Co. v. Washington*, the Supreme Court put forward a minimum contacts analysis, ruling that 'due process requires only that in order to subject a defendant to a judgment in personam, if he be not present within the territory of the forum, he have certain minimum contacts with it such that the maintenance of the suit does not offend 'traditional notions of fair play and substantial justice'. (*International Shoe Co. v. Washington*, 326 U.S. 310 (1945)) The minimum contacts doctrine was originally designed to address interstate activities, but it could easily apply to activities between nations.

31   *Doe I v. Unocal*, United States District Court C.D. California, 18 November 1998 (27 F. Supp. 2d 1174).

32   See also on this doctrine: O. De Schutter, 'The liability of multinationals for human rights violations in European Law', in: E. Brems & P. Vanden Heede (eds.), *Bedrijven en mensenrechten. Verantwoordelijkheid en aansprakelijkheid*, [Corporations and human rights. Responsibility and liability] (Maklu, Antwerp, 2003), p. 69-74.

33   See for example U. Mattei & J. Lena, 'U.S. jurisdiction over conflicts arising outside of the United States: some hegemonic implications', 24 *Hastings International and Comparative Law Review* (2001) 385-386.

34   *Contra: Doe I v. Unocal Corp.*, United States Court of Appeals Ninth Circuit, 18 September 2002, II. C., available on <http://www.ca9.uscourts.gov/>, holding that the Act of State doctrine does not necessarily preclude suit under the ATCA.

Universal jurisdiction under ATCA is not criminal, but civil in nature. This is an important difference between the U.S. and most continental-European legal systems, which, insofar as they provide for universal jurisdiction, mainly do this in a criminal law context.[35] This was the case with the Belgian Genocide Act. However, the difference should not be overstated since it is difficult to draw a strict line between civil and criminal jurisdiction.[36] This certainly holds true for the U.S. legal system, which, under certain circumstances, enables applicants to claim both compensatory and punitive damages in civil procedures. Such punitive damages are specifically allowed in cases under the ATCA, as these almost invariably concern intentional tort claims, arising from malice, or at least tort claims arising from gross negligence. In a number of ATCA cases, including a recent procedure against the Patriotic Front of Zimbabwe, considerable punitive damages were allowed.[37] In any event, the fact remains that ATCA procedures can never lead to typical criminal penalties such as imprisonment.

---

35   The question of whether civil universal jurisdiction for national courts is permitted under international law requires a more elaborate analysis that goes far beyond the present contribution. It has been contended that, if criminal universal jurisdiction may be accepted under international law, this should *a fortiori* be the case for civil universal jurisdiction. Interestingly, in 1928, in the *Island of Palmas* case it was held by the arbitrator, M. Huber: 'Sovereignty in the relations between States signifies independence. Independence in regard to a portion of the globe is the right to exercise therein, to the exclusion of any other State, the function of a State. This development [...] of international law [has] established this principle of the exclusive competence of the State in regard to its own territory in such a way as to make it the point of departure in settling most questions that concern international relations'. (Perm. Ct. Arb. 1928, *Island of Palmas* (U.S. v. Neth.), 2 R.I.A.A., 829). The reference to 'the function of a State' has brought some commentators to lay great emphasis on the alleged restriction of territorial sovereignty to public law. Private law, which regulates the relations between citizens and is not the function of a State, would be subject to the concurring competence of several States. See also M. Akehurst, 'Jurisdiction in international law', 46 *British Yearbook of International Law* (1972), (145), 177; L. Reydams, *Universal Jurisdiction. International and Municipal Legal Perspective* (Oxford, Oxford University Press, 2003), p. 3; B. Stephens, 'Translating Filartiga: a Comparative and International Law Analysis of Domestic Remedies for International Human Rights Violations', 27 *Yale Journal of International Law* (2000), (2), 44. See also A. Nollkaemper, 'Translating Principles of Public International Law into Principles of Corporate Liability', paper Hague Joint Conference, 2003, From Government to Governance: the Growing Impact of Non-State Actors on the International and the European Legal System (on file with the author), 9; *Restatement of the Law Third – The Foreign Relations Law of the United States*, Washington, American Law Institute (1990), p. 255; *Kadic v. Karadzic*, United States Court of Appeals Second Circuit (70 F. 3d 232).

36   See T. Meron, 'Is International law Moving Towards Criminalization?', 9 *European Journal of International Law* 1998, (18), 20. In this sense also B. Stephens, l.c., 27 *Yale Journal of International Law* (2000) 44-49. Stephens (18-21) rightly points out that, in a large number of legal systems, there is a certain independence, rather than a strict separation, between the civil and criminal law procedure. See B. Stephens, l.c., 18-21.

37   See *Adela Chiminya Tochiana et al.* v. *Robert Gabriel Mugabe, Zimbabwe African National Union Patriotic Front (ZANU-PF)*, U.S. District Court, S.D. New York, 11 December 2002. In this case, the judge condemned ZANU-PF and allowed damages totalling 71.250.453 $, comprised of 20.250.453 $ 'compensatory damages' and 51.000.000 $ 'punitive damages'. See for other cases allowing punitive damages: *Xuncax v. Gramajo*, 886 F.Supp. 162 (D.Mass. 1995); *Abebe-Jira v. Negewo*, 72 F.3d 844 (11th Cir. 1996).

Importantly, a number of features of U.S. civil procedure have proven to be incentives for the use of the ATCA. Unlike most European continental legal systems, the so-called 'class action' suit exists under U.S. law. This is a procedure whereby one or more plaintiffs with concurring interests file a claim on behalf of an entire 'plaintiff class'. The judgment in such cases is binding upon all members of the group as well as the adverse party, just as if one of the members had filed a claim individually.[38] Such a procedure against a large number of MNCs and banks, accused of complicity in the South African apartheid regime, was initiated by a South African organisation (*Khulumani*) on behalf of its 32 700 members and a number of individual victims[39] (supra, 2.), and by a person on behalf of all men and women who were victims of atrocities committed by Serbian military units under the command of Karadzic.[40] Under most continental-European laws, this would not be possible at all in view of the strict admissibility requirements, particularly requirements of interest, the plaintiff has to meet.[41] By way of a class action suit, high procedural costs are spread out over a large number of plaintiffs who, acting separately, would not be able to finance them.[42] Second, it provides procedural and economic advantages in that joining claims undeniably enhances efficiency. Third, a class-action suit may generate considerable publicity for the victims' situation. Noteworthy is the so-called *'pro bono'* regime, granting the lawyer payment from the damages allowed, a system that reduces the deterrence of excessive lawyers' fees, most importantly in the light of the American practice of contingency fees. Counsels for the plaintiffs may accept contingent fees and postpone payment until the suit is over. If the suit is lost, the lawyer receives nothing. If he wins, he receives a considerable percentage of the damages allowed. Although lawyers will be cautious in accepting contingency fees since losing the case may end their business, the threshold for the plaintiffs to start proceedings is much lower as they have nothing to lose.[43] Needless to say, this mechanism greatly enhances the risk of litigation in the United States.

---

38   For more information on this claim: see K.M. Clermont, *Civil Procedure* (West Group, St Paul, 1999, 5th ed.), p. 201-206; J.H. Friedenthal, M.K. Kane & A.R. Miller, *Civil Procedure,* (West Group, St Paul, 1999, 3d ed.), p. 736-755; International Financial Law Review (ed.), *United States Litigation. A guide for foreign corporations* (1995) 15-19.
39   *Khulumani et al.* v. *Barcleya National Bank Ltd. et al.,* 11 November 2002, United States District Court Eastern District of New York, complaint available on <http://www.nyed.us-courts.gov/02cv5952cmp.pdf.>
40   *Doe* v. *Karadzic,* United States District Court S.D. New York, 7 September 1994 (866 F. Supp. 734).
41   See for example Belgium: the plaintiff has to establish his interest in the action (Articles 17 and 18 Code of Civil Procedure). His interest should be personal and direct: Cour de Cassation [Supreme Court of Belgium], 25 October 1985, *Arr. Cass.* (1985-86) 249.
42   U. Mattei & J. Lena, l.c., 24 *Hastings International and Comparative Law Review* (2001) 395.
43   Especially in antitrust matters, contingency fees contribute to a litigation obsession. See W.S. Grimes, 'International Antitrust Enforcement Directed at Restrictive Practices and Concentration: The United States' Experience', in: H. Ullrich (ed.), *Comparative Competition Law: Approaching an International System of Antitrust Law* (Nomos, Baden-Baden, 1998), p. 234.

4   THE CONTROVERSY

As could be expected, the revival of employing the ATCA has generated controversy. Apart from the aforementioned problem of vagueness of this 18th-century legal text, recent litigation has revealed a number of shortcomings and drawbacks. First, although the burden of proof in civil cases is certainly more advantageous for the plaintiff than in criminal cases, he stands alone with it. Second, the victims may face difficulties in obtaining the execution of the judgment allowing damages. Third, the low procedural threshold to file a claim under the ATCA produces several drawbacks. Class actions are often initiated, or at least encouraged, by groups using the ATCA as a tool to influence politics and the media with a view to putting the situation in certain regimes on the agenda. Such use of the ATCA obviously harms its reputation. Precisely fear of rash or politically motivated claims, or both, foments political and corporate opposition to the ATCA. In Belgium, these claims contributed to the amendment and ultimate repeal of the Genocide Act.[44]

The universal character of the ATCA, like the Belgian Genocide Act, has been a very sensitive issue as well and has been challenged from ethical, legal, political and economic perspectives. Thus, it has been said that the ATCA enables U.S. courts to exercise jurisdiction extraterritorially[45], thereby unduly imposing American values on other States. By the same token, it has been argued that the ATCA's use boils down to a modern form of imperialism and an infringement upon the sovereignty of the State on whose territory the activities occurred.[46] Moreover, on the basis of this extraterritorial approach, the

---

44   C. van den Wyngaert, 'Valt de genocidewet nog te redden?' [Can the Genocide Act Still Be Saved?], *De Standaard*, 23 June 2003. See also the reaction of M. Verhaeghe, cited in 'Universele genocidewet is niet meer' [Universal Jurisdiction is Dead], *De Standaard*, 23 June 2003.

45   See the declaration of the presidency of the *International Chamber of Commerce*, 5 December 2002, supra note 25.

46   See U. Mattei & J. Lena, l.c., 382-383 and 388. A similar discussion arose in the Australian Parliament, in view of the extraterritorial character of the proposed *Corporate Code of Conduct Bill 2000* (available on <http://www.aph.gov.au/>): *Parliament of the Commonwealth of Australia, Report on the Corporate Code of Conduct Bill 2000*, Parliamentary joint statutory committee on corporations and securities, June 2001, §§ 3.37-109 en 4.47-4.53. More recently, the *'Universal Jurisdiction Rejection Act of 2003'*, a proposed bill introduced in the U.S. House of Representatives by Congressman Gary Ackerman on 9 May 2003, exemplified the opposition to universal jurisdiction. This proposal aimed at prohibiting any form of cooperation by the American Government with investigations or prosecutions on the basis of a law providing for universal jurisdiction. One could not fail to note that ATCA jurisdiction did not qualify for the definition of universal jurisdiction given by the proposal. In Section 10, the term 'universal jurisdiction act' was described as 'a statute of a foreign country that authorizes its judicial or prosecutorial authorities to investigate, prosecute, and punish genocide, war crimes, acts of torture, violations of human rights, or crimes against humanity that
(a) at the time of their actual or alleged occurrence, were not committed by or against the citizens or residents of that country or their property;
(b) did not occur on the territory of that country or territory under its control; or
(c) are otherwise prosecutable by an ad hoc international criminal tribunal established by the United Nations Security Council for the purpose of prosecuting such acts.'

U.S. legal system would run the risk of becoming the world's court of first instance for civil cases against perpetrators of human rights violations.[47] The analogy with the criticism of the Belgian Genocide Act ('the International Criminal Court's court of first instance') is once more striking.

Apart from that, political opposition to the ATCA is rife. The U.S. federal government, for instance, has recently attempted to block the *ExxonMobil* case (in which Indonesian peasants claimed damages from ExxonMobil for colluding in human rights violations committed by Indonesian army units), because allowing damages would harm foreign relations with Indonesia, a major ally in the war against terrorism.[48] In *Doe* v. *Unocal*, the U.S. Attorney General John Ashcroft filed an *amicus curiae* brief with the District Court, requesting it to revise its positive attitude toward the ATCA.[49] Dealing with this new generation of complaints would, according to this document, lead to unacceptable interference of U.S. courts in U.S. foreign policy. This *amicus curiae* brief has provoked vehement criticism from various human rights organisations and scholars, including Harold H. Koh, a Yale Law School professor and former Assistant Secretary of State for Human Rights under President Clinton.[50] While previous American administrations supported, or at least respected, the use of the ATCA in the fight against gross human rights violations, the current administration has apparently changed course.[51] In the administration's

---

47   T. Niles, 'The very long arm of American Law', *Financial Times*, 5 November 2002; D. Griswold, *Abuse of 18th century law threatens U.S. economic and security interests*, 25 January 2003, available on <http://www.cato.org/dailys/01-25-03.html>. The American legal system is exposed to a similar threat in antitrust matters. Drawing on the line of reasoning of the *Kruman* and *Empagran* cases, foreign plaintiffs could sue foreign defendants even when the anticompetitive conduct and effects occurred abroad, provided that the conspiracy also affected the U.S. market. Combined with the possibility of highly advantageous treble damages, one could easily understand the risk of a litigation rush to U.S. fora. See *Kruman* v. *Christie's Int'l PLC*, 284 F.3d 384 (2nd Cir. 2002), *Empagran, S.A.* v. *F. Hoffman-LaRoche Ltd.*, 315 F.3d 338 (D.C. Cir. 2003).

48   See J. Lobe, 'State Department Tries to Get ExxonMobil Suit Dropped', 7 August 2002, <http://www.corpwatch.org/news/PRT.jsp?articleid=3469>; S. Reddy, 'Individuals Struggle to Hold Corporations Accountable for Abuses', 8 August 2002, <http://www.globalpolicy.org/socecon/tncs/2002/holdtncsaccount.htm>

49   *Doe* v. *Unocal*, Appeal from the United States District Court for the Central District of California – Brief for the United States of America as Amicus curiae.

50   H.H. Koh, 'Wrong on Rights', 18 July 2003, *Yale Global*, available at <http://www.globalpolicy.org/intljustice/atca/2003/0721koh.htm>; made public as a paper during the ASIL/NVIR Hague Joint Conference on Contemporary Issues of International Law (July 2003), 'From Government to Governance: the Growing Impact of Non-State Actors on the International and the European Legal System. Koh remarked inter alia: 'The government's position is wrong, unnecessary, and damaging to meaningful efforts to promote corporate responsibility in the US and respect for human rights worldwide. Ironically this would also deny the US the right to try terrorist organizations for their action abroad'.

51   Compare with U.S. opposition to the International Criminal Court. See J. Wouters, 'Het Internationaal Strafhof doet de continenten uit elkaar drijven [The International Criminal Court drives the continents apart]', *De Standaard*, (17 August 2002).

view, the ATCA is merely an act that confers jurisdiction without necessarily granting a private right of action.[52]

Just as complaints against a number of businesses under the Belgian Genocide Act raised concerns with the Belgian business community[53], procedures under the ATCA met with resistance from the American and international business community. The National Foreign Trade Council, the U.S. Chamber of Commerce, the U.S. Council of International Business and the International Chamber of Commerce have all demanded a radical reform or even repeal of the ATCA, advancing various arguments. The possible precedent of the *Unocal* case (supra, 2) and its consequences for other MNCs is, of course, the main cause of concern. More in particular, the corporate world fears that the sole fact of being economically active or investing in a State in which gross violations of international law occur would suffice to be regarded as colluding in the violations under the current interpretation of the ATCA.[54] The business community considers the recent complaint against a number of banks for collusion in apartheid (supra, 2.) one of the most outrageous examples, as complicity in this case would emanate from the normal business activities of banks, namely granting loans.[55] MNCs fear that they will become the target of a spate of rash procedures, all the more so since an action against the foreign government concerned has almost no chance of success, due to the Foreign Sovereign Immunities Act. In their view, the threat of torts suits could considerably reduce foreign investment, which may provoke a backlash for U.S. and local economies.[56] Moreover, they fear that extraterritorial legislation such as the ATCA may undermine the competitive position of the companies to which it applies *vis-à-vis* the companies that are not subject to such legislation, a discrepancy that may contribute to the transfer of headquarters.[57]

Certainly, a blind eye cannot be turned to these concerns. However, they require considerable qualification in some respects. For instance, the risk of

---

52   Compare, for example, *Filártiga* v. *Peña-Irala*, holding that the ATCA indeed grants a private right of action, with the concurring opinions of the judges in *Tel-Oren* v. *Libyan Arab Republic*, United States Court of Appeals District of Columbia Circuit, 3 February 1984 (726 F. 2d 774), particularly judge Bork contesting that the ATCA grants a private cause of action. Basically, the federal government contends that any right of action would have to come from a federal statute, such as the Torture Victims Protection Act, which creates an explicit cause of action for aliens and U.S. for torture or extrajudicial killing.

53   See J. Wouters & L. de Smet, 'De strafrechtelijke verantwoordelijkheid van rechtspersonen voor ernstige schendingen van het internationaal humanitair recht in het licht van de Belgische genocidewet' [Corporate criminal responsibility for gross violations of international humanitarian law under the Belgian Genocide Act], in: E. Brems & P. vanden Heede (eds.), o.c., 309-338.

54   See L. Newman & D. Zaslowsky, 'The Alien Tort Claims Act: How Far Will It Go?', *New York Law Journal*, 2 (January 2003).

55   Idem.

56   D. Griswold, l.c., supra note 45.

57   See inter alia the discussion in the Australian Parliament with respect to the proposed *Corporate Code of Conduct Bill 2000: Parliament of the Commonwealth of Australia, Report on the Corporate Code of Conduct Bill 2000, Parliamentary joint statutory committee on corporations and securities,* June 2001, l.c., § 3.4.

rash procedures against MNCs is probably not as high as the corporate world tends to believe. It can reasonably be expected that U.S. courts would consider the mere presence of a MNC in a State in which gross violations of international law occur, to be insufficient to hold it liable under the ATCA. The Court of Appeals for the 9th Circuit made this clear in *Doe 1* v. *Unocal,* describing the liability standard as follows:

> practical assistance or encouragement which has a substantial effect on the prevention of the crime' and 'actual or constructive (i.e. reasonable) knowledge that the accomplice's actions will assist the perpetrator in the commission of the crime.[58]

Besides, American courts may resort to a number of mechanisms to dismiss rash claims in an early stage (see supra, 3.).

In addition, as far as the competitive position of American MNCs is concerned, one could agree with Human Rights Watch's opinion that leaving violations of the most fundamental human rights unpunished with a view to maintaining the competitive position of MNCs cannot be defended on ethical grounds.[59] Neither could the core of human rights and basic norms of international humanitarian law be neglected, norms that the international community as a whole accept as fundamental and universal. Beyond any doubt, these core rights include the rights sanctioned under the ATCA, such as the prohibition of genocide, crimes against humanity and war crimes. When legislation aims at the respect for these fundamental rights and freedoms, and the courts confine its enforcement to the territory of the enacting State, it can hardly be considered as imperialism or protectionism.

However this may be, academic, political and economic circles alike call for adjustments to or at least clarification on the ATCA, be it through Congressional intervention or through a judgment of the Federal Supreme Court.

5   COULD THE ATCA SERVE AS A MODEL?

Could the ATCA as a torts instrument serve as a model for European jurisdictions? The European Parliament, for its part, believes it could. As early as 1998, its Committee on Development and Cooperation, proposed conducting a study on the possibility of enacting a European version of the ATCA.[60] In ad-

---

58   *Doe I* v. *Unocal Corp.,* United States Court of Appeals for the Ninth Circuit, 18 September 2002, II, available on <http://www.ca9.uscourts.gov/ >.See also J. Wouters & L. De Smet, l.c., p. 309-338.

59   Human Right Watch, *Myths and facts about the Alien Tort Claim Act,* available on <http://hrw.org/campaigns/atca/myths.htm>.

60   *Report on EU standards for European enterprises operating in developing countries: towards a European Code of Conduct,* Committee on Development and Cooperation, 17 December 1998, p. 16.

dition, a recent resolution of the European Parliament[61] notes that Article 2 of the Brussels Convention,[62] now Regulation (EC) nr. 44/2001 (hereinafter 'the Regulation'),[63] already grants the courts of European Union Member States the option of hearing tort claims against MNCs registered or having their headquarters in a Member State, even when the damage has occurred in a third State. In the same resolution, the Parliament requests the Member States to introduce such extraterritorial jurisdiction in their national legislation, and requests the European Commission to conduct further research as to the application of this principle by national courts of the Member States.[64]

The Regulation, however, differs fundamentally from the ATCA. Unlike the ATCA, the Regulation only addresses violations by MNCs that are registered in or have their headquarters in a Member State.[65] Furthermore, the Regulation only designates the competent judge; it does not necessarily imply the application of international law. Whether the European Community is competent to turn this Regulation into a genuine European ATCA, is questionable, as a sufficient legal basis seems to be lacking in the current EC Treaty.[66] However, this does not prevent the Member States from introducing ATCA-like legislation at the national level. Nevertheless, as we have mentioned before, in the light of its peculiarities and problems, the ATCA can hardly be considered a 'model' for other national legal systems.

In any event, should a State contemplate introducing an ATCA-like system of universal torts jurisdiction, a thorough feasibility study for such a project under national and international law, as well as a broad parliamentary debate, weighing the pros and cons, should take place. Such a torts approach, compared with a criminal approach, probably has a number of advantages.[67] The victim, for instance, could take the initiative to bring a case before the

---

61   European Parliament, Resolution A5-0159/2002, 30 May 2002, Social Responsibility of Companies. Resolution of the European Parliament on the Green Book of the Commission, para. 50.

62   The Brussels Convention, a treaty dating from 1968, contains rules of jurisdiction (competent judge) and execution (enforcement of judgments in civil matters in other EU-countries).

63   Council Regulation (EC) nr. 44/2001, 22 December 2000 on jurisdiction and the recognition and enforcement of judgments in civil and commercial matters, OJ (2001) L12/1. See however for Denmark: considerations 21 and 22, and Article 1, para. 3.

64   Resolution A5-0159/20002, supra note 57, para. 50; *Report on EU standards for European enterprises operating in developing countries: towards a European Code of Conduct*, supra note 56, 16.

65   See for a more elaborate comparison of the ATCA and the Regulation: O. De Schutter, see note 32, p. 68-79.

66   To be true, Article 65 EC Treaty provides for the EC's competence to take measures in the field of cooperation in civil matters with transnational consequences. Yet these measures should be necessary for the proper functioning of the internal market. Article 308 EC Treaty as well, an article that allows the Council to take measures even if the EC Treaty has not provided the necessary powers, can only be invoked if action by the Community should prove necessary to attain, in the course of the operation of the common market, one of the objectives of the Community.

67   See N. Jägers, *Corporate human rights obligations: in search of accountability* (Intersentia, Antwerp, 2002), p. 213.

court, without having to wait for official action. In addition, although less certain, dealing with such cases, even when extraterritorial elements are involved, would be perceived as encroaching less upon the sovereignty of another State.[68] Moreover, the burden of proof is less cumbersome than in criminal cases. More specifically with respect to complaints against MNCs, a torts approach avoids the lingering controversy as to the criminal liability of MNCs.

On balance, however, universal torts jurisdiction, like universal criminal jurisdiction, is not a perfect instrument at all. In spite of its torts character, it cannot respond to a number of political and economic objections. In this respect, the manner in which a national system of universal (or otherwise extraterritorial) jurisdiction over gross violations of human rights and norms of international humanitarian law is established, rather than the choice between a torts and a criminal approach, is of utmost importance for its success. In practice, unfettered universal jurisdiction, as originally applied under the Belgian Genocide Act, or ambiguous legislative wording, as in the ATCA, can cause major problems, especially if they go hand in hand with user-friendly procedural mechanisms (such as the *plainte avec constitution de partie civile* with regard to the former legislation, and class actions with regard to the ATCA). Against this background, the time may have come to reconsider universal jurisdiction by national courts and to conceive international legal instruments and an international framework for dealing with gross violations of human rights and norms of international humanitarian law.

One of the multilateral mechanisms designed to tackle international crimes is the International Criminal Court (ICC). To be fair, with 92 ratifications, this court is no 'universal' tribunal and the refusal of a number of powerful States to become party to it or to cooperate is a reason for concern. An additional weakness of the ICC is its limited jurisdiction *ratione personae*, the ICC only having jurisdiction over natural persons.[69] Nevertheless, the ICC could

---

68   See L. Reydams, *Universal jurisdiction. International and municipal legal perspectives*, 3; J. Terry, 'Taking Filartiga on the road', in: G. Scott (ed.), *Torture as tort* (Portland Oregon, Oxford, 2001), p. 115-118.
69   Article 25.1 of the Rome Statute. Proposals for including legal persons have been discussed, though, at the Diplomatic Conference in Rome, but did not lead to any concrete results. A. Eser ('Individual criminal responsibility', in: A. Cassese, P. Gaeta & J.R.W.D. Jones (eds.), *The Rome Statute of the International Criminal Court: a Commentary*, I, (Oxford University Press, Oxford, 2002), p. 779, summarized the objections as follows: 'from a pragmatic point of view it was feared that the ICC would be faced with tremendous evidentiary problems when prosecuting legal entities, and from a more normative-political point of view it was emphasized that criminal liability of corporations is still rejected in many national legal orders, an international disparity which could not be brought in concord with the principle of complementarity'. K. Ambos ('Article 25', in O. Triffterer (ed.), *Commentary on the Rome Statute of the International Criminal Court* (Baden-Baden, Nomos, 1999) (475), 478) adds to this: 'The inclusion of collective liability would detract from the Court's jurisdictional focus, which is on individuals'. See, however, Article 25(3)(d) of the Rome Statute, which refers to 'a group of persons acting with a common purpose', which implies a certain recognition of the notion of criminal organization or entity.

deal indirectly with MNCs. Indeed, directors of MNCs could incur criminal liability for colluding in crimes over which the ICC has jurisdiction.[70] They could even incur torts liability under Article 75.2 of the Rome Statute, which provides that 'the Court may make an order directly against a convicted person specifying appropriate reparations to, or in respect of, victims, including restitution, compensation and rehabilitation'. Possible insolvency of the convicted person is addressed by Article 79 of the Rome of Statute, providing for the establishment of a trust fund, mainly based on voluntary contributions. The fund's Board of Directors was elected on 12 September 2003.[71] The ICC's Member States are required to criminalize international crimes, and, given the complementary role of the ICC,[72] are expected to exercise jurisdiction over these heinous acts, even when committed on behalf of MNCs. The ICC Statute does, however, not require Member States to exercise universal jurisdiction or to provide torts jurisdiction over these crimes. But if they do, bringing the case before the ICC has obvious advantages in terms of procedural expediency (combining both criminal and torts liability), defusion of political tensions and international recognition. It is true that the U.S. is not bound by the provisions of the Rome Statute, since it has decided not to become a party to the treaty. Nevertheless, the criminal and torts liability for which the Statute provides sends a forceful signal from the international community that international crimes by non-state actors, including MNCs, cannot remain unpunished. Let this be an invitation to the U.S. to consider very carefully any possible downscaling of the ATCA.[73]

---

70   On 23 September 2003, the Prosecutor of the ICC, Luis Moreno Ocampo, announced that he would also involve conniving companies in his investigations of complaints alleging international crimes in the Democratic Republic of Congo (a party to the Statute of the International Criminal Court).

71   Read more on this trust fund: <http://www.victimstrustfund.org>.

72   Article 17 Statute of Rome.

73   Article 12 Statute of Rome. It should be noted that the United States will never be willing to extradite their own nationals.

The concept of jurisdiction in the European Convention on Human Rights

Rick A. Lawson[■]

1 INTRODUCTION

The European Convention on Human Rights (ECHR) was adopted in 1950 in the framework of the Council of Europe. It contains a fairly limited set of 'classic' human rights and fundamental freedoms, such as the right to life, the prohibition of torture and the right to a fair trial.[1] Over the years, additional rights, such as the right to protection of property, have been added through protocols. What started as a project between ten mainly Western European States was joined by States in Central and Eastern Europe after the fall of the Berlin Wall. The Convention now embraces the Russian Federation and countries such as Armenia and Azerbaijan. In short, it has developed into 'a constitutional instrument of European public order (*ordre public*) for the protection of individual human beings'[2] to which 45 States have committed themselves – that is, *all* European States except Monaco (which is in the process of accession to the Council of Europe) and Belarus (which does not satisfy the Council's requirements in terms of democracy and respect for the rule of law). Over 800 million individuals enjoy the protection offered by the Convention, from Reykjavik to Wladiwostok.

The main feature distinguishing the Convention from other international human rights instruments is its supervisory mechanism. Both individual victims and States parties to the Convention may bring complaints to the European Court of Human Rights in Strasbourg. The Court's judgments have binding force, and the Council of Europe's Committee of Ministers supervises their execution in practice. If the Court finds that there has been a violation of the Convention, it may afford just satisfaction to the victim – including compensation of material damage, moral damage and legal costs. The Court operates on a full-time basis. In 2003, it registered over 38,000 fresh complaints. In the same year it delivered some 800 judgments and took over 17,000 admissibility decisions.

[■] The present paper was partially based on 'The Concept of Jurisdiction and Extraterritorial Acts of State', in G.P.H. Kreijen a.o. (ed.), *State, Sovereignty and International Governance* (Oxford UP, 2002), pp. 281-297, and on a paper 'Life After Bankovic – On the Extraterritorial Reach of the ECHR', presented at a conference in Maastricht, the Netherlands, in January 2003.

[1] For a recent description, see e.g. Jacobs & White, *The European Convention on Human Rights* (Oxford UP, 3rd ed., 2002, by C. Ovey & R.C.A. White).

[2] ECtHR, 23 March 1995, *Loizidou* v. *Turkey (prel. obj.)*, (Series A, vol. 310), §§ 75 and 93.

The territorial scope of the Convention, which was not much of an issue for decades, has received attention in recent case-law. It was especially the case of *Bankovic* (2001) that offered an occasion for the Strasbourg Court to address this matter in considerable detail.[3] I should mention here that I was involved in that case as legal advisor to the applicants, a factor which may of course influence my review of the Court's decision in that case.

At a technical level, the key question is how one should interpret the word 'jurisdiction' in Article 1 ECHR. Article 1 provides that the Contracting Parties shall secure to everyone 'within their jurisdiction' the rights and freedoms defined in the Convention. Accordingly, for an individual to be able to rely on the Convention, he must demonstrate that he was 'within the jurisdiction' of the State concerned at the relevant time. In the vast majority of cases, this is not even an issue: if someone complains that his trial before the Dutch courts was unfair, no-one will even think of the possibility that the applicant was not 'within the jurisdiction' of the Netherlands. But the question becomes crucial when a State conducts a military operation abroad and is alleged to have violated human rights in the process. Was the alleged victim 'within the jurisdiction' of the State concerned? Can he rely on the Convention?

This question is not devoid of practical relevance. Turkish armed forces have occupied northern Cyprus since 1974. Russian troops have been stationed in Transdniestria, a region of Moldova, since 1991. NATO forces carried out air strikes on Yugoslavia in 1999. Turkish security forces arrested Mr Öcalan, the leader of the Workers' Party of Kurdistan (PKK), in Kenya and transferred him to Turkey.

In each of these examples, it is clear that the conduct as such of the armed forces can be attributed to their State. But the question is whether the victims can invoke the rights and freedoms of the European Convention. The answer depends on the interpretation of the word 'jurisdiction' in Article 1 ECHR. Was Mr Öcalan 'within the jurisdiction' of Turkey at the moment of his arrest in Kenya? Clearly this raises some sensitive issues. We live in an interventionist age. Since September 11 the 'War on Terrorism' has been waged in Afghanistan and Iraq. The question whether the ECHR applies to armed forces on foreign soil is not a mere toy for academics.

In this contribution, I will address some early case-law relating to extra-territorial acts (§ 2 and 3). Against that background, paragraph 4 will discuss the leading case of the moment, *Bankovic*, as well as some recent decisions following *Bankovic*. Since, in my opinion, the Court's approach is unduly narrow, an alternative approach to the notion of jurisdiction will be proposed in § 5: the extent to which Contracting Parties must secure the rights and freedoms of individuals outside their borders, is commensurate with their ability to do so –

---

3   ECtHR, 12 Dec. 2001, *Bankovic a.o.* v. *Belgium and 16 Other Contracting States* (Appl. no. 52207/99; adm. dec.). All decisions and judgments of the Court can be found on <www.echr.coe.int>.

that is: the scope of their obligations depends on the degree of control and authority that they exercise.[4]

Some issues will *not* be discussed here: decisions concerning extradition or expulsion to third countries (which do not concern the actual exercise of a State's competence or jurisdiction abroad) and various forms of international judicial co-operation, such as the granting of *exequatur* to foreign judgments (which are not genuinely extra-territorial acts either). For similar reasons we will not address the human-rights dimension of the situation where a State raises the defence of sovereign immunity when summoned before a foreign court, or where domestic courts uphold foreign States' claims to immunity. Nor will attention be paid to intergovernmental co-operation in the context of the EU, although especially co-operation in police matters clearly entails an increasing number of cross-border operations and may raise complicated issues of imputability and proof. Exceptionally States place their organs at the disposal of another State. This situation also falls outside the scope of this paper, since the conduct of these organs will be attributed to the 'receiving' State. Instead, this paper will focus on genuine and often unsolicited operations on foreign soil, such as the bombing of a television station that was at issue in *Bankovic*.

As a last preliminary remark, it is noted that the concept of 'jurisdiction' takes on a somewhat different meaning here than in most other contributions in this book. Traditionally it has been the essence of statehood that there is a government exercising control over the persons, property and events within a territory: it sets the rules and secures compliance with them throughout the territory. Jurisdiction, then, is closely related to the national territory. Of course, there are exceptions. A State may have functional jurisdiction over an 'exclusive economic zone' beyond its borders; it may exercise criminal jurisdiction over its nationals abroad; it may even assume universal jurisdiction over acts of torture or genocide committed in a faraway country, without nationals being implicated at all. What these situations have in common (apart from being more or less exceptions to the rule) is that the State seeks to extend its jurisdiction so as to regulate situations and events outside its territory. This article seeks to explore in a way the reverse situation: a State conducts an operation outside its borders and assumes *de facto* control over individuals living in the territory of another State. Are these individuals thereby brought under the 'jurisdiction' of the former State?

---

4   For a more detailed discussion, see the articles mentioned in the author's note.

2   THE EARLY CASE-LAW CONCERNING STATE RESPONSIBILITY FOR EXTRA-
           TERRITORIAL CONDUCT

Not many early cases addressed extra-territorial conduct of the Contracting
Parties. An exception is a German case in which the Commission[5], not surpris-
ingly, observed that nationals of a Contracting State are within its 'jurisdiction'
even when domiciled or resident abroad, and that diplomatic or consular representatives of their country of origin perform certain duties with regard to
them which, under some circumstances, may give rise to liability under the
Convention.[6]

     In 1992 the Commission had to rule on a complaint by an individual who
had entered the Danish embassy in East Berlin, seeking diplomatic asylum.
The Danish ambassador had the individual handed over to the GDR police.
The Commission noted:

> It is clear, in this respect, from the constant jurisprudence of the Commission that autho-
> rised agents of a State, including diplomatic or consular agents, bring other persons or
> property within the jurisdiction of that State to the extent that they exercise authority over
> such persons or property. In so far as they affect such persons or property by their acts or
> omissions, the responsibility of the State is engaged'(...). Therefore, in the present case the
> Commission is satisfied that the acts of the Danish ambassador complained of affected
> persons within the jurisdiction of the Danish authorities within the meaning of Article 1
> of the Convention. (...).[7]

Much more controversial was the case of *Hess* v. *the UK*. Rudolf Hess, a former
Nazi leader, was convicted to lifelong imprisonment after the Second World
War. From 1947 he was detained in Spandau prison in Berlin. Pursuant to an
agreement concluded in 1945, the prison was administered and guarded jointly by the four allied powers: France, the Soviet Union, the USA and the UK. In
1973 Frau Hess brought a complaint about the continued detention of her husband. The UK being the only country concerned that had accepted the right to
individual petition, Mrs Hess directed her complaint against the UK alone. By
participating in the administration of the prison and the supervision of her
husband, Mrs Hess argued, the UK was responsible for a violation of Articles
3 and 8 of the Convention.[8]

---

5   Until 1998 complaints were first examined by the European Commission of Human
      Rights. The Commission's main task was to review the admissibility of the complaints
      and forward the most important ones to the Court. In an attempt to streamline the proce-
      dure, the Commission and the Court were merged into a single body in Nov. 1998.
6   ECommHR, 25 Sept. 1965, *X* v. *FRG* (Appl. No. 1611/62), *Yearbook ECHR* vol. 8 (1965), p.
      158.
7   ECommHR, 14 Oct. 1992, *W.M.* v. *Denmark* (Appl. No. 17392/90), not reported.
8   Art. 3 ECHR prohibits inhuman and degrading treatment or punishment; Art. 8 ECHR
      protects the right to respect for family life.

In its decision, the European Commission of Human Rights noted first of all that Mr Hess was not detained within the UK. But that was not necessarily a problem:

> a State is under certain circumstances responsible under the Convention for the actions of its authorities outside its territory [...]. There is in principle, from a legal point of view, no reason why the acts of the British authorities in Berlin should not entail the liability of the United Kingdom under the Convention.[9]

The Commission decided, however, that Mr Hess was not 'within the jurisdiction' of the UK, since the four powers were jointly responsible for the Spandau prison. The Commission observed:

> In regard to the administration of the prison, the Commission notes that changes therein can only be made by the unanimous decision of the representatives of the Four Powers in Germany or by the unanimous decision of the Four Governors. Administration and supervision is at all times quadripartite [...].
>
> The Commission is of the opinion that the joint authority cannot be divided into four separate jurisdictions and that therefore the United Kingdom's participation in the exercise of the joint authority and consequently in the administration and supervision of Spandau Prison is not a matter 'within the jurisdiction' of the United Kingdom, within the meaning of Article 1 of the Convention.[10]

There was a certain irony in the case: the UK, France and the USA were prepared to release Mr Hess on humanitarian grounds, but the Soviet Union was blocking this. The Commission may have been swayed by this background: to find that the UK had violated the Convention would put it in a position which it could do nothing by itself to change.

Yet one may wonder whether the argument on which the Commission relied was fully convincing. Assume that France, the Soviet Union and the USA had publicly stated that they favoured the release of Mr Hess, and that only the UK was opposed to this. Would it still be reasonable to say that Mr Hess was outside the UK's jurisdiction because of the joint authority? It is outside the scope of this paper to deal with the separate question of responsibility of States for conduct of organs common to a number of States, or for conduct of international organisations to which they belong. But in the instant case it would seem that the reason behind the Commission's decision was that the UK did not have any real power to bring about Hess' release.

3   'EFFECTIVE OVERALL CONTROL': THE NORTHERN CYPRUS CASES

The case-law discussed so far stems from the Commission. The *Loizidou* case offered the first opportunity for the European Court of Human Rights to express its views on extra-territorial conduct.

---

9   ECommHR, 28 May 1975, *Ilse Hess* v. *UK* (Appl. No. 6231/73), *DR* vol. 2, p. 73; *Yearbook ECHR* vol. 18 (1975), p. 174.
10   Ibidem.

The facts of the case are plain. Ms Loizidou claimed to be the owner of plots of land in northern Cyprus. Following the Turkish intervention she fled to the south and settled in what was left of the Republic of Cyprus. She brought a complaint against Turkey, stating that Turkish forces prevented her from returning to her property. Turkey rejected all responsibility for the situation. It advanced many arguments, the most relevant of which is for present purposes that:

> the question of access to property was obviously outside the realm of Turkey's 'jurisdiction'. [...] the mere presence of Turkish armed forces in northern Cyprus was not synonymous with 'jurisdiction' any more than it is with the armed forces of other countries stationed abroad. In fact Turkish armed forces had never exercised 'jurisdiction' over life and property in northern Cyprus.

Any complaints, Turkey argued, should be directed against the 'Turkish Republic of Northern Cyprus' ('TRNC') which was established in 1983. The Court rejected this preliminary argument as follows:

> [...] although Article 1 sets limits on the reach of the Convention, the concept of 'jurisdiction' under this provision is not restricted to the national territory of the High Contracting Parties. According to its established case-law, for example, the Court has held that the extradition or expulsion of a person by a Contracting State may give rise to an issue under Article 3, and hence engage the responsibility of that State under the Convention (see the *Soering* v. *the United Kingdom* judgment of 7 July 1989, Series A no. 161, pp. 35-36, § 91; [...]).
> In addition, the responsibility of Contracting Parties can be involved because of acts of their authorities, whether performed within or outside national boundaries, which produce effects outside their own territory (see the *Drozd and Janousek* v. *France and Spain* judgment of 26 June 1992, Series A no. 240, p. 29, § 91).
>
> Bearing in mind the object and purpose of the Convention, the responsibility of a Contracting Party may also arise when as a consequence of military action – whether lawful or unlawful – it exercises effective control of an area outside its national territory. The obligation to secure, in such an area, the rights and freedoms set out in the Convention derives from the fact of such control whether it be exercised directly, through its armed forces, or through a subordinate local administration.[11]

I believe that the outcome is fully in line with the object and purpose of the Convention, which the Court on this occasion described as 'a constitutional instrument of European public order (*ordre public*) for the protection of individual human beings'.[12] It would be morally wrong and legally unsound if, in the field of human rights, States were allowed to do abroad what they have undertaken not to do at home. 'Any other finding would result in a regrettable vacuum in the system of human-rights protection', as the Court put it in the later case of *Cyprus* v. *Turkey*.[13]

It is interesting to note the Court's focus on control over territory. It was not so relevant whether Ms Loizidou was actually prevented from returning

---

11   ECtHR, 23 March 1995, *Loizidou* v. *Turkey (prel. obj.)*, (Series A, vol. 310), § 62.
12   Ibidem, §§ 75 and 93.
13   ECtHR, 10 May 2001, *Cyprus* v. *Turkey* (Appl. No. 25781/94), § 78.

to her property by Turkish forces, or whether 'TRNC' officials were directly responsible. The Court could avoid difficult questions of proof by emphasising the fact that Turkey was in control anyhow. In its more recent *Cyprus* v. *Turkey* judgment the Court elaborated on this theme as follows:

> Having effective overall control over northern Cyprus, its [i.e., Turkey's] responsibility cannot be confined to the acts of its own soldiers or officials in northern Cyprus but must also be engaged by virtue of the acts of the local administration which survives by virtue of Turkish military and other support. It follows that, in terms of Article 1 of the Convention, Turkey's 'jurisdiction' must be considered to extend to *securing the entire range of substantive rights set out in the Convention and those additional Protocols* which she has ratified, and that violations of those rights are imputable to Turkey.[14]

This position has been confirmed on a number of occasions.[15]

The northern Cyprus saga might create the impression that effective overall control is required for a State to be held responsible for its acts abroad – or, more precisely, that effective overall control is needed to bring the persons concerned 'within its jurisdiction'. But this would be to ignore the existing case-law of the Commission. The lesson from Northern Cyprus must rather be that because Turkey exercises effective overall control over Northern Cyprus, and because it became thereby accountable for the conduct of the local administration, the Court did not have to determine whether Turkish forces actually exercised control in specific situations.

In addition, and quite significantly, the Court pointed out that Turkey must secure the entire range of substantive rights set out in the Convention. There is nothing that prevents Turkey from doing so. It seems fair to assume that if Turkey's control would not have extended that far, its obligation under Article 1 would have been more limited. Arguably, its responsibility would have been 'confined to the acts of its own soldiers or officials in northern Cyprus'. It would perhaps have been unreasonable to expect them to secure the entire set of Convention rights and freedoms.

4   THE CASE OF *BANKOVIC*

4.1   *The facts and the arguments of the applicants*

The facts of *Bankovic* are simple. On 23 April 1999, a building of *Radio Televizije Srvije (RTS)* was hit by a cruise missile launched from a NATO forces' aircraft. The attack occurred in the context of 'Operation Allied Force', a military campaign by NATO against the Federal Republic of Yugoslavia (FRY). Sixteen

---

14   Ibidem, § 77, emphasis added.
15   E.g. ECtHR, 31 July 2003, *Demades* v. *Turkey* (Appl. No. 16219/90). Note that this case originated in a complaint introduced in 1990; the Court apparently delayed its decision in this case (and in many other similar cases) in view of the political tensions caused by the Turkish reaction to its *Loizidou* and *Cyprus* v. *Turkey* judgments.

people were killed and another sixteen were seriously injured in the bombing of the RTS building. Five relatives of the deceased and a survivor of the bombing brought a complaint before the Strasbourg Court against the NATO Member States, in so far as they were bound by the ECHR. The applicants argued that the television station had not been not a legitimate target; they alleged breaches of notably Article 2 (the right to life) and Article 10 (the freedom to impart information).

The applicants primarily argued that the very bombing of the RTS building had brought them 'within the jurisdiction' of the NATO Member States. It would go too far to expect the respondent States to secure all rights and freedoms included in the ECHR, but at the very least one could expect these States to refrain from acts that endangered their right to life and their freedom to impart information.

It may be noted that the applicants did not express any view on the legality of 'Operation Allied Force' under public international law; they confined their complaint to the bombing of the RTS building. Similarly, the applicants did not dispute that in times of war the substantive norms of the Convention may have to be adapted. Even in the absence of a formal derogation under Article 15 ECHR, it is quite conceivable, for instance, that the Court leaves the States a wide margin of appreciation.[16] But these are issues related to the merits of the complaint; the first hurdle was to pass the admissibility test.

4.2   The arguments of the respondent States

The seventeen respondent States primarily contended that the applicants and their deceased relatives were not, at the relevant time, within their 'jurisdiction'. They argued that the exercise of 'jurisdiction' involves the assertion or exercise of legal authority, actual or purported, over persons owing some form of allegiance to a State or who have been brought within that State's control. They added that the term 'jurisdiction' generally entails some form of structured relationship normally existing over a period of time.

In addition, the respondent States referred *inter alia* to the fact that the FRY was not a party to the Convention and its inhabitants had no existing rights under the Convention. They also warned the Court not to assume competence to review the participation of Contracting States in military missions all over the world: 'The resulting Convention exposure would, according to the Governments, risk undermining significantly the States' participation in such missions'.[17] Apparently the respondent States feel that the conduct of their forces abroad is such that they should exclude it from any supervision by the Strasbourg Court.

---

16   Cf. ECtHR, 26 March 1987, *Leander* v. *Sweden* (Series A, vol. 116), § 59; ECtHR, 26 May 1993, *Brannigan and McBride* v. *the UK* (Series A, vol. 258-B), § 43.

17   ECtHR, 12 Dec. 2001, *Bankovic a.o.* v. *Belgium and 16 Other Contracting States* (Appl. no. 52207/99; adm. dec.), § 43.

4.3   The Court's decision

The Court, in a lengthy admissibility decision, decided that the applicants had not been 'within the jurisdiction' of the States concerned. Recalling that the Convention must be interpreted in the light of the rules set out in the Vienna Convention on the Law of Treaties (1969), the Court took as its starting point that the jurisdictional competence of a State is primarily territorial. Accordingly,

> 61. [...] Article 1 of the Convention must be considered to reflect this ordinary and essentially territorial notion of jurisdiction, other bases of jurisdiction being exceptional and requiring special justification in the particular circumstances of each case.[18]

The Court went on:

> 62. The Court finds State practice in the application of the Convention since its ratification to be indicative of a lack of any apprehension on the part of the Contracting States of their extra-territorial responsibility in contexts similar to the present case.[19]

The Court then addressed the situations in which it had recognised extra-territorial acts as constituting an exercise of jurisdiction. It summarised its jurisprudence as follows:

> 71. In sum, the case-law of the Court demonstrates that its recognition of the exercise of extra-territorial jurisdiction by a Contracting State is exceptional: it has done so when the respondent State, through the effective control of the relevant territory and its inhabitants abroad as a consequence of military occupation or through the consent, invitation or acquiescence of the Government of that territory, exercises all or some of the public powers normally to be exercised by that Government.[20]

Two important points must be noted here. First, the Court expressly reconfirms the extra-territorial reach of the Convention. *Loizidou* is still alive. The passage quoted here arguably opens the way for complaints about, for instance, peace-keeping operations where the armed forces of a Contracting Party exercise all or some of the public powers in a specific region.

Secondly, the Court silently modified *Loizidou* by introducing a new element in the last line: the exercise of 'all or some of the public powers normally to be exercised by [the] Government' of that territory. That requirement was not mentioned in *Loizidou*; nor was it in *Cyprus* v. *Turkey*. One wonders what the Court has in mind here. Is the exercise of normal public powers meant to be some sort of surrogate 'jurisdiction' within the meaning of Article 1 ECHR? Surely arrest and detention will fall under it, but what about alleged arbitrary killings? What if a Contracting Party occupies a territory and secures effective control over its inhabitants, but fails to exercise normal public powers, for in-

---

18   Ibidem, § 61.
19   Ibidem, § 62.
20   Ibidem, § 71.

stance at the early stages of the occupation? Will the individuals concerned remain unprotected as long as the occupying power allows an anarchy to last?

The potential relevance of this point may be illustrated by the occupation by British forces of areas in southern Iraq in the course of the 2003 war against Saddam Hussein. According to *Loizidou*, the inhabitants might come within British 'jurisdiction' if the British forces exercise effective control over the area. According to *Bankovic*, however, more would be needed: the test would be whether the British forces exercise all or some of the public powers normally to be exercised by the Iraqi Government. As long as they fail to do so, the Iraqi population would apparently remain outside British 'jurisdiction'. This would hardly be an incentive for the forces to assume their responsibilities vis-à-vis the civil population, despite their obligations under, for instance, the Fourth Geneva Convention.

Seen from a different angle, one could wonder about the consequences once the British forces exercised 'some' normal public powers in the parts of Iraq that they occupied in the summer of 2003. According to the Court in § 71 of *Bankovic* this would suffice to bring the local population within the 'jurisdiction' of the UK. Does this imply that the UK then had to secure *all* rights and freedoms of the Convention?

It remains to be seen if the 'normal public powers requirement' will be given an independent meaning.

Back to *Bankovic*. The Court then addressed the bombing of RTS. It did not explain the material difference between 'effective control ... as a consequence of military occupation' and air superiority, which NATO claimed it had over Yugoslavia during 'Operation Allied Force'. Instead, the Court focussed on the applicants' approach to Article 1 ECHR. The Court considered that this was 'tantamount to arguing that anyone adversely affected by an act imputable to a Contracting State, wherever in the world that act may have been committed or its consequences felt, is thereby brought within the jurisdiction of that State for the purpose of Article 1 of the Convention'. With some caution, the Court said it was 'inclined to agree' with the Governments' submission that the text of Article 1 does not accommodate such an approach to 'jurisdiction'. But without much caution it continued:

> 75. [...] the Court is of the view that the wording of Article 1 does not provide any support for the applicants' suggestion that the positive obligation in Article 1 to secure 'the rights and freedoms defined in Section I of this Convention' can be divided and tailored in accordance with the particular circumstances of the extra-territorial act in question and, it considers its view in this respect supported by the text of Article 19 of the Convention.[21]

This statement leaves little ambiguity. The Court added that the applicants' approach did not explain the application of the words 'within their jurisdiction' in Article 1 and it even went so far as to render those words superfluous

---

21   Ibidem, § 75.

and devoid of any purpose. The Court was not swayed either by the applicants argument derived from the fundamental nature of the Convention and the norms it seeks to protect.

> 80. The Court's obligation, in this respect, is to have regard to the special character of the Convention as a constitutional instrument of *European* public order for the protection of individual human beings and its role, as set out in Article 19 of the Convention, is to ensure the observance of *the engagements undertaken* by the Contracting Parties [...]
> It is true that, in its above-cited *Cyprus* v. *Turkey* judgment (at § 78), the Court was conscious of the need to avoid 'a regrettable vacuum in the system of human-rights protection' in northern Cyprus. However, and as noted by the Governments, that comment related to an entirely different situation to the present: the inhabitants of northern Cyprus would have found themselves excluded from the benefits of the Convention safeguards and system which they had previously enjoyed, by Turkey's 'effective control' of the territory and by the accompanying inability of the Cypriot Government, as a Contracting State, to fulfil the obligations it had undertaken under the Convention.
> In short, the Convention is a multi-lateral treaty operating [...] in an essentially regional context and notably in the legal space (*espace juridique*) of the Contracting States. The FRY clearly does not fall within this legal space. The Convention was not designed to be applied throughout the world, even in respect of the conduct of Contracting States. Accordingly, the desirability of avoiding a gap or vacuum in human-rights protection has so far been relied on by the Court in favour of establishing jurisdiction only when the territory in question was one that, but for the specific circumstances, would normally be covered by the Convention.[22]

At first sight the Court appears to accept in the last paragraph that breaches of human rights will remain unremedied if they do not take place in European countries. But a closer look reveals that the Court does *not* say this. The Convention was not designed to be applied throughout the world, but that does not mean that its application outside Europe is excluded. Hence the reservations ('essentially', 'notably', 'so far') that the Court makes. There are two arguments to believe that, despite the harsh wording of § 80, the Convention can have extra-territorial effect beyond the 'European legal space'.

Firstly, as we have seen, the Court continues to recognise the exercise of extra-territorial jurisdiction when a Contracting State, through the effective control of a territory and its inhabitants, exercises the public powers of the government of that territory (§ 71). There is no indication that the Court wished to limit this responsibility to the 'European legal space'. Similarly, the Court continues to accept that States may be responsible for acts producing effects in third countries (§ 69, not quoted here).

Secondly we must not forget that the Court made this statement in response to the applicants' argument that any failure to accept that they fell within the jurisdiction of the respondent States would defeat the *public ordre* mission of the Convention and leave a regrettable vacuum in the system of human-rights protection. Arguably the Court simply wished to indicate that this specific argument has its limits.

Yet it is this very passage that makes one wonder whether the respondent

---

22   Ibidem, § 80, emphasis in original.

States would have been responsible, had the RTS station been located within the 'European legal space'. One is inclined to think that the answer is affirmative. If Belgium bombs a TV station in the Netherlands, surely Belgium will be held responsible for any consequential violation of human rights (see *Cyprus v. Turkey*: 'any other finding would result in a regrettable vacuum in the system of human-rights protection'). But then the bombing in itself must be sufficient to bring the victims within Belgian 'jurisdiction'!

4.4   *Looking for an explanation*

A possible explanation for the outcome may be found in a speech of the Court's President, Mr Wildhaber, on the occasion of the opening of the judicial year 2002 of the European Court of Human Rights:

> Our perception of last year is coloured by the tragic events of 11 September and their aftermath. Terrorism raises two fundamental issues which human rights law must address. Firstly, it strikes directly at democracy and the rule of law, the two central pillars of the European Convention on Human Rights. It must be therefore be possible for democratic States governed by the rule of law to protect themselves effectively against terrorism; human rights law must be able to accommodate this need. The European Convention should not be applied in such a way as to prevent States from taking reasonable and proportionate action to defend democracy and the rule of law.[23]

More specifically on *Bankovic* he continued:

> We do have to realise that the Convention was never intended to cure all the planet's ills and indeed cannot effectively do so; this brings us back to the effectiveness of the Convention and the rights protected therein. When applying the Convention we must not lose sight of the practical effect that can be given to those rights.

Cohen-Jonathan too believes that the Court, which is already suffering from a heavy case-load, did not want to get involved in 'remote' conflicts that are politically sensitive.[24] This sounds plausible, but it remains curious that the Court in *Bankovic* did not allude at all to the warning of the respondent States that any decision to exercise review over military missions abroad would entail serious international repercussions. Would it not have been preferable for the Court to squarely address that concern and perhaps develop some sort of 'political question' doctrine, rather then to advance a number of semi-convincing arguments to deny jurisdiction?

---

23   Speech of 31 Jan. 2002.
24   G. Cohen-Jonathan, 'La territorialisation de la juridiction de la Cour européenne de droits de l'homme', 52 RTDH (2002), p. 1082.

4.5 Subsequent developments

Roma locuta, causa finita. The Court's interpretation of 'jurisdiction' in *Bankovic* was expressly repeated at various occasions. Thus the Court reconfirmed *Bankovic* in December 2002, when deciding the case of *Kalogeropoulou*. In this case a number of Greek citizens brought a claim for damages against Germany, before Greek courts, in connection with a Nazi massacre in World War II. The Greek courts found in favour of the plaintiffs, but Germany invoked its sovereign immunity and refused to pay. In rejecting a subsequent complaint against Germany, the Court referred to *Bankovic* and held that the Greek citizens had not been within German 'jurisdiction'.[25]

At the domestic level, *Bankovic* was followed by the Dutch Supreme Court.[26] The case concerned an appeal brought by a number of Yugoslav nationals who had started court proceedings in March 1999, seeking an injunction to restrain the State from participating in the military operations against Yugoslavia. In June 2002 the Advocate General argued that the appeal should be rejected. To the extent that the applicants invoked the ECHR, the Advocate General relied on *Bankovic* to find that they were not 'within the jurisdiction' of the Netherlands and hence not protected by the Convention. In November 2002, the *Hoge Raad* rejected the appeal, basing itself on Advocate General's opinion.

In March 2003 the Court decided the case of *Öcalan* on the merits. It remains to be seen whether this judgment is final: Turkey has announced that it will refer the case to the Grand Chamber, in accordance with Article 43 ECHR. One of Mr Öcalan's complaints concerned his arrest in Kenya by Turkish security forces, which he alleged was in breach of Articles 3 and 5 of the Convention. In its judgment the Court distinguished the *Öcalan* case from *Bankovic*:

> In the instant case, the applicant was arrested by members of the Turkish security forces inside an aircraft in the international zone of Nairobi Airport. Directly after he had been handed over by the Kenyan officials to the Turkish officials the applicant was under effective Turkish authority and was therefore brought within the 'jurisdiction' of that State for the purposes of Article 1 of the Convention, even though in this instance Turkey exercised its authority outside its territory. The Court considers that the circumstances of the present case are distinguishable from those in the aforementioned *Bankovic and Others* case, notably in that the applicant was physically forced to return to Turkey by Turkish officials and was subject to their authority and control following his arrest and return to Turkey (see in this respect the aforementioned decisions in the cases of *Illich Sánchez Ramirez v. France* and *Freda v. Italy*).[27]

The Court then proceeded to review the circumstances of Mr Öcalan's arrest under Articles 3 and 5 ECHR.[28] But the passage quoted here begs the question:

---

25   ECtHR, 12 Dec. 2002, *Kalogeropoulou a.o. v. Greece and Germany* (Appl. No. 59021/00; adm. dec.).

26   Hoge Raad, 29 Nov. 2002, LJN number AE5164, case C01/027HR.

27   ECtHR, 12 March 2003, *Öcalan v. Turkey* (Appl. No. 46221/99), § 93.

28   Ibidem, §§ 215-228 and 94-103 respectively.

does it matter, for the purposes of Article 1 of the Convention, that Mr Öcalan was forced to return to Turkey following his arrest? Two answers seem possible:

(a) No: 'directly after he had been handed over by the Kenyan officials to the Turkish officials the applicant was under effective Turkish authority and was therefore brought within the 'jurisdiction' of that State'; or

(b) Yes: the present case is distinguishable from *Bankovic* because Mr Öcalan 'was physically forced to return to Turkey by Turkish officials and was subject to their authority and control following his arrest and return to Turkey'.

It remains to be seen what the right answer is. The case of *Issa*, now pending before the Court, may shed further light on this issue. In *Issa*, Turkish forces, which had crossed into northern Iraq during an operation that lasted for approximately four weeks, allegedly arrested and killed a number of Iraqi shepherds.[29]

5   SOME CONCLUDING REMARKS

It follows from the existing case-law that there are four situations where extra-territorial acts of Contracting Parties may or may not bring an individual 'within the jurisdiction' of the State concerned:

(a) the 'northern Cyprus situation', where one State party to the Convention (State X) exercises effective overall control over part of the territory of another State party to the Convention (State Y). In this case State X must secure 'the entire range' of substantive rights and freedoms set out in the Convention. See *Loizidou* and *Cyprus* v. *Turkey*. It is conceivable, for instance, that complaints against Armenia are lodged relating to the situation in Nagorno-Karabakh.

(b) the 'Kosovo situation': same as (a), but here State Y is *not* a party to the Convention. One could think of post-conflict situations where armed forces are deployed (possibly in the framework of the UN, the NATO or the EU) to maintain law and order in an area during a (sometimes lengthy) phase of national reconstruction. One could also think of less settled situations, such as the occupation by British forces of areas in Iraq when the 2003 war was fought.

So far no case-law has emerged with respect to these areas,[30] even if the importance of accountability of the international forces has been un-

---

29   ECtHR, 30 May 2000, *Issa a.o.* v. *Turkey* (Appl. No. 31821/96; adm. dec.).

30   But see ECtHR, 16 Sept. 2003, *Behrami – France* (Appl. No. 71412/01; dec.). The applicant is a Kosovar, one of whose children was killed and another severely injured, when a group of children played with undetonated cluster bombs dropped during the NATO bombardments in 1999. The applicant maintains that France is responsible for the death, because the incident took place in the part of Kosovo which is under the jurisdiction and control of French KFOR troops, who had failed to mark the site and/or defuse the bombs, which they knew to be in the area. The Court decided to bring this case, relating to Article 2 ECHR, to the attention of the French government.

derlined repeatedly.[31] Two approaches are conceivable. One would be the isolationist element of *Bankovic*: 'the Convention was not designed to be applied throughout the world'. The other would base itself on the inclusive element of *Bankovic*: the recognition of extra-territorial jurisdiction 'when the respondent State, through the effective control of the relevant territory and its inhabitants abroad ... exercises all or some of the public powers normally to be exercised by that Government'. It is submitted that latter approach would better reflect the Convention's object and purpose to protect the basic rights of individual human beings.

Of course, the context in which national units function, and especially the extent to which they are able to regulate their own conduct (think of rules of engagement) will determine to what extent they should be held responsible for violations occurring within 'their' territory. In the case of UN forces acting under Chapter VII of the UN Charter, further complications may arise as the obligations flowing from UN Security Council resolutions may have precedence over other treaties.[32]

(c) the 'intra-European temporary operation', where agents of one State party to the Convention (State X) exercise *de facto* control over persons and property abroad in a more or less limited, incidental, *ad hoc* fashion in the territory of another State party to the Convention (State Y). There is limited authority, but it would seem that the old case-law mentioned in § 2 serves a guide: 'Insofar as the State's acts or omissions affect such persons, the responsibility of the State is engaged'.

(d) the 'external temporary operation': same as (c), but here State Y is *not* a party to the Convention. *Öcalan* suggests that State X must secure the Convention rights and freedoms, but *Bankovic* expressly points in the opposite direction.

Perhaps one should adopt an alternative approach. The least one may expect from States who intervene abroad in the name of the great ideals of freedom, democracy and the rule of law, is that they continue to abide by the same universal human-rights standards – whether they act at home or abroad. Taking into account the practical obstacles that may occur during extra-territorial operations, I believe that there is a good deal to be said in favour of a 'gradual' approach to the notion of 'jurisdiction': the extent to which Contracting Parties must secure the rights and freedoms of individuals outside their borders, is proportionate to the extent of their control over these individuals.

---

31   For a recent and in-depth discussion, see M.C. Zwanenburg, *Accountability under International Humanitarian Law for UN and NATO Peace Support Operations* (diss. Leiden, 2004).

32   See Art. 103 UN Charter. Cf., implicitly, ECtHR, 4 May 2000, *Naletilic v. Croatia* (Appl. No. 51891/99). See also Opinion 239 of the Parliamentary Assembly on the Accession of the FRY (24 Sept. 2002), § 18: the Secretary-General should 'explore with the authorities in Belgrade and with UNMIK ways to guarantee the applicability of the substantive norms contained in Council of Europe conventions and of their supervisory mechanisms in Kosovo, including access to the European Court of Human Rights, bearing in mind the special legal situation resulting from UN Security Council Resolution No. 1244'.

The first issue to be solved relates to the group of persons who are entitled to 'the benefit of the Convention's fundamental safeguards and their right to call a High Contracting Party to account for violation of their rights in proceedings before the Court'.[33] It would go too far to assume that anybody who is 'affected' by the conduct of a Contracting State is 'within the jurisdiction' of that State. A decision to cut development aid or to reduce quota for imports would then suffice to bring indeterminate numbers of people 'within the jurisdiction'. On the other hand, it would be too restrictive to require a formal legal relationship, or some kind of structured relationship existing over a period of time, between the State organ acting abroad and the individuals concerned. This would unjustifiably exclude State accountability in situations of *de facto* control or ad hoc operations on foreign soil.

Instead, it is suggested that if there is a direct and immediate link between the extra-territorial conduct of a State and the alleged violation of an individual's rights, then the individual must be assumed to be 'within the jurisdiction', within the meaning of Article 1, of the State concerned. What is decisive, is not so much whether the State happens to have control over territory (and, as a corollary, over those who happen to be in that territory), but whether the State has control over persons. The arrest of Mr Öcalan in Kenya would clearly fall in this category.

This 'direct and immediate link' test has two sources of inspiration. One is European Union law. According to Article 230 EC Treaty, an individual may bring proceedings before the European Court of Justice against decisions which, although in the form of a regulation or a decision addressed to another person, are 'of direct and individual concern' to the former.[34] In 2002 the Strasbourg Court adopted these very criteria when interpreting the scope of the right of access to court (Article 6 of the Convention).[35] The second source of inspiration for the 'direct and immediate link' test is the Court's judgment in the case of *Botta* v. *Italy*.[36] Admittedly, the context of *Botta* was rather different[37], but the 'direct and immediate link' test has been used in other cases,[38] and it may be useful to delimit the scope of the Contracting States' obligations in the context of extra-territorial situations.

The second issue is a substantive one: once it is accepted that persons

---

33 The quote is taken from *Cyprus* v. *Turkey*, supra note 13, § 78.
34 Art. 230, 4th indent, EC Treaty.
35 ECtHR, 24 Sept. 2002, *Posti and Rahko* v. *Finland* (Appl. 27824/95), §§ 53-54.
36 ECtHR, 24 Feb. 1998, *Botta* v. *Italy* (Reports 1998, p. 412), § 34.
37 A handicapped person complained under Art. 8 of the Convention that he did not have access to privately-owned beaches, due to a failure to implement and enforce domestic law requiring that facilities be offered. The Court found that 'the right asserted by Mr Botta [...] concerns interpersonal relations of such broad and indeterminate scope that there can be no conceivable direct link between the measures the State was urged to take in order to make good the omissions of the private bathing establishments and the applicant's private life' (§ 35).
38 E.g. ECtHR, 14 May 2002, *Zehnalová and Zehnal* v. *Czech Republic* (Appl. No. 38621/97; adm. dec.).

abroad may find themselves 'within the jurisdiction' of a State party to the Convention, how far do the State's obligations go? It is submitted that the extent to which Contracting Parties must secure the rights and freedoms of individuals outside their borders, is commensurate with the extent of their control. To take *Issa* as an example: no one would expect the Turkish forces in northern Iraq to secure 'the entire range of substantive rights set out in the Convention' (including positive obligations, et cetera) to the Iraqi shepherds over whom they assumed control. But insofar as they actually interfered with the shepherds' lives, the Turkish forces were obliged to respect their rights.

It is submitted that this 'gradual' and situation-specific approach to 'jurisdiction' had always been implicit in the Strasbourg case-law, even if it had not really been developed in the cases under review so far. As we have seen in § 2, the Commission stated repeatedly that the responsibility of the State is engaged 'insofar as' State agents affect persons or property.

Seen from quite a different perspective, the Strasbourg jurisprudence provides also other arguments for the flexible approach advocated here. According to well-established case-law, if the authorities arrest an individual, they are fully responsible for his well-being.[39] The very fact that the individual is brought under the authorities' full control, allows for – and demands – a far-reaching duty to protect him. If, on the other hand, the individual turns to the State and asks for protection against violence from a private party, the obligations of the State do not extend so far:

> the scope of the positive obligations must be interpreted in a way which does not impose an impossible or disproportionate burden on the authorities. Not every claimed risk to life can therefore entail for the authorities a Convention requirement to take operational measures to prevent that risk from materialising. For a positive obligation to arise, it must be established that the authorities knew or ought to have known at the time of the existence of a real and immediate risk to the life of an identified individual from the criminal acts of a third party and that they failed to take measures within the scope of their powers which, judged reasonably, might have been expected to avoid that risk.[40]

A similar approach may be taken, *mutatis mutandis*, if State agents operate on foreign soil. To avoid any misunderstanding: what is advocated here is *not* that States parties to the Convention assume all sorts of positive obligations when operating abroad. But the standard of review developed by the Court in the context of positive obligations may well be applied in an extra-territorial setting too – just because the State's powers will normally be much more limited during operations abroad. Hence, no 'impossible or disproportionate

---

39   See ECtHR, 28 July 1999, *Selmouni* v. *France* (Appl. No. 25803/94), §§ 87 ff.; ECtHR, 27 June 2000, *Salman* v. *Turkey* (Appl. No. 21986/93), § 99; ECtHR, 14 March 2002, *Paul and Audrey Edwards* v. *UK* (Appl. No. 46477/99), §§ 56-57.

40   ECtHR, 28 Oct. 1998, *Osman* v. *the UK* (Reports 1998, p. 3124), § 116; see also ECtHR, 24 Oct. 2002, *Mastromatteo* v. *Italy* (Appl. No. 37703/97), § 68. Likewise, the obligation to investigate alleged violations of Articles 2 and 3 ECHR is context-related: see, e.g., ECtHR, 10 May 2001, *Z a.o.* v. *the UK* (Appl. No. 29392/95), § 109; ECtHR, 26 Nov. 2002, *E. a.o.* v. *UK* (Appl. No. 33218/96), § 88.

burden' should be imposed, that is, one should not expect State agents to secure all Convention rights and freedoms where they are simply not in a position to do so. On the other hand, to the extent that they assume *de facto* control over individuals and interfere with their lives, they should take 'measures within the scope of their powers which, judged reasonably, might have been expected' to avoid violations of these individuals' rights.

Arguably, this standard is more demanding when the most fundamental of rights – such as the right to life[41] and the prohibition of torture[42] – are at stake.

In sum, it is submitted that if a State exercises effective overall control over an area, it is in a position to secure 'the entire range' of Convention rights – which includes positive obligations – and thus it should do so. In other situations, where no effective overall control is exercised, a lower standard applies. If there is a direct and immediate link between the extra-territorial conduct of a State and the alleged violation of an individual's rights, then the individual must be assumed to be 'within the jurisdiction', within the meaning of Article 1, of the State concerned. The State should then take 'measures within the scope of their powers which, judged reasonably, might have been expected' to avoid violations of the individual's rights. This is especially true where the most fundamental rights – notably the right to life and the prohibition of torture – are at stake.

---

41   In 2001 the Grand Chamber referred to the right to life as ' the supreme value in the international hierarchy of human rights' (ECtHR, 22 March 2001, *Streletz, Kessler and Krenz* v. *Germany* (Appl. No. 34044/96 a.o.), § 87; see also § 85). In 2002 the Court underlined 'the principle of sanctity of life protected under the Convention' (ECtHR, 29 April 2002, *Pretty* v. *UK* (Appl. No. 2346/02), § 65).

42   In *Al-Adsani*, the Grand Chamber accepted that 'the prohibition of torture has achieved the status of a peremptory norm in international law' (ECtHR, 21 Nov. 2001, *Al-Adsani* v. *the United Kingdom* (Appl. no. 35763/97), § 61).

ADR in a globalising world

Alex F.M. Brenninkmeijer and Natalia Shelkoplyas

1   INTRODUCTION

The history of adjudication shows that for quite a long period the administration of justice was linked with local or regional entities. In the modern democratic state, the court system mostly is part of the state organisation whose
functioning is based on the principle of separation of powers. Nowadays, we
see a tendency towards systems of judicial protection emerging on a higher
level than the level of the national state. Especially in the field of human rights
international systems of litigation have gained importance. The same can be
said in the context of European integration, although the role of courts within
the EU is more complex than the role of an international human rights court.
This development not only reflects the tendency of up scaling from local and
regional entities to national and nowadays international levels of conflict resolution. It also reflects the evolution of the basic notion of trust in society. The
court system is a fundamental element of the institutionalisation of trust within a community. This trust is, in a large variety of societies, intimately related
to two fundamental elements of the legitimacy of systems of dispute resolution. Firstly, the parties in the conflict should agree upon the rules, the law
which should be applied. Secondly, they should agree on the choice of the
neutral third party, judge or court who decides the case.[1] In the modern democratic state, conflict resolution is embedded within the concept of the rule of
law in which elements of the separation of powers are included. The law is
based upon a system of democratic decision-making. The legitimacy of court
decisions is, in other words, based upon the two fundaments of modern
states: the rule of law and democracy. And both theories contribute to trust in
those societies. However, the national state is apparently not the end of social
development.

Since World War II, we have witnessed an intensified growth of international and supranational co-operation. And with this development the question of trust in society is changing as well. The international protection of
human rights, for instance, through the European Court on Human Rights,
adds, in a significant way, legitimacy to the legal systems of the countries participating in the Council of Europe. Before the fall of the Berlin Wall this could
be said about the Western European countries. But since the accession of East-

---

1   M. Schapiro, *Courts, a comparative and political analysis* (The university of Chicago Press,
     Chicago, London, 1981). See as well J.Z. Rubin, D.G. Puitt & S. Hee Kim, *Social Conflict*
     (McGraw/Hill, New York etc., 1994).

ern European countries to this community, the case law of the ECHR, especially on Article 6 and Article 13 of the European Convention, has formed a standard for the quality of national court systems in those countries as well.

The enlargement of the European Union with the accession of Eastern European countries shows the same development. The *acquis communautaire* with regard to effective judicial protection, which is based upon the national legal traditions as well as Article 6 of the ECHR, forms a standard for the administration of justice.[2] The right to an effective remedy and to a fair trial is codified[3] in Article 47 of the Charter of Fundamental Rights of the European Union. This Charter is currently incorporated, as Part II, in the Draft Treaty establishing a Constitution for Europe.[4]

Those developments all stimulate the formation and improvement of public arrangements for conflict resolution. However, if we take a closer look at the aforementioned basic requirements of the legitimacy of systems of conflict resolution we can see that it is evident that not only state-based systems comply with those requirements. Systems of private conflict resolution can, to a certain extent, have advantages above public systems. In private systems, parties are free in selecting the rules that apply to their conflict. Furthermore, they can choose their own way in which a third-party-neutral should be involved. Although national courts systems improve their legitimacy, private systems are of growing importance as well. And, in the end, public systems appear to be time consuming and costly and for that reason parties might prefer ADR.[5]

There are more reasons for this development. Some of those reasons seem to bear no relation to the intensifying globalisation. Others are related to globalisation. In international trade and cross-border transactions, the choice for the applicable law and jurisdiction and, consequently, the courts which will apply the law, is related to the trust that parties have in the neutrality of national courts. When national courts suffer from a lack of quality, national bias or, even worse, from corruption, alternatives for public dispute resolution are highly preferable. Under national procedural law the application of national substantive law is evident, but the choice of the law which should be applied is in not evident in a globalising context.

Alternative dispute resolution (ADR) appears to represent the answer to the needs of the parties who are active in multiple jurisdictions. It functions as a neutral, non-judicial forum for their controversies and it produces solutions which are not necessarily arrived at by a strict application of the legal rules of

---

2   For a detailed discussion of various aspects of these EU-developments see for instance, J. Lonbay & A. Biondi (eds.), *Remedies for Breach of EC Law* (Chichester, 1997) or J. Wouters & J. Stuyck (eds.), *Principles of Proper Conduct for Supranational, State, and Private Actors in the European Union* (Antwerp, Groningen, Oxford, 2001).

3   See the Cases 222/84 (Johnston) [1986] ECR 1651; 222/86 (Heylens) [1987] ECR 4097; C-1/99 (Kofisa) [2000] ECR I-207 and T-222/99 (Martinez) [2001] ECR II-2833.

4   CONV 820/03 of June, 20, 2003.

5   E. Schmidt-Assmann & L. Harings, 'Access to Justice and Fundamental Rights' ERPL/REDP, vol. 9. No 3 (autumn/automne 1997).

national law which might be ill-suited to govern complex international transactions.

In this contribution we will reflect on some developments with regard to ADR from the perspective of its place in the process of globalisation.

2   PRIVATE ADR: BINDING AND NON-BINDING

Before looking at the role of ADR in an international context, it is perhaps appropriate to clarify what is understood under the broad heading of 'ADR'. On the one hand, arbitration, mediation, conciliation, and other forms of out-of-court settlement are often grouped under the same heading, i.e., 'Alternative Dispute Resolution'. This is justified when one takes the perspective of the court as a state-sponsored dispute resolution mechanism. Alternative here denotes the opposition between so-called private justice, which is achieved in ADR procedures, and justice achieved in courts.

On the other hand, arbitration can be regarded as a binding ADR and as such, it can be complemented by non-binding ADR methods. In some respects, arbitration occupies a middle ground between litigation and informal conflict resolution, partially incorporating features and characteristics of both, while not equivalent to either of them. While arbitration is consensual and private in nature (which puts it on the side of non-binding ADR), it functions as a binding method according to which the dispute is resolved through the decision of the private arbitral tribunal that superimposes its award on the parties who agree to the binding force of such an award.

In this respect, other non-binding ADR techniques contrast sharply with arbitration. Their main underlying methodology is based on the principle that the parties themselves resolve their dispute by reaching a new agreement ending the controversy (a settlement agreement). In contrast to direct negotiations, any ADR method presupposes that the settlement is achieved through the assistance of the neutral third party whose primary task is not to adjudicate on the parties' claims but to make parties arrive at a consensus on how the dispute can be remedied or eliminated all together. Compared to adjudicatory dispute resolution techniques the ADR method is often described as interests-oriented rather that rights-oriented.

3   INCREASING AWARENESS AND USE OF THE ADR FOR CROSS-BORDER
        CONTROVERSIES

It is possible to identify two major reasons leading to the global growth of mediation and other ADR techniques for resolution of disputes arising out of international transactions. The first relates to dissatisfaction with the costs, delays and uncertain outcomes of litigation systems. To a lesser extent, this dissatisfaction is also expressed with regard to arbitration, a traditional alternative to litigation, which has been gradually evolving under the influence of many factors in a more formal and judicialized method of resolving commercial conflicts. The second reason for the proliferation of ADR methods is connected with a deeper social transformation that calls for systems which can respond adequately to the speed, responsiveness, customer orientation and globalisation of business and technological change. Businesses are more likely than ever to need rapid decisions and dispute resolution procedures, which support rather than undermine business and customer relationships. Commercial as well as other forms of ADR are becoming popular because they appear to answer this business need as well as offset some of the shortcomings of the traditional dispute resolution systems.

The considerations of cost-efficiency, speed and unobtrusiveness of ADR are equally relevant in the context of its use in areas which do not pertain to the realm of commercial law, the traditional field of application of ADR. For example, family, labour and administrative disputes can all benefit from ADR.

There are however, other factors that, in the context of globalisation, make ADR especially relevant. Globalisation entails, among other things, the multiplication of the actual actors involved in cross-border transactions as well as an increase in volume of international trade. The latter is reflected in the number of international commercial agreements and, therefore, disputes arising under them. The number of judicial and non-judicial fora competing for jurisdiction over such disputes also increases. Initially, the multiplication of the number of participants in trans-border commercial transactions and the intensification of international trade resulted from the gradual removal of tariff and non-tariff barriers and the liberalisation of international trade in the framework of the World Trade Organisation. However, it is the development of electronic commerce that can be seen as being responsible for drawing into the orbit of international transactions the players, such as small business customers and consumers, who would probably not otherwise expand their interests beyond national frontiers.[6] For such a category of actors, litigation or arbitration presents only an unlikely alternative. The costs and complexity of these two traditional methods of dispute settlement projected onto an international plane would largely outweigh the benefits of having disputes resolved via them. Moreover, both litigation and arbitration require a certain degree of sophistication on the side of the parties, a feature which is often lacking in the case of consumers or small and medium-size enterprises.

The development of a global information society and e-commerce, apart from creating a larger class of ADR users, has contributed to innovative methods of dispute resolution in yet another way, namely by preparing the ground for the ODR, an ADR on-line. ODR is a term which might in fact denote two interrelated things.[7] Firstly, it may be used to denote resolution, by

---

6   F. Galinas, 'Arbitration and the Challenge of Globalisation', 17 (14) *Journal of International Arbitration* (2000), p. 117 at p.118.

7   R. Birke & L. E. Teitz, 'U.S. Mediation in 2001: the Path that Brought America to Uniform Laws and Mediation in Cyberspace', 50 *American Journal of Comparative Law* (2002), p. 181 at p. 206.

means of ADR, of the disputes arising in the context of e-commerce. In this case ODR by itself is not that different from other categories of ADR, simply by reason of its specific subject-matter. There are, however, attempts to introduce a genuine virtual ADR, a process which is partially or entirely conducted by electronic means and which is available for the resolution of disputes arising on- or off-line. In this regard it should be noted that the use of electronic means of communication might greatly contribute to the efficiency of ADR, making it even more informal, accessible and financially attractive for large categories of users such as consumers and small e-traders. However, the complete transfer of the mediation or any other ADR procedure to the on-line world seems to mean that those features that ensure the present success of ADR will only partially characterise a truly online ADR procedure. The latter would inevitably lack such features of a 'normal' ADR as personal presence and emotional contact between the parties and a neutral third party.

4 THE POSSIBLE FIELD OF APPLICATION OF ADR: INTERNATIONAL DISPUTES

It should be noted that mediation and other forms of non-binding ADR had first emerged and have come to flourish as a means of out-of-court settlement of disputes arising primarily in the context of domestic legal relationships, as the experience of the US shows.[8] Will ADR be equally successful as a method of resolution of disputes arising in a transnational context?

The answer is not straightforward. To begin with, the specific factors that may influence the role of non-binding ADR as a suitable means of international dispute resolution should be considered. It appears that in a national setting, the main motivation behind the choice in favour of ADR is based on efficiency considerations. ADR might be preferred to litigation or arbitration because it is more efficient in terms of cost and speed and preservation of the existing relationship between the parties. It also has the added value of flexibility. Resort to ADR in domestic agreements signifies that the parties are more predisposed to a non-judicial and informal way of settlement of controversies.

In an international setting, the dispute resolution clause is not only an indication of the parties' choice as to the method of dispute resolution. It also serves as a forum selection clause, or in other words, a choice-of-jurisdiction clause, which once agreed on, is binding and enforceable under the New York Convention on the recognition and enforcement of foreign arbitral awards of 1958.[9] An ADR clause with all its undeniably positive features and advantages cannot serve as a true forum selection clause because it does not deprive the courts of their competence to try the matter covered by the ADR clause. The main characteristics of ADR are its consensual character, which taints its ini-

---

8   M. Hunter, 'International Commercial Dispute Resolution: the Challenge of the 21 Century', 16 (4) *Arbitration International* (2000), p. 383.
9   Article II.

tial enforceability,[10] and the enforceability of the final outcome of a successful ADR attempt.

An ADR agreement or clause is not enforceable in the same sense as an arbitration agreement is. Enforceability of the ADR clause would mean, by analogy with enforceability of arbitration agreement, the stay of court proceedings and mandatory referral of the parties to ADR, notwithstanding the resistance of one of them. Clearly, as most of the beneficial features of ADR are premised on the voluntary nature of the parties' commitment and determination to pursue it, as well as on their cooperation, ADR can hardly be forced on the parties once the trust between them has disappeared.

It should be further recalled that the successful ADR procedure culminates in a settlement agreement, which, if formalised, has the binding force of a contract.[11] The question of enforceability of such an outcome is not decided uniformly even at the level of national ADR.[12] Some countries have introduced summary proceedings for enforcement of such settlement 'contracts'. Sometimes, settlement agreements can be accorded the force equivalent to judgement in some other ways, provided a number of conditions are met. However, this solution is more problematic in the case of settlement agreements in international ADR. Even with regard to foreign judgements, the global community has so far not reached an agreement on the universal system of recognition and enforcement.[13] The UNCITRAL Model Law on Conciliation 2002[14] has also left the question of enforceability of settlement agreements open.[15] Furthermore, there are still no uniform rules on the international jurisdiction under which the settlement agreements resulting from ADR could be enforced. It is inherent to the consensual character of the settlement contract as the result of ADR, that in most cases parties are willing to comply with their contractual obligations voluntarily. The mediation process itself does on the whole contribute to a mutual understanding between parties, and for that reason enforcement is mostly not an issue. However, with the further

---

10   Enforceability of an ADR agreement or clause would mean, by analogy with enforceability of arbitration agreement, the mandatory referral of the parties to ADR notwithstanding the resistance of one of the parties. Clearly, as most of the beneficial features of ADR are derived from the voluntary nature of the commitment to pursue it, ADR can hardly be forced on the parties once the trust in its use has disappeared.

11   C. M. Baker & A.H. Ali, 'A Cross-comparison of Institutional Mediation Rules', 57 (7) *Dispute Resolution Journal* (2002), p. 72 at p. 77.

12   See Guide to Enactment and Use of the 'UNCITRAL Model Law on International Commercial Conciliation', paras. 78-80.

13   The Convention on international jurisdiction and foreign judgements has been prepared under the auspices of the Hague Conference on Private International Law and it is still in the draft stage.

14   The Model Law was adopted by the UNCITRAL on 24 June 2002 at its 35th Session in New York, and was published as Annex I to the Report of the United Nations Commission on International Trade Law on its 35th session, Official Records of the General Assembly (A/57/17).

15   See Article 14 of the Model Law and the Guide to Enactment and Use of the 'UNCITRAL Model Law on International Commercial Conciliation', paras. 78-80.

development of ADR, the enforcement of settlement agreement is of growing importance.

The objective features of ADR make it overall a success story. It is likely that the use of ADR will proliferate further also as a means of settling cross-border disputes. Nevertheless, it can be argued that ADR should not be seen as obviating the need for making the forum selection choice, i.e., the choice between national courts of various countries potentially capable of assuming jurisdiction over the dispute or, what looks more like a standard in international trade, a non-judicial arbitration forum. Therefore, one can conclude that various ADR procedures can certainly complement existing means of settlement of international disputes but nonetheless cannot truly compete with them on an equal footing. This conclusion is confirmed by the fact that most international arbitration centres[16] nowadays provide a range of ADR services which can be used alongside binding arbitration or as a first step in the multi-tied dispute resolution process.

5   NON-BINDING ADR AND ARBITRATION COMPARED

The advantages of arbitration have often been described in much the same terms as the benefits of ADR. The cost and time efficiency, confidentiality, informality and flexibility of the procedure and its consensual character, as well as the less antagonistic attitudes of the parties and the high degree of voluntary compliance with arbitral awards have been emphasised as the features which ensure that arbitration has adequately responded to the international business community's demand for a forum for the resolution of their disputes. However, over time the arbitration process had to be institutionalised, formalised and has sometimes failed to deliver the advantages expected of it.

Nevertheless, certain characteristics still ensure that even a 'judicialised' arbitration method is especially suitable for the resolution of cross-border disputes. As Hunter put it, 'the general preference for arbitration in international transactions has nothing to do with the advantages of speed and cost-saving, which are often emphasised at arbitration conferences. In practice, these advantages apply only in the context of domestic arbitration before a sole arbitrator and even then only in specialised fields such as maritime, commodities, rent reviews, documents-only consumer arbitrations and a few others.' Among these advantages is a possibility to have the dispute resolved within the framework of the procedure, which is not a product of a legal system unknown to at least one of the parties. Another distinct advantage is related to the fact that arbitration is conducted in the language of the parties and various

---

16   The International Chamber of Commerce, the London Court of International Arbitration, the American Arbitration Association, the Permanent Court of Arbitration, the International Centre for Settlement of Investment Disputes, the WIPO Arbitration Centre, etc. See C. M. Baker & A.H. Ali, supra, for the comparison of mediation rules of various arbitration institutions.

documents and the proceedings themselves need not be translated into a foreign language of the country of the courts.

Secondly, arbitration mechanism ensures the necessary flexibility not only in the procedure itself but also in the choice and application of legal standards to the merits of the case. It is not news that the municipal systems of law were not prepared to face the rapid increase in and evolution of international commercial transaction. As the complexity of international transactions has grown steadily the inability, or rather a disincentive, of the national judges -generalist to get entangled in complicated commercial issues is rather understandable. This tendency is exacerbated by the presence of conflict of laws dimensions of cases, which often call for the application of the foreign law. The national judges applying foreign law are working simply as amateurs. In such instances, they do not contribute to the development or restatement of the existing law, both important functions of court adjudication. On the other hand, the a-national standards, loosely referred to as *lex mercatoria* have become the product of the active role that the arbitrators played in filling the gaps in the regulatory framework for the international business transaction.[17]

Lastly and most importantly, the finality and international enforceability of arbitration agreements and arbitral awards have been and will remain the advantages which are not easily outweighed by the drawbacks of the arbitration mechanism. Arbitration is a 'one stop' single instance dispute resolution method. No possibility of appeal means at least that the arbitration award will not be the subject of protracted multi-tiered appeal and review proceedings. Finally, the coherent framework for the international enforceability of arbitral awards established by the New York Convention of 1958 contrasts sharply with the disharmony that exists at the level of enforcement of court judgements or settlement agreements:

> The other positive feature of arbitration in the international context lies in the treaty obligation for enforcing arbitration awards across national boundaries. By contrast, it may be difficult to enforce a favourable judgement of a national court in another country, as there are no multilateral treaties covering the reciprocal enforcement of court judgements.[18]

6   EU AND ADR: LEGAL FRAMEWORK, PAST AND CURRENT INITIATIVES

For a long time, ADR was not considered as an area of particular Community interest; this is reflected by the fact that the EC Treaty does not devote much attention to ADR. Article 65 EC mentions simplification and improvement of recognition and enforcement of decisions in extrajudicial cases[19] as one of the measures in the field of judicial cooperation of the Member States in civil matters having cross-border implications.

---

17   F. Galinas, supra, p.118, 122.
18   M. Hunter, supra, p. 382.
19   I.e., arbitration.

Another article, Article 238 EC, provides that the ECJ should have competence to render a judgement pursuant to arbitration clause in the agreement concluded by or on behalf of the Community. Under this Article, the Court is accorded jurisdiction to resolve disputes arising under public procurement contracts, contracts related to projects financed by the Community, leasing contracts between the officials and the Commission.[20] Some doubts have been expressed whether under Article 238 EC the ECJ acts as a genuine arbitration tribunal or simply as a court. Despite the fact that in such proceedings the ECJ follows the rules of procedure established by the Rules of Procedure of the ECJ (which definitely lack the characteristics typical for arbitration rules) and the judges of the arbitration panel are not selected by the parties, some commentators maintain that ECJ acts nevertheless as a very specific, 'judicial arbitration', developed in the context of EC law.[21]

To complete the overview of Treaty provisions related to arbitration, Article 239 EC establishes the possibility to refer to the ECJ on the basis of special agreement of the parties the disputes between EU Member States related to the subject-matter of the Treaty. This article which may be interpreted as giving a competence for the ECJ to act as an arbitral tribunal in what will be public international arbitration, has never been used in practice.

Despite the near absence of the common Community framework, most of the EC Member States have been familiar with the 'alternative' means of settling disputes, such as arbitration or third-party-assisted negotiation and mediation. The level of development and the actual use of ADR methods across the countries of the EU largely vary. As was already mentioned, ADR has emerged as the practical response to the needs of various actors dissatisfied with the dispute resolution facilities offered by the courts. Therefore, such factors as the presence of ADR traditions (even if sector-specific), the degree of complexity, sophistication and affordability of the judicial process, case overload and overall efficiency of the national judicial system determine the attitude to ADR in a particular State. Until recently, development of ADR had primarily been attributed to the interests and enthusiasm of its users and sponsors. In the context of international commercial law, ADR has always been seen as a market-driven phenomenon.

Lately, however, the development of ADR at both at the national and EU levels has been also fostered by the efforts of public authorities. For example, recent EU initiatives indicate that apart from being based on such considerations as recognition of the virtues of ADR as a non-confrontational, result-oriented and cost-efficient way to settle various disputes, other important rea-

---

20   See further J.-F. Bourque, 'The Legal Framework of Arbitration in the European Union', *International Commercial Arbitration in Europe*, Special Supplement, *ICC Bulletin* (November 1994); L. Idot, 'Arbitration and EC Law' (1996) 5 IBJL, p. 561; M.-A. Gaudissart, J.-V. Louis & L. van den Hende, 'Dispute Settlement in International Agreements concluded by the European Communities', in: *Arbitration and European Law, Reports of the International Colloquium of CEPANI* (Bruylant, Bruxelles, 1997), 141.
21   L. Idot, supra, p. 586.

sons stand behind the increased interest and involvement of state and Community authorities in promotion of the consensual means of resolving disputes.[22] These include the conviction that ADR improves access to justice,[23] helps to solve the problem of judicial overload, and represents a more efficient way of resolving the disputes. Thus, the development of ADR has become a political priority, repeatedly declared by the European Union institutions. For instance, the European Council at Tampere in October 1999 stressed the importance it attached to alternative means of settling cross-border disputes.[24] The Laeken European Council in 2001 also drew attention to the role which voluntary mediation mechanisms might play in employment relations. This political priority was specifically asserted in the context of the information society, where the role of new on-line dispute resolution (ODR) services has been recognised as a form of web-based, cross-border dispute resolution.

The Commission has issued a Green Paper on alternative dispute resolution in civil and commercial law[25] which contains an inventory of the current state of development of non-binding ADR within Member States as well as in the Community. The Green Paper is meant to encourage the discussion on the topic of the desirability of the possible involvement of the Community in ADR by means of adopting regulatory measures, providing information support or creating a favourable environment. It appears that the preference of the Community now goes to non-binding forms of ADR, arbitration being expressly excluded from the Green Paper.[26]

7   ADR AND CONSUMER DISPUTES

Among the Community initiatives which have been already undertaken, the promotion of ADR in consumer disputes should be mentioned, especially in those concerning electronic commerce.[27] As was already pointed out, the globalisation of trade (and in the case of EU – further intensification of trade within the internal market) accompanied by changes in marketing and selling

22   See, for example, the reference to mediation as a possible alternative to a binding decision of a regulatory body in disputes arising between telecommunications operators. Articles 20(2) and 21(3) Directive 2002/21 on a common regulatory framework for electronic communications networks and services, [2002] OJ L 108/33.
23   Communication from the Commission on 'widening consumer access to alternative dispute resolution', COM (2001) 161 Final.
24   Tampere European Council 15-16 October 1999, Presidency conclusions, para. 30, available at <http://www.europarl.eu.int/summits/tam_en.htm#intro>.
25   COM (2002) 196 final.intro>.
26   Green Paper, para. 1.1 (2).
27   Communication from the Commission on 'widening consumer access to alternative dispute resolution', and, COM (2001) 161 Final. See also Directive 2000/31/EC of the European Parliament and of the Council of 8 June 2000 on certain legal aspects of information society services, in particular electronic commerce, in the Internal Market (Directive on electronic commerce).

techniques, i.e., by electronic commerce, has caused the emergence of a new category of international trade actors, consumers and small and medium businesses whose disputes have been labelled as 'small claims' or 'low value' disputes. The specificity of the disputes involving such actors is that neither of the traditional methods of dispute resolution, litigation or commercial arbitration, presents a feasible option for their resolution. The lack of professional expertise and information, insufficient financial resources, legal uncertainty and high costs of litigating (or arbitrating) cross-border disputes can effectively discourage such actors from entering into international agreements. Moreover, as in the case of purchases over the Internet, a consumer might remain unaware of the international dimension of the transaction and will be caught by surprise when confronted with the prospect of suing a party established outside of its place of residence. The negative experience may create a barrier to further participation of this category of actors in international exchange. On the other hand, while the individual stakes may be small, the aggregated power of the consumers and small companies and their influence on the economy is undeniably significant.

To bolster consumer confidence and to ensure that the small claims are resolved in an efficient manner, the Commission adopted a number of the soft law instruments. In two Recommendations, the Commission formulated principles applicable to dispute settlement procedures conducted respectively either by the third party, a special 'out-of-court' body, in Recommendation's terminology, which has a power to propose or impose the decision on the parties,[28] or by the third party who exercises a classic mediation function of assisting the parties to reach the settlement of their controversies.[29]

The first Recommendation formulates a number of principles applicable to bodies offering institutional ADR that reflect the specificity of consumer disputes. These are the principles of independence of out-of-court bodies, transparency and adversarial character of the procedure, effectiveness, legality, liberty and representation. As the Recommendation in issue concerns a range of ADR procedures which may result in a binding outcome, some of the above mentioned principles, such as, e.g., legality and liberty, guarantee that the minimum legal protection, which would have been otherwise available to the consumer in the national courts, is not undermined in ADR. For instance, the ADR bodies should ensure that the consumers do not waive their rights to judicial protection by an uninformed decision to resort to out-of-court schemes[30] and that the protection of consumers' rights reflected in mandatory provisions applicable to the consumer disputes is fully respected by the ADR decision.[31]

---

28   Commission Recommendation of 30 March 1998 on the principles applicable to the bodies responsible for out-of-court settlement of consumer disputes. [1998] OJ L 115/31.

29   Commission Recommendation of 4 April 2001 on the principles for out-of-court bodies involved in the consensual resolution of consumer disputes, [2001] OJ L 109/56.

30   Commission Recommendation of 1998, Article VI.

31   Ibidem, Article V.

The second Recommendation is addressed to bodies that can be seen as exercising mediation and conciliation functions lacking the power to render independent decisions. Consequently, the principles which are addressed to such bodies are slightly different from those formulated in the 1998 Recommendation and fewer in number. In particular, it is worth noting that the latter principle of independence is superseded by the principle of impartiality.[32] The principle of legality is relaxed into the principle of fairness which implies that the outcome of the procedure may not be based on the legal rules.[33]

The practical implementation of the principles laid down by both Recommendations has been ensured and monitored through the European extra-judicial network (EEJ-Net) which was launched by the Commission in 2001.[34] The EEJ-Net represents a platform consisting of the national contact points which provides consumers throughout the Community with the information on the national ADR bodies which meet the requirements of the Recommendations.[35] It also maintains the database of all the bodies which have been notified by the Member States as bodies complying with the principles contained in the Recommendations.

8   ADR AND THE EC INSTITUTIONS: JUDICIAL MEDIATION IN THE CFI PRACTICE

Moving to the practice of Community Courts, a recent study[36] has revealed that the CFI has been gradually embracing ADR techniques (mediation in particular) in its proceedings in order to bring the litigating parties to the settlement of their dispute.

The legal basis of the judicial mediation (that is mediation by the judges hearing the case) practised by the CFI is found in Article 77 of the Rules of Procedure of the ECJ, Articles 98 and 64 of the Rules of Procedure of the CFI. Articles 77 and 98 both envisage the possibility that the proceedings before the Courts can be ended by the settlement reached by the parties. Article 64 dealing with the powers of the CFI to take measures of organisation of procedure, mentions that those measures may pursue the goal of facilitating amicable settlement of proceedings.[37]

As the study demonstrated, out of approximately 40 cases of settlement most of them occurred in practice of the CFI.[38] Most of the settlements were

---

32   Commission Recommendation of 2001, Article A.
33   Ibidem, Article D(2)(b).
34   Council Resolution on a Community-wide network of national bodies for the extra-judicial settlement of consumer disputes, [2000] OJ C 155/1.
35   See Communication from the Commission on 'widening consumer access to alternative dispute resolution', COM (2001) 161 Final, p. 4.
36   S. J. Schønberg, 'Coping with Judicial Over-Load: the Role of Mediation and Settlement in Community Court Litigation' 38 CMLR (2001), 333.
37   Article 64(2)(d).
38   S. J. Schønberg, supra, p. 338.

concluded in staff cases (90 % of the total) and only a marginal number of settlement attempts, successful and otherwise were concerned with interim measures; with the non-contractual liability of the Community institutions; with
the legality of action taken by the institutions in the fields of competition law,
public procurement, financial aid granted under the Community funds, and
measures aimed at combating fraud and mismanagement. As was pointed
out,

> the reason why staff cases dominate the statistic is that they resemble classic civil litigation
> more than other cases coming before the Community courts. Staff cases do not always
> raise points of general legal importance, they rarely have wide-ranging financial implica-
> tions for the defendant Community institutions, and it will often be in the interest of the
> applicant to compromise in order to maintain a working relationship with his employer.
> By contrast, cases concerning the legality of measures taken by the Community institu-
> tions in the fields of agriculture and competition often have wide-ranging legal and finan-
> cial implications.[39]

It is interesting to observe that according to the Rules of Procedure of both the
ECJ and the CFI, second paragraph of Articles 77 and 98 correspondingly,
claims for annulment and actions concerning a failure to act cannot be subject
to settlement. Yet, this prohibition cannot bite since the applicant can always
simply withdraw his claims by sending a written request to the Court to dis-
continue the proceedings. It needs not indicate the reasons for the withdrawal.

It has been suggested that there are two reasons why the settlement option
was explicitly excluded in the cases mentioned above. First of all, in an annulment action or the action for failure to act there is a general public interest in
judicial pronouncement on these matters. The outcome of such claims might
potentially affect not only the position of the claimant but a broader category
of public. The second consideration is that in proceedings of this type, which
are vertical, the Community institutions by analogy with state bodies are
bound by the principle of legality. As correctly observed, 'by settling a dispute
over the legality of a Community measure, the institution might violate that
principle if the challenged measure was in fact lawful.'[40] Equally, if private settlement arrangements can deviate from mandatory rules, it seems less appropriate for the public authority to contract around mandatory rules addressed
to it. The study concludes that while there is a scope of judicial settlement in
practice of the Community courts, settlements of many disputes raising issues
of important legal principle of general application should not be encouraged.
This is a very important point: while the parties themselves can have different
incentives to resort nevertheless to settlement and to use their freedom of procedural disposition, it is not always consistent with the public function of the
judge to push the parties in this direction.

The question which remains is in how far 'judicial mediation' or traditional judicial settlement can be associated with true mediation? In our view, judi-

---

39   Ibidem, p. 339.
40   Ibidem, p. 336.

cial mediation, an example of which taken from the practice of Community Courts has been described above, cannot be regarded as a true mediation process. It is simply a part of the judicial process in which the judge employs some ADR techniques. In its true nature, judicial mediation emphasises the role of the judge as conciliator. The current revival of the interest in such functions of the Community judge should not obscure the fact that a judge in judicial mediation is not a neutral third party whose tasks are simply to assist the parties in negotiating the settlement.

9   CONCLUSION

In a globalising society national courts and national litigation do not answer the need for effective legal protection. Based upon best practices in different fields of social life ADR is becoming of increasing importance. The nature of mediation – informal, voluntary, time- and costs-saving, forms an explanation for the relative success of ADR. However, of more importance is that ADR can, in a non-formal way, bridge gaps between different legal systems. Complex questions regarding the competences of national courts can be avoided. The implementation of ADR in a global context is primarily based upon private initiatives. If multinational companies start challenging ADR-programmes, they contribute to the development of best practices, which can work as an example for others.

The EC initiatives in Europe have so far focused on the more or less traditional areas of civil law in the broad sense. The promotion of ADR by the Community has been especially noticeable in the field of cross-border consumer disputes. However, as the experience of other countries shows, and as was rightly remarked by the CEDR[41] in their response to the Commission's Green Paper on ADR,[42] there is a further scope for ADR expansion, both in terms of development of the new forms and into new areas, such as a use of 'consensus-building' ADR techniques to manage planning and environmental development discussions or 'regulatory mediation' where mediation is used to determine what regulatory sanctions are applied to a regulated company. In this respect Europe can draw on the experience of some other countries, such as the US and Australia, which have a far more developed ADR practice.

Globalisation means that societies become increasingly open to mutual trade, cultural and legal influences. In a world based on pluralism, ADR represents an indispensable element. While not providing a universal cure for all the ills in the field of cross-border conflict resolution in the global society, it creates a healthy competition to, and in some cases complements, the existing court system of dispute resolution. It further contributes to maintaining a self-

---

41   Centre for Effective Dispute Resolution.
42   Para 2.5, CEDR response to EU Commission Green Paper on Alternative Dispute Resolution, available at <www.cedr.co.uk>.

regulatory, efficient, non-confrontational and result-oriented approach to dispute resolution.

Seen in this light, the tasks of Community and national regulators in the field of ADR are challenging: to promote and encourage ADR without at the same time restraining its development and evolution by putting in place a rigid regulatory framework. The success of ADR so far has been often attributed to its flexible and self-regulatory nature allowing it to adapt itself rapidly to any changes in the society, economic, technological or legal. While based on the common core of principles, ADR techniques have also been able to evolve to meet the requirements of specific sectors, hence the diversity of forms of ADR and the ways the ADR procedure is conducted in different areas. In our view, the primary role of states and the Community should be in creating a favourable environment for the further evolution of ADR through accumulation and dissemination of the information on ADR, encouraging the schemes aimed at educating the potential users and the judiciary.

One final point which goes beyond the scope of the present contribution should nevertheless be mentioned in the conclusion. In the area of civil law relationships ADR is not really new. However, as long as it presents a kind of improved third-party-assisted form of negotiations, the ADR expansion into public law relationships raises some concern. It should be recalled that even the domain of arbitration does not extend so far as to embrace disputes involving rights which are not freely disposable. While arbitration, therefore, has always been precluded in certain areas, ADR seems to advance rapidly into the realm of public law. This is not surprising if ADR is understood as a number of techniques which are capable of bringing the parties to the consensus. However, many disputes touching upon public law issues are not really susceptible to negotiation, due to the vertical character of the underlying relationship. The question that remains is whether the distinguishing conflicts and settlement should be always seen as a kind of universal good which is beneficial for society at large. It can be hypothesised that in some instances and especially in the area of public law, the resolution of conflicts through public adjudicatory mechanisms would be still necessary to ensure the development of a given legal system and maintenance of the democratic balance in the society.

The Sarbanes-Oxley Act of 2002: A catalyst for global corporate change?

Kai I. Rebane and Joseph W. Marx[■]

1   INTRODUCTION

The passage of the Sarbanes-Oxley Act of 2002 ('SOA')[1] on July 30, 2002 in response to the corporate scandals at Enron Corp., Global Crossing Ltd., Tyco International Ltd., HealthSouth Corp., Worldcom Inc., and Qwest Communications International, among others, triggered heated debate over the application of U.S. corporate governance standards to U.S. publicly listed foreign companies.[2] Newspapers trumpeted the impending exodus of U.S. publicly listed foreign companies from U.S. capital markets to less restrictive corporate governance regimes. Many of these companies papered the United States Securities and Exchange Commission (the 'SEC') with letters demanding revisions to proposed rules, and foreign regulatory organizations hinted at reciprocal 'strikes' if the SEC did not exempt foreign companies from the SOA's most onerous provisions. Porsche AG made a highly publicized halt to its listing efforts on the New York Stock Exchange ('NYSE'),[3] as did Daiwa Securities Group Inc. and Fuji Photo Film, and the London Stock Exchange began a campaign to woo the many companies commentators agreed would soon seek markets with more lenient corporate governance standards.[4] In fact, in one study published in late 2002, 61% of European chief executive officers surveyed stated that over-regulation in the United States would cause them to leave U.S. markets.[5]

[■]   The views expressed in this article reflect the views of the authors and not of White & Case LLP.

[1]   Sarbanes-Oxley Act of 2002, Pub. L. No. 107-204, 116 Stat. 745 (codified in scattered sections of 15 and 29 U.S.C.) (2002).

[2]   Please note for purposes of this article that the terms 'U.S. publicly listed foreign company', 'foreign company', 'non-U.S. company' and 'foreign private issuer' (as defined later) will be used interchangeably.

[3]   Larry Schlesinger, *Sarbanes-Oxley Forces Porsche to Reverse* (Oct. 17, 2002), available at <www.managementconsultancy.co.uk/News/1131114>; Peter Gumbal, 'Tough Act to Follow – New U.S. legislation to combat corporate fraud provokes a backlash among European executives', *Time*, September 30, 2002, available at <http://www.time.com/time/europe/magazine/article/0,13005,901020923-351174,00.html>.

[4]   AccountancyAge.com, *Sarbanes-Oxley Helps LSE Campaign* (Jan. 7, 2003), available at <www.managementconsultancy.co.uk/News/1132056>; Andrei Postelnicu, 'Sarbanes-Oxley Act: A little breathing space', *Financial Times*, July 14, 2003, available at <http://www.ofii.org/newsroom/news/030704ft.cfm>; *Exchange offers more appeal for Japanese companies* (Dec. 9, 2002), available at <www.londonstockexchange.com/newsroom/releases/Jap09-12-02.asp>.

[5]   Larry Schlesinger, *Sarbanes-Oxley Scares Off European CEOs* (January 24, 2003), available at <www.managementconsultancy.co.uk/News/1132257>.

But corporate scandals are not solely a U.S. phenomenon anymore than corporate reform is a creation of the U.S. government. European companies have also experienced significant corporate failures, some of which were caused by questionable accounting practices, bad management and/or poor internal controls.[6] Names like Robert Maxwell, Polly Peck, Royal Ahold, Swiss Air, Phillip Holzmann, and Vivendi come to mind.[7] Therefore, restoring investor confidence by strengthening corporate governance is of great importance to the world's financial markets, not only to the United States and the European Union.[8] Other regions also have seen high-profile corporate scandals. In Asia, for example, Bank of China (Hong Kong) and Euro-Asia Agriculture (Holdings) Ltd. in Hong Kong, Yin Guang Xia in the People's Republic of China and the Daewoo Group in South Korea all have been investigated for accounting fraud within the past two years, while the past year saw the fall of HIH Insurance in Australia. Every day, it seemed, brought a new scandal and a renewed round of fingerpointing.

In part because of these high profile corporate scandals, calls for corporate reform in Europe and other regions of the world have gained much ground over the past two years. The European Commission (the 'Commission') issued a report in May 2003,[9] which would, among other items, require member countries to name independent regulators to enforce accounting rules and make company executives liable for publishing false accounts. From the Tabaksblat Report[10] in the Netherlands to the Higgs[11] and Smith[12] reports in

---

6   Speech by SEC Commissioner: The Sarbanes-Oxley Act of 2002: 'Goals, Content, and Status of Implementation', given by Commissioner Paul S. Atkins, *International Financial Law Review*, March 25, 2003, available at <http://www.sec.gov/news/speech/spch032503-psa.htm>.

7   Speech by SEC Commissioner: The Sarbanes-Oxley Act of 2002: 'Goals, Content, and Status of Implementation', given by Commissioner Paul S. Atkins, *International Financial Law Review*, March 25, 2003, available at <http://www.sec.gov/news/speech/spch032503-psa.htm>.

8   Speech by SEC Commissioner: The Sarbanes-Oxley Act of 2002: 'Goals, Content, and Status of Implementation', given by Commissioner Paul S. Atkins, *International Financial Law Review*, March 25, 2003, available at <http://www.sec.gov/news/speech/spch032503-psa.htm>.

9   'Modernising Company Law and Enhancing Corporate Governance in the European Union', Council Directive 2003/ /EC (not yet published), amending Council Directive 68/151/EEC (hereinafer, the 'Modernization Directive'), available at <http://europa.eu.int/comm/internal_market/en/company/company/official/conseil-ce-03620/03620_en.pdf>.

10   De Nederlandse corporate governance code: Beginselen van goede corporate governance en best practice bepalingen [The Dutch corporate governance code: Principles of good corporate governance and best practice provisions], available at <http://corpgov.nl/-page/downloads/Conceptcode%20Engels%20DEFINITIEF.pdf> (English version).

11   Review of the Role and Effectiveness of Non-Executive Directors (the 'Higgs Report'), available at <http://www.dtigov.uk/cld/non-exec-review>.

12   Audit Committees – Combined Code Guidance (the 'Smith Report'), available at <http://www.frc.org.uk/publications/content/ACReport.pdf>.

the United Kingdom and from the Bouton Report[13] in France to the Cromme Report[14] in Germany, European governments have addressed and are addressing a host of national corporate concerns specific to their home jurisdictions. Committees appointed by various other governments, from Canada[15] to Australia[16] to Japan[17], have issued proposals for reforming existing corporate regulations to mirror the changing corporate climate, and even non-governmental organizations have joined the movement.[18] While these agendas may not separately be as comprehensive as the SOA, they are a strong step toward addressing corporate and accounting problems and moving toward more enhanced global corporate governance standards.

In light of the current state of corporate reform, this article will examine recent developments in corporate governance. Part I will examine some of the most controversial aspects of the SOA for non-U.S. companies. Part II will offer a critical overview of these provisions of the SOA to the securities activities of U.S. publicly listed foreign companies and the reactions of these companies and foreign regulatory organizations. Part III will discuss in general some of the conflicts of the SOA with existing non-U.S. corporate governance rules and cultures. Finally, Part IV will examine corporate governance reform as a worldwide phenomenon and conclude that the SOA should not be viewed simply as an overreaction by the U.S. government to U.S. corporate scandals but, rather, as a constructive basis for improving global corporate governance standards on both sides of the Atlantic and around the world.

---

13   Pour un meilleur gouvernement des entreprises cotées: Rapport du groupe de travail présidé par Daniel Bouton, président de la Société Générale [Promoting Better Governance in Listed Companies](the 'Bouton Report') available at <http://www.eccg.-org/codes/country_documents/france/rapport_bouton_en.> (English version).

14   Regierungskommission Deutscher Corporate Governance Kodex [German Corporate Governance Code](the 'Cromme Report'), available at <http://www.corporate-governance-code.de/index-e.html>(English version).

15   The Law Commission of Canada, Annual Report 2002-2003, available at <http://-www.lcc.gc.ca/en/about/rapports/2003/ra2003/html/toc.asp>.

16   The Australian Corporate Governance Council issued 'Principles of Good Corporate Governance and Best Practice Recommendations' in March 2003, available at <www.asx.-com.au/about/pdf/ASXRecommendations.pdf>.

17   See the Revised Corporate Governance Principles published by the Japan Corporate Governance Committee (revising the Corporate Governance Principles produced by the Corporate Governance Committee in May 1998), available at <http://www.ecgi.org/-codes/country_documents/japan/revised_corporate_governance_principles.pdf>.

18   See, e.g. Organisation for Economic Co-operation and Development, *White Paper on Corporate Governance in South East Europe* (June 30, 2003), available at <http://www.-oecd.org/dataoecd/9/21/2790073.pdf> The White Paper calls for, among other things, increased protection for minority shareholders, an expanded role for boards of directors, and a continued shift toward international standards of accounting, auditing and transparency. See, e.g., International Corporate Governance Network, *Report Of The Corporate Governance Principles Review Committee – ICGN Statement On Global Corporate Governance Principles Adopted July 9, 1999 At The Annual Conference In Frankfurt, To Be Revised July 11, 2003, at the Annual Conference in Amsterdam*, available at <http://www.icgn.org/documents/CorpGovPrncples0503.pdf>

2   THE SARBANES-OXLEY ACT OF 2002

2.1   General applicability

The SOA generally applies to all foreign private issuers[19] that have securities registered under Section 12 of the U.S. Securities Exchange Act of 1934 (the 'Exchange Act') or foreign companies that are required to file so-called periodic reports under Section 15 of the Exchange Act. In addition, the SOA applies to companies that have filed a registration statement with the SEC under the US Securities Act of 1933 (the 'Securities Act') that has not yet become effective and that has not been withdrawn and privately-held companies that have registered debt securities with the SEC under the Securities Act.

2.2   Certification of financial reports

Arguably, the most contentious provision in the SOA is the certification of financial reports. Under the SOA, a foreign company's chief executive officer ('CEO') and chief financial officer ('CFO')[20] are required to certify financial and other information contained in that company's annual report filed with the SEC, known as a Form 20-F.[21] The two specific certifications are referred to as the Section 302[22] and Section 906[23] certifications. The implementing rules of Section 302 of the SOA require the CEO and CFO of a foreign company to certify their companies' annual report filed on Form 20-F and, in particular, the

---

19   A foreign private issuer is defined in the U.S. Securities Act of 1933, as amended (the 'Securities Act'), and the U.S. Securities Exchange Act of 1934, as amended (the 'Exchange Act'), as a foreign issuer other than a foreign government except an issuer that meets the following conditions:
      (1) More than 50% of the outstanding voting securities of such issuer are directly or indirectly held of record by residents of the United States; and
      (2) any of the following:
          (i)   the majority of the executive officers or directors are United States citizens or residents;
          (ii) more than 50% of the assets of the issuer are located in the United States; or
          (iii) the business of such issuer is administered principally in the United States.
20   Certification of Disclosure in Companies' Quarterly and Annual Reports, 17 CFR Parts 240, 249, 270 and 274, Securities Act Release No. 8124, Exchange Act Release No. 46427, Investment Company Act Release No. 25722, (Aug. 28, 2002) (the 'Certification Release'), available at <http://www.sec.gov/rules/final/33-8124.htm>. The exact wording of the Certification Release states that the parties responsible for the certification are 'the issuer's principal executive officer or officers and the principal financial officer or officers, or persons performing similar functions.'
21   Id. Reports that are current reports, such as reports on Forms 6-K and 8-K, rather than periodic (quarterly and annual) reports are not covered by the certification requirement. Disclosure controls and procedures, however, are required to be designed, maintained and evaluated to ensure full and timely disclosure in current reports.
22   Sarbanes-Oxley Act of 2002, §302.
23   Sarbanes-Oxley Act of 2002, §906.

CEO and CFO must personally certify that the financial statements 'fairly present in all material respects the financial condition, results of operations and cash flow' of the company and that they have established and maintained 'disclosure controls and procedures' and 'internal control over financial reporting' for the company.[24] The implementing rules of Section 906 of the SOA create a separate requirement for a foreign company's CEO and CFO to certify that the periodic report 'fully complies' with certain requirements of the Exchange Act, and that the information contained in the report fairly presents, in all material respects, the financial condition and results of operations of the company.[25] While the SEC has stated that a Section 302 certification does not apply to periodic reports other than a Form 20-F, it has not taken a clear view as to whether the Section 906 certification would apply to periodic reports on Form 6-K.[26] Section 302 of the SOA did not create any new civil or criminal liability penalties,[27] however, Section 906 enacts new criminal penalties in the U.S. penal code for CEOs and CFOs who file false certifications. CEOs and CFOs who certify statements 'knowing that the periodic report accompanying the statement does not comport with the requirements' may be fined up to US$1 million or imprisoned for no more than 10 years, or both.[28] Likewise, CEOs and CFOs

---

24   See the Certification Release, available at <http://www.sec.gov/rules/final/33-8124.htm>.
25   Idem.
26   On April 11, 2003, U.S. Senator Joseph Biden introduced a statement into the Congressional Record that asserts that Section 906 'is intended to apply to any financial statement filed by a publicly-traded company, upon which the investing public will rely to gauge the physical health of the company'. 149 Cong. Rec. S5325 (daily ed. Apr. 11, 2003). Although this language includes financial statements included in current reports on Forms 6-K and 8-K and annual reports on Form 11-K, idem at S5331, the language added to Title 18 by Section 906 refers to 'periodic reports containing financial statements', which in the SEC's final rules did not address Forms 6-K and 8-K. Certification of Disclosure in Certain Exchange Act Reports, Securities Act Release No. 33-8218; Exchange Act Release No. 34-47551 at fn. 37, available at <http://www.sec.gov/rules/proposed/33-8212.htm> The SEC is currently weighing the need for fulsome disclosure to investors against the possible chilling effect on information and substantial practical burdens the application of Section 906 to Forms 6-K, 8-K and 11-K would have. Management's Reports on Internal Control Over Financial Reporting and Certification of Disclosure in Exchange Act Periodic Reports, Securities Act Release No. 33-8238; Exchange Act Release No. 34-47986 (the 'Internal Control Release'), available at <http://www.sec.gov/rules/final/33-8238.htm>.
27   Even before the enactment of the SOA, a company's CEO and CFO could be held responsible as signatories for the company's disclosures under the Exchange Act liability provisions and can be liable for material misstatements or omissions under general antifraud statutes and under SEC authority to seek redress against parties who cause or aid or abet securities law violations. A CEO or CFO who now files a false Section 302 certification may be subject to SEC enforcement action under Section 13(a) and 15(d) of the Exchange Act and to both SEC and private actions for violation of Section 10(b) and Rule 10b-5 of the Exchange Act. In addition, if the annual report on Form 20-F in which the false certification was filed is incorporated by reference into a registration statement on Form F-3 or into a prospectus filed pursuant to Rule 424(b) of the Securities Act, the CEO and CFO may face liability under Sections 11 and 12(a)(2) of the Securities Act.
28   See the Certification Release, available at <http://www.sec.gov/rules/final/33-8124.htm>.

who 'willfully certify any statement... knowing that the period report accompanying the statement does not comport' with the Section 906 certification may be fined up to US$5 million or imprisoned for not more than 20 years, or both.[29]

2.3   Disclosure controls and procedures

2.3.1   Disclosure controls

The SEC adopted rules to implement Section 302 of the SOA which require foreign issuers to maintain 'disclosure controls and procedures' and, as of the end of the period covered by the annual report on Form 20-F, conduct an evaluation, with the participation of the foreign issuer's management, including the CEO and CFO, of the effectiveness of the design and operation of the foreign issuer's disclosure controls and procedures.[30] 'Disclosure controls and procedures' are controls and procedures required to be established and maintained by a foreign issuer that are designed to ensure that the information (financial and non-financial) required to be disclosed by a foreign issuer in the reports filed or submitted by it to the SEC under the Exchange Act, including Form 20-Fs and Form 6-Ks, is recorded, processed, summarized and reported, within the time periods specified in the SEC's rules and forms.

2.3.2   Internal control over financial reporting

The SEC adopted rules to implement Section 404 of the SOA to require an issuer's annual report[31] to include a report of management on the company's internal control over financial reporting.[32] In addition, a foreign issuer must now provide in its annual report on Form 20-F an internal control report attested to by the foreign issuer's auditors and must disclose any change in its internal control over financial reporting that occurred during the last fiscal quarter covered by the annual report, that has materially affected, or is reasonably likely to materially affect, the foreign issuer's internal control over financial reporting.

---

29   Idem.
30   Idem.
31   See the Internal Control Release, available at <http://www.sec.gov/rules/final/33-8238.htm>. In the case of foreign issuers, this Section 404 report will apply only to annual reports on Form 20-F, and not to reports on Form 6-K.
32   The term 'internal control over financial reporting' refers to a process designed by, or under the supervision of, the issuer's CEO and CFO, or persons performing similar functions, and effected by the issuer's board of directors, management and other personnel, to provide reasonable assurance regarding the reliability of financial reporting and the preparation of financial statements for external purposes in accordance with generally accepted accounting principles. Idem.

2.4   Standards relating to listed audit committees

2.4.1   Audit committee guidelines

The SEC adopted new rules to the Exchange Act to implement Section 301 of the SOA under which a national securities exchange may not list any security of any company, including a non-U.S. company, that is not in compliance with the following standards:
–   each member of the audit committee of the company must be independent according to specified criteria;
–   the audit committee of each company must be directly responsible for the appointment, compensation, retention and oversight of the work of any registered public accounting firm engaged for the purpose of preparing or issuing an audit report or performing other audit, review or attest services for the company, and each such registered public accounting firm must report directly to the audit committee;
–   each audit committee must establish procedures for the receipt, retention and treatment of complaints regarding accounting, internal accounting controls or auditing matters, including procedures for the confidential, anonymous submission by employees of the company of concerns regarding questionable accounting or auditing matters;
–   each audit committee must have the authority to engage independent counsel and other advisors, as it determines necessary to carry out its duties; and
–   each company must provide appropriate funding for the audit committee.[33]

2.4.2   Independence of audit committee members

Under the SEC rules,[34] each member of the audit committee must be independent. Members of the audit committee cannot be employed by the company, if they have worked for the company for the past three to five years (depending on which market the shares are listed on), or have been an employee or partner of the company's outside auditing firm within the past year. New Rule 10A-3 of the Exchange Act explicitly established two new standards for determining independence which include that the new audit committee member:
–   does not accept, directly or indirectly, any consulting, advisory or other

---

33   Standards Relating To Listed Company Audit Committees, Securities Act Release No. 8220; Exchange Act Release No. 47654; Investment Company Act Release No. 26001 (the 'Audit Committee Standards Release'), available at <http://www.sec.gov/-rules/final/33-8220.htm>.

34   Certification of Management Investment Company Shareholder Reports and Designation of Certified Shareholder Reports as Exchange Act Periodic Reporting Forms; Disclosure Required by Sections 406 and 407 of the Sarbanes-Oxley Act of 2002, Exchange Act Release Nos. 34-47262; Investment Company Release No. 25914 (the '406/407 Release'), available at <http://www.sec.gov/rules/final/34-47262.htm>.

compensatory fees, in any amount, from the company or any of its subsidiaries, other than fees (for which there is no limit) for serving as a
member of the board of directors or on any committee of the board, apart
from a few exceptions discussed later in this section; and
- is not an 'affiliate' of the company or any of its subsidiaries.[35]

In its final rules, the SEC has made some notable concessions to foreign companies, especially in some European jurisdictions, by providing exemptions in
certain specific areas in which foreign corporate governance arrangements
differ significantly from general practices among U.S. corporations, including
employee representation on the board of directors of a foreign issuer.[36] Under
the final SEC rules, a non-executive employee can sit on the audit committee
of a foreign issuer if such employee is elected or named to the board of directors or audit committee of such foreign issuer pursuant to the governing law
or governing documents, an employee collective bargaining or similar agreement or other home country legal or listing requirements applicable to such
foreign issuer.[37] In Germany, for example, the Co-determination Act of 1976
grants representation rights on the Supervisory Board to senior employees
working for companies subject to the regime of the Co-determination Act.[38]
According to the final SEC rules, there will be no other ability for a securities
exchange to exempt or waive foreign issuers from the requirements.[39] However, the SEC noted in the release relating to its final rules that it has the authority to respond to, and will remain sensitive to, the evolving standards of corporate governance throughout the world to address any new conflicts that may
arise from foreign corporate governance rules and practices.[40]

---

35   'Affiliated person' is defined as a person who controls, is controlled by or is under com-
      mon control with the company. Id. The SEC has defined 'control' as the possession, direct
      or indirect, of the power to direct or cause the direction of the management and policies of
      the company, whether through the ownership of voting securities, by contract or other-
      wise. Id. The SEC created a safe harbor, according to which a person would not be
      deemed an 'affiliated person' if he or she is both not a more than 10% holder of any class
      of equity securities of the company, and not an executive of the company. In addition, ex-
      ecutive officers, directors that are also employees of an 'affiliated person', general partners
      and managing members of an 'affiliated person' will be deemed to be 'affiliated persons'.
      Those who would be ineligible to rely on the safe harbor, but believe that they do not con-
      trol the company, still could rely on a facts and circumstances analysis. Idem.
36   See the Audit Committee Standards Release, available at <http://www.sec.gov/rules/-
      final/33-8220.htm>.
37   Idem.
38   §15, Nr. 1, Mitbestimmungsgesetz 1976 (the German Co-determination Act of 1976).
39   See the Audit Committee Standards Release, available at <http://www.sec.gov/rules/-
      final/33-8220.htm>.
40   Idem.

2.4.3   Audit committee financial expert

The SEC adopted Item 16A to the annual report on Form 20-F[41] to implement Section 407(a) of the Sarbanes-Oxley Act to require foreign private issuers to disclose in their annual report on Form 20-F that the issuer's board of directors has determined whether the issuer has one audit committee financial expert[42] serving on its audit committee, and if not, why not. If the issuer has a two-tier board of directors structure, the supervisory or non-management board would make the determination. In addition, the company must disclose the name of the audit committee financial expert (if there is one) and whether that person is 'independent' from management. The audit committee financial expert of a foreign private issuer must only be familiar with local GAAP, and not U.S. GAAP or reconciliation to U.S. GAAP (although that experience would be helpful).

The board of directors would have to determine whether an individual's qualifications, in the aggregate, satisfy the audit committee financial expert definition.[43] The fact that a person has previously served on an audit committee would not, by itself, justify the board of directors in designating such person as an audit committee financial expert. Once the board of directors determines that a particular audit committee member qualifies as an audit committee financial expert, it may, but is not required to, determine whether additional audit committee members also qualify as experts.

In addition, in its final rules relating to audit committees issued on April 9, 2003, the SEC amended the audit committee financial expert 'independence' requirement applicable to foreign companies. According to the amended rules, a foreign company listed in the United States will be required to disclose whether its audit committee financial expert is 'independent', as that term is defined by the U.S. securities exchange listing standards applicable to such foreign company. If the foreign private issuer is not listed on a U.S. securities exchange, it must choose one of the self-regulatory organization definitions of audit committee member independence that have been approved by the SEC in determining whether its audit committee financial expert, if it has one, is independent, and disclose which definition was used.[44]

---

41   Idem.
42   An audit committee financial expert must have the following 'attributes': an understanding of GAAP; the ability to assess the general application of GAAP in connection with the accounting for estimates, accruals and reserves; experience preparing, auditing or analyzing financial statements similar to those of the issuer, or actively supervising others engaged in these activities; an understanding of internal controls and procedures for financial reporting; an understanding of audit committee functions. Idem.
43   An audit committee financial expert must have gained such attributes through: education and experience as a principal financial officer, principal accounting officer, controller, public accountant or auditor, or experience in similar positions; experience actively supervising those functions; experience overseeing or assessing the performance of companies or public accountants with respect to the preparation, auditing or evaluation of financial statements; or other relevant experience. Idem.
44   The Audit Committee Standards Release, available at <http://www.sec.gov/rules/-final/33-8220.htm>.

2.5   *Auditor independence and SOA provisions affecting accounting firms*

The SOA imposes significant restrictions on all listed companies' relationships with their auditors in connection with providing audit services.[45] The SOA severely limits the scope of consulting services that auditors can offer to their audit clients. The SOA restricts any accounting firm that provides auditing services for a company from also providing non-audit services to that company, contemporaneously with the audit.[46] The SEC's final rules define the services which are prohibited contemporaneously with the audit as follows:

- Book-keeping or other services related to the accounting records or financial statements of the audit client;
- Financial information systems design and implementation;
- Appraisal or valuation services, fairness opinions, or contribution-in-kind reports;[47]
- Actuarial services;
- Internal audit outsourcing services;
- Management functions or human resources;
- Broker or dealer, investment adviser, or investment banking services;
- Legal services; and
- Expert services unrelated to the audit.[48]

Other non-audit services, such as tax services[49], may only be provided to the company if approved in advance by the audit committee of the company, ex-

---

45   Strengthening the Commission's Requirements Regarding Auditor Independence, Securities Act Release No. 8183; Exchange Act Release No. 47265; 35-27642; Investment Company Act Release No. 25915; Investment Advisors Act Release No. 2103 (the 'Auditor Independence Release'), available at <http://www.sec.gov/rules/final/33-8183.htm>.

46   It should be noted that the SEC and Public Company Accounting Oversight Board established by the SOA will be required to issue rules implementing the prohibition of the independent auditor's supply of such services within six months after the date of the commencement of the operations of the Public Company Accounting Oversight Board. Sarbanes-Oxley Act of 2002, Title 1.

47   The SEC rules prohibit the accountant from providing such services unless it is reasonable to conclude that the results of these services will not be subject to audit procedures during an audit of the audit client's financial statements. See the Auditor Independence Release, available at <http://www.sec.gov/rules/final/33-8183.htm>.

48   The SEC rules prohibit an accountant from providing expert opinions or other expert services to an audit client, or a legal representative of an audit client, for the purpose of advocating that audit client's interests in litigation or in a regulatory or administrative proceeding or investigation. An accountant's independence will not be impaired, however, by an accountant providing factual accounts or testimony or explaining the positions taken or conclusions reached during the performance of any service by the accountant. Idem.

49   Accountants will be able to continue to provide tax compliance, tax planning and tax advice to audit clients, subject to audit committee pre-approval requirements. There are, however, some circumstances where providing certain tax services to an audit client would impair the independence of an accountant, such as representing an audit client in tax court or other situations involving public advocacy. Idem.

cept those permitted non-audit services falling within a *de minimis* exception provided in the SOA. [50] Consideration of such non-audit services may be delegated to an independent director of the committee. Any such approvals by the audit committee of non-audit services must be publicly disclosed in the company's periodic reports under the Exchange Act. The SOA specifically notes that audit services may entail providing comfort letters in connection with securities underwriting in order to make clear that providing such a comfort letter is an audit service. In its final rules, the SEC included modified provisions, such as those limiting the scope of partner rotation and personnel subject to the 'cooling-off period,' in response to particular concerns raised about the international implications of these requirements. The final rules also gave non-U.S. accounting firms additional time to comply with rotation requirements. The final release also provides guidance on the provision of non-audit services by foreign accounting firms, including the treatment of legal services and tax services.

The SEC also adopted rules under Section 802 of the SOA requiring accounting firms to retain for seven years certain records relevant to their audits and reviews of issuers' financial statements, including workpapers and certain other documents that contain conclusions, opinions, analyses, or financial data related to the audit or review.[51] Because the only arguments received by the SEC from non-U.S. commentators, including the European Commission, noted that application of the rule to foreign auditors would place additional and differing layers of retention requirements on those firms but did not identify any direct conflicts with foreign requirements, no exemptions for non-U.S. auditors were provided in the final rule. A more significant problem, however, arises under the provisions of Sections 101, 102, 103, 104 and 105 of the SOA, which will be implemented by the Public Company Accounting Oversight Board (the 'PCAOB'). The charter of the PCAOB charges it with the oversight of the audits of public companies in order to protect the interests of investors and further the public interest in the preparation of informative, fair, and independent audit reports. The rules of the PCAOB, which must be approved by the SEC, require auditing firms, among other things, to register with the PCAOB and make available work papers in the event of investigations into audits.[52]

---

50   This exception waives the pre-approval requirements for non-audit services provided that all such services (1) do not aggregate to more than five percent of total revenues paid by the audit client to its accountant in the fiscal year when services are provided; (2) were not recognized as non-audit services at the time of the engagement; and (3) are promptly brought to the attention of the audit committee and approved prior to the completion of the audit by the audit committee or one or more designated representatives. Although not required to be pre-approved by the audit committee, non-audit services falling within the de minimus exception are nevertheless subject to a 'post approval' requirement. Idem.

51   Retention of Records Relevant to Audits and Reviews, Securities Act Release No. 8180; Exchange Act Release No. 47241; Investment Company Act Release 25911 (the 'Record Retention Release'), available at <http://www.sec.gov/rules/final/33-8180.htm>.

52   To see proposed and final rules of the PCAOB, as well as comments, see <http://www.pcaobus.org/pcaob_rulemaking.asp>.

3   CONFLICT WITH NON-U.S. CORPORATE GOVERNANCE RULES AND
         CULTURES

3.1   Historic background

The regulation of non-domestic companies by domestic regulators is not a recent phenomenon, nor one that is wholly a U.S. concept. In fact, when the United States first implemented securities regulation[53] following the stock market
crash in 1929, it lagged behind many European countries in so doing. The United States later provided for separate disclosure forms for foreign private issuers as foreign private issuers began to make an increasing number of offerings in the United States.[54] The SEC was forced to balance the need to provide
U.S. investors with fulsome disclosure against the desire to encourage foreign
companies interest in accessing U.S. capital markets.[55] The result was Form 20-
F, which allowed foreign companies to use either U.S. generally accepted accounting principals ('GAAP') or alternative accounting principles,[56] required
only a signature on behalf of the company, not by any particular officer, and
permitted various other variances from what was required by U.S. companies.
In September 1999, the SEC moved one step closer to aligning U.S. corporate
governance standards to European corporate governance standards when it
adopted revised disclosure requirements for foreign companies, including revisions to the definition of 'foreign private issuer' and the Form 20-F, to conform to the international disclosure standards endorsed by the International
Organization of Securities Commissions in September 1998.[57] Historically,
'[w]hile the SEC does not practice mutual recognition, it has made extra efforts
to provide accommodations for foreign market participants where possible
without sacrificing investor protections...' In a number of instances, the SEC
made adjustments for foreign issuers. Some examples include:
–   interim financial reporting is done on the basis of home country practice,
    rather than on a quarterly basis, as is required of U.S.-based issuers;
–   foreign private issuers are given longer deadlines for submitting annual
    reports;
–   foreign private issuers also use different registration forms for filing an-
    nual reports that are tailored particularly to their requirements and that
    take into account existing home requirements;
–   foreign broker-dealers are provided with an exception from registrations
    to facilitate dealing with certain U.S. institutional investors;
–   aggregate executive compensation disclosure is allowed for foreign pri-

---

53   1 Louis Loss & Joel Seligman, Securities Regulation 166-67 (3d ed. 1989).
54   2 Louis Loss & Joel Seligman, Securities Regulation 802 (3d ed.1989).
55   Idem at 803.
56   Idem at 807.
57   International Disclosure Standards, Securities Act Release No. 7745, Exchange Act Release
      No. 41936; International Series Release No. 1205, available at
      <http://www.sec.gov/rules/final/34-41936.htm>.

vate issuers, rather than individual disclosure, if permitted by the is-suer's home country.'[58]

In drafting the SOA, Congress removed much of the ability to interpret rules from the SEC. As a result, the SEC found itself in the difficult position of enacting rules under the SOA without the ability to tailor them to the realities of the global market. Many of the new rules not only imposed much greater disclosure requirements and fiduciary responsibilities, but, in several instances, conflicted with home country laws, forcing some companies into the uncomfortable position of making a choice between two legal regimes. Also, objections abound with the United States' rule-based approach to corporate governance, as opposed to the principles-based approach used in many non-U.S. jurisdictions. Ultimately, the SEC made a number of concessions for non-U.S. companies in the final rules it enacted to implement the SOA, including modifications of audit committee requirements to recognize variations in the laws and requirements of foreign jurisdictions, modifications of proposed definitions, and exclusion of certain non-U.S. attorneys from coverage of the SEC's attorney conduct rules. Nonetheless, even with the concessions made by the SEC, non-U.S. companies, organizations and governments have continued to lobby for more exemptions.

3.2   Section 302 and 906 certifications

In many non-U.S. corporate regimes, the entire board of directors of a company, not the individual, is collectively responsible for financial results. In giving its reason not to pursue its NYSE listing, Porsche AG cited the Section 302 and 906 certification requirements as its primary motivating factor.[59] Furthermore, many companies object to the certifications because they believe the United States should recognize the fiduciary duties already imposed on them by their home jurisdictions. For example, under Swiss law, numerous provisions prohibit company executives from making false or misleading statements in financial reports, rendering them liable not only under civil law but also under criminal law.[60] In Germany, deliberate falsifications of balance sheets are punished under the German Commercial Code and the Company Act.[61] Foreign companies noted that corporate officers in such instances also would face the uncomfortable prospect of dual liability. By requiring certifications from certain individual officers, the SEC is holding the few accountable in the United States for something which the many must account for elsewhere.

---

58   Speech by SEC Commissioner: 'Embracing International Business in the Post-Enron Era' by Commissioner Roel C. Campos at the Centre for European Policy Studies, Brussels, Belgium on June 11, 2003.

59   Larry Schlesinger, *Sarbanes-Oxley Forces Porsche to Reverse* (Oct. 17, 2002), available at <www.managementconsultancy.co.uk/News/1131114>.

60   Code pénal suisse (Swiss Penal Code), Art. 152, available at <http://www.admin.ch/-ch/f/rs/c311_0.html>.

61   Commercial Code (*Handelsgesetzbuch*), Art. 334.

3.3   Internal controls

Many home country laws place the responsibility for the accuracy of disclosure statements on a collective body, such as the board of directors, rather than
on individuals. In the United Kingdom, listed companies are also subject to
the internal control provisions of the UK Listing Rules.[62] In accordance with
the Combined Code on Corporate Governance,[63] compliance with the London
Stock Exchange Listing Rules Paragraph 12.43A[64] and the requirements of the
Turnbull Report of 1999,[65] boards of UK-listed companies must disclose in
their annual reports information on their internal controls, which includes a
description of risk assessment procedures and the processes that they have
adopted to review the effectiveness of their internal controls. Similarly,
Chilean companies are required by the Chilean Securities Exchange Act[66] and
the Chilean Corporations Act[67] to disclose, on a real time basis, a wide range of
information which such corporations determine may have an effect on the
market value of their stock. In Italy, companies have an independent board of
statutory auditors that, among other things, assesses the adequacy of internal
controls and oversees financial reporting.[68] Companies that violate such regulations face a broad range of sanctions, ranging from fines to, in extreme cases,
dissolution of the company.

3.4   Section 301 and 407 – Audit Committee and Financial Expert Disclosure

When the rules on Audit Committees and Financial Expert Disclosure were
initially proposed, many non-U.S. companies objected to the limitations on
which individuals could qualify as an 'Audit Committee Financial Expert.'
Their objections stemmed from the limited pool of qualified individuals from
which they would now be forced to draw, as many highly qualified financial
experts lack direct U.S. experience, which was required by the initial proposed
rule. In particular, multinational corporations argued that they needed to attract individuals with broad international experience in relevant business
areas, and that the rules, as proposed, would drastically reduce the pool of individuals on which they could draw.

---

62   Available at <http://www.fsa.gov.uk/pubs/ukla/chapt12-3.pdf>.
63   The Combined Code on Corporate Governance, July 2003, available at <http://www.frc.-
      org.uk/publications/content/CombinedCodeFinal.pdf>.
64   Available at <http://www.fsa.gov.uk/pubs/ukla/chapt12-3.pdf>.
65   Internal Control – Guidance for Directors on the Combined Code available at <http://-
      www.icaew.co.uk/viewer/index.cfm?AUB=TB2I_6342>.
66   Securities Market Law (Law No. 18,045), Art. 9, available at <http://www.-
      svs.cl/sitio/english/html/legisl_normativa/f_legis.html>.
67   Corporations Law (Law No. 18,046), Art. 46, available at <http://www.svs.cl/sitio/eng-
      lish/html/legisl_normativa/f_legis.html> (English version).
68   Legislative Decree 58/1998, Art. 149.1(c).

Many companies also pointed out that the proposed rules assumed a U.S. model of corporate governance.[69] In Japan[70], Sweden[71] and Canada,[72] for example, outside auditors are chosen by shareholders. In Chile, under the Chilean Corporations Act,[73] although Chilean companies have a Directors' Committee, which is analogous to a U.S. audit committee, under Chilean law, the Directors' Committee is permitted only to propose to the Board independent accountants for their consideration. The Board may or may not accept such proposal, and may make its own proposal, and submit both to the company's shareholders for consideration.

The concept of audit committee member 'independence,' in particular, was problematic for non-U.S. companies because home jurisdictions not only defined 'independence' differently from the proposed rules, but in fact, often legally required governance structures that directly violated such proposed definitions. In Chile, for example, under Chilean law a director may receive compensatory fees, other than director's compensation, or be an 'affiliated' person of the company, yet still satisfy the definition of 'independent' under Chilean law.[74] An even greater problem was faced by companies in Germany, Denmark, the Netherlands and Austria, which are required by law to have two separate boards – one for day-to-day management and the other for oversight. In Germany, for example, there is a two-tier board structure – a supervisory board (*Aufsichtsrat*) and a management board (*Vorstand*), which are separate (no individual may serve on both). The management board is responsible for managing a company's business in accordance with applicable laws and the company's charter and governing documents. The supervisory board appoints and removes members of the management board and works with the management board on, among other matters, financial matters, including the review and approval of financial reports and audits. Under the German Codetermination Act,[75] half of the members of the supervisory board represent shareholders and the other half represent employees. The employee representatives must be employees of the company, and at least one such

---

69   Letter from Nippon Keidanren (Japan Business Federation) to Mr. Jonathan Katz of the SEC (February 18, 2003), available at www.sec.gov/rules/proposed/s74002/-hendo1.htm>; Letter from NTT DoCoMo, Inc. to Mr. Jonathan Katz of the SEC (February 18, 2003), available at www.sec.gov/rules/proposed/s74002/ktachikawa1.htm>.

70   For a description of the Japanese provisions, see Letter from Financial Services Agency-Government of Japan to Mr. Jonathan Katz of the SEC (February 14, 2003) available at <http://www.fsa.go.jp/refer/sarbanes/e20030214-1.pdf>.

71   Aktiebologslagen, SFS 1975:1385 (Swedish Companies Act), Ch. 10, § 8.

72   Canadian Business Corporations Act, § 162, available at <http://www.canlii.org/-ca/sta/c-44/>.

73   Corporations Law (Law No. 18,046), Art. 50 bis, available at <http://www.svs.cl/-sitio/english/html/legisl_normativa/f_legis.html>.

74   Corporations Law (Law No. 18,046), Art. 50 bis, available at <http://www.svs.cl/-sitio/english/html/legisl_normativa/f_legis.html>.

75   §15, Nr.1, Mitbestimmungsgesetz 1976 (the German Co-determination Act of 1976). The law mainly applies to limited liability companies and joint stock companies with more than 2000 employees.

representative must be an officer. Under German law, the employee representatives must sit on the audit committee, and by definition, such members receive a salary from the company, which means that no member would satisfy the audit committee independence requirements under the proposed rule.

Even though the SEC in its final rules made it clear that the audit committee financial experts for foreign private issuers whose financial statements are prepared using home country accounting principles need only be familiar with such set of accounting principles, and revised the final rule to permit non-management employees to serve on audit committees, to allow shareholder selection and to permit alternative bodies to fulfill auditor oversight roles, non-U.S. companies still believe that their potential pool of directors remains unnecessarily restricted.

3.5 Auditor independence and provisions of the SOA affecting auditors

The general concerns expressed by non-U.S. companies and organizations with respect to auditor independence rules focused on two specific areas: first, the increased liability exposure for auditors and, second, the scope of prohibited non-audit services, in particular, the limitation on tax services.[76] Most significant of these concerns is not only that the SOA requirements would expose auditors to liability by virtue of their audit work for subsidiaries of U.S. companies, but more importantly, that auditors could also face criminal sanctions in their home jurisdictions if the SOA provisions required them to violate professional secrecy laws.[77] In Japan, for example, under the Certified Public Accounts Law,[78] CPAs are required not to disclose or misuse confidential informa-

---

76   See, Letter from EC Internal Market Director General to Mr. Jonathan Katz of the SEC (Nov. 29, 2002), available at ; Letter from from EC Internal Market Director General to Mr. Jonathan Katz of the SEC (Nov. 25, 2002), available at (discussing EU Recommendation on Auditor Independence and principles-based approach); Letter from Fédération des Experts Comptables Européens to Alexander Schaud, Director General of DG Internal Market of the EC (Sept. 26, 2002) available at http://www.fee.be/secretariat/-PDFs/FEE%20Letter%20&%20%20Position%20Paper/Sarbanes%20020926.pdf>; Letter from Mark Armour, Chairman of the Hundred Group, to Mr. Jonathan Katz of the SEC (January 13, 2003), available at <http://www.sec.gov/rules/proposed/s74902/marmour1.htm>; See, generally, the various comment letters available at <http://www.pcaobus.org/pcaob_rulemaking.asp>.

77   For a discussion of various secrecy law conflicts and a listing of various laws requiring auditor confidentiality, see Letter from Deloitte & Touche to Office of the Secretary, PCAOB (March 31, 2003), available at <http://www.pcaobus.org/pcaob_rulemaking.asp; Letter from Commissioner Frits Bolkestein of the EU to Mr. Charles M. Niemeier, Chairman of PCAOB (April 11, 2003), available at <http://www.pcaobus.org/pcaob_rulemaking.asp; See also, Letter from Fédération des Experts Comptables Européens to Alexander Schaud, Director General of DG Internal Market of the EC (Sept. 26, 2002) available at <http://www.fee.be/secretariat/PDFs/FEE%20Letter%20&%20%20Position%20Paper/Sarbanes%20020926.pdf>.

78   Art. 27, Certified Public Accountants Act of Japan (Law No. 103, 1948).

tion obtained through their services without justifiable reasons.[79] In many countries, such as Germany and Switzerland,[80] laws impose strict penalties for violations of secrecy laws. Many commentators to the proposed rules also believed that the SEC should have regard to home state rules in respect of foreign companies and their auditors, many of which have well-established oversight organizations.[81]

4 CORPORATE GOVERNANCE REFORM AS A WORLDWIDE PHENOMENON

4.1 European Union reform

4.1.1 Financial Services Action Plan

Corporate governance reform in the European Union ('EU') has been evolving for the past several years and touches upon many of the issues addressed by the SOA. Even before the recent string of accounting scandals, the EU formulated a Financial Services Action Plan (the 'Action Plan')[82] in which the Commission identified issues to be addressed and actions to be taken in order to improve European capital markets. In particular, the Action Plan placed priority on reducing market manipulation, improving the frequency and quality of information to investors, financial statements and auditing standards, and identifying and eliminating barriers created by variances in corporate governance regimes.[83] On January 28, 2003, the EU issued the proposed Market Abuse Di-

---

79 Letter from Financial Services Agency-Government of Japan to Office of the Secretary, Public Company Oversight Accounting Board (March 28, 2003), available at <http://www.pcaobus.org/pcaob_rulemaking.asp>.
80 Code pénal suisse (Swiss Penal Code), Arts. 162 and 321, available at <http://www.admin.ch/ch/f/rs/c311_0.html>.
81 See, e.g., Letter from Deloitte & Touche to Office of the Secretary, PCAOB (March 31, 2003), available at <http://www.pcaobus.org/pcaob_rulemaking.asp; Letter from Confederation of British Industry to Mr. Jonathan Katz of the SEC (Jan. 13, 2003), available at <http://www.sec.gov/rules/proposed/s74902/cedrupt1.htm>; Letter from The Japanese Institute of Certified Public Accountants to Mr. Gordon Seymour, Acting General Counsel, PCAOB (March 31, 2003), available at <http://www.sec.gov/rules/proposed/-s74902/cedrupt1.htm>.
82 The Financial Services Action Plan, COM(1999) 232, available at <http://europa.eu.int/-comm/internal_market/en/finances/general/actionen.pdf>.
83 The EU recognized that differences in corporate governance arrangements may create unnecessary uncertainty for both issuers and investors through conflicting regulations and unequal rights. As a result, the European Commission launched a review of existing codes of corporate governance with a view to identifying any legal or administrative barriers which could frustrate the development of a single EU financial market. The resulting 'Comparative Study of Corporate Governance Codes relevant to the European Union and its Member States' was published on March 27, 2002 and was used by the High Level Group of Company Law Experts in developing their report to the Commission. The study is available at <http://europa.eu.int/comm/internal_market/en/company/company/-news/corp-gov-codes-rpt_en.htm>.

rective,[84] which is aimed, among other things, at the establishment of an integrated regulatory and supervisory framework, involving a single authority in each member state, with a mandate to assist and share information with each other and to encourage a consistent approach to administrative and criminal sanctions for abusive market practices.[85] On March 26, 2003, the European Commission proposed a new Directive[86] to ensure transparency of information by requiring issuers to provide regular flows of information, facilitate proxy voting and require investors to inform issuers of acquisitions or dispositions of major holdings in companies. Under the proposed Directive, which cited the SOA as a model that 'sets a pace against which Community legislation must find a proper response for promoting European capital markets at international level,' the Commission revised the requirements for annual and interim financial reporting[87] and proposed that member states have in place adequate rules on identification of the responsible persons and bodies in a company and their liability for false information.[88] On May 16, 2002, the European Commission issued its Recommendation on Independence,[89] a principles-based Recommendation which addresses relationships and situations which could compromise an auditor's objectivity. The purpose of the Recommendation is to set 'a benchmark for Member States' requirements on statutory auditors' independence throughout the EU' and, in fact, much like the SOA, recommends that an auditor not perform certain tasks which might compromise such auditor's independence, including certain non-audit services.[90]

---

84   Council Directive 03/6/EC (2003), on insider dealing and market manipulation (market abuse). [2003] OJ L 96/16. The Directive was adopted by the Ecofin Council of Ministers on December 3, 2002 and is due to be implemented by member states no later than October 12, 2004. The Directive prohibits insider trading, market manipulation and dissemination of false information. The full text of the Directive can be accessed at <http://europa.eu.int/comm/internal_market/en/finances/mobil/com281en.pdf>.

85   The European Commission has published three working papers relating to the Directive which cover implementing measures aimed at (1) definitions of inside information and market manipulation as well as public disclosure of inside information by issuers; (2) fair presentation of recommendations and disclosure of relevant interests or conflicts of interest; and (3) a safe harbors, i.e., exemptions from the prohibitions of insider dealing and market manipulation in certain circumstances. The full text of these working papers can be accessed at <http://europa.eu.int/comm/internal_market/en/finances/mobil/market-abuse_en.htm>.

86   Proposal for a directive of the European Parliament and of the Council on the harmonization of transparency requirements with regard to information about issuers whose securities are admitted to trading on a regulated market and amending Directive 2001/34/EC, COM(03)138 final, available at <http://europa.eu.int/eur-lex/en/com/pdf/2003/-com2003_0138en01.pdf>.

87   Idem, art.4., at 12.

88   Idem, art 5.3.4, at 24.

89   Statutory Auditors' Independence in the EU: A Set of Fundamental Principles, Commission Recommendation 02/590/EC, [2002] OJ L 191/22, available at <http://europa.-eu.int/eurlex/pri/en/oj/dat/2002/l_191/l_19120020719en00220057.pdf>.

90   'A statutory auditor should not carry out a statutory audit if there are any financial, business, employment or other relationships between the statutory auditor and his client (including certain non-audit services provided to the audit client) that a reasonable and informed third party would conclude compromise the statutory auditor's independence'. Idem.

4.1.2   Lamfalussy Report

In February 2001, the Final Report of the Committee of Wise Men on the Regulation of European Securities Markets (the 'Lamfalussy Report')[91] was published with the committee's following recommendations: to create
(1) a broad framework of principles of securities market regulation;
(2) the creation of a high-level Securities Committee which would implement details of framework legislation with the assistance of an advisory Committee of European Regulators and under the oversight of the European Commission;
(3) a framework of enhanced cooperation and networking between regulators in the EU Securities Regulators Committee; and
(4) strengthened enforcement of EU law.
The Lamfalussy Report stressed the need to reform the EU regulatory system to correct what the committee perceived to be slow, rigid, overly detailed and inconsistently implemented regulations among member states. The six priority areas it identified were:
(1) setting up a single prospectus for issuers;
(2) modernizing admission to listing requirements;
(3) mutual recognition of markets based on home country supervision;
(4) updating rules for investment funds and provision finds;
(5) adopting of international accounting standards; and
(6) a single passport for recognized stock markets.[92]

The adoption by the EU of the Lamfalussy Report was perceived both as a step towards defragmenting the European financial services market and a model for the revision of broader issues.[93]

4.1.3   High Level Group Report

Following on the heels of the Lamfalussy Report, the Report to the High Level Group of Company Law Experts (the 'High Level Group Report'),[94] published on November 4, 2002, includes several recommendations on improving company law and corporate governance, including requiring listed companies to 'ensure that the nomination and remuneration of directors and the audit of the accounting for the company's performance within the board are decided upon exclusively by non-executive or supervisory directors who are in the

---

91   Final report of the Committee of Wise Men on the Regulation of European Securities Markets available at http://europa.eu.int/comm/internal_market/en/finances/-general/lamfalussyen.pdf>.
92   European Parliament DG Press Release, *Lamfalussy report on securities regulation – Economic Committee seeks transparency and 'call back'* (March 6, 2001), available at <www.europarl.eu.int/comparl/econ/press/20010306_lamfalussy_vote.pdf>.
93   Edward Bannerman, *The Stockholm Scorecard*, Centre for European Reform Bulletin, April/May 2001, available at <http://www.cer.org.uk/articles/n_17_bannerman.html>.
94   Available at <http://europa.eu.int/comm/internal_market/en/company/modern/consult/report_en.pdf>.

majority independent.'[95] Provisions on the role and responsibilities of audit committees (or any equivalent body), with respect to both the external and internal aspects of audit, should be included in the proposed Recommendation on the role of non-executive and supervisory directors.' The High Level Group Report, in essence, promoted greater cooperation among existing regulatory bodies, in contrast to the Lamfalussy Report, which advocated the creation of a 'European SEC.' In response to the High Level Group Report, and citing the recent financial scandals as a primary motivating factor, on May 21, 2003, the European Commission announced an action plan on 'Modernising Company Law and Enhancing Corporate Governance in the EU' (the 'Action Plan').[96] The Action Plan's main objectives are 'to strengthen shareholders' rights and protection for employees, creditors and other parties with which companies deal, while adapting company law and corporate governance rules appropriately for different categories of company [and]to foster the efficiency and effectiveness of business, with special attention to some specific cross-border issues.'[97] In particular, an important aspect of the Action Plan is an enhancement of directors' responsibilities for financial and key non-financial statements of companies.

4.2   National reforms

The UK government, which has long been considered a leading reformer in corporate governance matters, recently established committees to carry out two high level reviews – one to look at audit and accounting issues (the 'Smith Report') and the other to look specifically at the role and effectiveness of non-executive directors (the 'Higgs Report') – and also commenced a review of the Listing Rules of the Financial Services Authority. In response to the Smith Report and Higgs Report, on July 23, 2003, the Financial Reporting Council issued a revised Combined Code in July 2003,[98] which in particular enlarged the role of independent non-executive directors, strengthened the role of the audit committee in monitoring the integrity of the company's financial reporting and reinforced the independence of the external auditor. With respect to internal controls, the Turnbull Report published by the Institute of Chartered Accountants in England and Wales has been cited by the SEC as an example of a

---

95   Idem.
96   Council Directive 2003/ /EC (not yet published), amending Council Directive 68/151/EEC, available at <http://europa.eu.int/comm/internal_market/en/company/company/official/conseil-ce-03620/03620_en.pdf>.
97   *Company Law and corporate governance: Commission presents action plan* (May 21, 2003), IP/03/716, available at http://europa.eu.int/rapid/start/cgi/guesten.ksh?p_action.-gettxt=gt&doc=IP/03/716|0|RAPID&lg=EN&display=>.
98   'The Combined Code on Corporate Governance, July 2003,' available at <http://www.frc.org.uk/combined.cfm>.

suitable, recognized control framework.[99] In March 2003, the Australian Stock Exchange ('ASX') Corporate Governance Council issued its 'Principles of good corporate governance and best practice recommendations'[100] which, among other things, recommended establishing a system of internal control, creating a code of conduct and enacting procedures to safeguard financial reporting.

Other countries are enacting similar reforms to existing laws, many of which have not been significantly revised in decades and do not reflect modern business practices. In one such case, on January 10, 2003, the Italian government approved a reform of Title V of the Civil Code (*Codice Civile*),[101] which regulates stock companies and cooperatives. The reform, which will come into force on January 1, 2004, represents the first such legislative initiative since the enactment of the Civil Code in 1942.[102] The reforms were a reaction to globalization, and, among other things, introduced new governance models for stock companies, enhanced the role of company boards and independent directors within company boards, and required disclosure of directors' interest in transactions. In July 2002, the Singapore Companies (Amendment) Act was amended to require financial statements to comply with 'prescribed accounting standards' established by the Council on Corporate Disclosure and Governance.[103] Germany enacted the Transparency and Disclosure Law[104] on July 29, 2002, which requires the executive board and supervisory board of exchange-listed companies to declare once a year that the recommendations of the 'Government Commission on the German Corporate Governance Code' have been and are being complied with or which of the Code's recommendations are not being applied.

Countries are also reforming internal controls and sanctions for violations of corporate governance regimes. The recently proposed Dutch Corporate Governance Code would require the management board to report that internal risk management and controls are adequate and effective and provide

---

99 Speech by SEC Commissioner: Recent Experience with Corporate Governance in the USA, by Commissioner Paul S. Atkins, 2nd German Corporate Governance Code Conference, June 26, 2003, available at <http://www.sec.gov/news/speech/spch062603-psa.htm>.

100 'Principles of good corporate governance and best practice recommendations,' available at <http://www.asx.com.au/about/pdf/ASXRecommendations.pdf>.

101 Codice civile art. 2247 et seq., available at <http://www.jus.unitn.it/cardozo/Obiter_Dictum/codciv/home.html>.

102 Domenico Paparella and Vilma Rinolfi, *Company Law Reformed*, European Industrial Relations Observatory On-Line, available at <http://www.eiro.eurofound.ie/2003/02/Feature/IT0302101F.html>.

103 The reports of the three private sector-led committees which reviewed corporate governance practices, disclosure and accounting standards, and corporate regulatory framework in Singapore, and whose recommendations led to the amendments to the Companies Act, as well as the Singapore Exchange Listing Manual and the Public Accountants Act, are available at <http://www.mof.gov.sg/cor/>.

104 Gesetz zur weiteren Reform des Aktien- und Bilanzrechts, zu Transparanz und Publizitätsgesetz [Transparency and Disclosure Law], BGB1.I Nr. 50, 2681, available at <P>http://217.160.60.235/BGBL/bgbl1f/bgbl102s2681.pdf>.

substantiation of such disclosure.[105] In France, proposed rules would require the President of the board of directors or supervisory board to disclose the company's internal control procedures in the annual report.[106] Both the EU in general [107] and the Netherlands in particular[108], among others, have recommended barring management board and supervisory board members who publish misleading financial information from holding positions with European enterprises.

In Asia, a Revision to the Japanese Commercial Code advocated by the Legislative Council of the Ministry of Justice was passed into law in May 2002 and went into effect on April 1, 2003.[109] The adoption of the Revised Commercial Code is optional. The Revised Commercial Code requires companies opting to adopt the new system to establish nomination, audit and compensation committees and 'introduce the corporate executive officer system as a package.' The intention is to delineate between a board's oversight function and its business operation function, which is unclear under the previous Code.[110] In June 2003, Hong Kong proposed tighter governance standards, including the appointment of at least three independent directors,[111] after carefully reviewing the corporate governance rules and standards of various jurisdictions. Among the most important recommendations made in the resulting report are: the creation of nomination and remuneration committees; suggested best practices for directors' duties and responsibilities; that each board of directors have at least three independent non-executive directors. The report also makes mandatory the establishment of audit committees and requires that companies disclose individual director compensation, prohibits self-dealing by interested shareholders and undertakes to examine incompatibility of auditors with certain non-audit services.

Developed countries are not the only ones proposing reforms. In January 2002, the People's Republic of China drafted the first ever Code of Corporate Governance for Chinese Listed Companies,[112] whereby it established fiduciary duties of controlling shareholders and directors, reformed accounting procedures and the supervision of auditors, and expanded the information companies must disclose to shareholders. In addition to requiring a company to

---

105   DCGC, Art I.1.4. Available at <http://corpgov.nl/page/downloads/Conceptcode%20-
       Engels%20DEFINITIEF.pdf>.
106   Proposed L. 225-37 and 225-68.
107   The Modernization Directive.
108   DCGC, Annex 1, ¶16.
109   'Law for Partial Revision of the Commercial Code and Laws Concerning Special Exemp-
       tions to the Commercial Code as Related to 'Corporate Auditing' and 'Interim Plan for the
       Outline of Proposed Laws for Partial Revision of the Commercial Code'. See Ryoko Ueda,
       Corporate Governance and Reform of Japan's Commercial Code, *J-IRIS Research Newslet-
       ter* (October 2002), available at <http://www.j-iris.com/newsletter/nl02.pdf>.
110   For a discussion of the reforms, see Idem.
111   'The Corporate Governance Review by the Standing Committee on Company Law Re-
       form' available at <www.info.gov.hk/cr/download/scclr/cgr2_e.pdf>.
112   Available at <http://www.csrc.gov.cn/CSRCSite/eng/edeplt/rule/frzl02042901.htm>.

have independent directors on its board, the new Code also requires that audit committees be both chaired by an independent director as well as composed of a majority of independent directors, and that at least one independent director from the audit committee must be an accounting professional.

Reform is also not limited to corporate governance. The EU and several member nations are also addressing the issue of auditor independence in their proposals. The European Commission's Recommendation on Independence recommends, among other things, a two year 'cooling-off period' for key audit partners before joining an audited company in a key management position and audit partner rotation every seven years.[113] In the Netherlands, the government has proposed laws that would require independent public supervision of auditors.[114] The Commission de Opérations de Bourse in France has proposed new binding corporate governance rules to the French Commerce Code which would, among other things: prohibit statutory auditors from having direct or indirect interests in audited companies or providing non-audit services; require a five-year 'cooling-off period' before a company employee or manager may become a statutory auditor; and require disclosure by the statutory auditor to an audited company's board of any merger or contribution appraisals carried out within the previous two years.[115] Individual countries and the EU itself have also proposed the creation of their own accounting oversight boards to monitor audits and auditors.[116] Collectively, then, the various individual reforms are forming a mosaic that achieves the same wide-reaching goals as the SOA, simply at a more measured pace.

5   Conclusion

Corporate governance reform is not a recent phenomenon, nor is the SOA the most recent development. Corporate governance initiatives abound worldwide, as countries have begun to react to their own corporate scandals and an increasingly vocal and proactive body of investors. The particular corporate governance issues addressed by these various initiatives cover diverse issues with the common themes of transparency, independence and accountability. As a result, despite much saber rattling, the flight of foreign firms from the

---

113   Statutory Auditors' Independence in the EU: A Set of Fundamental Principles, Commission Recommendation 02/590/EC, 2002 OJ (L 191) 22 (May 16, 2002), available at <http://europa.eu.int/eurlex/pri/en/oj/dat/2002/l_191/l_19120020719en00220057.pdf>.

114   See DCGC, pmbl. (discussing Parliamentary Papers II 2002/03, 28 090, no. 5). Available at <http://corpgov.nl/page/downloads/Conceptcode%20Engels%20DEFINITIEF.pdf>.

115   Proposed L. 822-11.

116   See Letter from Swiss Institute of Certified Accountants to PCAOB Office of the Secretary (March 27, 2003), available at <http://www.pcaobus.org/pcaob_rulemaking.asp>. In Australia, there are proposals to make the Australian Financial Reporting Council responsible for audit oversight.

reach of the SOA to non-U.S. markets has failed to materialize and, in fact, the SOA has emerged as a forerunner of a growing number of corporate governance reform initiatives worldwide. As SEC Commissioner Paul Atkins recently noted, in a speech to the Second German Corporate Governance Code Conference, 'Europeans and Americans have fundamentally the same goals with respect to strengthening corporate governance. Despite the general thrust of Sarbanes-Oxley, the basic philosophy in the United States is for the states and the stock exchanges to determine their corporate governance requirements. Similarly, a group set up by the European Commission did not propose harmonization of corporate governance standards among the Member States. Instead, the group recommended that the Member States should each set forth minimum standards of conduct. The proffered rationale for this approach is that the corporate governance standards of the Member States are necessarily different and flexibility is critically important.'[117]

Although the SOA rattled the nerves of some, most non-U.S. issuers have come to realize that exiting the U.S. capital markets will not protect them from the advancing tide of corporate reform. As information technology allows investors to compare corporate governance regimes, and corporate transparency becomes expectancy, all companies, whether or not they wish it, will be forced to improve their own corporate governance.

---

117   Speech by SEC Commissioner: Recent Experience with Corporate Governance in the USA, by Commissioner Paul S. Atkins, 2nd German Corporate Governance Code Conference, June 26, 2003, available at < http://www.sec.gov/news/speech/spch062603psa.htm>.

Implementation of financial UN sanctions: Jurisdictional problems related to genuine global governance

Mielle Bulterman

1 INTRODUCTION

Most contributions to the seminar addressed jurisdictional problems related to the application of national or regional legislation to cross-border or global situations. While jurisdiction is still mainly allocated according to national borders, the importance of these borders in every day practice has decreased dramatically in recent years. This development has given rise to questions concerning the jurisdiction of States over the activities of multinational corporations and concerning the problems related to the simultaneous exercise of jurisdiction by different national authorities.

It may be thought that the introduction of global governance would solve many of the jurisdictional problems related to globalisation. The present contribution aims to address a phenomenon that could be qualified as genuine global governance, namely the adoption of binding decisions by the UN Security Council and their implementation in the UN Member States. To this end, the implementation of UN financial sanctions is taken as an example. The current practice of implementation of UN financial sanctions demonstrates that global governance calls for adjustments of the existing legal systems. This contribution focuses mainly on two jurisdictional problems: the absence of any legal remedies at UN level and the limited competence of national and regional courts to supervise UN sanctions.

2 THE UN FINANCIAL SANCTION REGIME

Since 11 September 2001, international terrorism has been perceived as one of the main threats to international peace and security. Since that date a variety of measures has been taken – at a global, regional and national level – in order to ensure that the 'fight against terrorism' has a successful outcome. One of the measures in this fight are the so-called 'financial sanctions' imposed by the UN Security Council. These sanctions aim to prevent the funding of terrorist activities, amongst other means by freezing the assets of terrorists and those of their sponsors. After the 11th of September existing UN financial sanctions against the Taliban and Osama bin Laden were tightened (§ 2.1) and supplemented by a general UN financial sanction regime (§ 2.2).

The UN financial sanctions are adopted by the UN Security Council exercising its power under Chapter VII UN Charter, which enables the Security

Council to take action 'with respect to threats to the peace, breaches of the peace, and acts of aggression'. Chapter VII UN Charter was originally designed for action against *States* that pose a threat to international peace and security. This has not prevented the Security Council, however, from making use of its powers under Chapter VII to adopt financial sanctions which have *individuals* as their target.[1] This exercise of the powers of the Security Council in the post-11 September era can be considered to be the ultimate form of global governance: at a truly global level decisions concerning individuals are taken and all UN Member States are obliged to comply with these decisions.

2.1   *The UN financial sanctions against Osama bin Laden c.s.*

The UN financial sanction regime against Osama bin Laden c.s. finds its origin in Resolution 1267(1999) of 15 October 1999. In this Resolution, the Security Council decided to impose financial sanctions against the Taliban in response to their refusal to extradite Osama bin Laden to the US. The UN Member States were called upon to freeze the assets of the Taliban and persons or entities associated with them, and to ensure that no funds are made available to them. A committee – Committee 1267, consisting of members of the Security Council – was established and granted the competence to decide which persons and entities fall within the ambit of Resolution 1267. Committee 1267 decides upon receiving 'relevant information' from UN Member States (in practice mainly the USA)[2] which persons and entities are put on the sanction list. It is unclear which criteria are used by Committee 1267 to evaluate whether this 'relevant information' justifies that a specific entity or person is put on the list. In the guidelines of the Committee it is stated that additions to the list should include 'to the extent possible, a narrative description of the information that forms the basis or justification for taking action'. In practice, however, persons and entities are added to the list without being given any explanation

---

1   One may question whether Chapter VII provides a sufficient legal basis for such action by the Security Council. Notwithstanding the importance of this question, it will not be dealt with in this contribution.

2   In the third report of the Monitoring Group it is observed in respect to the information provided by the Member States: 'Only a few countries have provided the names of the persons or entities they have identified as associated with Osama bin Laden and al-Qaida. Many countries have refrained completely from providing names of such persons or entities. Several reasons have been cited for this lacuna. Several Governments question the validity of placing persons or entities on the list without judicial findings of culpability. Several indicated that they lack established procedures for determining which names of individuals or entities should be communicated to the Committee. Some countries were barred by rules of confidentiality covering criminal proceedings or investigations. Some indicated a reticence to provide names of their own nationals. Some States were concerned that such action would require them to freeze the assets of the persons named, with dire consequences for their families'. Third report of the Monitoring Group established pursuant to Security Council resolution 1363(2001) and extended by resolution 1390(2002), S/2002/1338, § 17.

of the reasons for doing so. This can happen very quickly: a State may propose to put a person or entity on the list; this proposal is put before the members of the Committee and, if no-one objects, within two working days (or in case of urgency such shorter period as the Chairman may determine), the person or entity is on the list.[3]

In December 2000, the sanction regime of Resolution 1267 was expanded to Osama bin Laden and all persons and entities associated with him (Resolution 1333(2000)). Since 11 September 2001, Committee 1267 has been very active in expanding the list of persons that fall under the regime of Resolution 1267. When the Taliban regime fell, the Security Council adopted a new Resolution (Resolution 1390(2002) of 16 January 2002) abolishing the sanctions against the State Afghanistan and maintaining those against the Taliban and Osama bin Laden. In its supervisory tasks, the Committee 1267 is assisted by a monitoring group established pursuant to Security Council Resolution 1363(2001). The UN Member States have to report on the steps taken to implement the financial sanction regime.[4]

2.2 The UN general financial sanctions in the fight against terrorism

In addition to the financial sanctions against the Taliban and Osama bin Laden, since 28 September 2001, a general financial sanction regime has been established by means of Resolution 1373(2001). In this Resolution, the UN Member States are called upon to freeze all funds and other financial assets or economic resources of terrorists; to prohibit their nationals or any persons and entities within their territories from making any funds or financial services available for the benefit of terrorists. An important difference between Resolution 1373(2001) and Resolution 1267(1999) is that there is no UN list of the persons and entities that fall under the former resolution. This means that the UN Member States determine who qualifies as a terrorist and consequently falls under the scope of Resolution 1373(2001). The implementation of Resolution 1373(2001) is supervised by a sanction committee (the Counter-Terrorism Committee, CTC).[5] The UN Member States have to report regularly to the CTC on the steps they have taken to implement Resolution 1373.[6] The European Union sends in regular reports supplementing those of its Member States.

---

3   See the Guidelines of the Committee for the Conduct of its Work, adopted on 7 November 2002, § 8.
4   The State reports and other relevant documents are published on the internet site of Committee 1267 <http://www.un.org/Docs/sc/committees/1267Template.htm>.
5   The Counter Terrorism Committee must not be confused with Committee 1267 supervising the implementation of the UN financial sanctions against Osama bin Laden c.s. In order to clarify the respective roles of both Committees, on 28 July 2003 a press release was issued, approved by both the 1267 Committee and the Counter-Terrorism Committee (SC?7827).
6   The State reports and other relevant documents are published on the internet site of the Counter-Terrorism Committee <http://www.un.org/Docs/sc/committees/1373>.

3   IMPLEMENTATION OF UN SANCTIONS WITHIN THE EUROPEAN UNION

The UN Resolutions do not have immediate effect/are not self-executing; implementing measures need to be taken by the UN Member States in order to enforce the sanctions envisaged in the UN Resolutions. Within the European Union, financial UN sanctions are implemented as follows. First, a Common Position is adopted under the Second Pillar (the Common Foreign and Security Policy, CFSP) indicating that the UN sanctions are implemented by the EU. Subsequently, the financial sanctions are effectuated by an EC Regulation on the basis of Article 60 EC. This EC regulation has direct effect in the EU Member States.[7] This does not mean that no action is required of the EU Member States: they are obliged to supervise compliance with and to penalize violation of the EC sanction regulation. The EC sanction regulations in general contain a provision which states that each EU Member State shall determine the sanctions to be imposed where the provisions of the EC sanction regulation are infringed. As mentioned in the sanction regulations, such sanctions shall be effective, proportionate and dissuasive. This obligation still leaves the Member States a discretion in deciding how compliance with the EC sanction regulations is supervised; what penalties may be imposed in case of infringement of these regulations, and to take action in case a violation of the EC sanction regime occurs. Due to this discretion, there may be important differences between the EU Member States as regards the implementation of the EC sanction regulations.

The UN financial sanctions against the Taliban and Osama bin Laden and all persons associated with them (Resolution 1267), have been implemented at EU level following the scheme just described: by means of a Common Position (2002/402[8]), supplemented by a Community Regulation (881/2002).[9] These sanctions apply to all individuals and entities designated by Committee 1267 and listed in Annex I to this regulation. Annex I contains the names of the persons listed on the UN sanction list. Whenever Committee 1267 changes the UN-list, Annex I is amended accordingly.[10] At a national level measures need to be taken to ensure the enforcement of the Community Sanction Regulation.

---

7   Article 249 EC states 'a regulation shall have general application. It shall be binding in its
       entirety and directly applicable in all Member States'.
8   Council Common Position of 27 May 2002 concerning restrictive measures against Osama
       bin Laden, members of the al-Qaida organisation and the Taliban and other individuals,
       groups, undertakings and entities associated with them and repealing Common Positions
       96/746/CFSP, 1999/727/CFSP, 2001/154/CFSP and 2001/771/CFSP [2002] OJ L 139/4).
9   Council Regulation (EC) No 881/2002 of 27 May 2002 imposing certain specific restrictive
       measures directed against certain persons and entities associated with Osama bin Laden,
       the al-Qaida network and the Taliban, and repealing Council Regulation (EC) No
       467/2001 prohibiting the export of certain goods and services to Afghanistan, strengthen-
       ing the flight ban and extending the freeze of funds and other financial resources in re-
       spect of the Taliban of Afghanistan [2002] OJ L 139/9.
10   See e.g. Commission Regulation (EC) No 1184/2003 of 2 July 2003 amending for the 20th
       time Council Regulation (EC) No 881/2002 [2003] OJ L 165/21.

In the Netherlands this happens by means of a regulation on the basis of the Dutch Sanction Law.

The general UN financial sanctions regime as laid down in Resolution 1373(2001) has also been implemented within the European Union through a Common Position (2001/931)[11] and Regulation 2580/2001.[12] As stated above, implementation of the general UN financial sanction regime also entails that at a regional or national level it is decided who qualify as terrorists and consequently should be subjected to the UN financial sanction regime. A list of the persons and entities involved in terrorist activities to which the EU sanction regime applies has been added to EU Common Position of 27 December (EU sanction list). The Council may amend this list by unanimity.[13] Common Position 2001/931 lists the following criteria for listing persons or entities on the list:

> The list in the Annex shall be drawn up on the basis of precise information or material in the relevant file which indicates that a decision has been taken by a competent authority in respect of the persons, groups and entities concerned, irrespective of whether it concerns the instigation of investigations or prosecution for a terrorist act, an attempt to perpetrate, participate in or facilitate such an act based on serious and credible evidence or clues, or condemnation for such deeds. Persons, groups and entities identified by the Security Council of the United Nations as being related to terrorism and against whom it has ordered sanctions may be included in the list.
>
> For the purposes of this paragraph 'competent authority' shall mean a judicial authority, or, where judicial authorities have no competence in the area covered by this paragraph, an equivalent competent authority in that area.

Within the EU-list a distinction is made between 'intra-EU' and 'extra-EU' terrorist. Only the extra-EU terrorists (operating outside the European Union) are subjected to the regime of Regulation 2580/2001. 'Intra-EU' terrorists, such as ETA-activists, fall outside the scope of the EC financial sanction regime and are subjected to financial sanctions of the different EU Member States. As a reason for excluding 'intra-EU' terrorist from the EC sanction regime, it has been suggested that financial sanctions against intra-EU terrorist fall outside the scope of the Common Foreign and Security Policy.[14]

There is yet another important difference between the general UN financial sanction regime implemented by EC Regulation 2580/2001 (with the EU sanc-

---

11 Common Position of 27 December 2001 on the application of specific measures to combat terrorism [2001] OJ L 344/93.

12 Council Regulation (EC) No 2580/2001 of 27 December 2001 on specific restrictive measures directed against certain persons and entities with a view to combating terrorism [2001] OJ L344/70.

13 The list has been amended by e.g. common positions of 2 May 2002 [2002] OJ L 116/75 and 27 June 2003 [2003] OJ L 160/100.

14 This was at least suggested by the Dutch Minister of Foreign Affairs. Wijziging van de Sanctiewet 1977 met het oog op de implementatie van internationale verplichtingen gericht op de bestrijding van terrorisme en uitbreiding van het toezicht op de naleving van financiële sanctiemaatregelen, Nota naar aanleiding van het verslag, *Kamerstukken II* 2001/02, 28 251, nr. 5, p. 10.

tion list) and Resolution 1267 sanction regime implemented by EC Regulation 881/2002 (with the UN sanction list). The former regime leaves more discretion to the UN Member States not only in deciding to whom and what entities the sanction regime applies, but also in formulating exceptions to the application of the UN financial sanction regime. Community Regulation 2580/2001 explicitly provides for such exceptions. Articles 5 and 6 provide that the 'competent authorities of a Member State' may grant specific authorizations to use frozen funds; to make funds available to a person, entity or body included in the EU sanction list, to render financial services to such person. Originally, no such possibility was foreseen in Community Regulation 881/2002 implementing the UN financial sanctions against the Taliban and Osama bin Laden, since Resolution 1267(1999) did not foresee in the possibility to make exceptions to the UN financial sanction regime.[15] However, in response to criticism concerning the rigor of the UN financial sanction regime, on 20 December 2002 the Security Council adopted a Resolution introducing certain exceptions to the Resolution 1267 sanction regime. The necessary amendments to EC Regulation 881/2002 were introduced by means of a regulation adopted on 27 March 2003.[16]

4   GLOBAL GOVERNANCE AND THE RULE OF LAW

The system just described might seem very effective: at UN level the decision is taken to impose sanctions, the UN Member States are obliged to take the measures necessary to effectuate the UN sanctions. However, from the perspective of judicial protection for the persons and entities affected by UN financial sanctions, the system is less attractive. It is obvious that financial sanctions may have very severe consequences for their targets: that is their aim. In view of these consequences, on for instance the right to property, there is a clear need for judicial review. This is also recognized within the UN. In August 2002 a report of the Political Working Group on the United Nations and terrorism was published.[17] Recommendation 4 of this report reads as follows:

> All relevant parts of the United Nations system should emphasize that key human rights must always be protected and may never be derogated from. The independence of the judiciary and the existence of legal remedies are essential elements for the protection of fundamental human rights in all situations involving counter-terrorism measures.

---

15   Neither the relevant resolutions nor the guidelines of Committee 1267 mention the possibility of exemptions. In the third report of the Monitoring Group it is observed that Committee 1267 is 'considering guidelines to handle requests for exemptions, on humanitarian grounds' from the financial sanctions.

16   Council Regulation (EC) No 561/2003 of 27 March 2003 amending, as regards exceptions to the freezing of funds and economic resources, Regulation (EC) No 881/2002 imposing certain specific restrictive measures directed against certain persons and entities associated with Osama bin Laden, the al-Qaida network and the Taliban [2002] OJ L 82/1.

17   Doc. Nr. A/57/273, S/2002/875.

Within the UN similar views have been expressed by the High Commissioner for Human Rights, the Human Rights Committee and the General Assembly.[18] The importance of access to court in the context of counter-terrorist measures has also been stressed within the Council of Europe. According to Walter Schwimmer, Secretary-General of the Council of Europe: '[I]t is for the courts to ensure that the balance be struck between the obligation to provide protection against terrorist acts and the obligation to safeguard human rights.'[19] In the *Guidelines of the Committee of Ministers of the Council of Europe on human rights and the fight against terrorisme* the importance of a legal remedy is also emphasised.[20] This call for legal protection must not be interpreted as an argument against the use of UN financial sanctions as an instrument in the fights against terrorism. Obviously, neither the Council of Europe nor the UN aims to question the legitimacy of the reasons underlying the UN financial sanction regime. That is also not the purpose of this article. It is clear, however, that the current application of the UN financial sanction regime gives rise to important jurisdictional problems.

5   No legal remedy available at UN level

A first problem that can be identified concerns the fact that at UN level no legal remedies are available for individuals and entities that are put on the UN sanction list. There is no UN judge competent to rule on complaints of individuals or organisations who challenge the lawfulness of the financial sanctions imposed upon them by the UN Security Council. This lacuna is specifically felt under the Resolution 1267 sanction regime, where it is decided at UN level which persons and entities are subjected to financial sanctions. But as we shall see below, also under the general UN financial sanction regime, there is a need for a judicial authority at UN level.

The persons and entities on the UN-list of Resolution 1267 may request Committee 1267 to be struck from the list, but the chances of a successful outcome to such a request seem to be small. At least that was the experience of three Swedish nationals of Somalian origin. They were put on the UN sanction list by Committee 1267 on the basis of information provided by the USA. Their lawyer managed to convince the majority of the sanction committee that these individuals were wrongly put on the list. This was not sufficient, however, since three States objected and persons were only struck from the list if all Members of the Committee agreed. It needs no further explanation that the

---

18   A/RES/57/219, Protecting human rights and fundamental freedoms while countering terrorism, adopted on 27 February 2003.

19   Opening speech by the Secretary General of the Council of Europe, Mr Walter Schwimmer, 10th International Judicial Conference in Strasbourg from 23 to 24 May, <www.coe.int/T/E/Communication_and_Research/Press/Theme_files/Terrorism/>.

20   The *guidelines* were adopted on 15 July 2002 and can be found on the internet site of the Council of Europe: <www.coe.int>.

complete absence of any legal remedy at UN level is difficult to reconcile with the right of access to court and the basic notion of the rule of law. To some extent the situation has improved since 7 November 2002. On that day Committee 1267 adopted a guideline for the conduct of its work which includes the following 'delisting procedure':

> Without prejudice to available procedures, a petitioner (individual(s), groups, undertakings, and/or entities on the 1267 Committee's [the Committee]consolidated list) may petition the government of residence and/or citizenship to request review of the case. In this regard, the petitioner should provide justification for the de-listing request, offer relevant information and request support for de-listing.
>
> The government to which a petition is submitted ('the petitioned government') should review all relevant information and then approach bilaterally the government(s) originally proposing designation ('the designating government(s)') to seek additional information and to hold consultations on the de-listing request.
>
> The original designating government(s) may also request additional information from the petitioner's country of citizenship or residency. The petitioned and the designating government(s) may, as appropriate, consult with the Chairman of the Committee during the course of any such bilateral consultations.
>
> If, after reviewing any additional information, the petitioned government wishes to pursue a de-listing request, it should seek to persuade the designating government(s) to submit jointly or separately a request for de-listing to the Committee. The petitioned government may, without an accompanying request from the original designating government(s), submit a request for de-listing to the Committee, pursuant to the no-objection procedure.
>
> The Committee will reach decisions by consensus of its members. If consensus cannot be reached on a particular issue, the Chairman will undertake such further consultations as may facilitate agreement. If, after these consultations, consensus still cannot be reached, the matter may be submitted to the Security Council. Given the specific nature of the information, the Chairman may encourage bilateral exchanges between interested Member States in order to clarify the issue prior to a decision.

This procedure is a codification of the procedure already followed by the Committee in practice, for instance in the case of the Swedish Somalians. It is to be applauded that a formal delisting procedure has been established. However, given its political nature it is clear that this procedure does not fill the existing lacuna in legal protection at UN level.

6   NO EFFECTIVE REMEDY AT REGIONAL/NATIONAL LEVEL

The lack of any legal remedy to challenge financial sanctions at UN level is aggravated by the restricted possibilities of judicial review at the national and regional level – where legal remedies in general are available for individuals to challenge measures allegedly infringing upon their individual rights. The main problem, however, is that national and regional courts do not always have jurisdiction to supervise the implementation of UN sanctions.

Again the adventures of the Swedish Somalians may be taken as an example. When their efforts to persuade the 1267 Committee to strike them from the sanction list had failed, they decided to challenge the EC Regulation implementing the UN financial sanction regime before the Court of First Instance of the EC.[21] They claim amongst other things that the EU institutions have not examined why the 1267 Committee included them in its list and that they were not given any opportunity to apprise themselves and refute the allegations on which the decision to include them in Annex I to the EC regulation was based. This case gives rise to some pertinent questions relating to the jurisdiction of the European (or for that matter a national) court to supervise the implementation of financial UN sanctions.

A first question that needs to be answered in this respect is whether the ECJ is competent to review the decision of the 1267 Committee to put the Swedish Somalians on the UN-list. Or put in more general terms: is a national/regional court competent to rule on arguments challenging the lawfulness of a UN decision on financial sanctions? It is difficult to give an affirmative answer to this question without questioning the effectiveness of the UN sanction regime and more importantly the unequivocal obligation of Article 48 UN Charter for all UN Member States to take the measures necessary to carry out the decisions of the Security Council under Chapter VII. It is important to keep in mind that financial UN sanctions are not adopted by a simple administrative act, but by a decision of the Security Council; and that the sanction committees supervising the implementation of these sanctions have been established in a Security Council resolution.

Another jurisdictional problem concerns the competence of national/regional courts to review whether the national/regional measures implementing the UN financial sanctions regime are compatible with human rights norms. Is a national court competent to review whether the imposition of financial sanctions on a specific person is compatible with, for instance, his right to property as guaranteed under the ECHR? Or does Article 103 UN Charter constitute an obstacle for national and regional courts to review measures implementing UN sanctions under human rights treaties?[22] In several of its concluding observations the UN Human Rights Committee has expressed its concern about the human rights implications of national measures taken in the fight against terrorism and requested the State to ensure that these measures are fully in conformity with the Covenant on Civil and Political Rights. It observed with respect to the UK measures implementing Resolution 1373(2001): 'The State Party should ensure that any measures it undertakes in this regard are in full compliance with the provisions of the Covenant (...).'[23] This is easier said than done, specifically when the UN sanction regime as

---

21   Action brought on 10 December 2001 by Abdirisak Aden and Others against the Council of the European Union and the Commission of the European Communities. (Case T-306/01), [2002] OJ C 44/27.

22   Article 103 UN Charter provides: In the event of a conflict between the obligations of the Members of the United Nations under the present Charter and their obligations under any other international agreement, their obligations under the present Charter shall prevail.

23   Concluding observations of the Human Rights Committee: United Kingdom of Great Britain and Northern Ireland (CCPR/CO/73/UK; CCPR/CO/73/UKOT), § 6.

such is completely silent on the relation between the obligations under the UN sanction regime and existing human rights obligations.

The fact that currently a case is pending before the Court of First Instance in which Community legislation implementing UN sanctions is challenged, demonstrated that the problems just described are not merely of academic interest. In practice judges are confronted with cases where the implementation of UN financial sanctions is questioned on human rights grounds. One such case resulted in the *Segi* decision of 22 May 2002 of the European Court of Human Rights (ECrtHR). This case concerned a complaint of two organisations, Segi and Pro-Amnestia and persons associated with them against all EU Member States. Both organisations were put on the EU sanction list for reason of their alleged connections to ETA. As 'intra-EU terrorists' they were not subjected to financial sanctions at EU level. They complained that the Common Position concerned infringes their human rights as guaranteed by Articles 3, 6, 10, 11 and 13 ECHR. This complaint was declared inadmissible by the ECrtHR because they were not considered to be victim of any human rights violation as required by Article 34 ECHR. The fact that the name of the applicants is on the EU sanction list adopted pursuant to the Common Position does not have direct consequences for the applicants. The Court continues:

> Au demeurant, des mesures concrètes comme celles qui ont été adoptées ou qui viendraient à l'être seraient assujetties au contrôle juridictionnel établi sans chaque ordre juridique concerné, qu'il soit international ou national.

The qualification as terrorist is insufficient to succesfully rely upon the protection by the ECHR:

> Le seul fait que deux des requérant (*Segi* et *Gestoras Pro-Amnistia*) figurent dans la liste (...) en tant que 'groupe ou entités impliqués dans des actes de terrorisme' peut être gênant, mais constitue un lien beaucoup trop ténu pour justifier l'application de la Convention. (...) En définitive, les associations requérantes ne sont concernées que par la coopération renforcée des Etats membres sur la base des pouvoirs déjà existants et, de ce fait, doivent être distinguées des personnes présumées être réellement impliquées dans le terrorisme et visées aux articles 2 et 3 de la position commune.

The finding of the ECrtHR that Segi has to be distinguished from persons who are presumed to be really involved with terrorism is not correct. As mentioned above (§ 3), the distinction between organisations like Segi and organisations subjected to the EC financial sanction regime has to do with the division of competence between the European Union and its Member States. It does not aim to make a distinction – assuming that it is even possible to make such a distinction – between persons involved with terrorist acts and persons *really* involved with terrorism. Leaving this distinction aside, it can be concluded from *Segi* that the qualification as terrorist as such is insufficient to benefit from the human rights protection of the ECHR. Only the measures whereby the financial sanction regime is effectuated can be challenged on human rights grounds.

From the perspective of legal protection this is to be regretted. First of all, it means that the persons and entities concerned have to wait until implementing measures have actually been taken. If these measures are taken at a national level, it may in addition mean that they have to challenge different measures in various States. Furthermore, an action against the implementing measures does not always constitute an effective legal remedy to challenge the lawfulness of financial sanctions. It is hard to see how the lawfulness of these sanctions can be determined without saying anything about the decision (*i.c.* the Common Position) that is at the basis of the sanctions concerned. Finally, and most importantly, by declaring the complaint of Segi inadmissible, the ECrtHR, refrained from ruling on the substantive issues involved and thereby from giving much needed guidance on the requirements of human rights protection in the context of the fight against terrorism.

Eyes have now turned again to the European Court of Justice. On 13 November 2002, Segi brought an action against the Council of the European Union before the Court of First Instance seeking compensation for the damage that the organisation and its representatives suffered as a consequence of having been included in the EU sanction list.[24] Other cases challenging the EU measures implementing the general UN financial sanction regime in the fight against terrorism are *Kurdish National Congress* v. *Council*,[25] *People's Mujahidin of Iran* v. *Council*[26] *Chafiq Ayadi* v. *Council* in which Community regulation 881/2002 implementing the financial sanctions against Osama bin Laden c.s. is challenged.[27] It thus seems to be a matter of time before the first judgment of the ECJ is passed on the lawfulness of financial sanctions within the Community legal order.

7   CONCLUSION

Global governance requires global review, how can such review be realised? That seems to be the most important question evoked by the current practice of the UN financial sanction regime. It cannot be denied that the absence of any judicial review at UN level seriously undermines the legal protection – and thus the human rights – of the persons that are subjected to UN financial sanctions. The absence of any legal remedy at UN level puts pressure on national and regional courts to offer legal protection to those affected by UN financial sanctions. However, by claiming jurisdiction over questions concerning the lawfulness of the UN financial sanction regimes they may endanger the effectiveness and the supremacy of the UN system. It is also clear that the establishment of a UN tribunal to supervise the decisions of the Security Council – and other UN bodies – is not a sufficient mean to solve all jurisdic-

---

24   Case T-338/02, [2003] OJ C 7/24.
25   Case T-206/02, [2002] OJ C 247/13.
26   Case T-228/02, [2002] OJ C 247/20.
27   Case T-253/02, [2002] OJ C 289/5.

tional problems currently encountered in the implementation of UN financial sanctions. Since these sanctions are enforced at a national or regional level, a UN judge would not take away the need for legal remedies at a national or regional level. It is both impossible and undesirable that all disputes concerning the implementation of UN financial sanctions would be brought before a UN judge.

In this respect a parallel may be drawn with the respective roles of the national and European courts in the context of EC law. The national courts play an important role in securing that EC law is applied at the national level. However, when in a case before a national court a question arises on the interpretation of a specific rule of EU law, the national court may ask the European Court of Justice to clarify the matter; when the lawfulness of a Community act is challenged, a national court may not itself rule that the act is unlawful, but must refer the matter to the European Court of Justice.[28] A similar form of co-operation and division of competence would have to be established between the national courts and the UN judicial authority.

---

28   Case 314/85, *Foto-Frost*, [1987] ECR, 4199.

The contribution of International Labour Law to the challenge of globalisation

Gustav J.J. Heerma van Voss

1 INTRODUCTION

International competition has been a driving force for the internationalisation of Labour Law for a century. Yet, Labour Law depended highly on the regulation of national states and the power of unions in the national context. The recent development towards globalisation of economies seems to have had an important impact on Labour Law that is already in a process of reorientation as a result of changes in production methods: the industrial society is changing into an information- or service-society. At the turn of the century many labour lawyers expressed the idea that labour law was in some sort of identity crisis.[1] Are we watching the death-struggle of Labour Law or does it have answers?

2 HISTORY

Labour Law was developed since the 19th century as a result of the Industrial Revolution and the struggle of workers for better living conditions. By organising in unions and political parties the working class managed to influence the law. Labour Law was introduced as a new legal discipline that protected workers and compensated their unequal economic position towards employers.[2]

Soon it became clear that countries were depending on improving working conditions in other countries. If all countries were to develop labour standards it would not distort the competition on the world market: International Labour Law was born. At the end of World War I this idea was consolidated in the International Labour Organisation (ILO). The ILO developed a series of standards and is still doing so. Every year delegates from the ILO Member States (Governments as well as social partners) meet within the International Labour Conference at Geneva and formulate common standards. Every nation-state is free to accept the ILO-standards, and is encouraged to do so by the international community. However, this method meets two significant problems. Firstly, the standards set out in ILO-Conventions are worldwide stan-

---

1   Lord Wedderburn a.o., *Labour Law in the Post-industrial Era* (Aldershot, Dartmouth, 1994).
2   B. Hepple (ed.), *The Making of Labour Law in Europe, A comparative Study of Nine Countries up to 1945* (Mansell, London, 1986); H. Slomp, *Labor Relations in Europe, A History of Issues and Developments* (Greenwood Press, New York, 1990).

dards, and thus not always very effective in the developed western countries. Secondly, countries are free to accept or reject the standards. Many countries only accept ILO-Conventions that are in line with already existing legislation or with actual policies of the Government. However, there is no doubt that the ILO has done extremely important work by promoting its standards.[3]

Since World War II Labour Law has undergone a further development, especially in Europe: labour law became part of the constitution of several countries. Welfare states were developed. Within companies, the managerial prerogatives were restricted by the rule of law. A 'European social model' was designed: consultation of works councils, negotiation with unions, and protection of the incomes of the workers were generally accepted common elements of the systems, although every country has its specific features.[4] On the European level the European Social Dialogue is typical for this European Social Model of consultation rather than confrontation.[5] The basis for this system is considered to be found in two worldwide recognized constitutional rights of workers: the right to organize and the right to bargain collectively. The important role of the government, however, is specific for the European context.

> The acceptance of Labour Law in the European Society was clearly demonstrated when the Court of Justice had to decide whether labour conditions negotiated by unions in collective agreements with employer could be contrary to the Fair Competition-clause in the European Community Treaty. The Court concluded that a decision taken by organisations representing employers and workers in a given sector, in the context of a collective agreement, to set up in that sector a single pension fund responsible for managing a supplementary pension scheme and to request the public authorities to make affiliation to that fund compulsory for all workers in that sector does not fall within the scope of Article 81 EC-Treaty. Articles 3(1)(g), 10 and 85 of the EC-Treaty do not prohibit a decision by the public authorities to make affiliation to a sectoral pension fund compulsory at the request of organisations representing employers and workers in a given sector. Articles 82 and 86 EC-Treaty do not preclude the public authorities from conferring on a pension fund the exclusive right to manage a supplementary pension scheme in a given sector.[6] Thus, the Court gives room for exclusive pension schemes regulated by social partners that normally would not be excepted in a free market-economy. By this decision, the Court upholds the system of collective labour law, on which many of the EC-countries have basically based their labour relations.

But for the actual challenge of globalisation neither historic development provides an adequate answer.

---

3   M. Humblet a.o., *International Labour Standards, A global approach* (International Labour Organization, Geneva, 2002); N. Valticos & G. von Potobsky, *International Labour Law* (Kluwer, Deventer, 1995); L. Betten *International Labour Law, selected issues* (Kluwer, Deventer, 1993).

4   See for a theoretical basis for the European Social Model, M. Albert, *Capitalisme contre capitalisme* (Éditions du Seuil, Paris, 1991).

5   E. Franssen, *Legal aspects of the European Social Dialogue* (Intersentia, Antwerpen, 2002).

6   ECJ 21 September 1999, Cases C-115/97 to 117/97, Brentjens [1999] ECR I-6025. See also COJ 12 September 2000, Cases C-180/98 to CC-184/98, Pavlov [2000] ECR I-6451; ECJ 21 September 2000, Case C-222/98, Van der Woude [2000] ECR I-7111.

3   THE ACTUAL CHALLENGE OF GLOBALISATION

What is the problem? The construction of the identity of Labour Law has been tied to the nation-state.[7] But the economic markets are less and less regulated by nation-states. The influence of national government in Europe is restricted by the rules of the European Union. And the rules of the World Trade Organisation and the policies of the G-8 increasingly influence the European markets. Larger companies are either developing into multinational corporations or taken over by foreign investors. The impact of globalisation on Labour Law is not merely a matter of size or nationality. Globalisation also requires more flexibility. Companies have to adjust to market developments more rapidly than they were used to in the past. This requires fast adjustments of the workforce.[8] This has an impact on the employment contract. The relatively safe position of a worker with a full-time employment contract is threatened.[9] Employees have to be aware of the need to change the content of their work, their workplace or even their company more often than before. The traditional elements of Labour Law like the employment contract, dismissal protection and stable wage levels are under fire.[10] Labour relations are individualised. When people have to change jobs often, they feel no solidarity with the same group of workers, unions lose members and, finally, their influence.[11] Within the European Union, the emphasis on Economic Integration leads to less attention for Labour Law. The Economic and Monetary Union will lead to more integration in economic policies. The Labour Market will have to become more flexible as part of this policy. Labour Law as part of this development has not yet received much attention.

The ILO as an International Organisation is not able to meet the challenge. As was said before, the ILO is based on national Member States. Its conventions depend on the acceptance by the Member States and contain just basic norms. They do not influence the policies of multinational companies. Efforts to introduce codes of conduct to change this were not very successful. The codes of conduct are often not known, and their enforcement is not effective enough.

---

7   M. D'Antona, 'Labour Law at the Century's End: An Identity Crisis', in: J. Conaghan, R. M. Fischl & K. Klare, *Labour Law in an Era of Globalization, Transformative practices and possibilities* (University Press, Oxford, 2002), p. 31-49, 33.

8   R. Blanpain, 'The changing world of work', in: R. Blanpain & C. Engels, *Comparative Labour Law and Industrial Relations in Industrialized Market Economies* (Kluwer Law International, The Hague, 1998), p. 23-50.

9   T. van Peijpe, *Employment Protection under Strain*, (Kluwer Law International, The Hague, 1998).

10   R. Blanpain & M. Weiss (eds.), *Changing Industrial Relations and Modernisation of Labour Law* (Kluwer Law International, The Hague, 2003); J.R. Bellace & M.G. Rood (eds.), *Labour Law at the Crossroads: Changing Employment Relationships* (Kluwer Law International, The Hague, 1997); L Betten (ed.), *The employment contract in transforming labour relations* (Kluwer Law International , The Hague, 1995).

11   J. Conaghan, R. M.Fischl & K.Klare, *Labour Law in an Era of Globalization, Transformative practices and possibilities* (University Press, Oxford, 2002); L. Betten & D. Mac Devitt, *The Protection of Fundamental Social Rights in the European Union* (Kluwer Law International, The Hague, 1996).

4   THE SOCIAL POLICY OF THE EUROPEAN UNION

Within the EU efforts have been made to meet the challenge of globalisation,
even before the word as such was invented. The history of the European Social
Policy can be divided into three periods.

First period: 1957-1970 – Free Movement of Workers

During the 1960s the attention of the European Community in the field of
Labour Law was almost entirely focused on the introduction of the principle
of Free Movement of Workers.

Free Movement of Workers

The Free Movement of Workers was one of the four basic freedoms that were
necessary to establish the Common Market. The Free Movement of Workers
was part of the EC Treaty (at present the Articles 39-42). But it was finally more
precisely regulated in a Regulation of 1968 and in Directives on Movement
and Residence (1968) and on Public Order, Public Safety and Public Health
(1964). The co-ordination of social security systems was settled in regulations
of 1971 and 1972. Directives on the residence of retired workers, students and
other non-workers, and the protection of additional pensions completed this
system in the 1990s.[12] The policy introduced the principle of equal treatment
of EU citizens as worker in employment relations with national residents. The
equal treatment also includes social rights and residence rights for family
members. The case-law of the European Court of Justice gave a broad interpretation of these rights, giving EU citizens in other EC countries almost completely the same rights as national residents as soon as they find a job in that
country.

Second period: 1970-1990 – Social Action Programmes

During the 1970s the Governments of the Member States became aware of a
growing need to show the citizens that the European integration was not only
attractive for companies.
     The Commission launched Social Action Programmes to deal with this as-
pect. The Action Programmes originally related to two areas: the Restructuring of Enterprises and the Equal Treatment of Men and Women; later Health
& Safety was added.

---

12   See for a comparison with the US system: A.P. van der Mei, *Free movement of persons within
      the European Community: cross-border access to public benefits* (Hart, Oxford, 2002).

Restructuring of Enterprises

The developing internal market promoted the Restructuring of Enterprises. Some companies were merging with or taking over other companies, while others had difficulties to remain competitive on the growing European markets. The population was beginning to protest against the unilateral economic approach of the European integration. Mere economic integration would ask too high a price of the citizens in terms of insecurity of work. The policy of the AKZO-company which realised collective redundancies in the countries with the lowest level of worker protection made the population anxious about further economic integration. To make this development more acceptable for the workers three important directives were introduced, concerning:

- collective redundancies in 1975, requiring companies to consult workers' representatives and to inform government in case of mass dismissals.[13]
- the transfer of enterprises and acquired rights for workers in 1977, maintaining workers' jobs and other rights in case of a take-over.[14]
- insolvency of the employer in 1980, guaranteeing worker's wages during a short period after a bankruptcy.[15]

All three directives showed the ambiguity of labour law in a market-economy and within the EC as a primarily economic organisation. Although collective redundancies, transfers of enterprises and insolvency are accepted as normal, and even sometimes necessary events in a free market economy, the most direct and hard effects for the workers are postponed or reduced, in order to make time for the employees to enable them to adjust to the new situation.

Equal treatment

During the 1970s the European Community also introduced legislation in the field of equal opportunities for men and women on the labour market. Women demanded equal rights and the Commission saw room for social action programmes in this field. In addition to the already existing rule of equal pay for men and women according to the EC-Treaty (article 119, presently 141) directives were introduced to emphasise the equal rights of women:

- Equal pay in 1975
- Equal rights in employment in 1976
- Equal rights in Social Security in 1979
- Equal rights in Private Pension Systems in 1986
- Equal rights of self-employed in 1986

---

13   Council Directive 75/129/EEC of 17 February 1975, today replaced by Council Directive 98/59/EC of 20 July 1998, [1998] OJ L 225/16.
14   Council Directive 77/187/EEC of 14 February 1977, today replaced by Council Directive 2001/23/EC of 12 March 2001, [2001] OJ L 82/16.
15   Council directive 80/987/EEC of 20 October 1980, [1980] OJ L 283/23.

The non-discrimination policies were extended at the end of the century (Treaty of Amsterdam, 1997), by introducing new provisions in the EC-Treaty (Articles 13 and 14), broadening the scope to other forms of discrimination like nationality, race, religion, handicap, age and sexual orientation.

New Directives in this field at this time concerned:
- The division of the Burden of Proof in 1997
- Race discrimination in 2000
- General Framework discrimination at work in 2000.

Besides this, there is an international development of promotion of fundamental rights in labour law that seems to be quite universal. Anti-discrimination law and protection of the privacy of the worker are addressed within the EU as well as in other industrialised countries.[16]

Health and Safety

During the 1980s the need for a more general approach to Labour Law on the European level was felt. In the Single European Act of 1987 Qualified Majority Voting in the Council on Directives with regard to Health and Safety was accepted. During the 1980s a series of directives in this field was introduced, setting the standards for protection of workers in several specific areas. More general were the directives on:
- Framework Directive on Health and Safety of 1989,
- Protection of Pregnant Women at Work of 1992,
- Aspects of Organisation of Working Time of 1993 and
- Protection of Young Workers of 1994.

Third period: since 1990 – Overall social policy

At the end of the 1980s the call for an overall European social policy became more influential. The European Commission under the presidency of Jacques Delors introduced the 1992 project, aiming to complete the Internal Market. As a sequel to this, Delors also reanimated the 'social dialogue'. The Organisations of Employers and Workers on the European Level were invited to have regular meetings and encouraged to negotiate on agreements. On the basis of such an agreement a new decision-making process in the field of social policy was introduced. It was part of an Agreement on Social Policy that was related to a protocol annexed to the Maastricht Treaty of 1992 that allowed 11 of the 12 Member States to make further reaching decisions in the social field. At that time, the Conservative Government of the United Kingdom did

---

16   B. Hepple (ed.), *Social and Labour Rights in a Global Context, International and Comparative Perspectives* (University Press, Cambridge, 2002); M. Bell, *Anti-Discrimination Law and the European Union* (University Press, Oxford, 2002); J.D.R. Craig, *Privacy and employment Law* (Hart, Oxford,1999).

not accept this policy, as it also refused to agree with a Community Charter on the Rights of Workers that was endorsed by the other Member States in Strasbourg 1989. However, after the Labour Government took over in Britain in 1997, it accepted the social policy of the other countries and in the Amsterdam Treaty of that year the Social Policy provisions were placed in the EC-Treaty and became an integral part of European Law (Articles 136-145).[17]

The new procedures include the consultation of the European Social Partners on new initiatives in the social field. They have the option to choose to open negotiations before the Council of Ministers introduces legislation. Should the negotiations lead to an agreement, they can ask the Council to make that agreement binding in the form of European Law.

Employment Contract

The new procedure was used with respect to some agreements with regard to employment contracts:
- Directive and Agreement on Parental Leave
- Directive and Agreement on Part-time Work
- Directive and Agreement on Fixed-Term Contracts.

Also some sectoral agreements with regard to working hours in the Transport Sector followed this model.

In the field of Employment Contract Law in 1991 already the Directive on Information of Workers' rights was enacted.

Information and consultation

A new area of social policy is the field of information and consultation of workers.

Since the decision-making process of the large companies is more and more on a trans-national basis, national states are less able to influence them. Therefore, in 1994 the EC-Directive on European Works Councils was introduced.[18] Since 1999 every Community-scale undertaking must have a works council on the European level or another form of information and consultation procedure. The same goes for the newly introduced European Company

---

17　See for general overviews on European Labour Law in English: J. Kenner, *EU Employment Law, From Rome to Amsterdam and beyond* (Hart Publishing, Oxford, 2003); A C. Neal, *European Labour Law and Social Policy, Cases and Materials* (Kluwer Law International, The Hague, 2002); R. Blanpain, *European Labour Law* (Kluwer Law International, The Hague, 2002); C. Barnard, *EC Employment Law* (University Press, Oxford, 2000); R. Nielsen, *European Labour Law* (Djøf publishing, Copenhagen, 2000); E. Szyszczak, *EC Labour Law* (Longman, Harlow, 2000); B. Bercusson, *European Labour Law* (Butterworth, London, 1997); N. Burrows & J. Mair, *European Social Law* (John Wiley & Sons, Chichester, 1996).

18　Council Directive 94/45/EC of 22 September 1994 (EWC); R. Blanpain & P. Windey, *European Works Councils, Information and consultation of Employees in Multinational enterprises in Europe* (Peeters, Leuven, 1996).

(SE).[19] With regard to the European Company also rules for the influence of workers on the board of directors are included. In 2002 a Framework Directive was accepted with regard to Information and Consultation of Workers on the National Level.

The European Social Policy as a whole seems to be quite effective in the European context. Even though globalisation is going further than the European borders, every company with plants in Europe has to comply with the national rules that were introduced to comply with the directives. The European Commission and the Court of Justice ensured that these directives were transposed into national legislation and effectively enforced.[20]

As a result of globalisation, the arrangements for the EU-countries will be not enough and the need will grow for agreements with more countries about this issue.[21]

5   JURISDICTION PROBLEMS

Problems of conflicts of laws (private international law) within the European Union were settled in a Treaty, a Regulation and a Directive.[22]

Law on Contractual Obligations

The European Convention Regarding the Law Applicable to Contractual Obligations (hereinafter EC-Convention) dates from 1980 and at present has been adopted by all EC Member States.[23] In the future it will be replaced by a Regulation, making the European Court of Justice competent. At present that competence is dependent on the acceptance of an additional Protocol.

Labour Law used to fear that employers would abuse a complete freedom of choice of applicable law. On the other hand, the place of work as the only determining factor is also too simple. Therefore, the EC Convention prescribes in article 6, paragraph 1 that a choice of the parties in an employment contract for the law system of another country is valid, but 'shall not have the result of depriving the employee of the protection afforded to him by the mandatory rules of the law which would be applicable under paragraph 2 in the absence of choice'. Al-

---

19   See Council Directives 2001/86/EC of 12 March 2001(SE) and 2003/72/EC of 22 July 2003 (SCE).
20   J. Malmberg (ed.), *Effective Enforcement of EC Labour Law* (Iustus Förlag, Uppsala, 2003).
21   See in this respect also the Communication of the Commission to the Council, the European Parliament and the Economic and Social committeee promoting core labour standards and improving social governance in the context of globalisation of 18 July 2000, COM (2001) 416 final, also published in: A.C. Neal, *European Labour Law and Social Policy, Cases and Materials* (Kluwer Law International, The Hague, 2002), Volume II, p. 80.
22   See F. Gamillscheg & M. Franzen, 'Conflicts of Laws in Employment Contracts and Industrial Relations', in: R. Blanpain & C. Engels, *Comparative Labour Law and Industrial Relations in Industrialized Market Economies* (Kluwer Law International, The Hague, 1998), p. 161-179.
23   EC-Convention Regarding the Law applicable to Contractual Obligations of 1980.

though this might be seen as a form of protection of the national economic market, the rule is not simply providing the worker with the most favourable system. It just prevents the worker from being deprived of local labour protection and contributes to a fair competition within one Member State.

In the case of an absence of choice in the employment contract, article 6, paragraph 2 rules that the contract shall be governed:

> (a) by the law of the country in which the employee habitually carries out his work in performance of the contract, even if he is temporarily employed in another country; or
> (b) if the employee does not habitually carry out his work in any one country, by the law of the country in which the place of business through which he was engaged is situated; unless it appears from the circumstances as a whole that the contract is more closely connected with another country, in which case the contract shall be governed by the law of that country.

The result is that the place of work is normally decisive, but it is possible to argue that another factor is more connected.

If the law of another country is also involved article 7, paragraph 1 of the of the EC Convention prescribes:

> When applying under this Convention the law of a country, effect may be given to the mandatory rules of another country with which the situation has a close connection, if and in so far as, under the law of the latter country, those rules must be applied whatever the law applicable to the contract. In considering whether to give effect to these mandatory rules, regard shall be had to their nature and purpose and to the consequences of their application or non-application.

Execution of decisions

For the effective execution of decisions of courts in other European countries the European Union has Regulation 44/2001.[24] Articles 18-21 deal specifically with individual obligations on the basis of employment contracts. A case against an employer can be brought before a court in the place where the employee usually works or has worked or, when the worker has not worked in one single country, the court of the place where the affiliation is or was located that employed the employee (Article 19). Article 20 provides that the employer can bring his claim only before the courts of the Member State where the employee lives. The parties are only allowed to agree otherwise after a conflict has been raised.

Posting of workers

Specifically in the construction sector problems have occurred with regard to the working conditions of workers who were posted in another Member State. In the Rush Portuguesa case, Portuguese undertakings were made subject to

---

24   Regulation (EG) 44/2001 on execution of decisions in civil and commercial cases.

labour regulations of France. The Court of Justice decided in 1990 that an undertaking established in Portugal under the EC-Treaty providing services in the construction and public works sector in another Member State may move with its own workforce which it brings from Portugal for the duration of the work in question. In such a case, the authorities of the Member State in whose territory the work is to be carried out may not impose on the supplier of services conditions relating to the recruitment of manpower in situ or the obtaining of work permits for the Portuguese workforce.[25]

The European Council and Parliament reacted with a Directive on posting of workers.[26] In this Directive the Member States were entitled to guarantee workers posted to their territory the terms and conditions of employment covering the following matters which, in the Member State where the work is carried out, are laid down by law or collective agreements in the construction sector:

- maximum work periods and minimum rest periods;
- minimum paid annual holidays;
- the minimum rates of pay, including overtime rates;
- the conditions of hiring-out of workers;
- health, safety and hygiene at work;
- protective measures with regard to pregnant women or women who have recently given birth, and with regard to children and young people;
- equality of treatment between men and women and other provisions on non-discrimination.

By imposing this rule the 'gap' between EC-law and national labour regulation in this field was restored. Some people, however, would consider this Directive as a new form of national protection of the construction market against foreign competitors. A basic principle of European Law now seems to be that this competition should not lead to the so-called 'social dumping', which means that countries compete by lowering labour standards.

6   NEW FORMS OF SOCIAL POLICY IN THE EU

The relatively high unemployment in the European Union is sometimes considered to be a result of the high degree of protection given to workers in the EC. However, it is important to realise that the level of unemployment differs from country to country and the nature of the unemployment (young or old workers, men or women) often varies greatly. Unemployment is often still considered to be a national problem above a European one.

Since the issue is also politically sensitive on the national level, EC-Member States are not very willing to harmonise their employment policies. How-

---

25   ECJ 27 March 1990, Case C-113/89, Rush Portuguesa [1990] ECR I-1417.
26   Directive 96/71/EG of the European Parliament and of the Council of 16 December 1996 concerning the posting of workers in the framework of the provision of services, [1997] OJ L 18/1.

ever, this item seems to be getting more importance as a result of the introduction of the Economic and Monetary Union. As part of the integration of the national economies, the employment policy also needs more co-ordination. To promote this, in the Treaty of Amsterdam of 1997 a new approach was introduced in the new Employment Title of the EC-Treaty. Typical for this Title is the emphasis on voluntary co-operation between the Member States in tackling unemployment in the EC. New instruments are introduced such as peer reviews, benchmarking, good practices, guidelines and reports of the Member States, that are evaluated by the Commission and the Council.

The European Commission suggested that for an effective employment policy four pillars should be given priority, which also implies a culture change in Europe:

- Entrepreneurship (fewer labour costs, promoting self-employment)
- Employability (modernising education and training, lifelong learning)
- Adaptability (promoting new technologies and investment in human resources)
- Equal opportunities (men and women; reconcile work and family life; facilitate return to work).

In introducing the Employment Guidelines for 2000, the European Commission found inspiration in the idea that the 'knowledge economy' requires a new social policy. Basic assumptions are:

- the expectation that by 2010 half of all jobs will be in industries that are producers or intensive users of information technology
- young people should be educated for employment in the knowledge economy
- the belief that employment in the information society is less stable than in the past and more dependent on high skills and adaptability.

The Guidelines also include separate guidelines for each Member State. The Guidelines are incorporated in national Action Plans of the Member States and the effects on the employment figures are evaluated every year. On the basis of this evaluation new guidelines are formulated. The Guidelines focus for instance on youth unemployment, the participation of women, and the participation of older workers.

It is difficult to evaluate at this time the effects of the new forms of social policy that were introduced in the EC during the last five years. Sceptics argue that since the Member States are not prepared to empower the EC with the competence to formulate employment policies by majority decision, we cannot take this policy, mainly based as it is on the idea of 'shame and blame', seriously. On the other hand, we must realise that some aspects do not make the process completely voluntary. First of all, there is a link with the Economic Policy of the EC. The Labour Market is important for the health of the European economy as a whole, linked together as it is, especially since the establishment of the Euro as a common currency. Secondly, European politicians are often confronted their electorates' concerns with globalisation as a force that undermines their traditional certainties. They continuously have to assure to their citizens that Europe is not only an economic undertaking, but also a social one. They have to find new ways to maintain the so-called European social Model and to find new forms for it that fit into the economic developments in order to keep the confidence of the population.

7   CONCLUSION

In this paper I gave a general overview of the problems that result from the globalisation of the economy and also of labour markets. I also indicated how the European Union tries to cope with the problems resulting from this development. Most of the time the solutions of the European Union are just effective within the EU-territory. Multinational companies as well as workers from outside the EU will be affected by it, as far as they operate in EU-Member States.

    In the future this will not be enough. Globalisation reaches further than Europe and therefore we will need closer co-operation between industrialised countries on a global scale to tackle the issues mentioned in this paper. It will probably take a long time to make progress in this respect. Newly introduced means of policy-making with emphasis on co-ordination and evaluation of best practices might be helpful.

    The idea that globalisation leads to the death of labour law, as some analysts[27] suggest, seems too pessimistic. In my view, labour law has to adapt itself to the new situation, just as employees have to show flexibility these days. New forms of labour law may be created, fit for the 21st century. I choose for this option, not only to maintain my own job as a labour lawyer, but in the first place because I see it as essential for social cohesion in society to maintain or create an acceptable (or, even happy) working life for the actors on the globalising labour market.

---

27   H. Arthurs, quoted by D.M. Davies, in: J. Conaghan, R.M. Fischl & K. Klare, *Labour Law in an Era of Globalization, Transformative practices and possibilities* (University Press, Oxford, 2002), p. 159.

Optimal regulatory areas for securities disclosure

Merritt B. Fox[*]

1   INTRODUCTION

The corporate governance scandals of 2003 have brought renewed focus on mandatory disclosure. One of the most fundamental questions relating to this kind of regulation is the choice of regulatory area. The United States initially faced this question in the 1930s when, after intense debate, it decided to move from an exclusively state based system to one primarily relying on federal regulation. It is a hot issue today as well. The countries of Europe, for example, are currently deciding the extent to which the European Community, rather than its member states, should determine securities disclosure in Europe.[1] Canada is deciding whether to follow the path taken by Australia in the 1980s and to enlarge the role of the federal government in a system that has traditionally left disclosure regulation primarily to the provinces.[2] And advocates of issuer choice are urging the United States to reconsider its 1930s decision and to give issuers the option to choose among a reinvigorated set of state regulatory regimes.[3] The issuer choice school of thought is influencing the de-

---

[*]   The author wishes to thank the participants in the 2003 Hodge O'Neal Corporate and Securities Law Symposium of Washington University Law School, and in particular James Casteliano, Professor Hillary Sale and Professor Murray Weidenbaum, for their helpful comments on this paper.

1   See, e.g., Final Report of the Committee of Wise Men on the Regulation of European Securities Markets (February 2001) (the 'Lamfalussy Report'); Niamh Moloney, *EC Securities Regulation* 29-32 (2002).
2   See, e.g., 'Memorandum of Understanding Regarding the Regulation of Securities in Canada', 17 *Ontario Securities Commission Bulletin* 4401 (1994); Speech by Minister Throne in the Canadian House of Commons, House of Common Debates (February 27, 1996); J. G. MacIntosh, 'A National Securities Exchange for Canada?', in: T. Courchene & E. Neave (eds.), *Reforming the Canadian Financial Sector: Canada in Global Perspective* 185 (1997). Canada has periodically faced this question over the last several decades. Royal Commission on Banking and Finance, *Report* 561 (1964) (the 'Porter Report'); *CANSEC:* 'Legal and Administrative Concepts' November 1967 Ontario Securities Commission Bulletin 61. An excellent review of both past reform proposals and the current state of the debate can be found in: A.D. Harris, *A Symposium on Canadian Securities Regulation: Harmonization or Nationalization?* (University of Toronto Capital Markets Institute White Paper, 2002).
3   S.J. Choi & A.T. Guzman, 'Portable Reciprocity: Rethinking the International Reach of Securities Regulation' 71 S. Calif. L. Rev. 903 (1998); R. Romano, 'Empowering Investors: A Market Approach to Securities Regulation', 107 Yale L. J. 2359 (1998) (hereinafter *Empowering Investors*); R. Romano, 'The Need for Competition in International Securities Regulation' 2 Theoretical Inquiries L. 387 (2001) (hereinafter Need for Competition).

bates in Europe and Canada as well.[4] Finally, other advocates push for a move in the opposite direction, arguing that standards for issuer disclosure should be set at a global level.[5]

This article constructs an economic efficiency based theory of optimal regulatory areas for securities disclosure. While larger political and constitutional considerations unrelated to efficiency will inevitably also play a role in the resolution of the debates recounted above, efficiency considerations are important because they go to the capacity of capital markets to promote the generation of real wealth. The theory developed here can help identify the efficiency related trade-offs involved in choosing one level of government versus another and the information that is needed to choose intelligently.

The optimal structure of disclosure regulation over the world's issuers is determined by answers to two questions: With respect to any point on earth, what level of government, out of all the levels that have control over the point, should be the one regulating disclosure? And among all the units of government identified by the answer to the first question as the ones that should be engaging in disclosure regulation, which one or ones should regulate any given issuer?

Because all governmental units existing in the world today have a territorial base, answering the first question – the level of government to regulate securities disclosure – involves dividing the globe territorially, either more or less finely. What distinguishes one governmental unit from another is the territory associated with it. Thus the answer to the second question – which governmental unit or units at the chosen level regulates any given issuer – is going to depend on the issuer's ties to the chosen unit's territory. Potentially relevant territorial ties include where the issuer is located ('issuer location'), where its securities are being offered or traded ('transaction location'), and where the

---

4   See, e.g., Harris, supra note 2, at 84-86.
5   See, e.g.,U. Geiger, 'The Case for the Harmonization of Securities Disclosure Rules in the Global Market', 1997 Colum. Bus. L. Rev. 241 (1997); M. I. Steinberg & L. E. Michaels, 'Disclosure in Global Securities Offerings: Analysis of Jurisdictional Approaches, Commonality and Reciprocity', 20 Mich. J. Int'l. L. 207 (1999) at 261-65 (the world's country's, by self selection, would be divided into three groups – developed market, semi-developed market and emerging market – and each group would work out a uniform disclosure rule for its country's issuers that would permit sale and trading of their securities anywhere within the group). IOSCO, a worldwide organization of countries that provides a forum for meetings of the securities regulators of member states, initially undertook a straddle in which it urged countries either to adopt uniform rules (international uniformity) or reciprocity (essentially the issuer nationality approach). International Equity Offers, Report of the Technical Committee of IOSCO as cited in Steinberg & Michaels, supra note 2 at 241. IOSCO, in cooperation with IASC, is now seeking to develop a recommended set of international accounting standards and has developed a set of non-financial disclosure standards that could be used in a single uniform disclosure document for cross-border offerings, and thus has tilted toward international uniformity as the preferred result. See IOSCO, International Equity Offers, Report of the Technical Committee (Sept. 1989) (available from IOSCO at <www.iosco.org>) cited in M. Hurley, 'International and Debt and Equity Markets', 8 Emory Int'l. L. Rev. 701, 733 (1994), Steinberg & Michaels, supra, at 241, 243-46, and R. S. Karmel, 'The IOSCO Venice Conference' NYLJ 3 (Oct. 19, 1989).

purchasers or traders in the issuer's shares reside ('investor location'). Alternatively, as the issuer choice proposals suggest, the determination of which governmental unit regulates an issuer could be made to depend solely on its consent.

In prior writing, I have taken the answer to the first question – the level of government – as given. I have instead primarily focused on the second question – what kind of a tie an issuer needs to have to a territory to justify regulation of the issuer's disclosure by the government associated with the territory.[6] For example, I have assumed that for the United States, the proper level of government to be regulating securities disclosure is the one governing the territory of the nation as a whole. Given this assumption, I conclude that issuer location – the place where an issuer has its economic center of gravity as a firm – should be the territorial tie that triggers application of the U.S. regime to an issuer.[7] Thus the U.S. government should regulate the disclosure of all issuers located in the United States and no others except those who consent to U.S. regulation. The place or places where an issuer's securities are being offered or traded, and the place or places where the purchasers or traders in the issuer's shares reside, should, in my view, be irrelevant.

In contrast, the primary focus of this article is the proper level of government to regulate securities disclosure in a world with a high degree of international capital mobility. Part 1 briefly reviews the role of issuer disclosure in promoting economic efficiency and demonstrates that each issuer has a socially optimal level of disclosure. Part 2 identifies a regulatory structure for disclosure by the world's issuers as having two components: a division of the world into a set of areas and a rule of territorial tie that assigns issuers to these different areas for regulation by their respective governmental units. I suggest that the optimal world regulatory structure is the one that pairs issuers and governmental units in such a way that for each issuer, the persons who would ultimately benefit from the issuer being well regulated have residences that are, to the greatest extent possible, concentrated within the area of the regulating governmental unit.

Part 3 considers an ideal world conforming to assumptions that permit its division into geographic areas where there is very little economic integration across territorial lines except portfolio investment capital flows. I show that this division of the world, combined with an issuer location rule of territorial tie, results in an optimal regulatory structure. Use of an investor location or

---

6   See M.B. Fox, 'Securities Disclosure in a Globalizing Market: Who Should Regulate Whom', 95 Mich. L. Rev. 2498 (1997) (hereinafter 'Disclosure in a Globalizing Market'); M. B. Fox, 'The Political Economy of Statutory Reach: U.S. Disclosure Rules in a Globalizing Market for Securities', 97 Mich. L. Rev. 696 (1998) (hereinafter 'Political Economy'); M.B. Fox, 'Retaining Mandatory Securities Disclosure: Why Issuer Choice is Not Investor Empowerment', 85 Va. L. Rev. 1335 (1999) (hereinafter 'Retaining Mandatory Disclosure'); M. B. Fox, 'The Securities Globalization Disclosure Debate', 78 Wash. U. L.Q. 567 (2000); [hereinafter 'Disclosure Debate']; M.B. Fox, 'The Issuer Choice Debate', 2 Theoretical Inquiries L. 563 (2001) (hereinafter 'Issuer Choice Debate').

7   Fox, 'Political Economy', supra note 6, at 730-757.

transaction location rule of territorial tie is shown to result in regulatory structures less conducive to efficiency, as is also the case with issuer choice.

Part 4 considers the implications of the real world breakdown in the assumptions relating to each area that are used to construct Part 3's ideal world.
There are two sets of assumptions. One set is that most trade occurs within the
area, that labor and entrepreneurs have low mobility across territorial lines,
and that all issuers operating within the area have their economic centers of
gravity there. The second set is that the governmental unit associated with the
area is responsive to the needs of its residents and capable of effective application and enforcement of its rules, and that all issuers within the area have the
same optimal level of disclosure. Taking the political subdivisions present in
the real world, the first set of assumptions could only be met perfectly if the
world is a single large regulatory area. The second set of assumptions could
only be met, even approximately, if much smaller regulatory areas were employed. The discussion helps identify where the optimal point of tradeoff is
between the advantages of larger sized areas and the advantages of smaller
sized areas under various circumstances prevailing in different parts of the
world. The breakdown in assumptions is shown not to resurrect the case for
using investor location or transaction location as the rule for territorial tie or
the case for adopting issuer choice.

Part 5 concludes the article by sketching how the overall analysis can be
applied to current debates. It suggests that the United States should maintain
its nationally based system of regulation and that Canada should move from
a provincially based system to a nationally based one. It finds that for Europe,
the choice between Community level disclosure regulation and national regulation is a close one. Considerable problems are found with proposals for
regulation by some kind of global disclosure authority.

2   ISSUER DISCLOSURE AND ECONOMIC EFFICIENCY

The purpose of this article is to construct an economic efficiency based theory
of optimal regulatory areas for issuer disclosure. The necessary starting point
is an efficiency analysis of issuer disclosure in general. This analysis arises
from the observation that disclosure has both social benefits and social costs.[8]

---

8   I have analysed this question in more detail elsewhere. See Fox, 'Disclosure in a Globaliz-
       ing Market', supra note 6, at 2544-2550. See also M. Kahan, 'Securities Laws and the Social
       Cost of 'Inaccurate' Stock Prices', 41 Duke L.J. 977 (1992); P. G. Mahoney, 'Mandatory Dis-
       closure as a Solution to Agency Problems', 62 U. Chic. L. Rev. 1047 (1995).

2.1   Social benefits and social costs of disclosure

(1) *Benefits.* An act of disclosure by an issuer produces social benefits by improving how proposed new investment projects in the real economy are selected for implementation and how existing projects are operated.

Consider first the social benefits derived from an act of disclosure's effects on the issuer's own behavior. The disclosure produces these benefits directly when the issuer contemplates implementing a new project by means of a new offering of stock. Because of the disclosure induced increase in the accuracy of the price at which the shares will be sold, the firm's cost of capital is brought more in line with the social cost of investing society's scarce savings in the contemplated project, which increases the chances that the issuer will implement socially worthwhile projects and avoid socially unworthwhile projects.[9] The disclosure produces benefits through a second route as well, unrelated to whether the issuer is offering new shares, by increasing the effectiveness of several of the devices that limit the extent to which managers of a public corporation place their own interests above those of their shareholders. Additional disclosure assists in the effective exercise of the shareholder franchise and in shareholder enforcement of management's fiduciary duties.[10] It also increases the threat of hostile takeover when managers engage in non-share-value-maximizing behavior. It does so both by making a takeover less risky for potential acquirers and by reducing the chance that a value-enhancing acquisition will be deterred because the target has an inaccurately high share price. Finally, by reducing the riskiness associated with holding an issuer's stock in a less than fully diversified portfolio, additional disclosure increases the use of share price based management compensation, which also helps align the interests of managers and shareholders.[11]

Consider secondly how an issuer's disclosure produces additional social benefits derived from its effects on the behavior of other issuers. Information about one issuer helps investors understand better the prospects and operations of other issuers as well, particularly the issuer's competitors and major suppliers and customers. As a result, capital allocation and managerial agency cost reduction are improved for these other issuers as well through the same mechanisms described just above.

A plausible story can be told concerning how the benefits arising from the effects of the disclosure on the issuer's own activities are captured by the issuer through a higher sale price when, at the time of the primary market sale of its shares, it makes a commitment to provide such information on an ongo-

---

9   See Fox, 'Retaining Issuer Disclosure', note 6 supra at 1358-63.

10   See M.B. Fox, 'Required Disclosure and Corporate Governance' in: K.I. Hopt, et al.,(eds.), *Comparative Corporate Governance: The State of the Art and Emerging Research* (1998), p. 701-718.

11   See Fox, 'Disclosure in a Globalizing Market', note 6 supra at 2548-2550.

ing basis.[12] The issuer will not, however, be able to capture the benefits arising from the effects of the disclosure on the behavior of other issuers, since the prospect of such benefits will not make the disclosing issuer's shares any more attractive in the market. Thus the private benefits from an act of disclosure will be less than the social benefits.

(2) *Costs.* An act of disclosure entails costs as well. An individual issuer's disclosure involves for it two different kinds of costs, 'operational' costs and 'interfirm' costs. Operational costs are the out-of-pocket expenses and the diversions of management and staff time that issuers incur to provide the information. Interfirm costs arise from the fact that the information provided can put the issuer at a disadvantage relative to its competitors (by allowing them to compete more effectively) and to its major suppliers and major customers (by allowing them to bargain more effectively). The operational costs are the social costs of the issuer's act of disclosure: they are costs both to the individual firm and to society as a whole. The interfirm costs are costs only to the individual firm. They are not social costs because the interfirm disadvantages to the issuer from the disclosure are counterbalanced by the advantages the disclosure confers on the other firms. Thus, at all levels of disclosure, an issuer's private marginal costs will exceed its social marginal cost by an amount equal to these interfirm costs.[13]

2.2   An issuer's socially optimal level of disclosure

As a result of these benefits and costs, an issuer's level of disclosure affects the real returns generated by both it and other issuers. An issuer's socially optimal level of disclosure is the level at which the marginal social benefits just equal the marginal social costs.

Issuers will not disclose at their optimal levels if we rely on market forces alone. Under such a regime, an issuer's private benefits from disclosure will be less than its social benefits and its private costs from disclosure will be greater than its social costs. Thus, each issuer will choose to disclose at a level

---

12   See Fox, 'Retaining Mandatory Disclosure', supra note 6 at 1365.
13   I have considered this point in more detail elsewhere. See Fox, 'Disclosure in a Globalizing Market', supra note 6 at 2537-39 (1997). See also E.W. Kitch, 'The Theory and Practice of Securities Disclosure', 61 Brook. L. Rev. 763 (1995); J.C. Coffee, Jr., 'Market Failure and the Economic Case for a Mandatory Disclosure System', 70 Va. L. Rev. 717, 721-23 (1984), F.H. Easterbrook & D.R. Fischel, 'Mandatory Disclosure and the Protection of Investors' 70 Va. L. Rev. 669, 672-73 (1984); L.A. Bebchuk, 'Federalism and the Corporation: The Desirable Limits on State Competition in Corporate Law', 105 Harv. L. Rev. 1435, 1490-91 (1992).

below its social optimum.[14] This market failure constitutes the key efficiency based rationale for regulating issuer disclosure.[15]

3 THE APPROACH TO DETERMINING OPTIMAL REGULATORY AREAS

A regulatory structure for disclosure by the world's issuers can be identified in terms of two components: a division of the world into a set of areas and a rule of territorial tie for assigning issuers to these different areas for regulation by their respective governmental units. Global economic welfare is maximized when each of the world's issuers discloses at its socially optimal level. The goal therefore is a global regulatory structure in which each such issuer would be prompted to disclose as close as is cost effectively possible to its socially optimal level. Assume for now that governmental units are responsive to the needs of their residents. The regulatory structure that is likely to come closest to the goal is therefore one that pairs issuers and governmental units in such a way that for each issuer, the persons who would ultimately benefit from the issuer being well regulated – i.e. the persons who would be the ultimate beneficiaries of the greater real economic returns resulting from the issuer disclosing at its optimal level – have residences that are to the greatest extent possible concentrated within the governmental unit's area.

Each of the world's governmental units has associated with it a certain portion of the world's territory. Thus, any particular global regulatory structure implies a particular set of regulatory areas. The optimal set of regulatory areas is the one that corresponds to the best global regulatory structure.

4 OPTIMAL REGULATORY AREAS – THE IDEAL CASE

4.1 The starting point

It is easiest to see what each member of the optimal set of regulatory areas would look like by first considering an ideal case not found in the real world. This ideal case involves a division of the world into geographic areas where there is very little economic integration across territorial lines except in portfolio investment capital flows. More specifically, five assumptions apply to each regulatory area in this ideal case:

---

14   The analysis shows this conclusion to be true even if the issuer's managers completely identify with existing shareholders and seek to maximize share value.

15   It is, of course, possible that because of governmental failure, the cure would be worse than the disease, i.e., that governmental regulation would result in issuers disclosing at levels further from what is optimal than would reliance on market forces alone. This possibility does not eliminate the need to determine the optimal regulatory areas for securities disclosure. With respect to each of the world's issuers, we still need to determine what governmental unit should make the determination that governmental failure would exceed market failure.

(1) Trade in goods and services with persons outside the area is a small percentage of the area's GDP.
(2) Labor and entrepreneurs residing within the area have little mobility across the lines separating this area from the rest of the world.
(3) The governmental unit associated with the area is responsive to the needs of the residents of the area and is capable of effective application and enforcement of its rules.
(4) Each issuer that has any real economic activities in the area is 'located' in the area, which means that its economic center of gravity as a firm is located within the area. There are thus no multinational enterprises operating within the area. Indicators of an issuer's economic center of gravity would include where the issuer's headquarters are located, where it has its greatest concentration of physical capital and employees, and where its entrepreneurs resided at the time of the firm's founding.[16] Each issuer operating in the area would therefore be combining factors of production located primarily within the area to create goods and services that are primarily consumed within the area.
(5) Each issuer located within the area would be sufficiently similar in its corporate governance structure that it would have the same socially optimal level of disclosure.

It is possible, however, for the shares of each of these issuers to be offered to investors residing outside the area or to be traded among investors residing outside the area or traded on exchanges located outside the area. Thus, portfolio capital flows are global but real economic activity is local to the area.

In Part 4 we consider what the real world breakdown of these five assumptions would imply.

4.2   *The governmental unit as exclusive regulator of issuers located in the area*

In this ideal case, a regulatory incidence analysis strongly suggests that the level of government that corresponds to the unit associated with each of these areas should be the exclusive regulator of the disclosure of all issuers located in the area. We will see below that with this pairing of issuers and governmental unit, the ultimate beneficiaries of good regulation by any given regulating governmental unit will be primarily persons residing within its area. Thus, given the assumption that each governmental unit is responsive to the needs of the residents of its territory, this subdivision of the world, combined with an issuer location rule of territorial tie, involves the optimal regulatory structure.

The first step in seeing why this pairing of issuers and governmental units appropriately concentrates the benefits of good regulation, recall that, through its effects on capital allocation and the agency costs of management,

---

16   The issuer's jurisdiction of incorporation would not be a primary indicator.

an issuer's level of disclosure can enhance the real returns generated by both it and its competitors, major suppliers and major customers.[17] An issuer discloses at its optimal level when its disclosure's enhancement of these returns equals at the margin the disclosure's marginal social cost. Because of the assumption of little trade outside the area, we know that all the competitors, major suppliers and major customers of each issuer in the area will also be located in the area. Thus, if the governmental unit regulates in a way that prompts all the issuers located in the area to disclose at their socially optimal levels, the aggregate disclosure-induced net enhancement to the real returns generated by the area's capital utilizing enterprises would be maximized. There would be no enhancement of the real returns generated by issues located in any other area and the disclosure levels of the issuers in all the other areas would have no effect on this area's issuer returns.

This observation, however, does not complete the inquiry because a regulatory incidence analysis requires a determination of who are the ultimate beneficiaries from these enhanced returns. Analysis shows that it is not the investors in the area's issuers, who may or may not be residents of the area. Rather it is labor and entrepreneurs associated with the area's issuers, who do reside in the area.

(1) *Investors are not the ultimate beneficiaries.* In an efficient market, an issuer's share price takes into account the effect on the issuer's future expected cash flow from the particular disclosure rules imposed on the issuer and on its competitors, major customers and major suppliers. At the same time, if capital is relatively mobile internationally, competitive forces push capital toward receiving a single global expected rate of return (adjusted for risk). As a result, investors in all the world's issuers tend to get the same risk-adjusted expected return even though issuer disclosure-practices may vary widely from one regulatory area to another. Thus investors in issuers located in any given regulatory area will not receive any better returns whether issuers located in the area disclose at their optimal level or not.[18]

(2) *Entrepreneurs and labor residing in the area are the ultimate beneficiaries.* The higher returns that result from an area's issuers disclosing at their optimal level are real and must, of course, go to someone. Where they go is largely to the suppliers of the issuers' less mobile factors of production. These are the area's entrepreneurs, who will get higher prices when they sell shares in the firms they founded, and labor, who are likely to enjoy higher wages in an economy where capital is allocated and used efficiently. Thus, the persons in the world who primarily benefit from higher real returns when the area's issuers disclose at their optimal level are the area's entrepreneurial talent and

---

17   See I.A supra.
18   See, however, notes 19 and 25 infra.

labor, who are residents of the area, not the investors in these issuers, who may live anywhere.[19]

4.3   The inappropriateness of investor location as a territorial tie

In the ideal case, it is easy to see why investor location would be an inappropriate alternative to issuer location as a rule of territorial tie. Governmental units outside any given regulatory area should not attempt to regulate the disclosure of issuers located within this area even if the securities are sold to, or traded among, residents of the territories governed by these other units. This is because the disclosure level of issuers located within the area does not affect the welfare of residents of the territories governed by these other governmental units. For the same reasons, the government associated with the area should not attempt to regulate the disclosure level of issuers located outside the area even when the shares of these issuers are sold to, or traded among, residents of this area.

This rejection of investor location as a rule of territorial tie would appear to ignore another claimed benefit of mandatory disclosure – investor protection – which will be concentrated where an issuer's investors are concentrated. Investor protection, however, is not a sound justification for mandatory disclosure: disclosure is not necessary to protect investors against either unfair prices or risk. Consider first unfair prices. Under the efficient market hypothesis, securities prices are unbiased whether there is a great deal of informa-

---

19   If the area's issuers represent only a small portion of all equities available to investors in the world, investors would share in none of these gains. The area may be analogous to a single small firm in a perfectly competitive industry. Such a firm's level of production has no effect on price. Following this analogy, what the area produces is investment opportunities-dollars of future expected cash flow-just as the firm produces products. A disclosure improvement's positive effects on managerial motivation and choice of real investment projects will increase the number of dollars of future expected cash flow that the country has to sell. This benefits the entrepreneurs, who are selling the cash flow, and labor, who gain from the overall increase in the area's economic efficiency. See Fox, 'Disclosure in a Globalizing Market', supra note 6 at 2561-69. Because the area is like a small firm, however, the increase in the amount supplied is not great enough to lower the price at which a dollar of future expected cash flow is sold. Thus there is no benefit to investors, the 'buyers' of these dollars of expected future cash flow.
If the area's issuers represent a substantial portion of all equities available to investors in the world, as is the case with the United States, investors will share in some of these gains. A disclosure improvement's increase in the number of dollars of future expected cash flow that the area has to offer would be great enough to lower the price at which a dollar of future expected cash flow is sold, at least slightly. Thus all investors would gain from the improvement. This is equally true of investors from outside the area as for ones within the area and equally true for investors in issuers located within the area as for investors in issuers located outside the area. And it is equally true of disclosure improvements of issuers located within the area whose shares are primarily sold to, or traded among, only foreign investors as it is of issuers located within the area with primarily investors residing in the area. For more detailed discussions of these points, see, idem at 2552-2580 and Fox, 'Political Economy', note 6 supra at 732-739.

tion available about an issuer or very little. In other words, share prices will on average equal the actual value of the shares involved whether issuers are required to produce a lot of disclosure or only a little. Thus greater disclosure is not necessary to protect investors from buying their shares at prices that are, on average, unfair, i.e., greater than their actual values. Now consider risk. With less information available about an issuer, share price, while still unbiased, is less accurate, i.e., it is more likely to be significantly off one way or the other from the share's actual value. For an investor with a less than fully diversified portfolio, less share price accuracy can make the portfolio more risky. High quality disclosure would, to some extent, protect such an investor by reducing this risk. The investor, however, can protect him or herself much more effectively and at less social cost simply by diversifying more.[20]

4.4   The inappropriateness of transaction location as a territorial tie

The location of transactions in an issuer's shares is also an inappropriate rule of territorial tie. The analysis above shows that transaction location is irrelevant to where the benefits and costs of the issuer's disclosure practices are felt. Thus, governmental units outside any given regulatory area should not attempt to regulate the disclosure of issuers located within the area even if the issuers' securities are traded on exchanges located in territories governed by these other outside governmental units. Likewise, the area's government should not attempt to regulate the disclosure level of issuers located outside the area even when the shares of these issuers are traded on an exchange located within the area.

4.5   The inappropriateness of issuer choice

Finally, the analysis above shows that issuer choice, which eliminates any territorial tie at all, is inappropriate as well.[21] Under issuer choice, as proposed by Professor Romano and by Professors Choi and Guzman, each issuer in the world could choose whichever regulatory area's disclosure regime it wished.[22] Romano argues that issuer choice would lead to jurisdictions com-

---

20   In portfolio theory terms, issuer disclosure reduces firm specific ('unsystematic') risk. Firm specific risk can be completely eliminated by sufficient diversification. See B. Banoff, 'Regulatory Subsidies, Efficient Markets, and Shelf Registration: An Analysis of Rule 415', 70 Va.L.Rev. 135 (1984).

21   I have previously written extensively on the question of issuer choice. See Fox, 'Retaining Mandatory Disclosure', supra note 6 and Fox, 'Issuer Choice Debate', supra note 6. I will accordingly keep my remarks here brief. Professor Romano's reactions to these writings can be found in R. Romano, 'The Need for Competition in International Securities Regulation', 2 Theoretical Inquiries L. 387 (2001).

22   R. Romano, 'Empowering Investors', supra note 3 at 2361-62; Choi & Guzman, supra note 3 at 90.

peting to offer issuers regulations that maximize share value.[23] Choi and Guzman argue that it would lead to a diversity of available regimes and permit
each issuer to select the one best suited to its particular needs.[24] Neither argument, however, adequately takes account of the fact that issuer choice would
result in each issuer selecting a regime requiring it to disclose at less than its
socially optimal level. This is because each issuer will make its choice based on
its calculations of the private benefits and costs that would arise from complying with each area's required level of disclosure. As we have seen, an issuer's
private costs of disclosure exceed the social costs of its disclosure, while its private benefits are less than the social benefits. Under the standard assumption
that marginal costs rise and marginal benefits decline, the level of disclosure
at which the marginal private benefits equal the marginal private costs is
therefore lower than the socially optimal level, which is the level at which
marginal social costs equal the marginal social benefits.

Given this market failure, using an issuer location territorial tie will lead
to greater global economic efficiency than issuer choice unless the regulations
adopted by the selected governmental units cause issuers to deviate even
more (just in the opposite direction) from their optimal disclosure levels than
issuer choice would. Such suboptimal regulation is unlikely, given our assumptions. The analysis above shows that the persons who benefit from the
good regulation of the disclosure of issuers located in an area are concentrated in that area. And the governmental unit undertaking this regulation is assumed to be responsive to the needs of its residents.

4.6   Conclusion

In sum, if the world were divided into areas resembling the ideal case above
and each issuer's disclosure was regulated exclusively by the governmental
unit associated with the area in which the issuer was located, an optimal global regulatory structure would exist. The beneficiaries of any given issuer disclosing at its optimal level would be concentrated within the area in which the
issuer is located. The governmental unit associated with this area, which we
have assumed to be a responsive, would have full incentives to set the level of
disclosure at this level.

The disclosure level of issuers located outside a given area will have no effect on the welfare of the area's residents even when shares of these outside issuers are purchased or traded by residents of the area or traded on exchanges
located in the area. Thus, the fact that the governmental unit associated with
the area will not regulate the level of disclosure of these outside issuers is of no
matter to the residents of the area. Such a policy of forbearance also avoids
conflicts with other governmental units. This is because any effort by the

---

23   R. Romano, 'Empowering Investors', supra note 3 at 2362.
24   Choi & Guzman, supra note 3 at 916-17.

area's government to regulate the disclosure of outside issuers will affect the welfare of residents of the territories in which the outside issuers are located without these residents being able to participate as citizens in the process by which the regulations are set.

These conclusions hold over a wide range of assumptions concerning how global equity investing really is. We have assumed so far that equity investing is totally globalized and that investor location plays no role in who invests in which issuers. The conclusions hold at least as strongly, however, if global equity investing has not proceeded to the point where there is one global risk adjusted expected rate of return on capital. If investors exhibit some, or even a great deal of home bias, the concentration of benefits of good regulation at home is simply reinforced.[25]

5   AN OPTIMAL REGULATORY AREA: REAL WORLD CONSIDERATIONS

Real world considerations make it impossible to find a set of regulatory areas that fit the ideal assumed in Part 3. This can be seen by considering an extreme example. Imagine first that there is only one regulatory area: the whole world. In this 'division' of the world, some of the assumptions employed in Part 3 – most trade being within the area, low mobility of labor and entrepreneurs to outside the area, and all issuers operating within the area having their economic centers of gravity there – can be met perfectly. The remaining assump-

---

25   To the extent that globalization has not yet proceeded far enough to fully result in a single global risk adjusted expected rate of return on capital, the remaining market segmentation simply reinforces the point that the gains from an area's issuers disclosing at their optimal levels will be concentrated at home. An area whose issuers disclose at the optimal level of disclosure will have capital utilizing enterprises that produce higher returns net of costs of disclosure. If the single rate assumption is correct, the gains from getting the disclosure level right will primarily be enjoyed by the less mobile claimants on these returns, domestic entrepreneurs and labor, not by the suppliers of capital, who, wherever in the world they live, will at best enjoy a slight increase in the overall global expected return on capital. See supra note 19. If the assumption is incorrect, the reason would be that each area's investors still have a degree of bias against issuers from other areas. In that event, U.S. investors, for example, might share disproportionately in the gains from moving the U.S. issuer disclosure level toward its optimal level. The bias of foreign investors against U.S. issuers would mean that the increase in the number of expected dollars of future cash flow resulting from the change in required disclosure would be offered to a somewhat restricted market and push the price for them down more for U.S. investors than for other investors. Idem. To the extent that a U.S. issuer has U.S. shareholders, the fact that U.S. investors will share disproportionately in the gains from optimal disclosure simply creates an additional U.S. interest in the level of the issuer's disclosure. As for U.S. issuers whose shares are sold to and traded among only foreign investors, entrepreneurs and labor in the United States would, just as if there were a single global expected rate of return on capital, enjoy most of the gains from optimal disclosure. See Fox, 'Securities Disclosure in a Globalizing Market', supra note 6 at 2561-2569. Thus, in this example, the United States interest in the disclosure behavior of this second set of issuers would be as strong as it is shown to be under the assumption in the text.

tions – the governmental unit associated with the regulatory area being responsive to the needs of the residents of the area and capable of effective application and enforcement of its rules and all issuers having the same optimal level of disclosure – would, however, be wildly off the mark. Now imagine that we subdivide the world into smaller regulatory areas. As we make the regulatory areas smaller, the failure of this second set of assumptions is likely to become less severe. Problems begin to arise, however, with the first set of assumptions: there will be too much cross-border trade, too much factor mobility across area lines and too many issuers with no clear economic center of gravity. Thus, whatever the chosen set of regulatory areas, at least some of Part 3's five assumptions will not be met.

In this Part, we examine the implications of this breakdown in assumptions. This examination has two functions. First, it helps identify where the optimal point of tradeoff is between the advantages of larger sized areas and the advantages of smaller sized areas under various circumstances prevailing in different parts of the world. Second, it reveals that the breakdown of the assumptions, while making the world a messy place with no ideal solution to its division into regulatory areas, does not resurrect the case for using investor location or transaction location as the territorial tie to determine which government regulates which issuer, nor does it resurrect the case for issuer choice.

5.1   *Assumptions that fail as the regulatory areas grow smaller*

(1) *Trans-border trade.* The smaller a regulatory area, the greater the likelihood that there will be a substantial amount of trans-border trade. This creates problems even if labor and entrepreneurs are still relatively immobile. With substantial trans-border trade, many of the issuers located in a given area will count among their competitors and major suppliers and customers issuers located outside the area.

The existence of these out-of-area competitors, major suppliers and major customers biases the area's government downward when it compares requiring a higher level of disclosure to a lower one. The government knows that if it chooses the higher level, each of the area's issuers will both suffer costs and enjoy benefits. It will suffer the costs associated with *all* of its competitors, major suppliers and major customers finding out the additional required information. This is so whether the competitors, suppliers or customers are located inside the area or outside. It will benefit, however, from finding out the additional required information only from those of its competitors, major suppliers and major customers that are located inside the area and hence subject to the higher disclosure requirement. The area's issuers' competitors, major suppliers and major customers located outside the area are the ones who enjoy the rest of the benefits from the higher level of disclosure. Thus, there is a trans-border externality associated with the national government's decision to set the level of disclosure for its issuers. The government will choose the level that will maximize the welfare of its residents. The government will not account for the portion of the benefits from additional disclosure that would be enjoyed by its issuers' foreign competitors, major suppliers and major customers, just for the costs to its issuers of these outsiders learning the information.

Utilizing a larger regulatory area corresponding to a higher level of government reduces or eliminates this bias by internalizing some or all of these information externalities,[26] but doing so will entail the disadvantages of larger regulatory areas discussed below. This dilemma cannot be resolved by utilizing a smaller area but choosing investor nationality or transaction location as a territorial tie instead of issuer location. While choosing such ties would subject some issuers outside the area to regulation by the area's government, the set of outside issuers that would be regulated would bear no systematic relation to the ones whose disclosure levels affect the welfare of persons within the area. This is because regulation would be the result of an outside issuer having investors residing within the area or trades in its shares occurring on the area's exchanges. It would not be because of the outside issuer's status as competitor, major supplier or major customer of issuers located within the area.

The dilemma would also not be resolved by combining a smaller regulatory area with issuer choice. Because of the downward bias caused by transborder information externalities, regulation based on issuer location only partially, not fully, corrects for the market failure caused by the overall information externalities that justify regulation in the first place.[27] With issuer choice, this market failure would not be corrected at all.[28]

(2) *Factor mobility.* The smaller the regulatory area, the greater the likelihood that there will be significant mobility in labor and entrepreneurial talent across the area's borders. The greater this mobility, the more the returns to labor and entrepreneurs residing within the regulatory area will be affected by the demand for them outside the regulatory area. In essence, the greater the mobility, the more that the effective market for these factors can be seen as covering a territory larger than the regulatory area.

Because the returns to labor and entrepreneurs residing within the regulatory area are affected by demand outside the regulatory area, the benefits

---

26   I discuss these points in more detail elsewhere. See, Fox, 'Political Economy', supra note 6 at 747-749, 762-64.

27   See I.B supra.

28   See III.E supra. E. Kitch and S. Choi have each expressed the concern that the issuer location approach is undermined by these trans-border externalities. E.W. Kitch, 'Proposals for Reform of Securities Regulation: An Overview', 41 Va. J. Int'l L. 629, 651 (2001); S.J. Choi, 'Assessing Regulatory Responses to Securities Market Globalization', 2 Theoretical Inquiries L. 613, 646 (2001). They are in a sense correct, but they do not follow through to see its ultimate implications. The defect in my approach is that the system would only partially correct for a market failure that their issuer choice approach would not correct at all.

from regulation that prompts issuers located within the area to disclose at their optimal level are deconcentrated. Entrepreneurs and labor residing outside the area enjoy some of the benefit because of increased demand due to the more efficient utilization of capital by issuers within the area. At the same time, where issuers located outside the area are not subject to regulation that prompts them to disclose at their optimal levels, the returns to entrepreneurs and labor residing inside the area are lower than they otherwise would be.

This deconcentration of the benefits reduces the political incentive for the government associated with the regulatory area to undertake good regulation. This effect is different, and less pernicious, than the downward bias cause by cross-border trade. The government still does best by its residents by setting the required level of disclosure equal to socially optimal level of the issuers located within its area. The gain for doing so, however, is less and so other matters are more likely to take political priority. Thus, there is less likelihood that the government will make the full effort needed to get the disclosure level right.

This problem created by the breakdown of the labor and entrepreneurial talent assumptions would not be solved by utilizing investor nationality or transaction location instead of issuer location as the territorial tie. This is because the set of outside issuers that would be subject to the area's disclosure regulation under these approaches would bear no systematic relation to the ones whose disclosure levels would affect demand for entrepreneurial talent and labor residing within the area. Nor would the problem be solved by issuer choice. Again, issuer choice fails to address in the first place the market failure that prompts the need for regulation to correct what would otherwise be a suboptimal level of disclosure. The failure of the low mobility assumption simply means that the global regulatory structure will not be fully effective at correcting this market failure than would otherwise be the case.

(3) *Issuers with no clear economic center of gravity.* The smaller the regulatory areas, the more issuers in the world will have no clear economic center of gravity. This breaks down the assumption that every issuer has a clear economic center of gravity in one regulatory area or another. The consequences of this breakdown are very similar to those of the breakdown of the assumption of no significant labor and entrepreneurial talent mobility.

The benefits from an issuer with no clear economic center of gravity disclosing at its optimal level are experienced in significant part by persons residing in more than one area. If the issuer is regulated by a government associated with one of these areas, the benefits will be deconcentrated. This deconcentration reduces the political incentive for the government to undertake good regulation. In addition, even if the government does strive to regulate in a way that prompts its purely domestic issuers (i.e., issuers that clearly are located within the area) to disclose at their optimal level, the regulation is less likely to be right for the issuer with no clear center of gravity, which may well have a corporate governance arrangement that is different from that of most of the purely domestic issuers. A different corporate governance arrangement can imply a different (higher or lower) optimal level of disclosure.[29]

If the disclosure of the issuer with no clear economic center of gravity is regulated by governments associated with more than one of these areas, compliance by the issuer with multiple sets of regulation can be costly in terms of real resources. Moreover, while regulation by multiple governments decreases the chance that the issuer will end up disclosing at a level below its optimal level, it increases the chance it will be required to disclose above its optimal level.

Again, neither the investor location nor transaction location approaches have features that would address these problems. Issuer choice would have the advantage of assuring that no issuer would be regulated by a jurisdiction that requires disclosure above its optimal level because no issuer would choose such a jurisdiction. However, because issuer choice does not correct the market failure that leads to the need for mandatory disclosure in the first place, it is likely to result in most issuers being regulated by jurisdictions that require disclosure below their optimal levels.

5.2   *Assumptions that fail as the regulatory areas grow larger*

(1) *Responsive government with effective enforcement.* The larger the regulatory area, the less likely it is that the governmental unit regulating it will be responsive to the needs of the residents of the area. This proposition reflects the ideas behind the concept of 'subsidiarity' that regulation should be undertaken by the lowest level of government capable of handling the task properly. Citizen access to governments serving large numbers of geographically dispersed people is bound to be more difficult, everything else being equal. Also, while up to a point there may be economies of scale in terms of the resources necessary to develop a certain level of expertise on the part of governmental officials, beyond that point it is harder for government officials to be knowledgeable about the more diverse set of conditions likely to prevail in a regulatory area containing more people and a larger amount of territory.

These problems become most extreme when regulation is undertaken by some kind of multinational entity. Current political realities mean that national governments and transnational bureaucracies each need to play a large role in the governance of such entities if they are to have any meaningful influence. These intricacies lead to concerns about the 'democratic deficit' that critics claim is displayed by multinational bodies such as the European Community and the World Trade Organization. Such multinational entities are also likely to have particularly great problems effectively enforcing their rules. Even when they have their own enforcement authorities and institutions to apply their rules to specific cases, they are likely to require use of the legal systems of

---

29   See IV.B.2 infra.

their member states to impose any effective sanctions on persons they find to have violated these rules.

(2) *Issuers having the same optimal level of disclosure.* The larger the regulatory areas, the more likely it is that the assumption that all issuers have the same socially optimal level of disclosure will break down significantly. There are important differences among issuers worldwide in terms of the level of disclosure that will maximize the returns, net of the costs of this disclosure, that their capital utilizing productive activities generate. These differences in their socially optimal disclosure levels are significantly related to where the issuers are located. This is because differences in optimal disclosure levels arise out of differences in corporate governance arrangements and corporate governance arrangements tend to be different in different parts of the world. Disclosure is of more value, for example, in a market centered economy than in a bank centered one, and therefore, despite the higher costs of greater disclosure, issuers in a market centered economy will tend to have a higher socially optimal level of disclosure.[30] A single mandated disclosure level covering the issuers located in a larger regulatory area will therefore be further away on average from each individual issuer's socially optimal disclosure level.

Neither the investor location nor transaction location approaches have features that would address these problems. Each of these approaches would lead, for some issuers within a larger regulatory area, to their disclosure being regulated by a government outside the area. There would be no systematic relation, however, between the issuers subject to an outside government's regulatory regime and the issuers within the area that had socially optimal disclosure levels particularly far from that of the average issuer in the area. Again, relative to a larger regulatory area with issuer location as the territorial tie, issuer choice would have the benefit assuring that no issuer would be regulated by a jurisdiction requiring disclosure above the issuer's optimal level. Also again, however, issuer choice is likely to result in most issuers being regulated by jurisdictions requiring disclosure below their optimal levels.

6   CONCLUSION: APPLICATIONS

The choice of regulatory area for securities disclosure is, as noted in the introduction, a hot issue today around the world. The United States, which decided in the 1930s to move from an exclusively state based system to one primarily relying on federal regulation, is being urged by the proponents of issuer choice to reconsider and give issuers the option to choose among a reinvigorated set of state regulatory regimes. Canada is currently debating whether to

---

30   See Fox, 'Political Economy', supra note 6 at 758-760; A.N. Licht, 'International Diversity in Securities Regulation: Roadblocks on the Way to Convergence', 20 Cardozo L. Rev. 227, 237-253 (1998).

enlarge the role of the federal government in a system that has traditionally left disclosure regulation primarily to the provinces, a switch undertaken by Australia in the 1980s. The countries of Europe are deciding as well the extent to which the European Community, rather than its member states, should determine securities disclosure in Europe. Of the participants in the Canadian and European debates who urge that provincial or state level regulation be maintained, some simply seek to maintain the status quo. Others are proposing at the same time changes that would convert the regulatory structures for Canada and Europe into *de facto* issuer choice systems. There are also calls for making the whole world a single regulatory area where uniform standards are set for issuers around the world either by a multinational entity or through harmonization of state level requirements.

The theory of optimal regulatory areas set out here establishes a framework for analysing all these debates. While more definitive answers would require in-depth research concerning the specific features of each of the situations, application of certain commonly known facts is at least suggestive of the proper outcomes.

6.1   The United States and Canada

(1) *The United States.* Putting issuer choice aside for a moment, there seems to be no case for returning the United States to a state based regulatory structure. A large percentage of trade in goods and services in each state is with persons outside the state. There is sufficient mobility of labor and entrepreneurial talent between states that the market for them has a substantial national component. There is no strong evidence that state regulators would be significantly more responsive to the needs of their residents in the area of disclosure regulation than would be federal authorities. In the typical state, much of the economic activity is undertaken by issuers that cannot be characterized as having their economic center of gravity in the state. Whatever variation exists in the corporate governance structures of issuers across the country, little of it is geographically related. Thus, there is no reason to believe that issuers from one state would on average have a different optimal level of disclosure than issuers from another state.

A reinvigoration of state disclosure regulation would be called for if the United States were to adopt issuer choice. As we have seen, however, the economic efficiency case for mandatory disclosure is based on the market failure that arises from each issuer's private benefits from disclosure being less than the social benefits and its private costs being higher than the social costs. These divergences result in unregulated issuers disclosing at levels below their social optimum. Issuer choice does not correct for this failure. Thus, issuer choice cannot be justified on economic efficiency grounds unless the regulations adopted by the federal government have caused issuers to deviate even more (just in the opposite direction) from their optimal disclosure levels

than issuer choice would. I have argued elsewhere that the proponents of issuer choice have not made a persuasive argument that this is the case.[31]

(2) *Canada.* The economic efficiency case for Canada to be a single regulatory
area is strong, though not as strong as for the United States to be one. Quebec
and the western provinces may be more economically separate and distinct in
their corporate governance arrangements from the rest of the country than is
the case with any of the regions of the United States. Still, the overall situation
in Canada still seems close to that of the United States. There is a great deal of
trade between provinces and much mobility of labor and entrepreneurial talent across provincial lines. Many corporations have significant operations
across the country or at least in multiple provinces. The federal government
appears reasonably responsive and effective in its enforcement capabilities.
Any corporate governance differences among the country's issuers do not appear to be highly correlated with geography.

   A driving force behind reform is the inconvenience of the current regulatory structure whereby the provinces are the regulatory areas and investor location and transaction location are used in part as rules of territorial tie. This
can force issuers to comply with multiple disclosure regimes in order to participate in the national capital market. One solution to this problem is to move
to a single large national regulatory area, as suggested here. Other solutions
are to maintain the provinces as the regulatory areas but either to adopt issuer
location as the sole rule of territorial tie or to adopt issuer choice.

   Each of these alternative solutions would be as good for eliminating the
costly need to comply with multiple regimes as would be national regulation.
The theory of optimal regulatory areas developed here, however, suggests
that national regulation is superior to provincial regulation with issuer location as the sole territorial tie. The other alternative, issuer choice, cannot correct the market failures that lead unregulated issuers to disclose at a level
below what is socially optimal. As previously noted, issuer choice thus cannot
be justified on economic efficiency grounds unless the regulations that can be
expected to be adopted by the Canadian federal government would cause issuers to deviate even more from their optimal disclosure levels than would issuer choice.

   These potential problems with issuer choice are important to note. One
possible route that reform could take would be to retain the provinces as the
regulatory areas and to use issuer location to be the rule of territorial tie, but to
equate an issuer's location with the issuer's place of incorporation rather than
with its economic center of gravity. This sort of arrangement would establish
a *de facto* regime of issuer choice. An issuer could choose for its place of incorporation or reincorporation the province that has the disclosure rules it most
prefers and then go on to do business anywhere in Canada.

---

31   Fox, 'Retaining Mandatory Disclosure', supra note 6 at 1416-19.

(3) *A single combined regulatory area.* This discussion of the United States and Canada can be concluded with a provocative thought. A consideration of the five factors that need to be traded off in the construction of optimal disclosure areas suggests that perhaps the United States and Canada should be combined into a single regulatory area. The two economies are certainly highly integrated with free trade and significant labor and entrepreneurial talent mobility between the two. Their corporate governance systems are relatively similar. Establishing a responsive and effective regulatory entity might be difficult, but the closest substitute, harmonization of disclosure requirements, might be quite possible. Indeed, significant steps have already been taken in this regard. In 1991, the U.S. Securities and Exchange Commission (the SEC) adopted rules and forms implementing the Canadian multi-jurisdictional disclosure system, under which substantial Canadian issuers could offer securities in the United States based primarily on their Canadian disclosure filings.[32] The negotiations between the SEC and the various Canadian provincial securities commissioners leading up to implementation of the system resulted in the major provinces adding requirements that resembled what was already required in the United States, suggesting a certain kind of harmonization.[33]

6.2   Europe

The countries of Europe are also currently deciding the extent to which the European Community, rather than its member states, should determine securities disclosure in Europe. It is a close question whether there should be a single regulatory area encompassing the whole Community or multiple regulatory areas corresponding with the member states. While a much more detailed exploration is required to come to any definitive conclusions, several features of the situation stand out.

While the ambition of the Community is to have a highly integrated economy with large amounts of cross-border trade and high mobility of labor and entrepreneurial talent, the reality may lag behind. Overall, the level of economic integration appears not to be as great as in the United States or Canada, particularly with respect to the portion of the Community's territory constituting the new members. On the other hand, there is far more integration among the member states than among the regulatory areas in the ideal case discussed in Part 3 or even, as a general matter, between member states and countries outside the Community.

Compared to Canada or the United States, the European Community displays considerably more diversity in corporate governance arrangements.

---

32   Sec. Act Rel 6902, 49 SEC Dock. 260 (1991). The issuers are required, however, to provide a reconciliation between the published accounts and U.S. GAAP. They are subject to the U.S. liability system.

33   See E.F. Greene (et.al), *U.S. Regulation of the International Securities and Derivatives Market* §8.01 n. 1 (3rd ed. 1996).

Thus the U.K.'s market centered corporate governance looks quite different from Germany's bank centered one. And Italy, with its domination by family companies and relatively low protections for minority shareholders, looks quite different from either of the other two.

The Community level governmental institutions, with the continuing large role played by member states and by the central bureaucracy, may be substantially less responsive to the needs of its residents than are most member states' governments, whose top officials are chosen pursuant to direct democratic elections.

In sum, there are no simple answers to the question of the optimal regulatory area or areas for Europe. The underlying level of economic integration provides substantial arguments for a single regulatory area. The level of trade is sufficiently high to cause the kind of information externalities that would result in a significant downward bias in the level of disclosure that a member state is likely to require of its issuers. There is also enough labor and entrepreneurial talent mobility to reduce the incentives of member state governments to try to get the regulations right. On the other hand, the institutional factors argue the other way. The very large differences among countries in corporate governance arrangements suggest that their issuers have considerably different optimal levels of disclosure. And the bureaucracy in Brussels, that would be operating a Community wide regime, appears to be the subject of considerable resentment for its lack of responsiveness.

6.3   A single global regulatory area

The theory of optimal regulatory areas developed here strongly argues against a single global regulatory area, at least for all but the truly multinational issuers such as Daimler-Chrysler and BP-Amoco. Despite all the talk of globalization, we fall short today of having a truly integrated global economy.[34] This suggests that while the problems caused by the breakdown of the assumptions of low trade, low labor and entrepreneurial talent mobility and issuers with no economic center of gravity are substantial when we use countries or regional economic communities as the regulatory areas, they are not so substantial as to completely vitiate the logic set out in the ideal case in Part 3.

We just noted that problems relating to institutional factors raise serious questions concerning the desirability of a single European regulatory area. Such problems are far more grave when we contemplate the whole globe

---

34   Most of the world's issuers, even ones labeled 'multinational', for example have, still a distinct nationality of this sort in some country (particularly if the EC is for these purposes treated as a single country). In 1990, profits from foreign operations of U.S. corporations amounted to only about one-sixth of all corporate profits. See NIPA Table 6.16C, 72 Surv. Current Bus. No. 12 at 14 (1992). In 1989, overseas assets of even U.S. corporations designated as 'multinational' were only about one-fifth of their total assets, see J. Lowe & R. Mataloni, Jr.,'U.S. Direct Investment Abroad: 1989 Benchmark Survey Results', 71 Surv. Current Bus. No. 10 at 29 (1991) (data from Table 1).

being a single regulatory area. Setting up from scratch a responsive, effective multinational body to administer such a system would be a daunting task. Moreover, unlike with a nationally based system, dealings between the entrepreneurs or managers of the issuers and the officials regulating them would often not be between persons who share a common culture, language and understanding of business practices. Secondly, there are wide differences in corporate governance arrangements around the world that involve additional dimensions even beyond what we have seen in the comparison of the U.K., Germany and Italy.

In sum, the degree of world economic integration is not so complete as to vitiate the logic of national regulation and compel movement to a single regime. And the institutional factors argue strongly against such a move.

Personalia

Donald I. Baker, the senior partner of Baker & Miller, is a former Assistant Attorney General in charge of the Antitrust Division at the U.S. Department of Justice. He has also been a Professor of Law at Cornell University and has written two treatises and numerous articles and speeches. Mr. Baker is regularly honored by several national and international publications and organizations for his contributions to the antitrust field. Mr. Baker and his firm represented the Governments of the United Kingdom, Australia and Switzerland as amicus curiae in *Sosa v. Alvarez* and represents one of the petitioners in *Empagram* in the U.S. Supreme Court.

Pieter H.F. Bekker, Ph.D., LL.B. Leiden University, LL.M. Harvard Law School, practises public international law and arbitration at White & Case LLP in New York City. A former staff lawyer in the Registry of the International Court of Justice (1992-94), he chairs the Committee on Transnational Dispute Resolution of the International Law Association's American Branch and has served, since 1995, as ICJ Reporter for the American Society of International Law, whose Annual Meeting he co-chaired in April 2000. He is the author of three books and some 80 articles and notes on international law.

Alex. F.M. Brenninkmeijer (born 1951 in Amsterdam) is Professor of Administrative and Constitutional Law at the University of Leiden (NL) and former dean of the faculty of law. In 2002 he was appointed at the Albeda-chair for the law of civil service and ADR. Currently he is director of the research programme on conflict-resolution of the E.M. Meijers Institute of Leiden University. He is active as a mediator and is editor and co-author of the Handboek-Mediation and author of several articles on this subject. Brenninkmeijer is editor of several legal periodicals in The Netherlands among which the Nederlands Juristenblad (Dutch Legal Journal, weekly).

Mielle Bulterman is a Senior Lecturer in European law at the Europa Instituut of Leiden University. In 2001 she obtained her doctoral degree at Utrecht University for her doctoral thesis on human rights in the treaty relations of the European Community. Her current research interests include the implementation of UN sanctions by the European Union and the human rights protection with European and economic law.

Merritt B. Fox is Michael E. Paterson Professor of Law at the Columbia Law School. He is a graduate of Yale College and of Yale Law School; he also received a Ph.D. in economics from Yale University. His teaching and scholarly interests are in the areas of corporate and securities law, corporate and international finance, and law and economics. Before joining the Columbia Law School faculty, he practiced law with the New York City firm of Cleary, Gottlieb, Steen & Hamilton and taught at Yale University, Fordham Law School, Indiana University Law School in Bloomington and the University of Michigan Law School. At Michigan, he was the Director of the School's Center for International and Comparative Law. He is the co-director for Corporate Governance Studies for the William Davidson Institute at the University of Michigan Business School and past chair of the Business Associations section of the American Association of Law Schools.

Gustav J.J. Heerma van Voss (1957) is Professor of Labour Law and Social Security at Leiden University. In 1992 he defended his Ph.D.thesis on dismissal law in the Netherlands and Japan. He published on Dismissal law, Employer's obligations, Employee's Co-determination, the Employment Contract and European Labour Law. He also acts as chairman of labour arbitration committees, advises the Government and private parties and lectures for unions, works councils, employers' associations, lawyers and judges. He is editor of various Dutch Law Journals and Handbooks on Labour Law and Social Security.

Angus Johnston is a University Lecturer in Law at the University of Cambridge and a Tutor and Director of Studies in Law at Trinity Hall, Cambridge. He teaches and researches in the fields (*inter alia*) of Tort Law and European Union Law, with particular emphasis on the Constitutional structure of the European Union, the functioning of its judicial system and its law and policy in the Energy and Competition fields. His previous publications include (with Alan Dashwood) *The Future of the Judicial System of the European Union* (2001) and (with Simon Deakin and Basil Markesinis) *Markesinis and Deakin's Tort Law* (5th edn., 2003).

Rick A. Lawson holds the Kirchheiner Chair on Protection of the Integrity of the Individual at the *Europa Instituut* of Leiden University. He is a member of the EU Network of Independent Experts on Human Rights and editor of *NJCM-Bulletin*, the leading Dutch human-rights review. In 1999 he obtained a doctorate degree *cum laude* in Leiden for his PhD thesis *The European Convention on Human Rights and the European Communities – Towards a Responsibility Regime relating to the Conduct of International Organisations.*

Joseph W. Marx is a senior associate at White & Case LLP's Frankfurt, Germany office. He has previously worked as a Speech Writer in the Presidential Reelection Campaign of former U.S. President George Bush, as a Legislative Assistant and Speech Writer in the Office of United States Senator Thad Cochran and as Foreign Policy Assistant in the Office of former U.S. President Richard Nixon. His publications include the drafts of various foreign policy and political articles for Presidents Nixon and Bush in national newspapers and various articles in German newspapers on U.S. securities laws and Sarbanes-Oxley of 2002 Act issues. He also assisted former President Richard Nixon in drafting his *Seize the Moment: America's Role in One Superpower World* and *Beyond Peace*.

Johan Meeusen (Dr. iur. University of Antwerp, 1997; LL.M. University of California at Berkeley, 1993) is Professor of European Union Law and Comparative Private International Law at the University of Antwerp (Belgium). He is the author of numerous publications in the fields of EU law and private international law. In 2002, Professor Meeusen was granted an *ad personam* Jean Monnet Chair (2002-2005) by the European Commission.

Ralf Michaels is Associate Professor of Law at Duke University. Previously, he held positions as a fellow at the Max Planck Institute for Foreign and International Private Law in Hamburg, Germany, and at Harvard Law School. His current research deals with the impact of globalization on private international law, and alternatives to state-based approaches to conflict of laws problems

W. Todd Miller is the managing partner of Baker & Miller PLLC, a boutique firm that focuses a large portion of its practice on all aspects of antitrust counseling and litigation. Mr. Miller is also an adjunct professor at the Washington College of Law at American University, where he teaches a course on International and Comparative Antitrust Law. Mr. Miller has been internationally recognized as a leading antitrust attorney by such publications as *The Global Competition Review* and speaks and writes frequently on a variety of antitrust related topics.

Edward Powles is completing his professional legal training with Allen & Overy in Paris after having spent a year and a half in their London office. He graduated from Trinity Hall, Cambridge where he also read for the LL.M., focusing primarily on theoretical and practical aspects of public and private international law. His current interests include the law of restitution in the commercial sphere, as well as continued research into phenomena relating to constitutionalisation in public international law.

Kai I. Rebane is a senior associate at White & Case LLP's New York Office. After graduating from the Georgetown University, School of Foreign Policy in 1993, she graduated from the Fordham University School of Law in 1997. She has published on extradition and individual rights and has extensive legal experience in international equity and debt capital markets transactions.

Pippa Rogerson is a Senior Lecturer at Cambridge University Law Faculty, a Fellow, Tutor and Director of Studies in law at Gonville and Caius College, and a Solicitor of the Supreme Court in England and Wales. Her research interests are in conflict of laws and company law and she has published work in both areas.

Cedric Ryngaert is research fellow (Ph. D.) at the Institute for International Law (University of Leuven). His research focuses on jurisdictional issues of the relationship between the United States and the European Union and its Member States, as well as on legal and institutional issues of the process of globalisation.

Natalia Shelkoplyas LL.M., is Head of Legal Department at Amsterdam Trade Bank. She obtained a Ph.D (Tilburg University, the Netherlands) in Application of EC Law in Arbitration Proceedings. Her special research interests lie in the influence of European Community law on private contractual relationships and national civil procedures.

Piet Jan Slot is Professor of European and Economic Law at the University of Leiden, director of the Europa Instituut and editor of the Common Market Law Review. His areas of research and publication are: the substantive law of the EC, state aid, competition law, transport, energy and jurisdictional issues.

Leen de Smet is assistant at the Institute for International Law of Leuven University.

Patrick Wautelet is Professor of Law at the Law School of the University of Liège, where he teaches conflict of laws and international civil litigation. He is also a member of the Brussels Bar. Mr Wautelet has published extensively in the fields of conflict of laws, international litigation, international bankruptcy and international sales law. Mr. Wautelet has been a visiting researcher at Harvard Law School (2001-2002) where he worked with Prof. A. T. von Mehren. He also served as a recording secretary of the Special Commission of the Hague Conference for Private International Law dealing with jurisdiction and recognition and enforcement of foreign judgments.

Jan Wouters is Professor of International Law and the Law of International Organizations, Director of the Institute for International Law, KU Leuven; Of Counsel, Linklaters De Bandt, Brussels. He has published widely on international, European, company and financial law. He is the editor of the International Encyclopedia of Intergovernmental Organizations.

The following titles have appeared in the series published by the E.M. Meyers Institute for Legal Research of the Leiden University Faculty of law:

MI-1   T. Barkhuysen, *Artikel 13 EVRM: effectieve nationale rechtsbescherming bij schending van mensenrechten* (diss. Leiden), Lelystad: Koninklijke Vermande 1998, ISBN 90 5458 530 7.

MI-2   E.E.V. Lenos, *Bestuurlijke sanctietoepassing en strafrechtelijke waarborgen in de sociale zekerheid* (diss. Leiden), Lelystad: Koninklijke Vermande 1998, ISBN 90 5458 558 7.

MI-3   M.V. Polak (red.), *Geschillenbeslechting naar behoren. Algemene beginselen van behoorlijke geschillenbeslechting in traditionele en alternatieve procesvormen*, Deventer: Kluwer 1998, ISBN 90 2683 298 2.

MI-4   C.E. Smith, *Feit en rechtsnorm* (diss. Leiden), Maastricht: Shaker 1998, ISBN 90 4230 045 0.

MI-5   S.D. Lindenbergh, *Smartengeld* (diss. Leiden), Deventer: Kluwer 1998, ISBN 90 2683 324 5.

MI-6   P.B. Cliteur, G.J.J. Heerma van Voss, H.M.T. Holtmaat & A.H.J. Schmidt (red.), *Sociale cohesie en het recht*, Lelystad: Koninklijke Vermande 1998, ISBN 90 5458 618 4.

MI-7   M.H. Elferink, *Verwijzingen in wetgeving. Over de publiekrechtelijke en auteursrechtelijke status van normalisatienormen* (diss. Leiden), Deventer: Kluwer 1998, ISBN 90 2683 352 0.

MI-8   P.T.C. van Kampèn, *Expert Evidence Compared. Rules and Practices in the Dutch and American Criminal Justice System* (diss. Leiden), Antwerpen/Groningen: Intersentia 1998, ISBN 90 5095 049 3.

MI-9   N.C. van Steijn, *Mobil Oil III, een uitvinding of een ontdekking? Een onderzoek naar de gevolgen van de Mobil Oil III-beschikking van het Europees Octrooi Bureau van Nederland*, Den Haag: Jongbloed 1999, ISBN 90 7006 221 6.

MI-10   R.A. Lawson, *Het EVRM en de Europese Gemeenschappen; bouwstenen voor een aansprakelijkheidsregime voor het optreden van internationale organisaties* (diss. Leiden), Deventer: Kluwer 1999, ISBN 90 2683 463 2.

MI-11   J. Junger-Tas & J.N. van Kesteren, *Bullying and Delinquency in a Dutch School Population*, New York: Kugler Publications 1999 (or PB 97747, 2509 GC Den Haag), ISBN 90 6299 171 8.

MI-12   T. Hartlief & C.J.J.M. Stolker (red.), *Contractvrijheid*, Deventer: Kluwer 1999, ISBN 90 2683 511 6.

MI-13   P.W. Brouwer, M.M. Henket, A.M. Hol & H. Kloosterhuis (red.), *Drie dimensies van recht: rechtstheorie, rechtsgeleerdheid, rechtspraktijk*, Den Haag: Boom Juridische uitgevers 1999, ISBN 90 5454 026 5.

MI-14   T. Hartlief, *De vrijheid beschermd*, Deventer: Kluwer 1999, ISBN 90 2683 567 1.

MI-15   H.B. Krans, *Schadevergoeding bij wanprestatie*, Deventer: Kluwer 1999, ISBN 90 2683 557 4.

MI-16   H.I. Sagel-Grande & M.V. Polak (eds.), *Models of conflict resolution*, Antwerpen: Maklu 1999, ISBN 90 6215 651 7.

MI-17   H.J.Th.M. Van Roosmalen, *The King can do no wrong. Overheidsaansprakelijkheid naar Engels recht onder invloed van de jurisprudentie van het Hof van Justitie van de Europese Gemeenschappen*, Den Haag: Jongbloed 2000, ISBN 90 7006 223 2.

MI-18   R.A. Lawson & E. Myjer, *50 jaar EVRM*, Leiden: Stichting NJCM-Boekerij 2000, ISBN 90 6750 038 0.

MI-19   C.B. van der Net, *Grenzen stellen op het Internet. Aansprakelijkheid van Internet-providers en rechtsmacht*, Deventer: Gouda Quint 2000, ISBN 90 2683 622 8.

MI-20   R.P. Raas, *Het Benelux Merkenrecht en de Eerste Merkenrichtlijn: overeenstemming over verwarring?*, Den Haag: Boom Juridische uitgevers 2000, ISBN 90 5454 028 1.

MI-21   R.H. Haveman, P. Ölçer, Th.A. de Roos & A.L.J. van Strien (red.), *Seks, zeden en strafrecht*, Deventer: Gouda Quint 2000, ISBN 90 3870 798 3.

MI-22   W.J. Zwalve, *Qui solvit alii. Beschouwingen over betaling aan inningsonbevoegden*, Den Haag: Boom Juridische uitgevers 2000, ISBN 90 5454 033 8.

MI-23 Hans Krabbendam & Hans Martien ten Napel (eds.), *Regulating Morality. A Comparison of the Role of the State in Mastering the Mores in the Netherlands and the United States*, Antwerpen: Maklu 2000, ISBN 90 6215 736 X.

MI-24 Jan-Peter Loof, Hendrik Ploeger & Arine van der Steur, *The right to property. The influence of Article 1 Protocol no. 1 ECHR on several fields of domestic law*, Maastricht: Shaker Publishing 2000, ISBN 90 4230 103 1.

MI-25 D.L.M.T. Dankers-Hagenaars, *Op het spoor van de concessie. Een onderzoek naar het rechtskarakter van de concessie in Nederland en in Frankrijk*, Den Haag: Boom Juridische uitgevers 2000, ISBN 90 5454 042 7.

MI-26 T. Hartlief & M.M. Mendel (red.), *Verzekering en maatschappij. Juridische beschouwingen over de maatschappelijke rol van verzekeringen en verzekeringsmaatschappijen*, Deventer: Kluwer 2000, ISBN 90 2683 713 5.

MI-27 J.E.M. Polak, *Effectieve bestuursrechtspraak. Enkele beschouwingen over het vermogen van de bestuursrechtspraak geschillen materieel te beslechten*, (oratie Leiden), Deventer: Kluwer 2000, ISBN 90 2715 268 3.

MI-28 H.F. Munneke, *Recht en samenleving in de Nederlandse Antillen, Aruba en Suriname. Opstellen over recht en sociale cohesie*, Nijmegen: Wolf Legal Productions 2001, ISBN 90 5850 011 X.

MI-29 C.P.M. Cleiren, *Geding buiten geding. Een confrontatie van het geding voor de strafrechter met strafrechtelijke ADR-vormen en mediation*, (oratie Leiden), Deventer: Kluwer 2001 ISBN 90 3870 833 5.

MI-31 M.H. Wissink, *Richtlijnconforme interpretatie van burgerlijk recht*, Deventer: Kluwer 2001, ISBN 90 2683 763 1.

MI-32 X.E. Kramer, *Het kort geding in internationaal perspectief. Een rechtsvergelijkende studie naar de voorlopige voorziening in het internationaal privaatrecht*, Deventer: Kluwer 2001, ISBN 90 2683 784 4.

MI-33 P.B. Cliteur & V. Van Den Eeckhout, *Multiculturalisme, cultuurrelativisme en sociale cohesie*, Den Haag: Boom Juridische uitgevers 2001, ISBN 90 5454 093 1.

MI-34 C.P.M. Cleiren & G.K. Schoep (red.), *Rechterlijke samenwerking*, Deventer: Gouda Quint 2001, ISBN 90 3870 848 3.

MI-35 A.C. 't Hart, *Hier gelden wetten! Over strafrecht, openbaar ministerie en multiculturalisme*, Deventer: Gouda Quint 2001, ISBN 90 3870 847 5.

MI-36 U Drobnig, H.I. Sagel-Grande & H.J. Snijders, *Neue Entwicklungen im deutschen und niederländischen Involvenzrecht sowie Kreditsicherheiten an Mobilien*, Amsterdam: Rozenberg Publishers 2001, ISBN 90 6170 546 8.

MI-37 E.R. Muller & C.J.J.M. Stolker, *Ramp en recht. Beschouwingen over rampen, verantwoordelijkheid en aansprakelijkheid*, Den Haag: Boom Juridische uitgevers 2001, ISBN 90 5454 113 X.

MI-38 P.B. Cliteur, H.J. van den Herik, N.J.H. Huls & A.H.J. Schmidt (red.), *It ain't necessarily so*, Deventer: Kluwer 2001, ISBN 90 2683 854 9.

MI-39 E.R. Muller, *Conflictbeslechting: Kruisbestuiving van rechtswetenschap en bestuurskunde*, (oratie Leiden), Alphen aan den Rijn: Kluwer 2001, ISBN 90 1408 204 5.

MI-40 H.C. Wiersinga, *Nuance in benadering. Culturele factoren in het strafproces*, Den Haag: Boom Juridische uitgevers 2002, ISBN 90 5454 155 5.

MI-41 W. den Ouden, *De subsidieverplichting; wie betaalt bepaalt? Een onderzoek naar de rechtmatigheid van subsidieverplichtingen*, Deventer: Kluwer 2002, ISBN 90 2683 887 5.

MI-42 I. Sagel-Grande, *In the best interest of the child. Conflict resolution for and by children and Juveniles*, Amsterdam: Rozenberg Publishers 2001, ISBN 90 5170 572 7.

MI-43 W.M. Visser 't Hooft, *Japanese Contract and Anti-Trust Law. Sociological and Comparative Study*, Richmond Surrey: Curzon Press 2002, ISBN 07 0071 577 0.

MI-44 M. Dekker, *Het water meester. Het recht rond de overheidszorg voor de beveiliging tegen overstroming*, Den Haag: Boom Juridische uitgevers 2002, ISBN 90 5454 188 1.

MI-45 M. Lurks, W. Den Ouden, J.E.M. Polak & A.E. Schilder, *De grootste gemene deler. Opstellen aangeboden aan prof. mr. Th.G. Drupsteen ter gelegenheid van zijn afscheid van de Universiteit Leiden op 31 mei 2002*, Deventer: Kluwer 2002, ISBN 90 2684 004 7.

MI-46   S.C. Huisjes, *Over dode lijnen en een heuvel recht. De privaatrechtelijke aansprakelijkheid voor schade als gevolg van falende telecommunicatiedienstverlening*, Deventer: Kluwer 2002, ISBN 90 2684 003 9.

MI-47   M. Hallers, C. Joubert & J. Sjöcrona (eds.), *The Position of the Defence at the International Criminal Court and the Role of the Netherlands as the Host State*, Amsterdam: Rozenberg Publishers 2002, ISBN 90 5170 625 1.

MI-48   K.Teuben, *Rechtersregelingen als 'recht' in de zin van art. 79 Wet RO*, Den Haag: Jongbloed 2002, ISBN 90 7006 2313.

MI-49   M. Hallers, A.J. Mauritz, E.R. Muller & C.J.J.M. Stolker, *Beginselen van behoorlijk rampenonderzoek*, Den Haag: Boom Juridische uitgevers 2002, ISBN 90 5454 251 9.

MI-50   J.C. van der Steur, *Grenzen van rechtsobjecten. Een onderzoek naar de grenzen van objecten van eigendomsrechten en intellectuele eigendomsrechten* (diss. Leiden), Deventer: Kluwer.

MI-51   Y.L.L.A.M. Delfos-Roy, C. de Groot, P.A.C.E. van der Kooij, S.J.A. Mulder (red.), *Zekerheidshalve. Opstellen aangeboden aan Prof. mr. M.M. Mendel*, Deventer: Kluwer 2003, ISBN 90 268 40837.

MI-52   Barend Barentsen, *Arbeidsongeschiktheid. Aansprakelijkheid, bescherming en compensatie*, (diss. Leiden), Deventer: Kluwer 2003, ISBN 90 9000 061.

MI-53   A.F.M. Brenninkmeijer (red.), *De taakopvatting van de rechter*, Den Haag: Boom Juridische uitgevers 2003, ISBN 90 56454 279 9.

MI-54   H. Snijders & S. Weatherill, *E-commerce Law. National and transnational topics and perspectives*, Londen: Kluwer International 2003.

MI-55   F.B. Ronkes Agerbeek, *Zeg ik dat goed? EU-ambtenaren en hun vrijheid van meningsuiting*, Den Haag: Jongbloed 2003 ISBN 90 70062 33X

MI-56   A.C. Damsteegt, *De aansluiting van de Werkloosheidswet op het ontslagrecht*, Den Haag: Boom Juridische uitgevers 2003, ISBN 90 5454 312 4.

MI-57   P.Vos, *Kredietopvraging en insolventierisico. Overlevingskansen van bedrijven in financiële moeilijkheden en de Faillissementswet*, Deventer: Kluwer 2003, ISBN 90 1300 580 2.

MI-58   P.B. Cliteur & H.-M.Th.D. Ten Napel (red.), *Rechten, plichten, deugden*, Nijmegen: Ars aequi libri 2003, ISBN 90 6916 485 X.

MI-59   F.J.M. Feldbrugge (red.), *The Law's Beginnings*, Leiden/Boston: Martinus Nijhoff Publishers 2003, ISBN 90 0413 705X.

MI-60   A.F.M. Brenninkmeijer, *Effectieve conflictoplossing bij individuele arbeidsconflicten*, en L.C.J. Sprengers, *Collectieve belangen bij uiteenlopende geschillen* (oraties Leiden), Den Haag: Sdu 2003.

MI-61   A.H. Scheltema, *De goederenrechtelijke werking van de ontbindende voorwaarde*, Deventer: Kluwer 2003, ISBN 90 13 00744 9.

MI-62   W.H. Pokorný-Versteeg, *Milieu-effectrapportage in Nederland en de direct aangrenzende EU-lidstaten. Een rechtsvergelijkend onderzoek*, Deventer: Kluwer 2003, ISBN 90 13 00946 8.

MI-63   A.P.A. Broeders, *Op zoek naar de bron. Over de grondslagen van de criminalistiek en de waardering van het forensisch bewijs*, Deventer: Kluwer 2003, ISBN 90 130 0964 6.

MI-64   C.L.J. Caminada & K.P. Goudswaard, *Verdeelde zekerheid. De verdeling van baten en lasten van sociale zekerheid en pensioenen*, Den Haag: Sdu 2003, ISBN 90 1210 006 2.

MI-65   B.T.M. van der Wiel, *De rechtsverhouding tussen procespartijen*, Deventer: Kluwer 2004.

MI-66   A.J. Mauritz, *Liability of the operators and owners of aircraft for damage inflicted to persons and property on the surface*, Maastricht: Shaker 2003, ISBN 90 423 0234 8.

MI-67   T. Hartlief, Jac. Hijma & L. Reurich (red.), *Coherente instrumenten in het contractenrecht*, Deventer: Kluwer 2003 ISBN 90 1300 92 47.

MI-68   E.I. Helsloot, E.R. Muller, R. Pieterman & W.J.M. Voermans (red.), *Vervoer gevaarlijke stoffen in perspectief. Evaluatie van de Wet vervoer gevaarlijke stoffen 1996-2002*, Den Haag: Boom Juridische uitgevers 2003, ISBN 90 5454 420 1.

MI-69   W.J.M. Voermans, *Toedeling van bevoegdheid* (oratie Leiden), Den Haag: Boom Juridische uitgevers 2004, ISBN 90 5454 433 3.

MI-70   M.C. Zwanenburg, *Accountability under International Humanitarian Law for UN and NATO Peace Support Operations*, diss. Leiden 2004.

MI-71   M. Kuijer, *The Blindfold of Lady Justice. Judicial Independence and Impartiality in Light of the*

Requirements of Article 6 ECHR, Nijmegen: Wolf Legal Productions 2004, ISBN 90 5850 074 8.

MI-72   V.J.A. Sütö, *Nieuw Vermogensrecht en rechtsvergelijking; de reconstructie van een wetgevingsproces (1947-1961)*, Den Haag: Boom Juridische uitgevers 2004, ISBN 90 5454 467 8.

MI-73   Paul Cliteur, Hans Franken & Wim Voermans (red.), *Naar een Europese Grondwet*, Den Haag: Boom Juridische uitgevers 2004, ISBN 90 5454 471 6.

MI-74   S.L. Kuipers, *Cast in Concrete? The Institutional Dynamics of Belgian and Dutch Social Policy Reform*, Delft: Eburon Academic Publishers 2004, ISBN 90 5972 028 8.

MI-75   Piet Jan Slot & Mielle Bulterman (ed.), *Globalisation and Jurisdiction*, Den Haag: Kluwer Law International 2004, ISBN 90 411 2307 5.

Overige publicaties van het E.M. Meijers Instituut:

H.D. Ploeger, *Privaatrechtelijke aspecten van de aanleg van boortunnels*, Kluwer Rechtswetenschappelijke publicaties, Deventer: Kluwer 1997, ISBN 90 2683 122 6.

T. Heukels, N. Blokker & M. Brus (eds.), *The European Union after Amsterdam; A Legal Analysis*, The Hague: Kluwer Law International 1998, ISBN 90 411 1131 X.
(together with the Europa Instituut, Universiteit Leiden)

T. Barkhuysen, M.L. van Emmerik & P.H.P.H.M.C. van Kempen (eds.), *The Execution of Strasbourg and Geneva Human Rights Decisions in the National Legal Order*, The Hague: Kluwer Law International 1999, ISBN 90 411 1152 2.
(together with Van Asbeck Centrum, Universiteit Leiden)

H. Peter van Fenema, *The International Trade in Launch Services, The Effects of US Laws, Policies and Practices on its Development*, Leiden 1999 ISBN 90 901 3064 0.
(together with International Institute of Air and Space Law)

E.C. Nieuwenhuys & M.M.T.A. Brus, *Multilateral Regulation of Investment*, Den Haag: Kluwer Law International 2001 ISBN 90 411 9844 X.

E. Nieuwenhuys, A. Toussaint & M. Valstar, *Verslag van het symposium Internationale Dimensies van Maatschappelijk Verantwoord Ondernemen*, Leiden: E.M. Meijers Instituut 2002, ISBN 90 9016 080 9.

E.R. Muller & J.P. Coenen, *Parlementair onderzoek in Nederland*, Den Haag: Sdu Uitgevers 2002, ISBN 90 1209 700 2.